HANDBOOKS

VIRGIN ISLANDS

SUSANNA HENIGHAN

VIRGIN ISLANDS

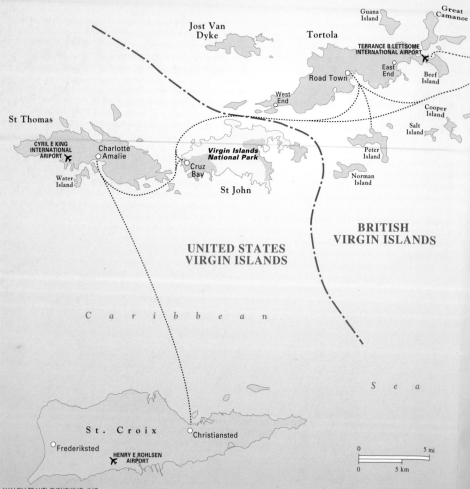

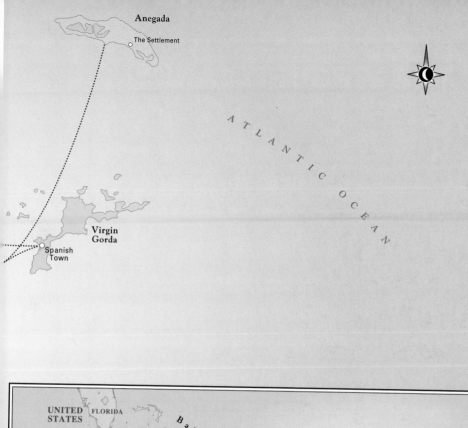

Anegada

○ The Settlement

A T L A N T I C   O C E A N

Virgin
Gorda

○ Spanish
Town

UNITED
STATES
FLORIDA

Florida Keys

B a h a m a s

A T L A N T I C

O C E A N

CUBA

G r e a t e r

A n t i l l e s

HAÏTI

DOMINICAN
REPUBLIC

VIRGIN
ISLANDS

JAMAICA

PUERTO
RICO

L e s s e r   A n t i l l e s

HONDURAS

NICARAGUA

C a r i b b e a n   S e a

Aruba Curaçao
Bonaire

Margarita

COLOMBIA

VENEZUELA

DISCOVER
THE VIRGIN ISLANDS

The colors are the first things you notice in the Virgin Islands. The shimmering sea is a palate of blue, green, and purple. Bright white sand and green coconut palms create a picture so pleasing to the eye it is difficult to look away. When the sun shines brightly from above, the tropical colors intensify until they dance beneath the light.

At other times of day, color is more muted, but no less beautiful. At dawn, curls of orange and pink glow from behind the mountains. After the sun drops below the horizon in the evening, the sky turns a deep, dark blue so pure it could swallow you. At night, the sky is black – the perfect backdrop for the extravagance of stars above.

But the Virgin Islands are much more than beautiful. They are alive. Step off the plane and you are bombarded by the lyrical and

Fort Frederik, St. Croix

seemingly undecipherable tongue of the islanders – an English awash with colorful phrases, colloquialisms, and a dialect that is part West African, part American, and part Caribbean. Study this language long enough and you have studied the Virgin Islands in their entirety.

The Virgin Islands are much more than beaches, bare feet, and piña coladas. They are quiet villages, bustling shopping districts, financial services centers, and the exciting convergence of people from around the world. They are societies built almost miraculously from the embers of the brutal West Indian plantation system. Today's Virgin Islanders are worldly, educated, and alert to opportunity. Thankfully, they are also learning to prize what makes their island home unique, and visitors are the beneficiaries of this.

a North Coast beach, Anegada

One of the greatest things about the Virgin Islands is their sheer variety. Each island is distinct. You can choose to drop off the map on isolated and quiet Anegada or immerse yourself in the pleasant bustle of St. Thomas' Charlotte Amalie. Pick your way through St. Croix's numerous museums and historic attractions, or set sail from Tortola to one of the British Virgin Islands' remote cays.

Subtler differences distinguish the British and U.S. Virgin Islands. The U.S. islands are more closely linked to the U.S. mainland, culturally, politically, and economically. You will see yellow ribbons commemorating U.S. troops overseas and islanders celebrating Independence Day and Thanksgiving. In the British islands you will sense the reserve so long associated with the British, but don't expect a proper cup of English tea.

Virgin Islanders across the border have more in common than they have differences, however. The common Virgin Islands culture is one that prizes self-reliance, honesty, and hard work in equal mea-

Jost Van Dyke Methodist Church

sure to friendliness, warmth, and generosity. Many people lament that this traditional culture is being erased in favor of the American culture depicted on television sets and movie screens. But you can find traditional Virgin Islands culture in the fungi music, fried fish dinner, or just in a conversation you strike up with your friendly bartender, taxi driver, or the guys under the tree.

The heart of a Virgin Islands experience is in the details: the spicy jerk chicken bought from a roadside stand, the sound of scratch band music wafting through the night, or the sight of a solitary bright red bromeliad deep in the forest. For someone else, the moments they remember may be the cool bite of an early morning swim, the winding cobblestone alleys of the islands' old towns, and the sound of tree frogs chirping at night.

Many visitors simply want respite and relaxation. And there is nothing wrong with that. Indeed, when the first travelers began "discovering" the Virgin Islands, emptiness and obscurity were their greatest attraction. Despite decades of growth, it is still possible

Tortola's annual Festival Parade

to find the same quietude that so delighted the first visitors to the Virgin Islands. At the right places and the right times, there is a stillness so powerful it steadies your own mind and heart. In the middle of the forest of St. John, on a quiet beach on St. Croix, at the heart of a seaside village on Tortola the stillness surrounds you. Dust settles, no one moves, and the world pauses just long enough for you to notice.

Life exists in equal measure to silence: comings and goings on the harbors; dancing under the stars; a delightful mélange of cultures; the exciting start of a regatta. The joy of the Virgin Islands is that you choose your proportions: two parts stillness, one part life – chill and serve. Yield: paradise.

relaxing along the Baths, Virgin Gorda

Contents

The Lay of the Land 14

Planning Your Trip 17

Explore the Virgin Islands 19

Best of the Virgin Islands 19

The Seven-Day Family Vacation 21

Past and Present: 10 Days of History and Culture 22

Beach Lover's Tour 23

Two-Week Sailing Adventure 24

Wildlife and Wilderness 26

St. Thomas 29

Sights 32

Entertainment and Events 44

Shopping 46

Sports and Recreation 47

Accommodations 51

Food 54

Practicalities 57

St. Croix 61

Sights 65

Sports and Recreation 84

Entertainment and Events 89

Shopping 91

Accommodations. 92
Food. 96
Practicalities 99

St. John. 103
Sights 106
Entertainment and Events. 119
Shopping. 120
Sports and Recreation 121
Accommodations. 126
Food. 129
Practicalities 132

Tortola 136
Sights 141
Entertainment and Events. 161
Shopping. 165
Sports and Recreation 166
Accommodations. 173
Food. 178
Practicalities 183

Virgin Gorda. 188
Sights 192
Entertainment, Events, and Shopping. 199
Sports and Recreation 200

Accommodations. 202
Food. 205
Practicalities 207

Jost Van Dyke. 210
Sights 213
Entertainment and Recreation 219
Accommodations. 221
Food. 222
Practicalities 224

Anegada 226
Sights 231
Sports and Recreation 235
Accommodations. 237
Food. 239
Practicalities 240

Background. 243
The Land. 243
History 258
Government and Economy. 273
The People 276

Essentials 283
Getting There and Around...283
Visas and Officialdom.. 288
Tips for Travelers 291
Health and Safety 294
Information and Services...296

Resources..302
Suggested Reading...302
Internet Resources 306

Index.. 308

13

MAP CONTENTS

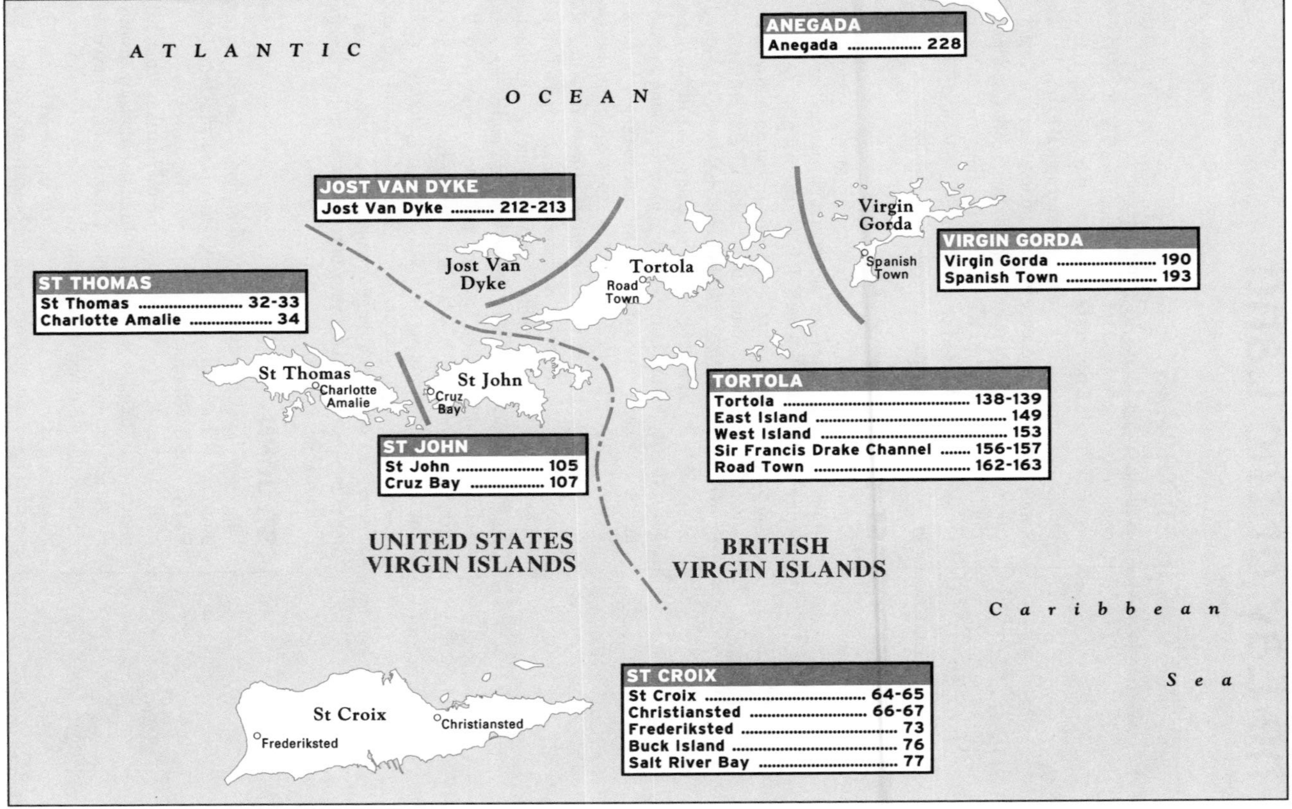

ATLANTIC OCEAN

Caribbean Sea

BRITISH VIRGIN ISLANDS

UNITED STATES VIRGIN ISLANDS

Anegada

Virgin Gorda — Spanish Town

Tortola — Road Town

Jost Van Dyke

St John — Cruz Bay

St Thomas — Charlotte Amalie

St Croix — Christiansted, Frederiksted

ST THOMAS
St Thomas 32-33
Charlotte Amalie 34

JOST VAN DYKE
Jost Van Dyke 212-213

ST JOHN
St John 105
Cruz Bay 107

ANEGADA
Anegada 228

VIRGIN GORDA
Virgin Gorda 190
Spanish Town 193

TORTOLA
Tortola 138-139
East Island 149
West Island 153
Sir Francis Drake Channel 156-157
Road Town 162-163

ST CROIX
St Croix 64-65
Christiansted 66-67
Frederiksted 73
Buck Island 76
Salt River Bay 77

The Lay of the Land

ST. THOMAS

Bustling, crowded, and highly commercial, St. Thomas is the hub of the Virgin Islands and the entry point for most travelers to the region. Historic **Charlotte Amalie** is the main attraction, although beachfront resorts on the east end appeal to travelers who want a Caribbean experience in the confines of familiar American culture. Beach and nature lovers will be better served seeking out a quieter, less developed island, however. Duty-free **shopping** for watches, jewelry, and crystal is a major draw for the millions of cruise ship passengers who visit here annually.

ST. CROIX

Overlooked by many, St. Croix has a lot to offer visitors of all stripes. The "Big Islands" has the greatest physical and cultural diversity of all the Virgin Islands. It is also the best place for visitors who want to balance natural beauty and recreation with an exploration of Virgin Islands history and culture. **Christiansted** and **Frederiksted** are classic West Indian harbor towns. The island's countryside invites quiet exploration. **Buck Island National Monument,** just off shore, is an ideal place for hiking and snorkeling. Two weeks is a good amount of time to explore St. Croix. Devote a couple days to exploring Christiansted's historic attractions, shops, and museums, then drive out to Frederiksted, the epicenter of St. Croix's dramatic history. Rent a car and follow the island's heritage trail, stopping at sugar mill ruins and greathouse museums. Beaches and bays on the wild and undeveloped east end are accessible only on foot, and well worth the journey. The lush, damp forest in the island's northwest corner is a perfect contrast to the sunny, sandy beaches of the western shore. St. Croix is the most gay-friendly of the Virgin Islands, and its diverse community supports a range of cultural activities and events, including an annual Half Ironman competition and a rollicking Christmastime Carnival.

ST. JOHN

Rapid development has not spoiled St. John's natural beauty, protected—thankfully—by the **Virgin Islands National Park.** But development has changed the feel of this island from a laid-back "Love City" to a tropical Martha's Vineyard, populated by trendy restaurants, multimillion-dollar mansions, SUVs, and lots of beautiful people. The influx of moneyed developers and landowners has pushed the price of vacationing here through the roof. Despite this, there remain (at least for the time being) affordable and exquisite beachfront camps within the park, plus a few small inns and guesthouses around **Cruz Bay.** St. John has the best beaches in the U.S. Virgin Islands, and the best hiking in the whole archipelago. You could spend two weeks here and snorkel at a different beach each day. Activities organized by the National Park Service are ideal for families and outdoor enthusiasts who want to not only have fun but learn about the island at the same time.

TORTOLA

Home to the capital of the British Virgin Islands, Tortola is an island of steep hills, remarkable vistas, quiet beaches, and a somewhat unkempt, unique harbor town. As the hub of the British islands, Tortola is the most developed. It is also the capital of the British Virgins' massive **sailing** industry, with marinas dotting the southern coast from West End to East End. Thousands of travelers arrive on Tortola annually to depart on sailing vacations that meander throughout the Virgin Islands. Land-based tourists delight in the quiet beaches of the north shore, surfers congregate on **Little Apple Bay,** beach bums favor **Cane Garden Bay,** and nature lovers can have their pick of a half dozen other undeveloped, quiet white sand beaches. Nightlife on Tortola is laid-back, except on the full moon when full moon parties ignite the night with infectious Caribbean music and creative libations. For a change of scenery, catch a ferry to one of the out islands across the Sir Francis Drake Channel, or spend a day exploring the world-famous **Wreck of the *Rhone*** dive site.

VIRGIN GORDA

One of the Virgin Islands most visited attractions, the **Baths National Park** draws thousands of tourists to Virgin Gorda every year. Here, giant boulders create grottos and pools all along the island's southwestern shore. On the other end of the island, **North Sound** is a sailor's paradise: a community without roads, where the fastest way between two points is over the water. Here you can learn to sail, take up water sports like windsurfing and kiteboarding, or simply paddle to a quiet beach and spend the day. In between, Virgin Gorda has some of the region's nicest upscale hotels, a series of unspoiled beaches, and a quaint, neat, and friendly town. **Gorda Peak National Park,** home to the world's smallest lizard, is good for hiking. Virgin Gorda's main attractions can be seen in a day or two, but if you really want to acclimate to the rhythm of this friendly island, plan on a week or more.

JOST VAN DYKE

This tiny island has more goats than people, and more visitors than year-round residents. Sailors especially delight in Jost Van Dyke, which boasts some of the warmest and most unique beach bars around. **Great Harbor** is picturesque—its main street is a sandy path lined by palm trees. **White Bay** is one of the most beautiful beaches in the Virgin Islands. Stay onboard your charter boat, or come ashore for a few nights at a beach-front campground, island inn, or upscale villa. Jost Van Dyke is exceptionally quiet, except for the days around the New Year when thousands flock here for Foxy Callwood's world-famous **New Year's Eve** bash. For those interested in leaving the beach behind, Jost Van Dyke is ideal for exploring—on water and on land. The Virgin Islands' best water sports and eco-tours outfit is here, guiding visitors to offshore cays and little-known attractions, like **Little Jost Van Dyke, Bubbly Pool,** and **Sandy Cay.** Plan about two or three days here if you want to blend beachfront relaxation with some outdoor exploration.

ANEGADA

The most unusual of the Virgin Islands, Anegada is a universe unto itself. Totally flat, very dry, and sparsely populated, this coral island 14 nautical miles north of Virgin Gorda is famous for miles of coastline, its endangered **iguana,** and the **fresh lobsters** fishermen harvest from reefs around the island. Anegada is also a sportfisher's mecca: elusive **bonefish** live in the shallows around the island, and wahoo, marlin, jack, and tuna live in the nearby **North Drop,** where sportfishing boats from all over the Virgin Islands head to troll for fish. Anegada makes a good day trip from any of the Virgin Islands. Come here for a longer stay if you want time to contemplate the endless horizon, listen to the sound of wind in your ears, or explore the unique dry, scrubby interior—a **wilderness** of wild orchids, flowering frangipani, and bright yellow century plants. Anegada is an island waiting to be discovered by birders, fishers, and outdoor enthusiasts.

Planning Your Trip

Don't make the mistake of planning your trip to the Virgin Islands down to the last day, let alone hour. The best trips are somewhat uncharted—you are, after all, in the islands. For most visitors it is not about squeezing more things *into* your day, but taking things *out*. Life here is best when you keep things simple; complexity often breeds confusion, disappointment, and frustration.

Small islands, by their nature, pose a unique challenge to visitors. There are no road trips, for example. There are, however, boats, and these are the best way to get around if you want to see all, or even some, of the Virgin Islands on one trip. If length and breadth are your concerns, forget about ferries (slow, limited and expensive), car rentals (expensive), and planes (very expensive). Charter a boat and away you go.

Don't underestimate the pleasure of looking at the same view every day of your vacation, either. No one said you had to travel hither and yon to experience the Virgin Islands. You can count the grains of sand on the beach in front of your hotel too, if you'd rather. Muster up the energy for a few day trips around the island of your choice, and you'll come home with a suntan, some stories, and a few less worries.

There is, of course, a middle ground. Choose a home base (or two), and pick a few other islands that strike your fancy for day trips. Just don't forget to temper the exploration with relaxation. Find the right balance for you, and you'll be—as the islanders say—all right.

The Virgin Islands are not the place to come if you're looking for exciting nightlife, shopping, modern cities, or world-class museums. Also, leave your impatience at home. The pace of life here is slow, and the attractions are the great beaches, excellent sailing waters, and hundreds of snorkel and dive sites. Islands including St. John, St. Croix, and Tortola have a wide offering of other outdoor pursuits: hiking, kayaking, biking, birding, windsurfing, and surfing among them. Charlotte Amalie on St. Thomas and the entire island of St. Croix are rich in history, and all the islands have unique bars and restaurants—some elegant, some ramshackle, and lots in between. Peace and quiet are the major attractions of the remote out islands of the British Virgins.

WHEN TO GO

Life in the Virgin Islands follows a distinct rhythm defined by the travel patterns of those who visit the region. Winter (November–March) is the "high" season, when North Americans and Europeans come to escape cold weather back home. This coincides with the dry season in the islands, and the season of the best sailing winds and coolest, most comfortable temperatures. It is also when you will find the greatest variety of things to do and places to eat and stay; many establishments shut down and limit hours during the slow season.

During the summer (May–September) travelers will find bargains. Most hotels offer discounts of up to 40 percent during summer, and airfare tends to be less then too. It is hotter, however, and the winds tend to die down for sailing. Otherwise, there is little difference. Do be aware of the hurricane season (June–November), and be sure to buy trip insurance if there's chance you could be blown off course by a storm or storm warning.

The so-called "shoulder seasons" between summer and winter may be the best time of all to visit the islands. March and October typically enjoy pleasant weather (not too hot), lower prices, and fewer tourists (you'll have the beaches to yourself). Some hotels offer discounts, too, although not as deep as those in summer.

WHAT TO TAKE

Beginning in 2007, all Americans need a passport to return to the United States from the British Virgin Islands and other Caribbean countries (but not the U.S. Virgin Islands). While a passport is not necessary for a visit to the U.S. Virgin Islands, some form of government-issued ID is. It is always a good idea to pack not only your passport, but also a photocopy of it. Also bring evidence of your hotel reservations and return passage home.

Light, loose-fitting clothes are best; pack a few long-sleeved shirts and light pants for the evenings, especially in the winter. Some elegant restaurants have dress codes that require slacks and button-up shirts for men, and dresses for women. You will probably sweat a lot during the days, so plan on at least a few extra changes of clothes. Launderettes are easy to find, but if you're going to do a lot of moving around consider bringing clothes you can wash in the bathroom sink.

Virgin Islanders tend to dress neatly. If you are going to attend a business function you will need smart office clothing: a tie for men and a suit for women. Around town, you will want to look presentable, although casual is fine. Short-shorts and skimpy tank tops are best saved for the beach. After dark, you may wish to dress up, especially if you are going to soak up whatever nightlife there is on your island. Leave your best jewels at home; there is no need for them here, and you are just inviting trouble.

If you plan to do a lot of swimming, snorkeling, or scuba diving, bring two bathing suits;

there is nothing worse than putting on a wet suit because you forgot to hang it up to dry the night before. Water booties, aqua shoes, or similarly water-happy sandals are handy, too. Fast-drying shorts that you can get wet comfortably are also very useful, especially if you're going to be entering and exiting dinghies and small boats. Bring a comfortable pair of shoes you can wear on the streets of historic Charlotte Amalie or the hiking trails of St. John. You will probably find that a pair of sandals or flip-flops is indispensable. Scuba divers and surfers do not need to bring their own gear; there is plenty available for rent around the islands. If you're going to be camping, pack a raincoat or poncho.

Be sure to prepare for the sun: bring sunscreen, sunglasses, a wide-brimmed hat and lip balm (sunburned lips really hurt). A refillable water bottle is especially handy, so you don't always have to stop for water. If you're going to do hiking, a CamelBak-type water jug is best. If you want to take photos, bring extra film to avoid paying high island prices. If you are interested in birds, plants, or marinelife, bring an identification manual with you.

The beach is a great place to catch up on your reading, so don't forget a few books. You can always trade them in at book swaps around the islands when you're finished.

Explore the Virgin Islands

BEST OF THE VIRGIN ISLANDS

If you have three weeks and an ample budget, you can hit the most important attractions in the Virgin Islands, from historic sites to empty beaches. You take in each island's greatest hits: Charlotte Amalie and Magen's Bay on St. Thomas; Christiansted National Historic Site and the Buck Island on St. Croix; and St. John's petroglyphs and idyllic Trunk Bay.

In the British Virgin Islands, highlights include a day trip to The Baths, a high-powered day sail to Jost Van Dyke's beach bars, and a final respite on Anegada's North Coast.

Most visitors may prefer to be more selective; island-hopping like this is very pricey and can be tiring too. But if you really want to taste all that the Virgin Islands have to offer, this trip is for you.

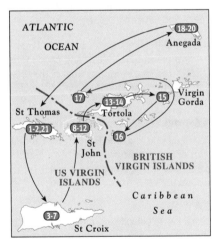

Bay on the north shore for the afternoon. Have dinner at a **Frenchtown** bistro.

DAY 3
Catch a ferry to St. Croix, and check into a hotel near Christiansted for five nights. Spend the afternoon sightseeing around **Christiansted National Historic Site.**

DAY 4
Rent a car and drive around St. Croix, stopping at Cramer Park and Point Udall in the east before heading west. Go for an afternoon swim along one of the west coast beaches, and watch the sunset.

DAY 5
Tour St. Croix's historic attractions: visit **Whim Greathouse Museum,** Lawaetz House, and **Fort Frederik Museum.**

DAY 6
Take a day trip to **Buck Island,** where you can snorkel and hike to the top of the island. In the late afternoon, head to Cane Bay on the north coast for a late swim and sunset cocktails.

DAY 1
Arrive at Cyril E. King International Airport in St. Thomas, and check into a hotel in or near Charlotte Amalie for two nights.

DAY 2
In the morning, walk around **historic Charlotte Amalie** and visit the museums, historic sites, and galleries. Head to **Magen's**

DAY 7

Pack a picnic and hike to **Jack and Isaac Bays** on the east end. Catch some local scratch music in the evening.

DAY 8

Take the seaplane back to St. Thomas and catch a ferry to St. John. Stop by the National Park Service office to get your bearings and then check into a hotel or beachfront campsite for five nights. Go to **Trunk Bay** for an afternoon swim.

DAY 9

Rent a car and take the long way around to Salt Pond Bay on the southern coast of the island. Hike to **Ram's Head**, beach comb at Drunk Bay, and sunbathe at Salt Pond Bay. Spend the evening listening to local blues and bluegrass in **Coral Bay.**

DAY 10

Take a guided hike on the Reef Bay Trail to the **petroglyphs** and Reef Bay sugar mill ruins.

DAY 11

Take a guided tour of the Cinnamon Bay sugar mill ruins, then go to Annaberg to watch traditional St. John basket-making, baking, and gardening. Spend the afternoon relaxing on the beach closest to your hotel.

DAY 12

Go on an early morning birding expedition at Francis Bay Pond. Hike to Waterlemon Bay and snorkel around **Waterlemon Cay.**

DAY 13

Take a ferry to West End, Tortola, and check into an island hotel for five nights. Enjoy sunset cocktails along the north shore.

DAY 14

Rent a car and drive to **Sage Mountain National Park** for an early hike. Picnic at Mount Healthy and drive by the **Fahie Hill Mural** before heading down to Cane Garden Bay for an afternoon swim.

DAY 15

Take a day trip to Virgin Gorda. Catch a ferry from Road Town to **Spanish Town,** take an island tour stopping at **Coppermine Point,** and spend the afternoon at **Baths National Park.**

DAY 16

Take a day sail to **Norman Island** and Cooper Island. Snorkel at the Caves.

DAY 17

Rent a powerboat and sail to Jost Van Dyke. Stop at the **beach bars** in **White Bay** and **Great Harbour.** Say hello to Foxy Callwood, and leave your T-shirt at Sidney's Peace and Love.

DAY 18

Catch a plane to Anegada and check into a hotel for three nights. Spend the day watching the **North Coast** horizon at Cow Wreck Beach.

DAY 19

Rent a bicycle and tour The Settlement and stop at the **Iguana Headstart Facility** before heading out on a circular route around the **Western Salt Ponds.**

DAY 20

Take a taxi to Loblolly Bay and spend the day snorkeling and sleeping in a hammock. Enjoy your last lobster dinner.

DAY 21

Take an early morning flight back to St. Thomas, and head back home.

THE SEVEN-DAY FAMILY VACATION

The Virgin Islands are a great place for children, especially children who enjoy being outside and like the water. A family vacation in the Virgin Islands should be heavy on swimming and snorkeling, with a dash of history and sightseeing. St. John is the perfect home base, since frequent moves will just add stress to your trip. Leave the Gameboy at home, but bring the camera to record your family's encounters with sea creatures like turtles, dolphins, rays, and conch.

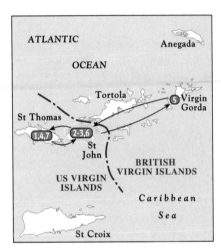

includes exhibits about St. John. Grab an ice cream and watch the waterfront abuzz with activity. If you have teenagers, let them loose in Cruz Bay for some shopping.

DAY 3

Hike the Reef Bay Trail with or without a ranger guide, stopping at the **petroglyphs** on the way down.

DAY 4

Take a day trip to St. Thomas. Visit **Coral World** and Fort Christian Museum. Back on St. John, attend the evening campfire presentation at Cinnamon Bay.

DAY 5

Take a day sail to the **Baths** on Virgin Gorda. Keep a tally of all the fish you see while snorkeling.

DAY 1

Fly to Cyril E. King International Airport on St. Thomas, and take a ferry to St. John. Check into a campsite or hotel, which will be your home base for the entire trip. Go to the closest beach.

DAY 6

Spend the day at Cinnamon Bay. The more active among you can learn to windsurf.

DAY 2

Take the guided snorkel tour at **Trunk Bay.** Drive to Cruz Bay in the afternoon and visit the National Park information center, which

DAY 7

Go for a morning swim before catching the ferry back to St. Thomas for your departure flight.

PAST AND PRESENT:
10 DAYS OF HISTORY AND CULTURE

Historical tourism has long been overshadowed by the natural beauty of the Virgin Islands. And the islands' history—heavy as it is on slavery and oppression—makes for difficult beach conversation. But more and more travelers are finding stories of hope and redemption within the islands' rich history. St. Croix is the best base for historical and cultural exploration. It has more to see, more resources for learning, and more people who are interested in preserving heritage. Historical tourists on the other islands will need a little persistence and ingenuity to tap into all the resources, but if you do, you will be rewarded.

Cultural attractions mix readily with historical ones. Fungi, or quelbe, music is one of the best manifestations of Virgin Islands culture still in existence. Island carnivals are also an excellent time to see the present-day manifestations of African, South American, and European cultures.

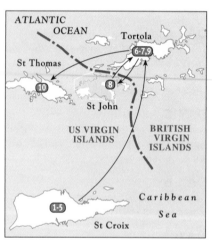

DAY 3

Rent a car and follow the Heritage Trail around the island, stopping at **Whim Greathouse** and the Lawaetz Museum.

DAY 4

Explore Frederiksted. Go to **Fort Frederik Museum** and Sprat Hall. Eat *ital* food at one of the Rastafarian restaurants. Seek out some live music in the evening.

DAY 5

Hike at Salt River Bay, the Columbus landing site. Spend the afternoon at a pig roast and traditional music concert at Mount Victory Camps in the Caldonia forest.

DAY 6

Travel to Tortola. Check into a hotel on the west end for the next four nights, and then take a drive along the Ridge Road, stopping at the **Fahie Hill Mural.** Drive along the north coast, stopping at the Callwood Rum Distillery in Cane Garden Bay and the North Shore Shell Museum in Carrot Bay. Eat fresh local fish at one of Carrot Bay's local restaurants.

DAY 1

Fly to Henry Rolsten Airport on St. Croix. Check into a hotel in or around Christiansted for five nights. Walk along the waterfront at sunset.

DAY 2

Explore **Christiansted National Historic Site** on foot. Stop at **Fort Christiansvearn** and the **Steeple Building.**

DAY 7

Rent a powerboat and sail out to **Salt Island.** Hike around the salt pond and tend the graves of those who perished in the Wreck of the *RMS Rhone.*

DAY 8

Catch a ferry from West End to St. John for a day trip. Take an island tour, stopping at the Annaberg Sugar Mill and Ione Sprauve Museum. Watch the sun set as you sail back to Tortola.

DAY 9

Explore **Main Street** in Road Town, and visit Old Government House Museum. Head to the Trellis Bay, Beef Island **Full Moon Party** with local fungi musicians.

DAY 10

Return to St. Thomas. Spend the morning exploring **historic Charlotte Amalie** before catching an afternoon flight home.

BEACH LOVER'S TOUR

There are beaches for every taste in the Virgin Islands: small crescents of sand and broad hard-packed shores; crowded, high-spirited coasts and empty, private retreats; beaches with reefs to snorkel and walls to dive; beaches with fine white sand and high-colored grains; hot sandy beaches and shaded escapes. Beach lovers can set for themselves the singular task of finding the best beach—it is a project that could take months, or a lifetime.

For travelers with less time, consider this, the greatest hits. Stops include Trunk Bay on St. John; Magen's Bay on St. Thomas; Cane Garden Bay on Tortola; and the Baths on Virgin Gorda. Stray a bit off the beaten path to discover Smugger's Cove, Spring Bay, and Hawksnest Beach. Finish it all off with the beach to beat all others: Anegada's North Coast.

DAY 1

Arrive at Terrance B. Lettsome International Airport, Beef Island, British Virgin Islands. Check into a beachfront hotel or campsite for seven nights. Take a sunset beachcombing walk along Long Bay, Tortola.

DAY 2

Go for an early swim at Cane Garden Bay before heading to Little Apple Bay where you can watch surfers (or join in).

DAY 3

Catch a ferry to St. John. Rent a car and hit the best beaches: **Trunk Bay,** Cinnamon Bay, and Hawksnest Beach.

DAY 4

Take a day sail or ferry to Virgin Gorda, and spend the day at the **Baths** and **Spring Bay.**

DAY 5

Fly to Anegada for the day and head straight to the **North Coast,** an unbroken strand of white sand.

DAY 6

Take a ferry to St. Thomas and head to

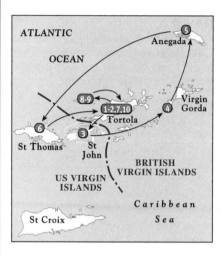

Magen's Bay Beach. Stop at Coki Point in the afternoon for a snorkel.

DAY 7

Spend the day at Smuggler's Cove Beach on Tortola.

DAY 8

Take a ferry to Jost Van Dyke and check into a beachfront campsite for two nights. Relax on **White Bay.**

DAY 9

Take a guided eco-tour to Little Jost Van Dyke, the **Bubbly Pool,** and **Sandy Cay.**

DAY 10

Swim at **Long Bay, Beef Island,** before you catch your departing flight from Beef Island.

TWO-WEEK SAILING ADVENTURE

No format is better suited for exploring the Virgin Islands than sailing. It makes it easy to get around and captures the real natural attraction of the place. It is also exciting and fun. Plan as long a sailing trip as you can—you will lose a day on each end to checking in and checking out.

This two-week itinerary includes a few land-based days on Anegada and St. Croix, and many short sails between bays and cays. Plan your sailing vacation early—get a chart and plan your course at home—and be sure to get a skipper if necessary. You don't want to spend your vacation worried about wrecking a multimillion-dollar boat.

DAY 1

Fly to Terrance B. Lettsome International Airport, Beef Island. Check in with your charter boat company, provision your yacht, and plan your itinerary.

DAY 2

Set sail to **Norman Island.** Snorkel at the Caves and pick up a mooring at the Bight for the night.

DAY 3

Rendezvous with the dive boat, and dive the *RMS Rhone.* Nondivers in your party can dinghy ashore to Norman Island and hike to the top of Spyglass Hill.

DAY 4

Sail to **Salt Island.** Go ashore and hike around the salt pond. Sail to Manchineel Bay, Cooper Island, for the night.

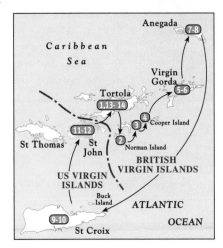

DAY 5

Pick up a day-use mooring at Fallen Jerusalem, where you can snorkel and hike over the rocks. Sail to **North Sound,** Virgin Gorda, for the night.

DAY 6

Dinghy around North Sound. Pack a picnic and take it ashore to Prickly Pear Island for a day of exploring.

DAY 7

Sail to Anegada. Treat yourself to a real bed at Neptune's Treasure Guesthouse.

DAY 8

Take a taxi tour of the island and stop at Loblolly Bay on the **North Coast** for the best snorkeling on the island.

DAY 9

Sail to St. Croix. Pick up a mooring in Christiansted Harbor. Celebrate your successful sail at a waterfront eatery.

DAY 10

Sail to **Buck Island** for the day. Return to Christiansted at night, and come ashore for a night of live music.

DAY 11

Sail to **Coral Bay,** St. John. Eat dinner at a seaside café and swap sailing stories at the bar.

DAY 12

Sail to Francis Bay, St. John. Swim ashore to the beach, and hike the Francis Bay Trail.

DAY 13

Sail back to Road Town, Tortola, and come ashore for dinner at a beachfront restaurant. Dance under the stars at Cane Garden Bay.

DAY 14

Check out with your charter boat company and travel to Beef Island for your flight home.

WILDLIFE AND WILDERNESS

Every trip to the Virgin Islands incorporates some element of nature. But real nature-lovers can see truly remarkable sites if they look carefully and stray from the beaten paths. On St. Croix, the Caldonia Rainforest and north coast, underwater Wall are among the attractions. St. John, home of the Virgin Islands National Park, is the best island for hiking and snorkeling. In the British Virgin Islands, remote Jost Van Dyke and Anegada have unique wilderness attractions.

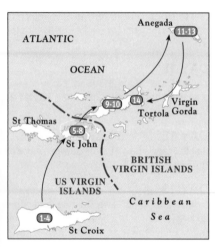

DAY 4

Dive the famous north shore **Wall** with one of the local dive shops.

DAY 5

Take the seaplane to St. Thomas, and catch a ferry to St. John. Check into a campground for four nights.

DAY 6

Hike the Reef Bay Trail, stopping at the **petroglyphs** along the way. If you want, continue on to Lameshur Bay for snorkeling.

DAY 7

Hike from Annaberg to Coral Bay. Stop at **Waterlemon Cay** along the way to snorkel.

DAY 1

Fly to Cyril E. King Airport on St. Thomas and catch the seaplane or a ferry to St. Croix. Check into a campground or hotel for four nights.

DAY 2

Rent a four-wheel-drive vehicle and take the scenic drive through the Caldonia Rainforest. Visit Sandy Point Wildlife Refuge, and look for endangered turtle nests.

DAY 3

Pack a picnic and hike to **Jack and Isaac Bays** on the east end. Bathe in the nude.

DAY 8

Rent a dinghy in **Coral Bay** and explore the east end of St. John. Snorkel in a mangrove swamp.

DAY 9

Take a ferry to Tortola and check into a hotel for two nights. Hike the trails at **Sage Mountain National Park** in the morning, and visit the **J.R. O'Neal Botanical Gardens** in the afternoon.

DAY 10

If you're staying near the east end, take a day sail to the Dog Islands for snorkeling and diving. If you're nearer the west, sign up for an eco-tour with Jost Van Dyke Watersports to Great Tobago island.

DAY 11

Catch an early-morning flight to Anegada. Check into a hotel for three nights, and visit the **Anegada Iguana Headstart Facility** in The Settlement. Go to Loblolly Bay on the **North Coast** for an afternoon snorkel.

DAY 12

Hike through the **Anegada Outback,** keeping a lookout for wild orchids, birds, butterflies, and flowering frangipani.

DAY 13

Rent a kayak and paddle around the southern shore of Anegada. Search for **bonefish** in the shallows.

DAY 14

Catch an early-morning flight back to Beef Island and transfer to St. Thomas for your departure.

ST. THOMAS

St. Thomas is an inkblot, about 12 miles long and three miles wide. It is the second largest of the U.S. Virgin Islands and the most populous. A steep spine stretches from east to west, with the highest point at Crown Mountain, on the western third of the island.

Charlotte Amalie is one of the West Indies' most picturesque harbors: layers of historic and modern homes, businesses, and churches rim the broad harbor. This is the center of business and government, plus an inviting historic town. The international airport is a short drive west, and ferries and seaplanes leave regularly with service to St. Croix, St. John, and Tortola.

Historically and today, St. Thomas is the hub of the Virgin Islands. As the center of business, commerce, services, and transport, St. Thomas long ago lost the quiet island feel of the other Virgin Islands. This is the "big city" of the Virgins—the place where people come to shop, celebrate, and meet up. At the same time, for those who call this island home, it is a small town where everyone knows each other.

The island's long history has left historic attractions dating back to the earliest days of colonization—old churches and forts that bring an Old World feel to the capital, Charlotte Amalie, an attraction that is often overlooked in favor of the beaches of the east end and north shore. Magen's Bay, the best beach on the island, is broad and quiet. On the east end, Coki Point and Sapphire Bay are alive with tourists and island residents.

St. Thomas is one of the best islands for family vacations. There are plenty of activities for children, ranging from underwater observatories to

© SUSANNA HENIGHAN

HIGHLIGHTS

《 Historic Downtown Charlotte Amalie: Narrow, winding cobblestone streets are lined by old churches, forts, and warehouses that face the gleaming waterfront (page 35).

《 Frenchtown: Traditionally the home of French-speaking fishermen, this tiny waterfront community is now known for its classic architecture, fine dining, and hip nightlife (page 39).

《 Magen's Bay: This public beach is the jewel of St. Thomas, with more than a mile of packed white sand, coconut palms, and clear water (page 41).

《 Coral World: This family-friendly ocean park makes it easy to enjoy the wonders of the undersea environment. Come here to see sea turtles, rays, sharks, iguanas, colorful fish, and much more (page 43).

《 St. Thomas Carnival: Calypso music, colorful costumes, local food, long nights, and traditional games and sports – that's just some of St. Thomas's annual Carnival (page 44).

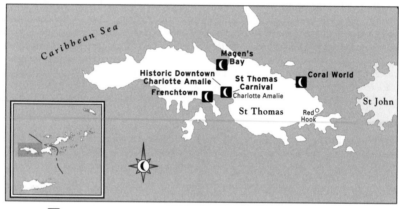

LOOK FOR **《** TO FIND RECOMMENDED SIGHTS, ACTIVITIES, DINING, AND LODGING.

snorkeling, and parents will find pleasure in the dining, nightlife, and shopping of the city. Modern comforts like a large movie theater, fast-food restaurants, and American shopping malls will appeal to travelers who want to maintain a link to a familiar American culture.

You can also head off the beaten path to St. Thomas's western end, where a small Rastafarian community lives, and drive through the winding, narrow mountain roads that pass vistas rivaling any in the Virgin Islands.

PLANNING YOUR TIME

You can see St. Thomas's major sights in a few days, but plan to stay longer if you want to have time to sample all the restaurants, attractions, and duty-free shopping. History buffs will want one or two days to soak up all that St. Thomas has to offer.

Most visitors to St. Thomas stay at the large chain resorts along the beaches of the east and southern coast. But St. Thomas's unique appeal is in **historic Charlotte Amalie,** where travelers will find an increasing number of small, independent hotels, many with excellent views of Charlotte Amalie harbor. The old world ambience of these hostelries cannot be beat. You will want a rental car to explore the island, go to the beach, and get around town at night, when street crime can be a problem.

CRUISING TO FORTUNE?

By design, no island in the Virgins is as touched by cruise ships as St. Thomas. More than 1.6 million cruise ship passengers visited St. Thomas in 2005, making it one of the most popular cruise ship destinations in the Caribbean. Put simply, on St. Thomas, cruise ships rule.

Cruise ships represent the bread and butter of the St. Thomas economy. Taxi drivers, excursion companies, downtown shops, and roadside vendors depend on the constant traffic of cruise ship passengers for a livelihood. The industry is credited with bringing in $600 million annually for the island, 40 percent of its tourism revenue. Surveys have shown that the average cruise party of two spends more than $550 during a day on St. Thomas.

Cruise ships are an important source of revenue for the local government too. Ships pay a $7.50 head tax for each cruise ship passenger they bring to the island. Revenue from these taxes is used to finance expensive port development projects required by bigger and bigger cruise ships.

In 2006, St. Thomas opened a new port facility at Crown Bay which cost some $31 million to build. On St. Croix, which suffered complete abandonment by cruise ships in 2002, the Public Finance Authority has invested $14 million on a waterfront revitalization project at Frederiksted for the express purpose of enticing cruise ships back to the city.

Cruise ships have a social and cultural impact on the island, too. While Charlotte Amalie feels like a busting city during the days, it can be a ghost town at night after the ships have sailed away. The popularity of St. Thomas as a cruise ship destination has encouraged the development of a more gimmicky tourism product there, one that tends to exploit popular misperceptions and stereotypes of the Caribbean rather than break them down.

The size of the cruise sector has also led many islanders to develop a narrow view of what tourists are and can be. Perhaps most sadly of all, the high-volume nature of the cruise ship economy precludes any real exchange of culture between visitor and resident.

St. Thomas is one of the most popular cruise ship stops in the Caribbean—recent years have seen upwards of 1.6 million cruise ship passengers passing through, or 35 times the population of the island itself. From Thanksgiving to Easter, the island is marked by traffic jams and many of the so-called attractions are swamped by hordes of slow-moving cruise ship passengers. Most head to Charlotte Amalie's shopping district before picking up an open-air taxi to **Magen's Bay,** the island's best beach. Plan your day to avoid these areas between 10 A.M. and 2 P.M., the height of the cruise ship day.

St. Thomas is a family-friendly destination. Plan an itinerary of water sports, hiking, kayaking, and sightseeing to entertain the children. While adventurers will find **Coral World Ocean Park** too tame, it is ideal for young children and adults who don't feel comfortable snorkeling or diving on their own. Other "snorkel substitutes" on St. Thomas include a submarine reef tour and underwater scooters.

Dining and nightlife are two favorite attractions for many visitors. Restaurants range from seaside grills to old world gourmet to local food stands. Gourmands should head to **Frenchtown,** where sophisticated cuisine turns into hot nightlife in the wee hours. For a closer look at St. Thomian culture, plan your visit for late March or early April when the annual **St. Thomas Carnival** is in full swing. The annual parade is one of the longest and most colorful in the islands.

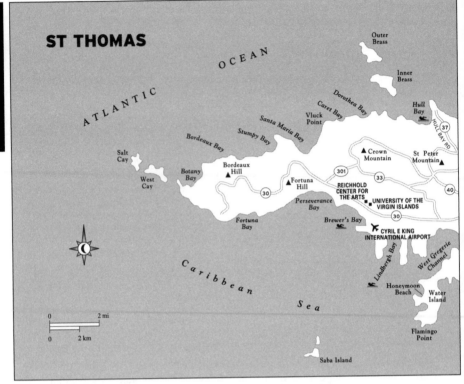

ST THOMAS

Sights

Explore Charlotte Amalie on foot or by taxi. The rest of the island is best explored by car. The countryside is widely developed, with the exception of the west end. Highways are generally well maintained, but routes are confusing and traffic can be very heavy. Drivers make liberal use of their horns and hand gestures to communicate with other drivers.

To reach the East End, take Route 30 (Frenchman's Bay or Bovoni Road), which follows the southeastern coast, runs into Route 32 (Red Hook Road), and continues along the shoreline past the best beaches and large resorts before becoming Route 30 (Smith Bay Road). To get to the north shore, take Route 35 (Mafolie Road) and follow it to Magen's Bay. Route 40 (Valdemar Hill Drive, also called Skyline Drive) follows the island's backbone from Charlotte Amalie to the east end. Take Route 30 as far west as you dare to explore the west end.

CHARLOTTE AMALIE

The capital of the U.S. Virgin Islands, this harbor town is one of the loveliest in the region. The wide bay plays host to huge cruise ships, small pleasure boats, and the small fishing skiffs of traditional fishermen. Long, narrow warehouses, built to store hogsheads of sugar, line the waterfront and have been converted into one of the largest shopping districts

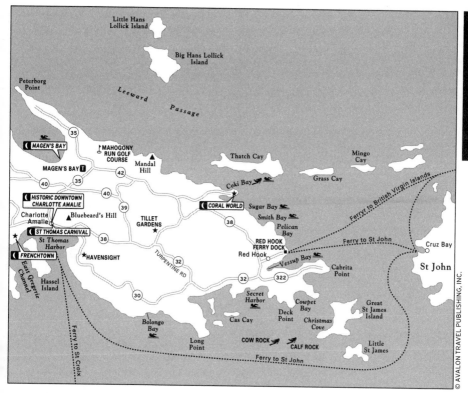

© AVALON TRAVEL PUBLISHING, INC.

in the Caribbean. Behind the shops, quiet side streets evoke the town's long history.

Charlotte Amalie is also a hub for dining, entertainment, and nightlife. Dozens of restaurants cater to all kinds of tastes, and during the annual St. Thomas Carnival, a colorful parade makes its way up Main Street.

There are three main roads in Charlotte Amalie. Waterfront Drive, also called Veteran's Drive, fronts the harbor and extends from Havensight Mall to Frenchtown. This four-lane road is best navigated by car or taxi. Main Street, also called Dronnigen's Gade, and Norre Gade, run parallel to the waterfront. Back Street, also called Wimmelskafts Gade, is one block farther inland, also parallel to the shoreline. Street names in the town are remnants of the island's Danish past.

Parking is available at the large public lot near Fort Christian. From 7 A.M. to 6 P.M. Mon.–Fri., you will pay $1 for the first hour, $.75 for each additional hour, or $5 for the whole day. Parking after hours and on weekends is free.

History

Charlotte Amalie was founded in 1781, when four artisans built homes next to the new Fort Christian and were granted licenses to operate inns. The settlement was named after the Danish Queen, but for the first century of its existence, Charlotte Amalie was better known as Taphuus, or pub. That probably says a lot. From the early days, Charlotte Amalie was a lively place. Early visitors described it variously as a freewheeling and exciting place, or as a den of pirates and scoundrels.

Charlotte Amalie grew steadily after its establishment. Warehouses were built along the

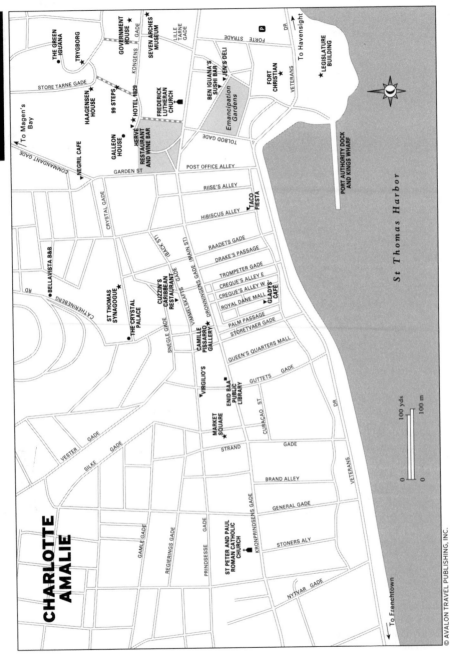

CHARLOTTE AMALIE

St Thomas Harbor

To Magen's Bay

To Havensight

To Frenchtown

THE GREEN IGUANA
TRYGBORG
GOVERNMENT HOUSE
SEVEN ARCHES MUSEUM
LEGISLATURE BUILDING
STORE TARNE GADE
HAAGENSEN HOUSE
99 STEPS
HOTEL 1829
FREDERICK LUTHERAN CHURCH
BEN IGUANA'S SUSHI BAR
JEN'S DELI
FORT CHRISTIAN
Emancipation Gardens
GALLEON HOUSE
HERVE RESTAURANT AND WINE BAR
NEGRIL CAFE
GARDEN ST
TOLBOD GADE
POST OFFICE ALLEY
PORT AUTHORITY DOCK AND KINGS WHARF
COMMANDANT GADE
RIISE'S ALLEY
CRYSTAL GADE
HIBISCUS ALLEY
TACO FIESTA
BELLAVISTA B&B
RAADETS GADE
DRAKE'S PASSAGE
TROMPETER GADE
CREQUE'S ALLEY E
CREQUE'S ALLEY W
ROYAL DANE MALL
GLADYS' CAFE
CATHERINEBERG RD
ST THOMAS SYNAGOGUE
THE CRYSTAL PALACE
CUZZIN'S CARIBBEAN RESTAURANT
PALM PASSAGE
CAMILLE PISSARRO GALLERY
STORETVAER GADE
QUEEN'S QUARTERS MALL
SNEGLE GADE
VIRGILIO'S
GUTTETS GADE
ENID BAA PUBLIC LIBRARY
MARKET SQUARE
CURACAO ST
VESTER GADE
SILKE GADE
STRAND
BRAND ALLEY
VETERANS DR
GENERAL GADE
GAMLE GADE
REGIERINGS GADE
PRINDSESSE GADE
KRONPRINDSENS GADE
ST PETER AND PAUL ROMAN CATHOLIC CHURCH
STONERS ALY
NYTVAR GADE

LILLE TARNE GADE
KONGENS GADE
FORTE STRADE
VETERANS DR
VIMMELSKAFTS GADE
DRONNINGENS GADE
BACK ST
MAIN ST
GADE

100 yds
100 m
0
0

© AVALON TRAVEL PUBLISHING, INC.

waterfront on long, narrow lots, which allowed for the most efficient use of the valuable waterfront. Homes were built on the hillward side of Main Street, and the residential portion of town steadily expanded up Denmark and Government Hills, and in the valley between them. Authorities did not manage this growth, and many homes were built very close together along narrow, precarious lanes. In the mid-1700s it became clear that additional residential space would be required in the town, and Danish authorities subdivided the valleys west of Denmark Hill and east of Government Hill.

Many of the early residents of Charlotte Amalie were free black people. These former slaves often bought their freedom, although some were manumitted by their owners. Many were skilled artisans, and others started shops that catered to the demands of a growing town. Savanne, the area west of Denmark Hill, near the market square, was the heart of the free black population. Today the area is called Savan (Sa-VON).

The absence of a building code and general unplanned nature of Charlotte Amalie made it susceptible to fire. No less than six fires destroyed more than half the town between 1804 and 1832. Eventually, following the last of these devastating fires, authorities put in place a restrictive building code that prohibited wood buildings on Main Street and required that all new roofs be covered with fire resistant materials. Many of the buildings still standing today date from the period of rebuilding after 1832.

◖ Historic Downtown Charlotte Amalie

Historic Charlotte Amalie encompasses the area from Fort Christian in the east to the Market Square in the west. Amble along a narrow alley to the top of Government or Denmark Hills for a view of the historic district. Old churches, many of which date to the early days of Danish colonization, are among the most distinctive landmarks. Fortifications around the historic town have been converted into tourist attractions and provide some of the best views of the harbor.

Today, most visitors concentrate on the

Fort Christian is one of St. Thomas's oldest standing buildings.

HISTORIC CHARLOTTE AMALIE WALKING TOUR

Despite the throngs in Charlotte Amalie's shopping district, you will have the town's historic attractions mostly to yourself. The sights listed here are organized from east to west and make a nice walking tour. Plan on one to three hours, depending on the amount of time you spend at each attraction. Wear a hat and bring plenty of water.

Brick-red and imposing, **Fort Christian** on the eastern end of the Charlotte Amalie waterfront is the oldest building in use on St. Thomas and a National Historic Landmark. Built between 1672 and 1680 by African laborers under direction of Danish colonialists, the fort was the center of political and community life during the early years of Danish colonization of the Virgin Islands. The fort housed the governor's residence, town hall, court, and jail, as well as its first church. It is now home to a museum. The lime-green building across Waterfront Drive from Fort Christian is the **V.I. Legislature Building.** This building dates back to 1874, when the Danes built it atop the site of a two-story wooden army barracks. Aside from its color, the building is notable for its red roof, white banding, and cast-iron rails. It served as the Charlotte Amalie High School before it became the seat of V.I. Senate.

Catty-corner from Fort Christian is the inviting, shady square of **Emancipation Gardens,** built in commemoration of the island's 1848 emancipation. Lignum vitae trees provide shade. Today, it is as pleasant place to rest and people-watch. Public concerts and other events are frequently held in the gazebo here.

Across the street from the park is the restored **Grand Hotel,** now the Grand Galleria, a complex of shops and restaurants. The original hotel opened in 1840 as the Commercial Hotel and Coffee House. Across Norre Gade (Main Street) from the Grand Galleria is **Frederik Lutheran Church,** the earliest church still standing on St. Thomas. Lutheranism was the official religion of the Danish colony, and while other faiths were tolerated, Lutheranism was encouraged. The first Lutheran congregation met in the Fort Christian courtyard. In 1754, a church was built outside the fort, but it was destroyed by hurricane 18 years later. Work began on Frederik Lutheran Church in the 1780s, and it was dedicated in 1793. The orginal church was in the simple Georgian style. It was gutted by fire in 1825 and rebuilt, with the addition of some Gothic-style trim. A hurricane in 1870 blew off the roof, which was rebuilt.

Take one of the narrow, steep walks up to Government Hill, the heart of Charlotte Amalie's historic district. **Government House** is the largest and most conspicuous building on Government Hill. The present structure, the fourth official residence of the chief executive, was built in 1867 by St. Croix carpenter Richard Bright. It was designed by a local merchant, Otto Marstrand. Built of white brick, Government House is most notable for its covered balconies with slender, fluted columns and ironwork rails. Pop your head in to see if you can take a look around the interior; the security guards may let you as long as no official function is going on.

There are several long staircases in this part of Charlotte Amalie, the most famous being **99 Steps** (wrongly named – there are 103), which takes you farther up Government Hill to **Trygborg,** better known as Blackbeard's Castle. Join a $12 walking tour offered by the

shops and stores of historic Charlotte Amalie. The old warehouses have been restored and air-conditioned and now boast a large selection of duty-free jewelry, perfume, crystal, and other fine wares. However, even nonshoppers will appreciate the ambience of these old buildings and the narrow, cobblestoned walks between them.

Explore Charlotte Amalie on foot in the morning or late afternoon for the best experience. The noonday sun combined with slow-moving taxis that congest Main Street detract from the overall experience at other times of day. The town must be explored on foot—traffic is just too tight and parking too scarce to attempt driving, except at night, when street

Inn at Blackbeard's Castle and you can climb to the top of this Danish military structure, which dates back to 1680.

Back at the bottom of 99 Steps is **Hotel 1829.** Formerly the Lavalette House, the hotel was built around 1831 by a wealthy French merchant, Alexander Lavalette. Set well above street level, this old home now houses a small hotel and bar. Visitors are welcome in the afternoon, when the bar opens.

At the corner of Nye and Crystal Gades, about two blocks from Government Hill, is the **St. Thomas Reformed Church,** formerly the Dutch Reformed Church. This 1844 church is unique among Charlotte Amalie structures in that it has survived largely intact since its construction. An imitation Roman temple, the church was built at the height of the classical revival period, with plaster colored and grooved to resemble red sandstone. The interior reflects the colonial woodwork styles of the period. A unique feature of this building is that it is a lumber core covered by masonry, a building style that has prevented cracks experienced by pure masonry structures during the region's frequent earthquakes.

One of Charlotte Amalie's most unique historic buildings is the **St. Thomas Synagogue** (Crystal Gade, tel. 340/774-4312, hebrew-cong@islands.vi, www.onepaper.com/synagogue, 9 A.M.-4 P.M. Mon.-Fri.), more properly called the Synagogue Beracha V'shalom V'gimilath Chasidim (Blessing, Peace, and Acts of Piety). Built in 1833 to replace an older structure, this house of worship continues to serve St. Thomas's small Jewish population. It is the oldest Hebrew congregation in the United States and the second oldest in the Western Hemisphere. The building, which underwent restoration in 2000, has been designated a National Historic Landmark. The sand floor is believed to reflect a tradition brought by early Sephardic Orthodox congregants, who worshiped on this site since 1796. Visitors are welcome as long as no service or other event is in progress; a small museum recounting the history of the Jewish community is set in the back of the church. Donations are welcome.

Near the corner of Dronnigen's Gade and Guttet Gade is the **Enid M. Baa Public Library** (Main Street, tel. 340/774-3407, 9 A.M.-5 P.M. Mon. and Fri., 9 A.M.-8 P.M. Tues.-Thurs., 10 A.M.-4 P.M. Sat.), built in 1818 by Baron von Bretton. The ground floor of the building contained shops and a courtyard, while the second floor was used as a residential quarters. A third story over the middle portion of the building had good views of the harbor. As a public library, the building is open to the public.

Just west of the public library is the **Market Square,** the traditional center of trade and commerce in town. During the days of slavery, it was also where slave auctions were held. A few years ago a large truck backed into the market building, damaging it so badly it had to be taken down. Despite this, the area is still a good place to find local farmers and artisans selling produce, arts, and crafts, especially on Saturday morning.

About two blocks farther west along Main Street is **St. Peter and St. Paul Roman Catholic Church.** Consecrated in 1848, this building replaced earlier churches destroyed by fire and hurricanes. The interior murals were painted in 1899 by Father Leo Servais and Brother Ildelphonsus.

crime can be a problem. See the *Historic Charlotte Amalie Walking Tour* sidebar in this chapter for the best route through the town and its historic attractions.

Museums

The **Fort Christian Museum** (Veterans Drive, 340/776-4566, 9 A.M.–4 P.M., $3 adults) houses simple exhibits with information about the history of the fort and the Virgin Islands, as well as the natural history, flora, and fauna of the islands. You can also climb to the top for impressive views of Charlotte Amalie harbor and step inside the first church, now furnished with antique West Indian mahogany furniture.

Tucked along a narrow alley next to the

ST. THOMAS'S IMPRESSIONIST MASTER

Camille Pissarro was born on July 10, 1830, on St. Thomas. The son of a Sephardic Jewish father and Dominican mother, Pissarro went to Paris at age 12 to attend school. There, his advisor told him to take "advantage of his life in the tropics by drawing coconut trees." When Pissarro returned to St. Thomas at age 17, he took this advice to heart. He spent the next five years of his life drawing images of island life: donkey carts, Negro women washing, harbor life, and the Danish forts.

Pissarro's parents did not embrace his avocation, and they required him to continue with daily chores to assist with the family business. The young artist became frustrated, and at age 23 ran away to Venezuela with the Danish painter Fritz Melbye. Pissarro later said he "bolted to Caracas in order to get clear of the bondage of bourgeois life."

Soon, Pissarro's parents resigned themselves to his choice of profession, and he returned to St. Thomas. He later returned to Paris to study art, where he was influenced by early impressionists. His own style was developing, too – one in which light was as essential as the subject being painted.

Pissarro developed friendships with other artists on the vanguard of the impressionist movement. In 1874, he joined Monet in organizing independent exhibitions to avoid the scrutiny of the status quo, which was highly critical of this new kind of art.

After Pissarro moved to Paris, his parents followed, having left their St. Thomas business in the hands of a caretaker. His parents employed a young maidservant from Burgundy, Julie Vellay, who became Pissarro's lifelong companion.

Despite scathing reviews and poverty, Pissarro remained dedicated to the impressionist method. He became something of a teacher, providing inspiration for artists such as Renoir, Monet, Degas, and Cézanne. By the end of his life, Pissarro had finally begun to receive critical praise for his work. He died of blood poisoning in November 1903.

Lieutenant Governor's Office on Government Hill is the **Seven Arches Museum** (Knud Hansen Alley, 340/774-9295, 10 A.M.–4 P.M. Mon.–Sat., $5), which provides a unique glimpse into the island's past. First surveyed in 1805, early structures on this spot were destroyed by hurricanes in the first half of the nineteenth century. Italian Andre Bonelli constructed the present building in 1857 as a gift to his daughter, Annette Margareth. A number of prominent black St. Thomas families owned the house over the next decades, including the Corneiro family. Museum proprietors Barbara Demaras and Philibert Fluck bought the building in 1993 and turned it into a museum. It is also their home, and when you go you will be greeted by the couple's friendly family of dogs and cats. The museum is furnished with West Indian mahogany furniture. Recent archeological work at the site has suggested that part of it was once a communal cooking area for the free black community of Charlotte Amalie.

One of the fathers of impressionist painting, Camille Pissarro, was born and raised on St. Thomas. His life and work is immortalized at the **Camille Pissarro Gallery** (14 Dronnigen's Gade, 340/774-4621, 10 A.M.–5 P.M. Mon.–Sat., 10 A.M.–1 P.M. Sundays (when a ship is in), free), housed in the old Pissarro home. The son of a St. Thomas businessman, Pissarro was schooled in Paris but returned to St. Thomas after his graduation. The young artist painted and sketched in his spare time, creating lovely depictions of island life, prints of which are on sale at the gallery. You can also see the rooms where Pissarro painted.

Named after the first black bandmaster in the U.S. Navy and St. Thomas native, the **Alton Augustus Adams Music Research Institute** (1-B Kongens Gade, 340/715-5680, 10 A.M.–12:30 P.M. and 1:30–4 P.M. Tues.–Fri., www.cbmr.org, free) is a resource center about black Caribbean music styles. A part of Columbia College's Center for Black Music Research, this center was founded in 2001 and houses a database of information about traditional Virgin Islands music. The center also organizes occasional public performances of local music and dance styles.

Tours

You can climb to the top of Trygborg, or **Blackbeard's Castle,** and tour four old West Indian town houses on a walking tour offered by Historic Blackbeard's Castle (340/776-1234, www.blackbeardscastle.com, $12), although you will find this attraction shuttered on days when there is no ship in town. You can join an organized tour, leaving between 9 A.M. and 10 A.M., or take your own self-guided tour anytime between 9:30 A.M. and 3 P.M. Call the day before to confirm the departure time if you want to join the guided tour. Stops include **Villa Notman,** built in 1860 by Scottish engineer James Notman; **Britannia House,** the onetime home of the British consul to the Danish West Indies; **Haagensen House,** an 1827 home built for the Danish banker Hans Haagensen; and **Hotel 1829** on Government Hill. You also get a cold drink about halfway through the tour. Each of the historic homes has been furnished with period furniture and decor. If you take the self-guided tour, curators are on hand at Haagensen House and Britannia House to answer your questions.

While you can enter Hotel 1829 without paying for the $12 tour, a tour ticket is required to view the other homes and buildings. If you're interested in history, or just want a chance to savor Charlotte Amalie's style and charm, this is a good thing to do. Take the self-guided tour to avoid being part of a crowd and to move at your own pace; the guides know their script but little else— the curators are more knowledgeable.

◖ Frenchtown

In response to large-scale desertion of the plantations following the end of slavery, colonial authorities attempted to attract immigrant labor to fuel the agricultural economy, especially on St. Croix. These attempts were largely unsuccessful; the immigrants were often just as uninterested as the newly-freed slaves in laboring in sugar cane fields.

In the 1870s, a large group of laborers of French origin left St. Bartholomew and settled in St. Thomas in two distinct communities: Frenchtown, west of Charlotte Amalie, and along the north shore. "Frenchies," as they are called today, were fishermen and artisans, known for their straw hats. Today, Frenchtown remains a quaint, tight-knit community of fishermen and their families. The fish market here is especially lively.

Located in the heart of Frenchtown along the western side of the harbor, the **French Heritage Museum** (Rue de St. Barthelemy, 340/774-2320, 9 A.M.–6 P.M. Mon.–Fri., free) is dedicated to preserving the traditions and history of St. Thomas's French inhabitants. Housed in a yellow building next to the Josephe Aubain Ballpark in Frenchtown, this is the place to come to learn about this unique St. Thomas community.

Water Island

At 500 acres, Water Island is the larger of the two islands in Charlotte Amalie harbor. A quiet, mostly residential place, Water Island has several miles of paved road good for walking or biking, some nice beaches, and an interesting history. There is regular ferry service from Frenchtown.

Often referred to as the fourth Virgin Island, it bears the distinction of being the site of a series of black-owned plantations, dating back as early as 1769 when a free mulatto named Jean Renaud had a plantation there with 18 slaves. In 1793 the plantation was sold to another free black man named Peter Tararyn, the commander of the Free Negro Corps, established by the Danes to capture runaway slaves.

In 1799 another free black established a second plantation on Water Island, and the two plantations existed side by side until the end of slavery in 1848, when the island was deserted. In 1944, the U.S. Department of Defense bought Water Island for $10,000 and began to build Fort Segarra, a military fort with barracks, gun emplacements, watchtowers, and underground bunkers. World War II ended while construction was under way; Fort Segarra was abandoned midstream, but not before basic infrastructure including roads, water pipes, a sewage system, and power lines were put in place. Following the end of the war, the Army's Chemical Warfare Division used Water Island to test poisonous gases.

In 1950, the Department of Defense leased Water Island to a private developer, who built a hotel and private homes on the island. In 1965 the lease was sold to Edward McArdle, who expanded the hotel and operated it until 1989, when Hurricane Hugo struck the islands. The hotel was badly damaged and was not rebuilt. In 1996, the federal government transferred Water Island to the local government, and all residents were allowed to buy their land and remain. The 2000 census revealed a year-round population of just about 150 people.

Water Island's greatest attraction is **Honeymoon Beach,** also known as Druif Bay, a protected, clean, and quiet beach along its southwest shore. Honeymoon Beach is within walking distance of the ferry that runs regularly between St. Thomas and Water Island, and it makes a good day-trip destination, especially if you are staying near town. **Sprat Beach** is a little farther off the beaten path.

Get to Water Island on the Water Island Ferry (340/715-2186 or 340/775-5770).

Hassel Island

The smaller and closer of the islands in St. Thomas harbor, Hassel Island was once connected to the main island via a narrow isthmus. The Danish government first separated it from St. Thomas in 1860, and the U.S. Army Corps of Engineers deepened the channel by dredging in 1919. Originally called Hurricane Hole, the island later came to be known as Hassel Island after its owners, the Hazzel family. There are several historical ruins on Hassel Island, but no organized or easy way to view them.

On the northern tip, close to where the Tortola and St. John ferries pass on their way into the harbor, are remains of the earliest steam-powered marine railway in the Western Hemisphere. Opened in 1844, the marine railway lifted large vessels out of the water for cleaning and repair. It used technology that, while common today, was brand new in the 1840s. St. Thomas was one of the first ports to install a marine railway, which testifies to the island's importance in the realm of shipping. The marine railway operated almost continuously for 120 years. From 1911 until 1954 it was operated by the Creque family of St. Thomas. During World War II it was leased to the U.S. Navy. The last recorded ship was hauled out there in 1965.

Other ruins on the island include early 19th century English fortifications, dating back to their brief occupation of the islands during the first Napoleonic War. The British built Fort Shipley, or Shipley's Battery, on the highest point of the island.

Hassel Island is 135 acres, and mostly abandoned. It is forested by dense, drought-resistant cacti and grasses, and the coastline is rocky and mostly impenetrable. A few residences are visible along the coast facing St. Thomas—although they are not widely used today. Most of the island—122 acres—is owned by the Virgin Islands National Park.

Havensight

Havensight is the shopping district around the cruise ship dock, on the eastern end of Charlotte Amalie harbor. A large outdoor mall and additional stores in the vicinity attract shoppers nearly every day of the year. The **Paradise Point Tramway** (340/774-9809, 9 A.M.– 5 P.M. Thurs.–Tues., 9 A.M.–9 P.M. Wed., $16 adults, $8 children 6–12, under 6 free) departs from Havensight and carries passengers in a tram to Paradise Point, an overlook with nice views of the harbor, plus a bar, restaurant, and more shops. The tramway is open only when a cruise ship is in harbor. If you are land-based, you can also drive to Paradise Point.

Beaches

The best beaches on St. Thomas are along

the eastern end. Nevertheless, if you're staying near town consider these beaches, which are closer to home.

Brewer's Bay Beach, past the airport and right across the highway from the University of the Virgin Islands, is a popular and pleasant beach, especially among college students who come here between classes. There are no facilities, but a food bus or two usually parks here on the weekends, selling cold drinks and snacks. You also get the thrill of watching planes swoop down to land at the nearby airport.

Located just east of the airport, **Lindbergh Bay** is a long, narrow beach popular with families and locals. A public playground right next door is an added attraction. The bay got its name in 1929 when Charles Lindbergh landed at the nearby field during a goodwill tour of the region following his 1927 solo crossing of the Atlantic.

On Water Island, **Honeymoon Beach** is appealing and quiet. On weekends, there is sometimes a food van selling burgers and drinks; otherwise walk uphill 10 minutes to the local deli. There is nice snorkeling along the southern end of the beach.

For a resort experience, head to **Morningstar Beach** at Frenchman's Reef Hotel, on the eastern end of Charlotte Amalie harbor. The beach is long, thin, and manicured. The Reef, as it is called, operates a ferry to and from the Charlotte Amalie waterfront. Round-trip fare is $5 for adults and $3 for children 3–12. It operates Mon.–Sat. and departs Charlotte Amalie every hour on the hour between 9 A.M. and 5 P.M.

NORTHSIDE

The north shore of St. Thomas is quiet, crisscrossed by narrow roads, and punctuated by remarkable vistas. A series of bays wind in and out, but none is better than Magen's Bay, the broad, long public beach about midway along the island's north coast.

Overlooks

On St. Thomas, a good view is an entrepreneurial opportunity. The best vistas are popular with itinerant vendors, drink retailers, and other businesspeople out to make a buck. When the cruise ship dock is full, expect the overlooks to be teeming with tourists and locals trying to sell them something.

The most famous overlook is **Drake's Seat,** located at the crossroads of Routes 40 and 33. The legend that Sir Francis Drake stopped here is probably not true, but never mind. The view of Magen's Bay is fantastic, and there's a bench where you can sit to thoroughly enjoy it. Come here early in the morning or late in the afternoon to avoid crowds.

Mountaintop (St. Peter Mountain Road, 340/774-2400), which proclaims itself "world famous," is really a small shopping mall on top of one of St. Thomas's highest points. When there's a cruise ship in, taxis disgorge hundreds of cruise ship passengers here; when there's no ship, the place is a ghost town. The view from the front balcony is excellent; on a clear day you can see Tortola and the other British Virgins. There are also restrooms, and a bar, which specializes in banana daiquiris, supposedly invented here.

St. Peter Greathouse

You can tour a luxurious great house overlooking Magen's Bay at St. Peter Greathouse and Gardens (St. Peter Mountain Road, 340/774-4999, 8 A.M.–4 P.M., $10 adults, $5 children). The great house, which is also used for private functions and parties, is decorated with the work of local artists. Guests get a free rum punch with their admission, which you can enjoy on the balcony overlooking the north shore.

◖ Magen's Bay

This beach is special in part because it is so big, beautiful, and calm, and in part because it has escaped the fate of all the other superb St. Thomas beaches: resort development. The park attracts a diverse crowd of tourists and locals, and it can be a place for quiet relaxation or high-spirited fun.

The beach itself is about one mile long and slightly heart-shaped. It is wide, gently sloping, and almost always calm. Even on days when there are a lot of people here, you can be sure

ST. THOMAS

COURTESY OF U.S. VIRGIN ISLANDS DEPARTMENT OF TOURISM

Magen's Bay, the best beach on St. Thomas

to find a quiet corner of shade (or sun). This is a popular place for an early morning jog or walk. A small enterprise at the eastern end of the park rents water sports gear and kayaks, but most people are content lolling around in the crystal, calm water.

Magen's Bay is owned by the territorial government and administered as a public park; visitors must pay $3 per adult, $.25 per child, and $1 per car to get in. The fee collection booth is open about 7:30 A.M.–6 P.M. daily. Funds go to maintain public restrooms, picnic tables, shelters, and collect garbage. There is a small bar and snack shop near the entrance.

For a more secluded experience, head to **Little Magen's Bay** along the eastern end of the bay. Nudity is common at this small beach.

Hull Bay

This caramel-colored beach is the only place to catch surf on St. Thomas. During the winter months small swells are just big enough to provide a diversion for surfers, although many head to better breaks on Tortola when they can. Hull Bay is the epicenter of the north shore French community, and the bay is often scattered with small fishing boats.

The bay here is almost always quiet, and there is plenty of shade. The beach bar is as friendly as they come, with games such as horseshoes to while away an afternoon.

Hans Lollik

A 500-acre undeveloped island two miles from the St. Thomas coastline, Hans Lollik and its neighboring Little Hans Lollik have long been the apple of developers' eyes. The local government refused to give one developer the necessary building permits. In 2004 the islands were sold to another developer, who says he plans to build a resort and marina on Hans Lollik. Adventurers can kayak or windsurf there from Hull Bay or Magen's Bay.

RED HOOK AND THE EAST END

St. Thomas sheds its historic ambience and multicultured feel on the East End, where resorts line adjacent bays and numerous bars and restaurants cater to hotel guests and resident expats. This is also where you will find the best water sports and the island's most popular attraction, Coral World. Red Hook, the sprawling town on St. Thomas's easternmost tip, is where most people come to catch ferries to St. John and Tortola. Farther inland, Estate Tutu and the surrounding areas are the most populated portions of St. Thomas, with large shopping malls and traffic jams.

◖ Coral World

Coral World Marine Park and Undersea Observatory (Coki Point, 340/775-1555, fax 340/775-9068, www.coralworldvi.com, $18 adults, $9 children 3–12) puts the wonder of underwater sea life within reach of everyone. An undersea observatory allows you to get eye-level with the coral reef without getting wet; other exhibits showcase specific marine creatures, including green turtles, sharks, and sting rays. There is even an exhibit showing the nighttime reef—including phosphorescent coral. In addition to the marine exhibits, Coral World features a short nature trail with tropical plants, endangered tortoises, and lots of iguanas.

At first blush, Coral World may seem like a tourist trap—there are plenty of opportunities to spend money here—but the park is serious about its educational mission. If you are equally serious about learning, Coral World provides a great opportunity for education. Exhibits feature lots of information about animals, oceans, and environmental threats, but you have to stop and read them. Staff members also present information about the animals at the many daily feedings (which are scheduled throughout the day, so you are bound to see something cool while you're there).

Coral World also offers an activity it calls Sea Trekkin', similar to what is called Snuba elsewhere. You put on a bathing suit and wear a special helmet that allows you to breathe normally while you're underwater. The set-up allows you to swim around underwater, like a scuba diver, without wearing a tank on your back.

If you are doing a lot of snorkeling or diving on your own, you probably won't get much out of Coral World. But for people who either

Coral World is a unique underwater observatory.

© SUSANNA HENIGHAN

don't have time or can't manage the challenge of snorkeling, Coral World is an excellent place to come. It is ideal for families, small children, and older travelers. Coral World tends to be busy, especially when a lot of cruise ships are in port. To avoid the crowds, come early or late. Also look out for ubiquitous coupons, available in many of the free tourist trade magazines you see around, which offer $3 off adult admission and $1 off a child's. You can also find them on the Coral World website.

Tillet Gardens

Located in Estate Tutu, near the shopping mall that houses Kmart and other attractions, Tillet Gardens (Anna's Retreat, 340/779-1929) is an arts community named for its founder, silkscreen artist Jim Tillet. Tillet founded the arts center on an old Danish farm in the 1960s. Today, the surrounding area has morphed into a busy shopping district, but Tillet Gardens is still a quiet oasis. You can visit with an artist at work, buy locally made art, or relax in a café. Tillet's protégé, Sonny Thomas, carries on the silkscreening tradition. Even the wall surrounding the complex has been turned into a canvas for art: colorful murals stand out from the surroundings.

Beaches

There is a series of nice beaches along the island's east and southern coast, but most are occupied by resorts. Nonguests are tolerated at such beaches, but you may be asked to pay for a beach chair or feel compelled to buy lunch from the local beachfront restaurant.

The best public beach in the area is **Coki Point Beach,** next to Coral World. Look for signs to Coral World on Route 38 (Smith Bay Road) and take the short, potholed road to the beach. Parking is haphazard and unsecured; leave your valuables at the hotel. There is excellent snorkeling here, and an excellent dive shop is right next door. There is also an array of beach vendors selling snacks, trinkets, cold drinks, and, if you look carefully, marijuana. The beach gets crowded on weekends and when a cruise ship is in town.

One of the best resort beaches is at **Sapphire Bay,** a long beach near Red Hook. Locals flock here on Sunday afternoons when bands play hot soca and calypso tunes. There is also usually a game of beach volleyball going on. The view here is especially nice, and snorkeling is good.

Another good resort beach is on the southern shore. **Bolongo Bay,** home to the eponymous resort, is a welcoming and appealing crescent of sand along Route 30. Bolongo Bay has a popular beach bar and good water sports center. You can also pass the day just relaxing on the sand and enjoying the ocean view.

Vessup Bay Beach near the end of Route 322 on the far side of Vessup Bay is a long, broad string of sand especially popular among water sports enthusiasts. There is a bar nearby.

Sugar Bay, at the Wyndam Sugar Bay Resort, is a compact but broad ribbon of sand opposite Coki Point. The resort has beach chairs for guests, but nonguests can partake in the water sports, crystal water, and sand.

Secret Harbour is a calm bay off Route 322. The same-named resort and restaurant are the backdrop, and you can take advantage of the resort's water sports shop.

Entertainment and Events

◖ St. Thomas Carnival

St. Thomas has the largest Carnival in the Virgin Islands—it is bold, colorful and festive. Held in late March and early April, St. Thomas Carnival attracts islanders from St. Croix, St. John, Tortola, Virgin Gorda, and even farther afield. The Carnival Village is set up in the large public parking lot next to Fort Christian in downtown Charlotte Amalie. Admission is free, and there is top-notch live entertainment nightly, plus lots of local food and drink on sale.

The Lionel Roberts Stadium in the Hospital Ground area of Charlotte Amalie is the venue for many of the shows and contests, including a series of calypso contests climaxing with the finals, where the island's Calypso Monarch is crowned. The King and Queen of the Band is a contest for the most elaborate colorful, feathered costume, and the annual steel pan concert features the island's best steel pan bands. A Quelbe Tramp is held down Main Street, where people dance behind a traditional quelbe band, but the crowds come out for the massive early morning Jouvert, when soca and calypso bands pump out loud, pulsating grooves.

The climax of the Carnival is the Adult's Parade (the Children's Parade, held one day before, features lots of majorettes and children's steel band orchestras), which wends from Western Cemetery to the Lionel Roberts Stadium. Ground zero is Post Office Square, the broad stretch of road in front of the main downtown post office, where judges and dignitaries watch the parade on risers. Onlookers line Main Street from early in the day, staking claim to shady spots with foldout chairs and coolers.

Check with the U.S. Virgin Islands Department of Tourism (340/77408784, www.usvitourism.vi) for a schedule of the upcoming Carnival. During the fete, check the local papers for details about start times, performers, and parking restrictions.

Rolex Regatta

The St. Thomas Yacht Club (340/775-6320) hosts the International Rolex Regatta every March. The Rolex is part of the Caribbean Ocean Racing Triangle, which also includes the St. Maarten Heineken Regatta and the BVI Spring Regatta.

Reichhold Center for the Arts

The premier performance venue in the Virgin Islands is the Reichhold Center for the Arts (No. 3 Brewer's Bay, 340/693-1559, www.reichholdcenter.com), an open-air amphitheater affiliated with the University of the Virgin Islands. The 2,000-seat center was built in the late 1970s and has hosted performers as varied as the Moscow Ballet and Ray Charles. The Center's annual arts series runs from October to May and features performances by top jazz, Latin, and reggae performers. Other shows include dance, classical, and local quelbe music. Tickets can be bought online in advance.

Cinemas

St. Thomas's lone cinema is **Caribbean Cinemas** (Weymouth Rhymer Highway, 340/776-3666), located in the same shopping center as Cost-U-Less between Charlotte Amalie and Estate Tutu. First-run movies show nightly, with matinees on the weekend.

Nightlife

Frenchtown is the home of the most sophisticated nightlife on St. Thomas. Many people gather at **Oceana** (340/774-4262) for lively after-work conversation at the bar. On Thursdays, Fridays, and Saturdays all the beautiful people head to **Epernay** (Rue de St. Barthelomy, 340/774-5348) for dancing and mingling into the wee hours. There is a $5 cover charge to get in on Friday and Saturday nights. People look chic and stylish here—blue jeans and sandals would be out of place. The crowd is multicultural and mature.

On the other side of the spectrum is **The Green House,** (Waterfront, 340/774-7998) the first choice for many island residents looking for a night out. Its two-for-one happy hour is the first attraction, followed by live music on weekends. The dance floor here is hot and crowded, moving to the rhythm of reggae, calypso, and soca. If midweek has you down, stop by the Green House on Tuesday night for one of the liveliest school-night parties around. Ladies, beware the sharks.

You can easily ping-pong between the **Offshore Bar** (Port of Sale Mall, 340/779-6400) and **Shipwreck Tavern** (Al Cohen's Mall, 340/777-1293) two popular nightspots near Havensight, to find the best party. The Offshore brings in live rock and blues bands regularly and attracts a lively, young, mostly expat crowd. This place feels like a live music bar in College Town, U.S.A. The Shipwreck is darker, danker, and a bit more laid-back, with a pool hall and video games.

In the parking lot of Red Hook Plaza on the east end, **Duffy's Love Shack** (340/779-2495) is a landmark. This is your genuine froo-froo drinks and limbo party place, and people looking for fun come here like moths to the flame. The open-air bar is a popular hunting ground for those searching for companionship, whether for the night or a little longer.

Shopping

Charlotte Amalie

Downtown Charlotte Amalie is the heart of St. Thomas shopping. Stores selling jewelry, gems, crystal, electronics, perfume, liquor, and souvenirs line Main Street and many of the narrow alleys between Main Street and the Waterfront. The territory's duty-free status means you can find significant savings on these big-ticket items.

In addition to low prices and lots of selection, another big draw for shopping downtown is the historic ambience. Many shops are built within the long, narrow warehouses once used to store sugar, rum, and other goods ready to sail to Europe and America. Cobblestoned walks, old stone walls, and classic West Indian architecture lend to the enjoyment of being downtown.

Many downtown shops are chain stores. **Diamonds International** (340/774-1510), **Little Switzerland** (340/776-2016), and **Cardow Jewelers** (340/776-1140) are the biggest names in jewelry. **A.H. Riise** (340/776-2303) sells liquor and perfume. **Boolchands** (340/776-0302) has a wide selection of cameras and other electronics.

Tucked among these big names, you will find some smaller shops selling island-style clothing, handcrafted jewelry, and art. Among the independent and interesting shops are the **Pissarro Gallery,** (340/774-4621) where you will find reproductions of Pissarro prints and other works of art, and **Native Arts and Crafts,** (Emancipation Gardens, 340/777-1153) which sells locally made lace, dolls, and other crafts. **Down Island Traders** (340/775-7019) stocks an intriguing selection of Caribbean arts, crafts, spices, and more.

Vendor's Plaza, located on the waterfront next to Emancipation Gardens, is the place for cheap goods: colorful sarongs, St. Thomas T-shirts, jewelry, and handbags. You can also usually find people here offering to braid your hair into dreadlock-like braids.

Havensight

Havensight is newer and feels like a regular outdoor mall. Located next to the West Indian Company cruise ship dock, this mall was built to capitalize on cruise ship passengers as soon as they get off the boat. Many stores have shops both downtown and at Havensight. Parking is generally good here.

In addition to stores selling jewelry, watches, perfume, and liquor, you will find the island's best photo shop (**Blazing Photos,** 340/776-5547), bookstore (**Dockside Books,** 340/774-4837), and art supply center (**The Draughting Shaft,** 340/776-1822) here.

Red Hook

Red Hook is an increasingly popular place to shop. There are no jewelry or watch stores here; shops at American Yacht Harbour, the big waterfront building near the ferry dock, specialize in things like island-style clothing, footwear, unique handmade jewelry and art. **Keep Left** (340/775-9964) has hats, sunglasses, backpacks, sandals, and all sorts of "active lifestyle" accessories. **The Blade and Key** (340/775-3254), located west of American Yacht Harbor, sells brand-name cutlery, knives, and Leathermans. On Route 38, near the turnoff to Coki Point, is **Kilnworks Pottery and Art Gallery** (340/775-3979), which produces unique island-style pottery.

Sports and Recreation

WATER SPORTS

Snorkeling

The best place on St. Thomas for snorkeling is Coki Beach. A healthy, fringing reef runs parallel to the beach, with a narrow sandbar in the middle. Gear plus orientation, if you want it, is available from **Coki Beach Dive Club** (340/775-4220), located on the road to Coki Beach.

You can also snorkel around Cas Cay and the other islands near St. Thomas's east end. You will need a boat to get to these sites, however, or sign up for a kayak tour of the area.

Snorkeling Substitutes

St. Thomas specializes in snorkeling substitutes, activities that let you explore the underwater world with more ease and comfort than normal snorkeling. Purists look down their noses at these activities—after all, snorkeling is really quite easy. But for families, people not in optimal health, or folks who want to be able to fit some underwater sightseeing into a busy day of shopping, touring, and dining, these activities make sense.

In **Sea Trekkin'** (Coral World Underwater Observatory, 340/775-1555) you put on your swimsuit and a special helmet that keeps you supplied with oxygen and then descend about 30 feet to walk amid the coral reef. **Bob Underwater Adventures** (Port of Sale Mall, Havensight, 340/715-0348, www.bob-usvi.com) puts you on an underwater scooter to explore in water about 7–10 feet deep. Your hair even stays dry, and you can wear glasses or contacts without a problem.

The **Atlantis Submarine** (Havensight, 340/776-5650, www.atlantisadventures.com, $76 adults, $38 children) offers 50-minute underwater tours of reefs around St. Thomas aboard the *Atlantis 15* submarine. The narrated tours go out to Buck Island off the southeast shore of St. Thomas.

Diving

Several wreck and reef dive sites are accessible by boat from St. Thomas. Only **Coki Beach** has good diving from the beach.

Offshore, divers can explore a number of wrecks along the island's southern coast. *Miss Opportunity,* an old Navy hospital barge, lies in about 55 feet of water south of the airport. One of the most popular wreck dives is the *Witshoal II,* an old tank landing ship that spent 32 post–World War II years hauling wood pulp on the Great Lakes but sank during Tropical Storm Klaus in 1984. Today, it lies in between 90 and 30 feet of water west of Saba island off St. Thomas and is home to a thriving artificial reef. Three other wrecks, the *Witconcrete II, Grainton,* and *Witservice IV* lie around Saba island.

There is another cluster of snorkel and dive sites around Buck and Capella islands, off the southeast coast of St. Thomas. Not to be confused with St. Croix's Buck Island, St. Thomas's Buck is small, rocky, and home to a lighthouse. The west end of the island offers year-round protected reef diving and snorkeling. The *Cartanza Senora* (sometimes called the *Cartenser Senior*) was sunk here as an artificial reef in 1979. Submarine sightseeing tours bring visitors to this area, especially the north shore of Buck Island.

The **Cow and Calf,** another popular dive site, is named for its resemblance to an adult and baby whale. Below water, this dive site is a maze of arches, ledges, and tunnels.

In addition to sites mentioned here, many St. Thomas operators sail to sites around St. John and even to the British Virgin Islands. **Chris Sawyer Diving Center** (Compass Point Marina, 340/775-7320 and Red Hook, 340/777-7804, www.sawyerdive.vi) is one of the largest St. Thomas dive operators, offering a whole range of dive packages, instruction, and night snorkels and dives. The company also has an office at the Wyndam Sugar Bay resort.

Another favorite St. Thomas dive shop is **Coki Beach Dive Club** (340/775-4220, www.cokidive.com), located along the road to

Coki Beach. These folks offer some of the best and friendliest dive instruction and specialize in the reef just offshore Coki Beach. Other dive shops include **Underwater Safaris** (Havensight Mall, 340/774-3737) located inside Water World Outfitters and **Blue Island Divers** (Crown Bay Marina, 340/774-2001, www.blueislanddivers.com).

Kayaking

Bovoni Cay, Patricia Cay, and Cas Cay lie within the protected mangrove lagoon offshore the community of Nadir and are ideal for exploring in a kayak. **V.I. Ecotours** (Estate Nadir, 340/779-2155, www.viecotours) offers guided kayak tours of the area, plus boat trips to Cas Cay. Most tours include snorkeling, and some include hiking.

The Cas Cay trip is $60 for adults, $35 for children 4–13. The kayak and hike tour is $75 for adults and $45 for children 4–12. Children under 4 are free.

Fishing

St. Thomas is the base of the largest sportfishing fleet in the Virgin Islands. Sportfishers depart daily from marinas along the east end of the island, many headed to the North Drop, a famed fishing ground in the British Virgin Islands. Most sportfishing expeditions last at least a few hours; many last all day. Prices, which range from $800 and up per day, are quoted per boat, not per person. All bait, tackle, fuel, and beverages are included.

Marlin season is in the summer, when the waters are at their warmest. Marlin are tagged and released. Other sport fish, such as barracuda, wahoo, tuna, mahimahi, and jacks can be kept; most boats will cut a fillet for you if you ask.

Black Pearl Charters (Sapphire Marina, 340/775-9982) has been in business for 30 years and operates out of a 38-foot sportfishing yacht with a full galley, air-conditioning, and head. Other sportfishers are **Marlin Prince** (340/693-5929), captained by Eddie Morrison, and **Prowler II** (340/775-7205 or 340/344-6212), captained by Mark Lamborn. Captain Don Mertens runs **Bluefin II** (American Yacht

Harbor, 340/775-6691), and Captain Red Bailey is at the helm of **Abigail III** (Sapphire Beach Marina, 340/775-6147). Other sportfishers include **Double Header Sportfishing** (Sapphire Marina, 340/777-7317) and **Peanut Gallery Sportfishing** (Crown Bay Marina, 340/775-5274).

The **Virgin Islands Game Fishing Club** (Red Hook, 340/775-9144) organizes fishing tournaments, including the Offshore Marine Dolphin Derby in April, the July Open, and Wahoo Wind-Up every November. Another good source of information about sportfishing charters, upcoming tournaments, and recent catches is **Neptune Fishing Supply** (American Yacht Harbor, 340/775-0115), which also sells fishing supplies and can help you get your BVI fishing license.

SAILING

You can rent a powerboat for the day or go on a day sail on St. Thomas.

Powerboat rentals are available from **Nauti Nymph** (American Yacht Harbor, 340/775-5066). They have 25-, 29-, and 31-foot powerboats, which come equipped with a bimini top, ice cooler, and freshwater shower. Rates range $285–480 for a half day, $335–530 for a full day. This is a very popular way to explore St. John and the British Virgin Islands.

Day sail operators typically take visitors to St. John and the British Virgin Islands. Most serve lunch and drinks, and all provide snorkel gear and instruction if necessary.

The **Winifred** (340/775-7898) is a 43-foot wooden sailboat that takes a maximum of six passengers to St. John. The 50-foot **Nightwind** (340/775-4110 or 779-2877) provides breakfast, lunch, and an open bar to passengers on its day sail to St. John.

For a smooth ride, try **Scubadu** (340/643-5155), a 40-foot catamaran. Captain Max skippers the **Lou** (340/775-7467), taking no more than six people on his day sails to St. John. **Fantasy** (340/775-5652) boasts President Bill Clinton as a passenger when he visited the Virgin Islands. Fantasy sails to St. John and offers breakfast, lunch, and an open bar.

Marinas

St. Thomas's marinas are found almost exclusively on the east end of the island, although there are a few around Charlotte Amalie Harbor. The brand new Yacht Haven USVI, between Havensight and Charlotte Amalie, is due to open in 2006. This new marina is built on the site of the first Yacht Haven, a once grand facility badly damaged in Hurricane Marilyn. **Yacht Haven USVI** (Long Bay, 340/774-5030, fax 340/774-5035, www.yachthavenusvi.com) will have slips large enough for 400-foot mega yachts, plus shopping, dining, and office space. It also boasts state-of-the art high-speed communications and in-slip refueling.

Near Charlotte Amalie, **Crown Bay Marina** (Gregorie Channel, 340/774-2255, fax 340/776-2760, www.crownbay.com) is a 96-slip full service marina and host to the annual Charter Yacht Society boat show. There is a chandlery and repair shop plus shops, restaurants, high-speed communication, fuel, water, electricity, and pump-out service. Crown Bay can accommodate vessels of up to 200 feet long and 15-foot drafts.

American Yacht Harbour (Red Hook, 340/775-6454, fax 340/776-5970, www.ayhmarina.biz) is a 105-slip, full-service marina in the heart of Red Hook. Amenities include refueling, pump-out, communications, ice, water, and electricity. AYH can accommodate boats up to 110 feet long, with a 10-foot draft.

The 67-slip **Sapphire Beach Resort and Marina** (North of Red Hook, 340/775-6100 x8142) can accommodate boats of up to 65 feet with 10-foot draft. **Pirate's Cove Marina** (Benner's Bay, 340/774-4655, www.piratescove.vi) is a 30-slip marina across from Food Town grocery store in Estate Fredenhoj. This friendly marina can accommodate boats and has an inn on-site.

Frenchtown Marina (VHF Channel 16, 8 A.M.–5 P.M.) can accommodate vessels 30–150 feet, with depths of up to 18 feet. Water, electricity, and showers are available, and you're right next to some fantastic dining.

Anchorages

St. Thomas has 11 official anchorages, including Bolongo Bay, Charlotte Amalie Harbor, Cowpet Bay, Hull Bay, Jersey Bay, Long Bay, Muller Bay, Nazareth Bay (Secret Harbor), Red Hook, Benner Bay, and Vessup Bay.

On Water Island, you can anchor at Elephant Bay, Flamingo Bay, and Honeymoon Bay. On Hassel Island, anchor at Careening Cove. You can also anchor at Christmas Cove on Great St. James Island off the eastern tip of St. Thomas.

The Reef Ecology Foundation of St. Thomas and St. John has set up a limited number of moorings for public use to protect the coral reef from anchor damage. These blue-striped buoys are free but restricted to boats less than 60 feet long. They are located at Thatch Cay, Grass Cay, Congo Cay, Carvel Rock, Great St. James, Little St. James, Cow and Calf, Capella Island, Flat Cay and Saba Island.

These moorings are intended for day use only and not in storm conditions. There is a three-hour time limit on use.

Yacht Clubs

The **St. Thomas Yacht Club** (Cowpet Bay, 340/775-6320, www.ctyc.net) organizes regattas and social events year-round. The International Rolex Regatta in March is the biggest sailing event of theid year, but the Yacht Club hosts a number of other smaller-scale regattas from October to May.

LAND PURSUITS
Golf

Mahogany Run Golf Course (340/777-6006, U.S. toll free 800/253-7103, www.mahoganyrungolf.com) is St. Thomas's only golf course. The 18-hole, par 70 course was first built in 1980 but has undergone recent renovations and improvements. Nestled in a small valley near Magen's Bay on northeast St. Thomas, Mahogany Run is compact and highly engineered. It was designed by George and Tom Fazio. The course is best known for the Devil's Triangle, the challenging 13th, 14th, and 15th

ST. THOMAS

The Nature Conservancy trail to Magen's Bay

holes, where golfers battle the windswept Atlantic coast of St. Thomas.

Tee-time reservations are accepted up to two months in advance with full prepayment. Golf course amenities include a newly renovated clubhouse, restaurant, and pro shop. Greens fees (including cart rental) range from $145 per pair in winter to $125 per pair in the summer.

Hiking

Until 2004 there was no bona fide hiking trail on St. Thomas. That was when the Nature Conservancy opened the **Magen's Bay Trail,** a 1.5-mile trail through the Magen's Bay valley. The trail passes through a dry tropical forest on its way to the western end of Magen's Bay beach.

The trailhead is located along Route 35, the road to Magen's Bay. Look very carefully for a low stone pillar and yellow sign marking the entrance to the hike. There is a small parking area at the trailhead.

The best way to experience this hike is to hike down, go for a swim, and catch a taxi from Magen's Bay back up to your car.

Tennis

There are six public tennis courts on St. Thomas—two at Crown Bay (Subbase), two at Bordeaux, and two at Long Bay. They are open on a first-come, first-served basis.

Several hotels also have tennis courts. Near Charlotte Amalie, the **Marriott's Frenchman's Reef** (340/776-8500 ext. 6818, $10 per hour) has four lighted courts. **Bluebeard's Castle Hotel** (340/774-8990, $6 per hour) has two lighted courts.

Bolongo Bay Beach Club (340/775-1800 ext. 468, $10 per hour) has four lighted courts. **Mahogany Run Tennis Club,** (340/775-5000, $8–10 per hour), next to the same-named golf course, has two lighted courts.

Near the east end, there are courts at **Sapphire Beach Resort and Marina** (340/775-6100, $10 per hour) and the **Ritz-Carlton** (340/775-3333, $60 per hour).

Spectator Sports

St. Thomas has local basketball, softball, and soccer leagues, plus regular horse races, tennis competitions, and golf tournaments. Check the Emile Griffith ball field across from the ferry dock in Charlotte Amalie for local softball and little league action. Basketball takes place on community courts around the island; tournaments are held at the University of the Virgin Islands gym at Brewer's Bay. Check the local papers for upcoming sporting events.

Horse racing is one of the most popular local sports. Races are held monthly at **Clinton Phipps Racetrack** (Esate Nadir, 340/775-4355).

© SUSANNA HENIGHAN

Accommodations

There are two kinds of accommodations on St. Thomas: large chain resorts and small independent hotels and guesthouses. Most people who come here stay in the large resorts; they have the longest advertising reach, and many offer attractive package deals. Hotel chains including Best Western, Holiday Inn, Marriott, Wyndham, and Antilles Resorts have hotels on St. Thomas. They are not listed here.

Travelers looking for something more unique and offbeat would be wise to steer clear of chain resorts. Rooms in Charlotte Amalie's historic district are affordable, and some are quite luxurious. There are also a few independent beachfront hotels for a range of budgets.

Villas

St. Thomas has hundreds of villas for rent. The best-known villa agent is **McLaughlin Anderson** (Bluebeard's Castle, 340/776-0635, www.mclaughlinanderson.com). Also try **Calypso Realty** (340/774-1620, fax 340/774-1634, www.calypsorealty.com).

HISTORIC CHARLOTTE AMALIE
Under $125

One of the best values on St. Thomas, **The Crystal Palace** (12 Crystal Gade, 340/777-2277, U.S. toll free 866/502-2277, www.crystalpalaceusvi.com, $109–139 winter, $89–109 summer) is a five-room bed-and-breakfast located in a historic Charlotte Amalie town house. The double-breasted colonial manor is furnished with 18th- and 19th-century West Indian pieces and is set in a neighborhood of equally impressive colonial-era town houses, churches, and shops. All rooms are air-conditioned; two come with private baths. Guests share a kitchenette, and a continental breakfast is served overlooking the Charlotte Amalie harbor every morning. Host Ronnie Lockhart is a treasure trove of local history and tips for visiting St. Thomas.

Perched on the edge of Government Hill,

Galleon House Bed and Breakfast (Government Hill, 340/774-6952 or 800/524-2052, www.galleonhouse.com, $79–139 winter, $69–99 summer) offers moderately priced rooms in walking distance to downtown shopping and historic attractions. Rooms lack personality but are equipped with air-conditioning, cable TV, and telephones. The cheapest rooms have shared bathroom facilities; the most expensive have private balconies. Guests receive complimentary breakfast and have access to the pool. Views are of downtown Charlotte Amalie; you have to walk out of the hotel and to the main road for harbor views.

For budget accommodation, try **The Danish Chalet Inn** (Gamble Nordsidevej, 340/774-5764, fax 340/777-4312, www.danishchalet-inn.com, $98–160) a 15-room, family-run hotel overlooking historic Charlotte Amalie. The inn is close to the red-light district; be

the Governor's Office in Charlotte Amalie

© SUSANNA HENIGHAN

sure to take a taxi at night. Rooms are air-conditioned and come with cable TV.

Another budget choice is the **Bunker Hill Hotel** (7A Commandant Gade, 340/774-8066, fax 340/774-3172, www.bunkerhillhotel.com, $98–130 winter, $79–98 summer). Located about a block away from Government Hill, Bunker Hill Hotel is a 15-room inn with two pools, full complimentary breakfast, and views of downtown. Rooms are air-conditioned with cable TV and telephone. Some have private balconies.

$125-175

Next door to Government House and in the middle of Charlotte Amalie's historic district, ◖ **Hotel 1829** (Government Hill, 340/776-1829 or 800/524-2002, www.hotel1829.com, $105–220 winter, $75–160 summer) is a departure from typical beachfront or hillside accommodations. Built by a wealthy French sea merchant for his bride in 1829, the three-story building remained a private home until 1906 when it became a hotel. The original kitchen has been turned into a bar and dining room where visitors can play backgammon or sip cocktails while looking out over the Charlotte Amalie harbor. The view is especially lovely at night. Decor includes original hand-painted tiles, life-size Italian chess pieces, and a Tiffany stained glass mural. Rooms are furnished with mahogany furniture, cedar ceilings, and bamboo platform beds. The hotel's 15 rooms include several suites with private balconies overlooking the harbor, as well as smaller rooms that overlook the hotel courtyard and pool. Despite amenities including air-conditioning and cable TV, the hotel holds on to its historic atmosphere and Old World charm.

The Green Iguana Hotel (37B Blackbeard's Hill, 340/776-7654 or 800/484-8634, www.thegreeniguana.com, $119–149 winter, $89–129 summer) wraps around the side of Blackbeard's Hill with views of Crown Bay and parts of downtown Charlotte Amalie. The rooms are clean and cozy and come equipped with modern amenities, including satellite TV, microwaves, coffeemakers, air-conditioning,

and telephones. Large rooms have full kitchens. Guests can use the pool at neighboring Blackbeard's Castle Hotel. The Green Iguana is within walking distance of downtown Charlotte Amalie, although climbing Blackbeard's Hill on your way back will keep you in shape.

$175-225

Gourmet full breakfasts are served overlooking Charlotte Amalie at ◖ **Bellavista Bed and Breakfast** (2713 Murphy Gade, 340/714-5704, fax 340/776-7308, www.bellavista-bnb.com, $150–230 winter, $130–195 summer). This four room B&B is located in an exclusive part of town—the Governor's private residence is right around the corner—but you are overlooking the red roofs of historic Charlotte Amalie. Guests have access to the pool, an above-average collection of vacation reading, and the invaluable advice of hostess Wendy Snodgrass. Rooms are cozy and comfortable, but you will probably find yourself relaxing in the spacious sitting rooms and balcony. Amenities include air-conditioning, cable TV, and nightly turndown service. No detail goes unnoticed here.

OUTSIDE CHARLOTTE AMALIE

There are a number of hotels and inns on the outskirts of Charlotte Amalie. Some are nestled in quiet residential communities, and others are right on the beach.

Under $125

You get a lot for your money at **Mafolie Hotel,** (340/774-2792, U.S. toll free 800/225-7035, fax 340/774-4091, www.mafolie.com, $109–149 winter, $85–115 summer) a 22-room inn overlooking Charlotte Amalie. All the rooms here are air-conditioned, with cable TV, phone, refrigerators, and tasteful decor. Guests get continental breakfast and use of a pool and a daily hotel shuttle to Magen's Bay or downtown. The more expensive rooms have balconies overlooking the picturesque harbor below, but no matter where you stay you are never far from the impressive panorama below you. The hotel is set on a busy road perched well above town; walking to town is out of the question. It can be a bit noisy, especially at rush hour.

$125-175

The **Island Beachcomber Hotel** (Lindbergh Beach Rd., 340/774-5250, fax 340/774-5615, www.st-thomas.com/islandbeachcomber, $139–159 winter, $90–120 summer) is located on Lindbergh Bay, next to the St. Thomas airport, about a five-minute drive to Charlotte Amalie. The 47-room hotel is well suited for business travelers who want to be able to relax on the beach at the end of the day. It is also one of the best values for beachfront accommodation on St. Thomas. Rooms are not noted for their character but come well equipped with air-conditioning, satellite TV, wireless Internet, refrigerator, phone, coffeemaker, and hair dryer. There is a restaurant and bar on the premises.

The **Bellavista Scott Hotel** (No. 5 Estate Thomas, 340/714-5500, fax 340/714-5501, www.bellavistascotthotel.com, $125–170 winter, $119–160 summer) is a 24-room, concrete block hotel located in a busy residential and commercial neighborhood on the east side of Charlotte Amalie. The location is convenient to Havensight, and some rooms have views of the cruise ship dock. All rooms have kitchens, air-conditioning, cable TV, and phones. There is a large freshwater pool on the premises.

RED HOOK AND THE EAST END

The East End is where you will find large beachfront resorts, including chain resorts operated by the Ritz-Carlton, Wyndham, Antilles Resorts, and Equivest, the time-share company. Listed here are hotels with a more independent feel.

$225-300

⚡ Bolongo Bay Beach Club (340/775-1800, U.S. toll free 800/524-4746, www.bolongobay.com, $255 winter, $199 summer) is a beachfront resort that doesn't really feel like a typical resort. The amenities are top-notch, but the atmosphere is decidedly casual. Bolongo's genuinely friendly staff, active water sports program, and popular restaurants make this the sort of place where fun is priority number one. The family-run resort has 75 oceanfront rooms, each with its own private balcony. The hotel is set on Bolongo Bay beach, a broad, curved ring of sand shaded by coconut palms.

Set is a sheltered, crescent-shaped bay near Red Hook, **Secret Harbour Beach Resort** (6280 Estate Nazareth, 340/775-5550, U.S. toll free 800/524-2250, fax 340/775-1501, www.secretharbourvi.com, $275–315 winter, $149–189 summer) is a 60-room, full-service resort. Rooms overlook Secret Harbour and are appointed with tasteful rattan furniture, tile floors, and exposed beams in the ceiling. Amenities include a water sports center, tennis courts, pool, on-site restaurant, and gift shops. Rooms are air-conditioned, with cable TV and phone. Many have balconies overlooking the ocean.

Point Pleasant Resort (6600 Estate Smith Bay, 340/775-7200, U.S. toll free 800/524-2300, fax 340/776-5694, www.pointpleasantresort.com, $255–355 winter, $180–255 summer) is part of the Antilles Resort family, but it retains a unique feel. Originally a family-owned resort, Point Pleasant is a series of individual villas perched over Water Bay and overlooking Coki Point. All suites come with a full kitchen, satellite TV, a/c, private balconies, and ocean views. Suites range in size from junior suites perfect for two adults to deluxe suites for as many as five people. There are pools, a beach, and walking trails leading to nearby beaches and overlooks. In addition, there are two popular restaurants on-site.

...s catering to tourists are generally high...ity and expensive. More outgoing diners will enjoy trying local eateries as well.

CHARLOTTE AMALIE
Downtown

Across the street from Emancipation Gardens, near Fort Christian, **Jen's Deli** (43–46 Norre Gade, 340/777-4611, $5–10) is a popular stop for lunch or breakfast among the downtown crowd. This small storefront shop tends to get crowded at peak hours; otherwise it is nice place to sit with a drink and read the morning paper. Sandwiches range from traditional favorites to imaginative wraps. The daily soup special is also a big favorite.

Just around the corner from Jen's is **Ben Iguana's Sushi Bar** (Grand Galleria, 340/777-8744, 11:30 A.M.–3 P.M. and 5–9 P.M., $5–12 per sushi roll), the best place for sushi on St. Thomas. You can sit inside near the tiny bar or outside in the courtyard.

In the midst of bustling A.H. Riise Mall in historic Charlotte Amalie you will find **Café Amici** (340/776-5670, $12–18), a popular lunch spot that serves Continental-style pasta, pizzas, salads, and sandwiches for $12 and up. The bar does a bustling business of cold drinks and frozen concoctions.

For West Indian food, your first choice should be **C Cuzzin's Caribbean Restaurant & Bar** (No. 7 Back Street, 340/777-4711, Mon.–Sat. 11 A.M.–5 P.M. lunch, Tues.–Sat. 5–9:30 P.M. dinner, $13–20). This is the place to come for authentic Virgin Islands and West Indian cuisine, served in a friendly setting. Located in a restored 19th-century livery stable and cook shop, Cuzzins has local favorites like stewed chicken, mutton curry, and conch salad, as well as standards like steak and seafood. Try the conch Creole, and don't forget to order an authentic local drink like mauby, ginger beer, or sea moss.

You can taste Jamaican food at **Negril Café and Cocktail Lounge** (6A Comman-dante Gade, 340/774-4830, 11:30 A.M.–late, $6–15), a cozy eatery in the colorful neighborhood behind Government Hill. Try the Jamaican-style jerk chicken, pork, curry, and other favorites. On Wednesday and Saturday they serve saltfish and ackee, a Jamaican stand-by. This is not in the best part of town, so steer clear at night.

If you follow the "where the locals eat" philosophy of dining, then head to **Petite Pump Room** (Veteran's Drive, 340/776-2976, 7 A.M.–4:30 P.M. Mon.–Sat., $9–15) for breakfast or lunch. This waterfront restaurant is located upstairs the Wilmouth Blyden Ferry Terminal and draws a large lunchtime crowd from downtown offices.

For a more informal lunch or dinner, get some of the tastiest island-style barbecue at **Open Pit Bar-b-Que,** (Waterfront, 340/513-4582, 11 A.M.–11 P.M. Mon.–Thurs., 11 A.M.–midnight Fri., 5 P.M.–midnight Sat., $4–8), a mobile food stand that sets up along the waterfront. Look for it across from FirstBank at lunchtime, and across from the Lottery Building after 5 P.M. The barbecue comes with traditional sides including potato salad, coleslaw, and macaroni and cheese.

Taco Fiesta Bar and Grill Express (Hibiscus Alley, 340/774-6600, 6 A.M.–10 P.M., $3–10) serves a lot more than just tacos. You can get a hearty breakfast here for $7, or a sandwich for less than $8. Try the jerk chicken wrap ($7) or tofu burger ($6). Of course, there are also tacos (including mahimahi, shrimp, and tofu), burritos, and Mexican-style combination platters. Look for Taco Fiesta behind Banco Popular on the Waterfront.

One of the most popular downtown restaurants is welcoming **C Gladys' Cafe** (Royal Dane Mall, 340/774-6604, 7 A.M.–4:30 P.M. Mon.–Sat., 8 A.M.–2:30 P.M. Sun., $5–12). Set in a restored waterfront warehouse, Gladys' draws a crowd of loyal regulars for her traditional breakfast, served with lots of hot coffee and even the morning paper, if you like. At lunch, retreat into the air-conditioning for sandwiches, soups, and salads, or order from the West Indian menu of saltfish, mutton stew, or conch and fungi. Buy a bottle of Gladys's own hot sauce as a souvenir.

One of St. Thomas's longest-standing fine restaurants, **Hervé Restaurant and Wine Bar** (Government Hill, 340/777-9703 ext. 11, $22–34) serves Caribbean favorites with a European touch. Entrées include pan-seared Norwegian salmon, grilled rabbit, and Creole red snapper. Budget diners can sample the world-class fare at lunch, when the menu features fresh quiche, seafood crepes, cold roast duck salad, and even a sirloin burger on a sesame-seed bun. Lunch costs $8–15. Hervé's wine list is among the best on the island.

For classic Northern Italian cuisine, come to **Virgilio's** (18 Dronnigan's Gade, 340/776-4920, 11:30 A.M.–10:30 P.M. Mon.–Sat., $22–40). Set in the heart of historic Charlotte Amalie in a beautiful old building with vaulted ceilings, this is a romantic and sophisticated place to dine. Soft music and expert service create a refined ambience. Dinners are expertly created: lobster ravioli, rack of lamb, and some of the most luxurious desserts on the island.

Frenchtown

Some of the island's best restaurants are found in Frenchtown. Walk around this peaceful neighborhood and take your pick.

A Frenchtown landmark, **Alexander's Bella Blu** (340/774-4349, $9–28) has a dizzying array of choices: Austrian specialties, pasta, Mediterranean dishes, salads, sandwiches, and daily comfort food specials. One diner can try souvlakia (skewered lamb) while another has veal Jaeger Schnitzel. This is a great stop for a filling lunch; the daily $12 special features favorites like a roast beef platter and chicken parmesan.

C Craig and Sally's (3525 Honduras, 340/777-9949, 11:30 A.M.–3 P.M. Wed.–Fri., 5:30–10 P.M. Wed.–Sun., $17–45) is an intimate, romantic restaurant known for imaginative cuisine. Specials change daily, according to the whims of chef Sally and availability of

the best ingredients. Imagine roast pork with clams or pan-seared jumbo scallops. You can also choose from one of the best wine lists on the island.

You can nibble from the extensive tapas menu, or dine more formally on fresh seafood, lamb, or beef at **Oceana** (8 Honduras, 340/774-4262, 5–10 P.M. Mon.–Sat., $21–35) located in Villa Olga on the tip of Frenchtown. The downstairs bar attracts a lively after-work crowd. Upstairs, diners choose from a seafood-heavy menu with specialties like pan-fried trout and mussels in white wine sauce. The downstairs tapas menu includes crostinis, cheese platters, and the like.

Most people head to **Epernay** (Rue de St. Barthelemy, 340/774-5348, 11:30 A.M.–11:30 P.M. Mon.–Sat., $28–40) for the late-night dancing, but it is a good place to eat as well. Try the sesame-crusted tuna with sticky rice. Champagne and vintage wine are served here by the glass.

Take a break from sophistication and pretense at **Frenchtown Deli** (Frenchtown Mall, 340/776-7211, 7:30 A.M.–8 P.M. Mon.–Fri., 7:30 A.M.–5 P.M. Sat., 7:30 A.M.–4 P.M. Sun., $5–9), home of the best sandwiches and fresh coffee on the island. Grab a bagel here for breakfast, or choose from a thick sandwich or hearty salad at lunch or supper.

Havensight

The malls around the cruise ship dock house several casual eateries. If you feel like pizza, go where the locals go: **Pizza Amore** (340/774-2822, 9 A.M.–8 P.M. Mon.–Thurs., 9 A.M.–9 P.M. Fri., 10 A.M.–9 P.M. Sat., $3–10) in Al Cohen's Plaza, across the street from Havensight Mall. In addition to whole pizzas ($14 for a large cheese) and slices ($2.25), Amore does salads and sandwiches. Takeout is popular; no deliveries.

Shipwreck Bar and Restaurant (Al Cohen's Plaza, 340/777-1293, 11 A.M.–4 A.M. Mon.–Sat., 11:30 A.M.–2 A.M. Sun., $5–9) is a dark, smoky bar with monster-sized burgers. This is a favorite hangout for young Americans who live on St. Thomas. Come here for bar food at its best: quarter-pound hot dogs, fries, nachos—you get the picture. **Gourmet Gallery** (340/774-3001, 7 A.M.–9 P.M. Mon.–Sat., 8 A.M.–8 P.M. Sun., $4–10) at Havensight is an upscale grocery store with a good takeout deli. Come here for sandwiches, salads, or cold pasta dishes. This is a popular white-collar lunch stop.

For vegetarian food, walk about two blocks from Havensight proper to Mandela Circle, the traffic light intersection easily identified by the presence of fast-food eatery Wendy's. This is where you will find **Natural Food Grocery** (Mandela Circle, 340/775-3737, 7:30 A.M.–6 P.M. Mon.–Fri., 9 A.M.–6 P.M. Sat., $6–10), whose deli serves vegetarian and vegan platters, plus the best veggie burgers on St. Thomas. It also serves tuna, turkey, and roast beef sandwiches.

Outside Town

Havana Blue (Morningstar Beach, 340/715-2583, 5–10 P.M., $24–32) serves Latin American-Asian fusion at a lovely beachfront location. Leave your flip-flops home for this trendy and elegant dining experience. Try a bowl of soba noodles to start and Polynesian duck or Havana pollo for your entrée. Sides of black beans, braised bok choy, and jasmine rice are available.

For pizza, sandwiches, salads, and gourmet coffee drinks, try **Kokopelli Cafe** (Market Square East, 340/715-5280, 11 A.M.–10 P.M., $9–15). Located in a shopping center along Route 38 (the same shopping center as the movie theater), Kokopelli is a casual, American-style café with booths, tables, and a play area for children.

Rub elbows with the sailing set at **Tickles Dockside Pub** (Crown Bay Marina, 340/776-1595, $10–22). This open-air waterfront eatery is casual and welcoming; it serves a menu ranging from bar food to fresh seafood and steak. It is also a great place for a cold drink on a hot afternoon. This is the sort of place where everyone knows your name after a few visits.

Many St. Thomians make **Sib's Mountaintop Bar and Restaurant** (Mafolie Road, 340/774-8967, 5–10 P.M. daily, 10 A.M.–2 P.M. Sun., $7–25) a pit stop on their way home. You can choose to eat around the bar or in the sit-down restaurant next door. Come here for fresh red snapper, great burgers, pizza, chicken-fried steak, and more.

One of the most surprising restaurants on St. Thomas, **Randy's Bar and Bistro** (Al Cohen's Plaza, 340/775-5001, 11 A.M.–3 P.M. and 5:30–10 P.M. Mon.–Sat., $12–37) is a gourmand's delight tucked into a commercial storefront at the top of Raphune Hill. Happy hour is popular here—especially among martini fans—and many drinkers migrate to the tables set amid wine crates for meals of roasted lamb, fresh salmon, mussels, and more. Lunch is more casual and more affordable.

Markets

The high-end Gourmet Galleries at Havensight and Crown Bay stock hard-to-find items and fresh meat and produce. More general grocery items can be found at any of the Pueblo stores. The most convenient is at Long Bay, near Havensight.

NORTHSIDE

The best gourmet dining on St. Thomas is found near Mahogany Run Golf Course on the Northside. **Old Stone Farmhouse** (Mahogany Run, 340/777-6277, Tues.–Sun. 5:30–9:30 P.M., $18–35) is housed in a restored plantation great house. You can choose the chef's multicourse tasting menu or order à la carte from the ever-changing menu. There is also a full sushi menu daily. Save room for the homemade desserts.

Few places on St. Thomas capture island style better than 🄲 **Hull Bay Hideaway** (Hull Bay, 340/777-1898, 10 A.M.–10 P.M. daily, $8), serving sandwiches, burgers, and fries. Come in bare feet and don't dare hurry. This open-air, laid-back bar and restaurant caters to beachgoers, families, and people just looking for a little company. Games like horseshoes and dominos are popular ways to spend the afternoon. If you're hungry, the famed "Arthur burger," named after the proprietor, is the way to go.

RED HOOK AND THE EAST END
Red Hook

For a casual bite on the run, **Burrito Bay Deli** (American Yacht Harbor, 340/775-2944, 6 A.M.–8 P.M. Mon.–Sat., 6 A.M.–6 P.M. Sun., $6–12) is the best choice in Red Hook. Try the hearty huevos rancheros for breakfast. For lunch and dinner choose from the Tex-Mex menu, order from the daily specials, or just grab a sandwich. Dine in and watch the boat traffic in and out of Red Hook.

In the parking lot of Red Hook Plaza, **Duffy's Love Shack** (340/779-2495, 11 A.M.–midnight, $12–25) is a landmark. Besides froo-froo drinks, it serves standard American fare with a Caribbean twist, like mahimahi sandwiches, burgers, steak, or chicken salad.

East End

The **☪ Blue Moon Cafe** (Secret Harbour Resort, 340/779-2262, 8 A.M.–10 P.M., $14–25) transforms from a casual beachfront café into a refined dinner spot at night. The breakfast menu features traditional favorites. At lunch, you can try sandwiches, portobello mushroom salad, or coconut shrimp. For dinner, the menu includes seafood dishes, pasta, risottos, and grill favorites, including New York strip steak, ribs, and chicken breasts.

Voted best for seafood by readers of the local newspaper, **Bonnie's by the Sea** (Elysian Resort, 340/774-8868, 7 A.M.–10 P.M., $15–35) has nightly specials and a twice-monthly West Indian pig roast buffet. Proprietor Bonnie Erb has been in the restaurant business on this very beach for more than 20 years, and she knows her stuff. Tuesday night is all-you-can-eat shrimp; Wednesday is prime rib night.

Smith Bay

Imagine an English pub in the middle of a West Indian community. That's the **Toad and Tart** (Smith Bay Rd., 340/775-1153, 5:30–10:30 P.M. Tues.–Sat., $15–32), where you can get genuine English pub fare: roasts, bangers and mash, fish and chips. And just like an English pub, the welcome is real and the atmosphere homey. There is also beer on tap, and the bar opens at 3 P.M.

Practicalities

INFORMATION AND SERVICES
Tourist Offices

The Department of Tourism operates an information office at Havensight, near the cruise ship dock, but don't seek it out—it's pretty useless unless all you want are numerous advertising handbills.

Maps and Charts

The free pocket map of St. Thomas and St. John widely available at tourist information booths, hotels, and car rental agencies is clear and well drawn. Pick one up when you arrive—it will be adequate for most people's purposes. There is also a map inside *St. Thomas This Week,* the free tourist magazine. Maps are also available at Dockside Bookshop in Havensight Mall.

Libraries

The **Enid M. Baa Public Library** (Main St., 340/774-3407, 9 A.M.–5 P.M. Mon. and Fri., 9 A.M.–8 P.M. Tues.–Thurs., 10 A.M.–4 P.M. Sat.) is located on Main Street next to Market Square in the historic Bretton House. You can still see the original "charge desk" dedicated in 1943 by poet Edna St. Vincent Millay, who was a frequent visitor to the Virgin Islands at the time. There is public Internet access here for $2 an hour.

Media

The *Virgin Islands Daily News* publishes Mon.–Sat. and is the best source for up-to-date news and events information. A weekend section on Thursday includes a dining guide and entertainment calendar. The *Daily News* is for sale at numerous establishments, plus along the roadside for people on their morning commute.

You can also buy the *St. Croix Avis* at many places on St. Thomas. Also try the bright-yellow *St. Thomas-St. John This Week* for useful visitor information.

Emergencies

There is a full-service hospital on St. Thomas. The Roy L. Schneider Hospital (Estate Thomas, 340/776-8311, www.rlshospital.org) recently expanded to include a cutting edge cancer treatment facility. Schneider Hospital has a decompression chamber for diving accidents; call 340/693-6215 to reach it directly. Despite the advances, many island residents still feel better traveling to Puerto Rico or the mainland United States for specialist and even routine services.

Walk-in medical centers can help with minor health problems and are convenient for visitors. The **Walk-In Medical Center** (Sixth St., Estate Thomas, 8 A.M.–6 P.M. Mon.–Fri., 340/775-4266) is a good choice.

Police headquarters is located in the Alexander Farrelly Justice Center on the waterfront, next to the Fort Christian parking lot. You can reach police by calling 340/774-2211. Dial 911 in an emergency.

Mariners can call for help on Channel 16, or call Virgin Islands Radio on Channels 24 or 85.

Banks

U.S., Canadian, and Puerto Rican banks do business in the U.S. Virgin Islands. You will find Banco Popular (340/693-2777) branches at Hibiscus Alley in downtown Charlotte Amalie, at Red Hook Plaza, and Lockhart Gardens, near Havensight. The Bank of Nova Scotia (340/774-0037) has branches at Havensight, Tutu Park Mall, and Nisky Center (west of town). FirstBank (340/775-7777) can be found at Red Hook and Port of Sale Mall, Havensight.

Post Offices

There are five post offices on St. Thomas. The main post office, DeLugo Post Office, is located at 5046 Norre Gade in central Charlotte Amalie and is open 7:30 A.M.–5 P.M. Mon.–Fri. and 7:30 A.M.–noon on Saturday. The Havensight post office is open 9 A.M.–5 P.M.

Communications

Beans, Bytes, and Websites (Royal Dane Mall, 340/776-7265, 7 A.M.–6 P.M. Mon.–Sat., 7 A.M.–1 P.M. Sun.) in downtown Charlotte Amalie has high-speed Internet access for 15 cents a minute. Little Switzerland (340/776-2010) offers free Internet access for 15 minutes 9 A.M.–5 P.M. daily. There are also several different call centers and cybercafés across the street from Havensight Mall, catering to cruise ship crew members who want to call home during their time off the ship.

Customs and Immigration

People arriving in St. Thomas from the British Virgin Islands or other international destinations must clear immigration and customs on their arrival. People returning to the U.S. mainland from St. Thomas undergo immigration and customs screening on their departure, although a passport is not required (a government-issued ID is, however). There are customs and immigrations officers stationed at the Weymouth Blyden Ferry Terminal on the Charlotte Amalie waterfront 8 A.M.–4:30 P.M. daily. They meet all ferries arriving from international destinations (principally the British Virgin Islands) and any private yachts that need to check in. Call 340/774-2378 to reach the immigration office at the ferry dock.

In addition, there are customs, immigration, and other border security officials at the Cyril E. King International Airport. For more information, call Customs (340/693-2250, U.S. toll free 800/981-3030) or Immigration and Naturalization (340/774-1390). The INS has an administrative office at Nisky Center on the western outskirts of Charlotte Amalie.

Launderettes

There are many different launderettes on St. Thomas, most with long hours. Almost all provide drop-off service in addition to letting you do your own wash. One of the largest is **La Providence Laundromat** (Tutu Park Shopping Center, 340/777-3747, 6 A.M.–11 P.M.) behind Tutu Park Mall. La Providence also has a location in American Yacht Harbor in Red Hook. Near town, try **Lover's Lane Laundromat** (Barbel Plaza, 340/714-1658, 5:30 A.M.–6:30 P.M.). Plan on about $1.75 a wash.

GETTING THERE
By Air

More direct flights from the mainland arrive in St. Thomas than any other Virgin Islands. During the winter travel season, Delta, U.S. Airways, American, and United fly nonstop from major U.S. cities including New York, Baltimore, Miami, Charlotte, and Chicago.

The Cyril E. King International Airport (STT) is located near Lindberg Bay, about four miles west of Charlotte Amalie. You will pay $6 for a taxi from the airport to town, and between $10 and $13 to the East End resorts. Car rental companies Avis and Hertz have desks at the airport.

By Sea

Most people who visit St. Thomas come aboard a cruise ship. Nearly every major cruise line calls on the island, including Carnival, Holland America, Norwegian, Royal Caribbean, Princess, and Celebrity. Cruise ships dock at the West Indian Company Dock in Havensight or the Crown Bay Marina on the west side of Charlotte Amalie. Check the back cover of *St. Thomas This Week* for an up-to-date cruise ship schedule.

GETTING AROUND
Buses

The public bus system, Vitran (340/774-5678), has routes covering St. Thomas from the far west to the far east. Country buses ($1) travel between Red Hook and town every hour beginning at 5:30 A.M. and ending at 8:30 P.M. Additional buses travel from town to Bordeaux in the west. City buses (75 cents) travel between the hospital on the east side of town to the western end of town between 6:15 A.M. and 10:15 P.M. Some travel to the airport and UVI. In general, Vitran is unreliable, however. If you happen to catch a bus, be sure to have exact change.

But don't be disheartened—there is another way. For budget travelers, one of the delights of St. Thomas is its dollar buses. These unofficial, highly efficient buses follow a set route including Red Hook, Tutu Park Mall, Charlotte Amalie, and the University of the Virgin Islands. They do not go to the north side, beaches, or west end. Passengers pay $1 for a ride, no matter how long or short it is. Dollar buses are actually the same open-air "safari" taxis—converted from pick-up trucks—that bus cruise ship and other tourists around the island. The only difference is the makeup of the passenger base and the route they follow.

Dollar buses stop at established Vitran bus stops, marked with a brown and white sign. Some of the easiest places to catch a dollar bus are in Red Hook, next to the ferry dock; in front of Tutu Park Mall; in front of the Fort Christian parking lot and in front of the Roy L. Schneider Hospital.

Dollar buses are not really designed for tourists; you need to be sprightly, confident, and have some knowledge of the geography of the island to ride comfortably. Some buses may pass you by since you probably don't look like their average passenger. You can always stick your arm out as a signal to stop, but if you are on a road frequented by the taxis catering to tourists (especially Waterfront Drive in Charlotte Amalie) you may well be picked up by a tourist taxi. When in doubt, just ask, "Is this the dollar bus?" and someone will set you straight.

Taxis

Taxis are readily available at the airport, around Charlotte Amalie, and at resorts and major attractions. Many taxis are 6–12 passenger vans; others are open-air "safari" buses, ideal for sightseeing.

Taxi rates are set by the government. Official licensed taxis have a special license plate beginning with the letters TP, and the drivers will display their taxi commission ID card. Per-person taxi rates are lower if you have more than one person going to the same destination. The single-person rate from Charlotte Amalie to Red Hook is $10, to the airport is $6, and to Magen's Bay is $8.50. For a complete list of current taxi rates, check *St. Thomas This Week*.

In addition to licensed taxis, there is a booming industry of unofficial taxis, called gypsies. There is no really good way to identify a gypsy taxi because they look just like regular cars; taxi drivers stand outside grocery stores and shopping malls waiting for someone who looks like they need a taxi. Gypsy taxis generally charge less than the official published rates, but you are taking a risk in using them. There have been a few cases of violence perpetrated against gypsy taxi passengers, especially single women. If you do take an unlicensed taxi, don't take one alone, don't take one at night, and don't take one to remote or unpopulated areas. Gypsy taxis are found outside Tutu Park Mall, around the Red Hook ferry dock, and outside other shopping areas on the island; they do not frequent tourist-oriented places, like the airport.

Car Rental

Taxi fares add up, so renting a car is the best way to get around St. Thomas if you want to explore the beaches, overlooks, and out-of-the-way restaurants and don't want to depend on other, cheaper, means of getting around. If you are staying in town, consider renting a car for a few days of your vacation.

Often, the best rental rates are available from the major car rental chains, especially if you book well in advance. Per-day rental rates for an economy class car will run $30 and up from most rental agencies; some will quote rates as high as $60 a day. There is a $2.50 per-day government tax on car rentals, and additional fees for those rented at the airport. For most people, four-wheel drive will not be necessary; St. Thomas roads are well maintained.

Chain rental companies include **Avis** (340/774-1468), **Hertz** (340/774-1879), **Budget** (340/776-5774), and **Thrifty** (340/776-1500). You could also try **Dependable Car Rental** (340/776-2253).

ST. CROIX

The largest of the U.S. Virgin Islands is the richest in history, culture, and landscapes. St. Croix (pronounced Croy) lies 40 miles south of St. Thomas and St. John, on the other side of the cavernous Virgin Islands trough. The 84-square-mile island is shaped like a baseball pennant, slightly ruffled by the surrounding Caribbean Sea. It is 22 miles long and six miles wide. Beaches line the straight west coast, giving way to a dense tropical forest in the northwest. To the south, rolling hills slope toward the sea. The island tapers to a point at its extreme east end, where the spare landscape is dominated by cactus and wild frangipani trees.

St. Croix is rich in natural resources. The Taino, one of the island's earliest groups of inhabitants, called the island Ay-Ay, meaning The River. The Kalinago, who lived on St. Croix several centuries later, named it Cibuquiera, or The Stony Land. Frederiksted, on the west coast, is a quiet, Victorian-style town where Crucians (Cru-shuns) come to enjoy the sunset and some of the island's hippest bars. Christiansted, on the north coast, is a bastion of historic sites, shopping, and creative eateries. In between, the countryside is dotted by great house and windmill ruins, built by African slaves when the island was a major sugar-producing colony. Place names like Work and Rest, Humbug, All for the Better, and Patience Grove evoke the island's grand, and often tragic, past.

St. Croix sees the fewest tourists in the U.S. Virgin Islands, and its economy is the most diverse. One of the largest oil refineries in the Western Hemisphere, HOVENSA, sits on the southern shore, a cityscape of smokestacks and

© SUSANNA HENIGHAN

HIGHLIGHTS

◖ Christiansted National Historic Site: Once St. Croix's economic and administrative core, Christiansted is still the center of its historic attractions. Fort Christiansvaern, the Steeple Building, and other attractions make this the best place to begin exploring the island's rich past (page 67).

◖ Fort Frederik Museum: The brick-red colonial era fort in Frederiksted houses a museum that interprets St. Croix's rich history, especially the painful story of slavery (page 73).

◖ Buck Island: Protected by the National Park Service, Buck Island is surrounded by a huge barrier reef. Hiking trails cut through dry, tropical brush (page 75).

◖ The Wall: This massive underwater ledge on the north coast plunges 3,200 feet. Teeming with marine life, it is a perfect playground for divers (page 78).

◖ Whim Plantation Museum: St. Croix is dotted with great house, sugar factory, and windmill ruins, but Whim is the only place where you can see a fully restored great house, windmill, and sugar mill, even down to the working cookhouse (page 79).

◖ Jack and Isaac Bay Preserve: These beautiful, unspoiled bays on the east end of the island are the place to come for seclusion, white beaches, turquoise water, and peace (page 82).

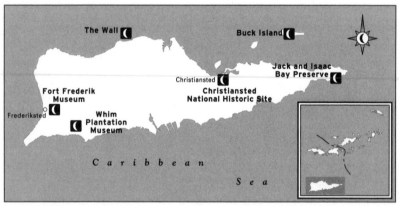

LOOK FOR ◖ TO FIND RECOMMENDED SIGHTS, ACTIVITIES, DINING, AND LODGING.

concrete. Senepol cattle graze in pastures, and rum is distilled and exported worldwide. Tourism, while critical to the St. Croix economy, has never held the revered status that it has on other islands. St. Croix is foremost a place where people live, not a place where people visit.

Just over 53,000 people make their home on St. Croix, a bit more than St. Thomas, but the island's ample proportions mean a lot more elbow room. Descendants of St. Croix's African slaves make up the majority of the pop-ulation, but successive waves of Caribbean immigrants, many from Puerto Rico and the Dominican Republic, have enriched the native society. Other settlers from the Middle East, U.S. mainland, Canada, and Europe, including Danes who can trace their roots back to the days of slavery and sugar, complete the island's diverse population.

Nowhere is St. Croix's diversity more evident than in its music, food, and arts. You can spend an evening dancing to the infectious sounds of traditional scratch music or grooving to Trinidadian-style steel pan. Meals range from sophisticated French cuisine served in an Old World–style town house to fresh roti or jerk chicken served from an open-air booth.

St. Croix is the most overlooked of the U.S. Virgin Islands, in part because it has been unwilling to smooth out all of its kinks for the benefit of tourists. Visitors who recognize the value of this realism will be rewarded by a dynamic, fascinating, and ultimately awesome island. While the Big Island is unable to match the pizzazz of St. Thomas or the exceptional natural beauty of St. John, it has something neither of the other islands does: a whole package.

PLANNING YOUR TIME

They don't call St. Croix "The Big Island" for nothing. It can take all day just to circle the island, and weeks to tap into all the attractions and activities it has to offer. If you must limit your time to less than a week, do so with the knowledge that you will have to leave without visiting some of its great attractions.

St. Croix's two greatest strengths are its historical sites and the diversity of its landscape. Visits to the island should make time to touch on each of these areas: history and nature.

On the historic side, brick-red **Fort Frederik** in Frederiksted is a good starting point for understanding the island's history. The **Whim Plantation Museum** puts a sharper focus on life on an 18th-century sugar plantation, showing both the elegance and misery of the time. **Christiansted National Historic Site** showcases the urban face of the Danish plantation society.

St. Croix's natural beauty is on display nearly everywhere you look, although nowhere better than at unspoiled **Jack and Isaac Bays** on the east end. Choose a small, intimate boat for the daylong outing to **Buck Island,** where the primary attraction is snorkeling on its glorious reef. If you're an experienced scuba diver, or if you've ever wished to be one, St. Croix, with wreck, reef, pier, and, especially, its famous **Wall** dives, is the perfect place to suit up.

St. Croix puts on some great annual events,

and it is worth considering whether you can plan your visit to coincide with one. The annual Crucian Christmas Festival, which begins in mid-December and continues until Three Kings Day in January, is the biggest showcase of Crucian culture, arts, and music. The Agriculture Fair in late February, Half Ironman in April, and Mango Melee in July are also worthwhile.

DRIVING TOURS

A daylong driving tour of St. Croix will take you through each of its major landscapes. This tour starts and ends in Christiansted but can be picked up anywhere in the 55-mile loop. Plan for a full day, especially if you want time to explore one or two sights along the way and break for lunch.

Travel east from Christiansted on Rte. 82, which follows the northern coast. Continue on to Point Udall, pausing to stretch your legs at Cramer Park and gawk at the giant Base Array Telescope on the way.

Retrace your path to the intersection with Rte. 60 and turn left, heading south over a few hills before striking out along the southern coast. Stop at Divi Carina Bay Casino for a few hands of blackjack, or press on, admiring the wide, open vistas before you.

At Great Pond, an important wetland ecosystem, turn onto Rte. 624 and then left on Rte. 62, which continues along the coast. Look out for the red Senepol cattle, which are easy to spot against the green hillsides. The road takes a sharp left turn at Canegarden Bay, and you will see the smokestacks of the HOVENSA Oil Refinery before you. Prepare to navigate through the most congested part of St. Croix.

Continue straight on Rte. 62 (the road narrows) until it runs into Rte. 70. Turning left, you will pass Sunny Isle Shopping Center before the traffic thins out and the road widens; you are now on the Melvin Evans Highway (Rte. 66), a limited access four-lane road. Continue on the highway until it intersects with Rte. 64, or Airport Road. Turn right, and follow Rte. 64 north until it intersects with Centerline Road, also called the Queen Mary Highway (Rte. 70). This is a straight road

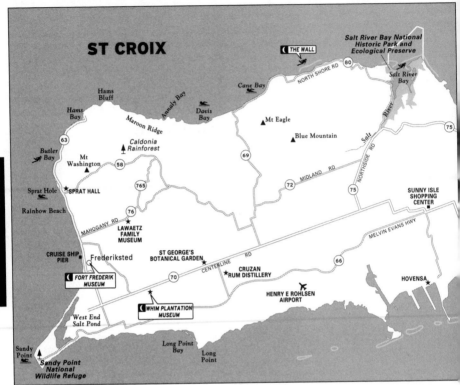

that passes gas stations, farmland, residential neighborhoods, and convenience marts. If you have time, stop for a stroll through the St. George Village Botanical Gardens or **Whim Plantation Museum.** If it's time for a snack, try Armstrong's Homemade Ice Cream, near Frederiksted. Continue on Rte. 70, which makes a right-hand turn at a traffic light. The road then reaches a T intersection; bear left, and then turn right again. You are now entering Frederiksted, where you can stop for lunch or coffee at one of Frederiksted's great eateries, or a walk along the cruise ship pier (when there's no ship in). You could also spend an hour or so at the **Fort Frederik Museum.**

Head north from Frederiksted on the coastal Rte. 63, then turn right onto Mahogany Road (Rte. 76), which will take you through the Caldonia Rainforest. The Mt. Pellier Domino Club makes a great pit stop. After you leave the rainforest, navigate your way through a residential neighborhood, jogging left on Rte. 705 before turning left onto Rte. 69, which passes Carambola Golf Course and winding down to Cane Bay. Follow the Northshore Road (Rte. 80) all the way to Salt River Bay, where the road intersects with Rte. 75, which will take you back to Christiansted. For a refreshing finish, stop at Pelican Cove beach for a swim before calling it a day.

St. Croix Heritage Trail

One of the most unique attractions on St. Croix is the Heritage Trail, a 72-mile route around St. Croix that takes you by sights of historic, cultural, and natural importance. Brown Heritage Trail signs mark the trail around the island. Trail guides are available from visitor

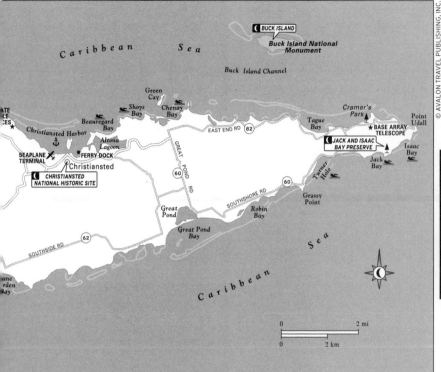

information booths or the Heritage Trail Office (Hotel Caravelle, 340/713-8563, www.st-croixheritagetrail.com). It's worth the trouble to get your hands on one of these guides. It is a handy and informative resource for visitors, who can either set out to follow the whole trail in a day, or dip in and out over the course of a few days, or weeks.

Sights

CHRISTIANSTED

Picturesque and brimming with history, the first city of St. Croix is an oasis of sophistication with a small-town feel. By day the sidewalks fill with people exploring the town's historic sites and browsing its unique shops. By night, people from all over St. Croix come to dine at fine restaurants and enjoy lively nightlife.

Christiansted was planned by St. Croix's first Danish governor, Frederik Moth, in 1734, the year following Denmark's purchase of the island. Many of the buildings in the center of the town were built in the decades the followed, as Christiansted became the capital for trade into and out of the growing Danish colony. Thanks to a protective building code, many of these original structures remain, giving the town an appealing Old World atmosphere.

Exploring Christiansted on foot is a pleasure. It is compact and easy to navigate, and most

CHRISTIANSTED

Christiansted

Harbor

Protestant Cay

HOTEL ON THE CAY

CHRISTIANSTED NATIONAL HISTORIC SITE

SCALE HOUSE/NATIONAL PARK INFORMATION CENTER
CUSTOM HOUSE
KING CHRISTIAN HOTEL
SEAPLANE TERMINAL
CLUB COMANCHE
DANISH WEST INDIA AND COMPANY WAREHOUSE
HOTEL CARAVELLE
INTERNET CAFE
STEEPLE BUILDING
THE BEAN MON
BACCHUS
LORD GOD OF SABAOTH LUTHERAN CHURCH
DANISH MANOR HOTEL
GOVERNMENT HOUSE
PINK FANCY
TURTLES DELI
ST CROIX ARCHAEOLOGY MUSEUM
PARADISE CAFE
KENDRICK'S
APOTHECARY MUSEUM
POST OFFICE
ZENY'S RESTAURANT
HOLY CROSS CATHOLIC CHURCH
SUNDAY MARKET SQUARE
ST JOHN'S ANGLICAN CHURCH
To West Island
75
FRIEDENSTHAL MORAVIAN CHURCH
70
NORTH RD
To West Island

MARKET ST
WEST ST
WATERGUT ST
STRAND ST
KING ST
COMPANY ST
SOBOETKER ST
CONTENTMENT RD
QUEEN ST
HILL ST
MARKET ST
EAST ST
FISHER ST
PRINCE ST
KING CROSS ST
QUEEN CROSS ST
NEW ST
LITTLE ST

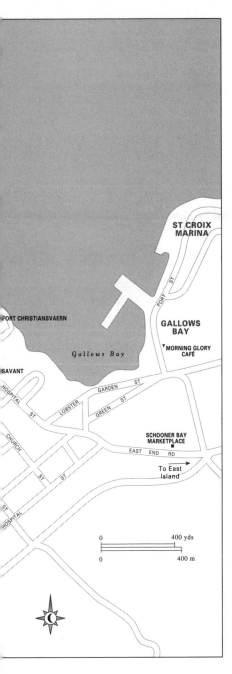

ST CROIX
MARINA

FORT CHRISTIANSVAERN

GALLOWS
BAY

MORNING GLORY
CAFÉ

Gallows Bay

SAVANT

HOSPITAL ST

LOBSTER ST

GARDEN ST

GREEN ST

CHURCH ST

ST

ST

SCHOONER BAY
MARKETPLACE

EAST END RD

To East
Island

HOSPITAL ST

0   400 yds

0   400 m

ST. CROIX

sidewalks are shaded. Leave your car at one of two public parking lots in town and plan on at least a day to explore the town's attractions.

Orientation

Most attractions and restaurants in Christiansted are found within the four-square-block area contained by King Cross Street on the west, Queen Street at the south, and the waterfront on the north and east sides. A boardwalk extends from the seaplane terminal to the old wharf.

Use common sense if you explore areas outside of this central area—Christiansted is well acquainted with urban problems like street crime, vandalism, and drug abuse, especially in the areas untouched by tourism. Avoid the areas beyond Market Street and Hill Street at night.

◖ Christiansted National Historic Site

Comprising five historic structures dating to the earliest days of Danish colonization, Christiansted National Historic Site (340/773-1460, www.nps.gov/chri, adults $3, children under 16 free) is the natural starting point for any exploration of historic Christiansted. The park is open 8 A.M.–5 P.M. Mon.–Fri. and 9 A.M.–5 P.M. on weekends and federal holidays. It is closed on Christmas Day and Thanksgiving. To visit the park, go first to Fort Christiansvaern to buy a ticket that will grant you entry to the fort and the nearby Steeple Building. You don't need a ticket to view the other parts of the park. A park map and guide is available at the park shop housed in the old Scale House near the waterfront.

Built on the site of an earlier French fortification, **Fort Christiansvaern** (Christian's defenses) was designed to protect the port from attacks, enforce collection of customs duties, house Danish troops, and prevent slave insurrections on the island. Its bright yellow color was typical of Danish construction of the day.

The fort was completed in 1749, with significant additions made between 1835 and 1841. After 1878, when laborers rioted

ST. CROIX

© SUSANNA HENIGHAN

the Christiansted wharf

throughout the island, the fort was converted into a police station and courthouse. The National Park Service has restored the fort to its 1830s appearance.

The tour of the fort is self-guided, although park rangers are around if you have any questions. Some rooms have been furnished with period furniture to depict the lifestyle of the Danish soldiers and officers. There is also an arsenal stocked with typical small arms of the day and equipment for the fort's numerous cannons. The tour also takes you to the underground cells, where slaves and convicts were punished, and to the fort's toilets, which flushed right into the sea. There are nice views of Protestant Cay and the Christiansted waterfront from the second floor.

The attractive, white **Steeple Building** was the first Danish Lutheran Church on St. Croix. During the early years of Danish colonization, church services were held in a rehabilitated French church in the town. When that building was destroyed by hurricane in 1738, services moved first to a room in the fort and then to a warehouse near the wharf.

Construction of the Steeple Building began in 1750, and the building was consecrated in May 1753 as the Church of the Lord of Sabaoth. The distinctive tower, with its four-tiered octagonal cupola, was added 40 years later. Lutheranism was the official religion of the Danish, so church attendance by military officers, government officials, and members of Danish colonial society was considered mandatory. During the time the Steeple Building functioned as a church, there were two Sunday services. The first, at 9 A.M., was conducted in Danish for the white congregation. The second, at noon, was conducted in Dutch Creole for nonwhites.

In 1831 the congregation moved to a new church building at the corner of King and Queen Cross Streets, where it remains today. Many of the original church furnishings are still in use at the present-day church. The Steeple Building was then used variously as a warehouse, hospital, bakery, and school before becoming part of the National Historic Site.

Visitors to the building can view a life-size mural depicting the way the building would

FAMOUS SON

Alexander Hamilton, the first Treasury Secretary of the United States and one of the authors of the Federalist Papers, grew up in obscurity in Christiansted, the illegitimate son of a shopkeeper. Hamilton's years on St. Croix, from age 10 to 18, provide a glimpse into social realities of the time; his story provides insight into the early influences of one of America's most important early statesmen.

Hamilton's mother, Rachel Faucett, moved to St. Croix when she was 16 and was married to John Lavien, who owned a cotton plantation in the new colony. Rachel and John's marriage was not a happy one. In 1749 John publicly accused Rachel of infidelity and had her jailed at Fort Christansvaern for several months. When she was released, Rachel left St. Croix for St. Kitts, where she met and fell in love with James Hamilton, a Scotsman. Alexander Hamilton was born in 1755, the second of two sons born to Rachel and James, who never married. In 1765, the family moved to St. Croix, where James had some business. Soon after the move, James moved out and later returned to Nevis. He never saw his sons again.

Rachel rented a house and shop in Christiansted at No. 34 Company Street. Alexander helped his mother with the business while his brother was apprenticed to a carpenter. In February 1768, Rachel caught yellow fever and died at the age of 38. Alexander was 11 years old. What little property Rachel had was inherited by Peter Lavien, the legitimate son she had with her ex-husband. Alexander and his brother were left penniless.

Alexander moved in with a local merchant, Thomas Stevens, and began working as a clerk for an import-export house, Beckman and Cruger, located at Nos. 7–8 King Street. Alexander's natural intelligence and business sense attracted the attention of his employers, and soon he was making important decisions for the company. Hamilton later told his children that his years at Beckman and Cruger were "the most useful part of his education."

During this time Hamilton also developed a friendship with Presbyterian Rev. Hugh Knox, who shared with him his library of books on philosophy, reason, and law. Hamilton's account of a 1772 hurricane published in the *Royal Danish America Gazette* so impressed those who read it that Hamilton's friends and supporters raised money for him to travel to the United States for an education. In June 1773, Hamilton sailed from St. Croix for New York, where he would spend one year at the Barber Academy before enrolling in King's College, the institution later to become Columbia University.

ST. CROIX

COURTESY OF LIBRARY OF CONGRESS/JOHN TURNBULL

Alexander Hamilton spent his teenage years on St. Croix.

have been laid out during a church service. There are also a few small exhibits, and National Park Service staff and volunteers are present to answer your questions.

From 1733, when the Danes bought St. Croix, until 1754, the island was administered by the Danish West India and Guinea Company, a royally chartered slave-trading monopoly. The **Danish West India and Guinea Company Warehouse,** located across Company Street from the Steeple Building, was the administrative and commercial headquarters of the company. During the second half of the 18th century, the warehouse complex would have been about three times its present size, housing offices, warehouses, and quarters for company staff and slaves. The open yard in the center of the warehouse was used for slave auctions. Today the warehouse contains offices and public restrooms.

The two-story **Scale House,** steps from the waterfront, is where imports and exports were weighed for the purpose of taxation. Hogsheads of sugar and puncheons of rum were weighed before being loaded on ships to Europe and North America. Like today, St. Croix imported most of the food and supplies it needed; these goods were also weighed, logged, and taxed at the Scale House. The building you see today was built in 1856 and replaced a wooden weighing house first built in 1740.

A scale dating from 1861 is on display on the ground floor, which also houses a National Park Service gift shop and information desk. This is where you will find free guides to the three national parks on St. Croix and lots more useful information for visiting St. Croix.

The taxes levied at the Scale House were paid at the **Customs House** next door. Part of the first floor dates to 1751, when it was part of a row of buildings in the Danish West India and Guinea Company's warehouse. The existing structure was completed in 1841. The Customs House was the site of the town's post office until 1927 and then housed the public library until 1972. Today, it houses the headquarters of the National Park Service on St. Croix.

Government House

This imposing U-shaped building, at Nos. 2–3 King Street, still functions as the U.S. Virgin Islands' governor's living quarters and office when he is on St. Croix. Governor-General Peter von Scholten combined two large town houses and added the eastern facade in 1830 to create the building as it appears today.

As long as no official function is going on, visitors may walk through the courtyard, up the outside staircase, and into the great ballroom, where there is a painting of von Scholten. Admission is free.

St. Croix Archaeology Museum

The local Archaeological Society maintains the tiny St. Croix Archaeology Museum (No. 6 Company St., 340/692-2365, 10 A.M.–2 P.M. Sat., free), which is dedicated to exploring the island's pre-Columbian past. In addition to displaying artifacts from the island's Taino and Saladoid periods, it recounts the events that took place when Christopher Columbus's fleet sailed into Salt River Bay.

Apothecary Museum

Calling this a museum is a little bit of a stretch, but it is worth a stop nonetheless. Located in Apothecary Hall at No. 4 Queen Cross Street, the glass-enclosed exhibit shows an apothecary's office from the 19th century. The exhibit is maintained by the St. Croix Landmarks Society, which has a shop and offices in the same building.

Market Square

The market square (7 Company St.) was included in Frederik Moth's 1734 plan of Christiansted and served as one of the focal points for the sale of fresh fruits, vegetables, and wares produced by skilled artisans. The market was busiest on Sunday, the day slaves were free from field work and could come to town with any produce they were able to grow in their own kitchen gardens.

It was here in 1852, four years after emancipation, that a military company of blacks, known as the Frikorps, opened fire to disband a Christmas Eve gathering that had been forbidden due to fears of a yellow fever epidemic. A number of revelers were killed or injured, and in the aftermath some blacks called for revenge by bloodshed or arson. To restore order, the Danish governor disbanded all militia units. It was not until 45 years after the Christmas Eve Massacre, as it became known, that the government raised another militia in the Danish West Indies.

Today, the market square is largely deserted, except on Saturday mornings when you will find local farmers selling fruits and vegetables.

Sunday Market Square

Not to be confused with the primary Market Square, the town's other historic market area is Sunday Market Square. This broad street and commercial district on Market Street, between King and Company Streets, underwent a $2.4 million renovation in 2005. The revived square is expected to encourage future economic development in Christiansted and to discourage the kind of illicit activities that gave the area its more common nickname, Times Square.

Historic Churches

St. Croix's oldest extant church, the **Lord God of Sabaoth Lutheran Church** (4 King St., 340/773-1320) was built around 1740 as the Dutch Reformed Church. When the Lutheran congregation left the Steeple Building in 1831, they moved in here. The most distinctive feature is the neoclassical tower, built in 1834.

The **Holy Cross Catholic Church** (20 Company St., 340/773-7564) was built in 1755 and extensively altered in the 1850s. Holy Cross combines the molded facades of San Juan's 17th-century churches with the neo-Gothic elements favored in the 19th century.

St. John's Anglican Church (27 King St., 340/778-8221) sits prominently at the entrance to downtown Christiansted. St. John's was built in the mid-19th century, replacing a 1772 building. A fire in 1866 destroyed much of the church's original interior, but the exterior reflects the fidelity to the Gothic Revival style prescribed for Anglican churches around the world.

Moravian missionaries arrived in St. Croix in the 1730s to minister to enslaved Africans. Christiansted's **Friedensthal Moravian Church** (New St., 340/772-2811) was founded in the 1750s. The parish house, or manse, was built in the 1830s, and the present church was built between 1852 and 1854. The manse was used as both a home and a school.

Protestant Cay

Located in the middle of Christiansted harbor, Protestant Cay is a tiny islet home to a small, inviting beach, water sports center, restaurant, and hotel. Most people who live in and around Christiansted frequent this handy beach, and it often becomes crowded on weekends.

To get there, hop on the ferry (adults $3 round-trip) that runs 7 A.M.–midnight daily. The ferry departs from the Christiansted wharf in front of the old Customs House. Look for a small step labeled Hotel on the Cay near a bench, where you can sit while you wait. The ferry does not run according to schedule; as

© SUSANNA HENIGHAN

The Steeple Building was one of the first churches on St. Croix.

ST. CROIX

soon as the captain sees anyone waiting on either side, he comes out to carry you across.

FREDERIKSTED

Frederiksted is a city on the comeback. Long in the shadow of larger, busier, and more classically Caribbean Christiansted, St. Croix's other city is in the midst of a cultural and economic rejuvenation.

The waterfront town is home to some of the island's most interesting restaurants and coolest clubs, as well as the best sunsets on St. Croix. Dive shops in and around the town specialize in the island's west coast dives, including the Ann Abramson Pier. A number of gay-friendly establishments lend to the trendy ambience and make this the place for travelers seeking something a little bit off the beaten track.

History

Frederiksted was founded in 1751 to put a stop to the growing illegal trade taking place along the island's western coast, where merchants could easily skirt import taxes. It was here that Governor General Peter von Scholten, faced with thousands of slaves demanding freedom, read the emancipation proclamation in 1848. Thirty years later, black laborers again marched into Frederiksted to protest unfair working conditions. They didn't like what they heard, and they set fire to the town and 30 neighboring estates in what is now called the Fireburn. The town was rebuilt in the Victorian style of the day, with elaborate gingerbread trims, wide porches, and covered sidewalks. This classic architecture is still evident today.

In modern times, Frederiksted became the port of call for cruise ships visiting St. Croix. These visits provide the town with its economic bread and butter, so when cruise ship visits dropped off in 2004, Frederiksted teetered close to devastating economic decline.

But Frederiksteders are used to struggle, and the dedicated people of organizations like the Frederiksted Economic Development Association aren't giving up anytime soon. Events like the monthly Sunset Jazz on the waterfront, the Crucian Christmas Festival, and the Emancipa-

sidewalk scene in Frederiksted, St. Croix

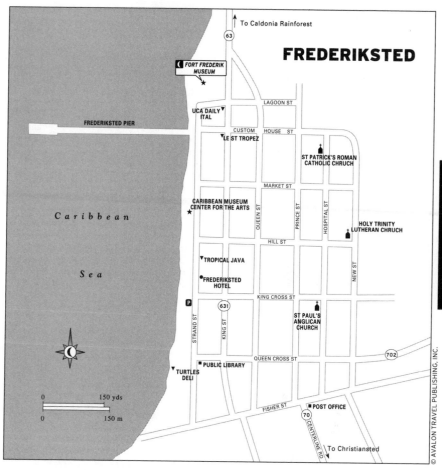

tion Day events in July bring people to Frederiksted. In 2005 the government undertook a major waterfront revitalization project in Frederiksted, which created a superb waterfront park for walking, sitting, people-watching, and public events. Tourism officials are optimistic that cruise ships will soon return to St. Croix in great numbers.

Frederiksted has not completely overcome its ghosts, however. Unemployment and poverty remain problems in Frederiksted, as they do in all of St. Croix. Visitors should be careful if they venture into parts of Frederiksted away from the waterfront. There are still a number of run-down and empty storefronts, but a huge amount of potential.

◖ Fort Frederik Museum

The Fort Frederik Museum (340/772-2021, 8:30 A.M.–4:30 P.M. Mon.–Fri., $3) is well worth a visit. Set on the town's waterfront, this deep red fort served as the focal point of two of St. Croix's most important historic events: the 1848 abolition of slavery and the 1878 labor riots, known locally as the Fireburn. The fort houses exhibits that describe these events, as well as a UNESCO exhibit entitled The Slaver

ST. CROIX

FREEDOM CITY

Moses Gottlieb, better known as General Buddhoe, is the hero of the 1848 St. Croix slave uprising that led to emancipation in the Danish West Indies. He is credited with not only leading the uprising, but also keeping the peace during the days after emancipation was achieved.

As a skilled sugar boiler, Buddhoe often traveled from plantation to plantation. He was known and respected by slaves around the island, so when he argued that slaves should

Slaves on St. Croix demanded their freedom in 1848.

demand their freedom in a peaceful and organized way, they listened.

Late on July 2, 1848, it was a conch shell that told slaves around the island that the rebellion had begun. By the morning of July 3, more than 2,000 slaves were on the roads, making their way to Frederiksted. Legend has it that as they marched, the black men, women, and children sang, "Mek way, we comin fo ah we freedom." Before midday, General Buddhoe arrived from Estate La Grange atop a white horse, dressed in full military uniform.

Buddhoe was the spokesman for the slaves, telling the authorities that their demand was simple: freedom. A deadline of noon came and went with no sign of freedom, so the slaves tore up the hated whipping post and threw it in the sea. Buddhoe gave the authorities a final ultimatum: If the slaves did not receive their freedom by 4 P.M., the town would burn. Minutes before 4 P.M., Governor General Peter von Scholten rode into Frederiksted, quickly consulted with the planters inside the fort, and came outside to make his announcement. His words are still famous today: "From this day onward, all unfree in the Danish West Indies are today free."

With the objective met, Buddhoe set about keeping the peace. He interceded to save the life of Fire Marshal Jacob Gyllich and even helped round up former slaves who continued to loot. But Buddhoe was not thanked for his efforts. After the discord ended, Buddhoe was imprisoned at Fort Christiansvaern. He was not tried but was deported to Trinidad on January 8, 1849. There are reports he eventually made his way to the United States.

Fredensborg, which remembers the slave trade by re-creating the 1768 journey of the slave ship *Fredensborg* from Copenhagen to Christiansted via the Gold Coast of Ghana. The museum also houses two excellent photographic exhibits depicting the island's market women and Puerto Rican community.

In addition to housing exhibits, the fort

is an attraction in itself. Built between 1752 and 1760 to discourage smuggling along the island's western shore, the fort was named for the reigning Danish monarch of the day, Frederik V. It was built on the site of an earlier earthen fortification, Fort St. James, built by the English in the 1640s and later used by both the Spanish and the French.

COURTESY OF LIBRARY OF CONGRESS/H.L. STEPHENS

Unlike Fort Christiansvaern, which is owned by the federal government, Fort Frederik is maintained by the local government. Until 1973, the fort housed government offices. Between 1974 and 1976 the fort underwent restoration before being opened as a museum.

Caribbean Museum Center for the Arts

After several itinerant years, The Caribbean Museum Center for the Arts (10 Strand St., www.cmcarts.org, 340/772-2622, 10 A.M.–5 P.M. Tues.–Sat., free) found a permanent home in 2005. The center contains a small gallery that exhibits the work of local artists and organizes art classes for children and adults. It also produces a wall calendar featuring the work of local artists and sells note cards, prints, and original artwork.

Historic Churches

Holy Trinity Lutheran Church, at Hill and Hospital Streets, is the oldest church in Frederiksted. Built in 1792 to replace an original wood structure built 25 years earlier, Holy Trinity has changed some over the years but still reflects the original design. The Frederiksted town cemetery is across the road from Holy Trinity.

At Market and Hospital Streets, **St. Patrick's Roman Catholic Church** was built in 1848, the same year as emancipation, and was expanded shortly after to accommodate a growing congregation. Built from local cut stone, the church shows elements of Gothic Revival, neoclassical, and Spanish Baroque. The church cemetery contains a monument to 14 sailors from the *U.S.S. Monongahela,* who perished in the 1867 tidal wave that deposited their vessel several hundred yards inland.

St. Paul's Anglican Church, at King Cross and Prince Streets, was completely restored after a fire in the 1990s. The church combines an 1812 West Indian hipped roof structure with a neo-Gothic three-tiered tower built in 1848. The tower was constructed with local limestone and Danish brick.

Beaches

There are good beaches both north and south of Frederiksted. To the north, the coast is really one long stretch of sand, but most people swim at the beaches in front of one of the three popular beach bars in the area. **Sprat Beach,** in front of the Sunset Grill, is a good choice, as is **Rainbow Beach,** in front of Changes in L'Attitude.

On the south side of Frederiksted, the beach just past the fish market is popular with local residents, especially on weekends and holidays. There are picnic tables and shelters here. Less than 100 yards farther south is **Sandcastle Beach,** in front of the hotel by the same name.

◖ BUCK ISLAND

Buck Island, a 180-acre island surrounded by almost 20,000 acres of protected coral reef and seabed, is located less than two miles from St. Croix's northern coast. Noted for excellent snorkeling, hiking, and one of the nicest beaches on St. Croix, Buck Island packs a lot of punch for nature-loving visitors. The island and surrounding reef make up **Buck Island National Monument** (340/773-1460, www.nps.gov/buis, 6 A.M.–6 P.M.), which was declared thus by President Kennedy in 1961. President Clinton added 18,135 acres of seabed and reef to the monument as part of the U.S. Coral Reef Initiative in 1998.

Buck Island is a nesting ground for the endangered brown pelican, hawksbill, leatherback and green sea turtles, and the threatened least tern. The barrier reef that surrounds the majority of the island has extraordinary coral formations, deep grottos, abundant reef fishes, sea fans, and gorgonians. An underwater snorkel trail on the east end showcases a small part of the reef, while hiking trails cut through the dry forest and provide views of the surrounding sea.

The National Park Service manages Buck Island, and human activity is limited on and around the island. A half dozen concessionaires are licensed to provide day trips to the island. Private boats must adhere to strict regulations; fishing is very limited. Anchoring is by permit only. Meanwhile, the Park Service has installed

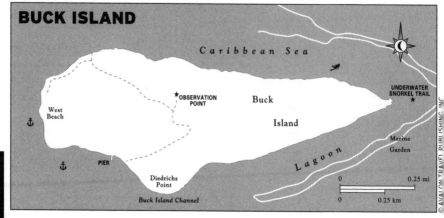

basic infrastructure to give the public access to Buck Island's attractions. There are moorings near the underwater snorkel trail and a concrete dock at Diedrich's Point on the western shore. Picnic tables and pit toilets are at the western end of the island.

A hiking trail traverses the island's western end, passing flowering frangipani, Turks head cacti, and orchids. The trail climbs to an observation point at mid-island, where you can see St. Thomas, St. John, and the British Virgins on a clear day.

Getting There

Licensed concessionaires offer half- and full-day trips to Buck Island. Half-day trips include snorkeling on the underwater trail and a short visit to the western beaches. Full-day trips give visitors more time underwater and enough time to hike the island's trails.

It is easy to feel like a member of the herd at Buck Island, especially since the Park Service requires tour operators to guide you through the underwater trail. For the best experience, try to get on a trip with fewer than six people. If you want to hike the complete trail, be sure to tell the tour operator of your wishes so you will get on a trip that will give you at least 1.5 hours on the island.

Most concessionaires leave from Christiansted, and the trip to Buck Island takes be-

tween 30 and 80 minutes, depending on the type of boat. Other trips leave from Green Cay Marina east of Christiansted. Trips to the island are shorter from here. Expect to pay between $40 and $75 for a half-day trip and between $60 and $100 for a full day.

Mile Mark Watersports (59 King's Wharf, Christiansted, 340/773-2628, www.milemark-watersports.com) offers full- and half-day trips on sailboats or powerboats. It is the only concessionaire to offer diving as well as snorkeling, although diving at Buck Island is not highly recommended due to accessibility and weather conditions.

Big Beard's Adventure Tours (Queen Cross St., Christiansted, 340/773-4482, www.bigbeards.com) provides a beach barbecue on full-day trips.

Two smaller operators leave from Green Cay Marina and get to Buck Island much more quickly. They are *Teroro II and Dragonfly* (340/773-3161) and *Diva*, (340/778-4675) which has a passenger limit of six.

Private boats must obtain a permit from the National Park Service before anchoring or mooring at Buck Island. There is no anchoring inside the reef; the only anchor zone is off West Beach, where the bottom is sandy.

NORTH SHORE

Heading west from Christiansted, the focus turns quickly from history to nature. Northshore Road winds along the shore of Salt River Bay before striking out along the dramatic northern coast. Offshore and underwater, the celebrated Wall teems with marinelife, beckoning divers.

Estate Little Princess

Located less than two miles west of Christiansted, the ruins of Estate Little Princess are under the stewardship of the Nature Conservancy (3052 Estate Little Princess, 340/773-5575, www.nature.org). Visitors can amble through the 250-year-old plantation ruins or examine the cutting-edge green technologies the Conservancy is showcasing on-site. This is also the site of the Nature Conservancy's Eastern Caribbean headquarters.

St. Croix's first governor, Frederick Moth, bought the estate in 1738 and gradually established a full-fledged sugar plantation and factory. It operated as a sugar plantation for nearly 200 years. In the 1950s an American couple bought the 25-acre estate, and in 1990 the property was bequeathed to the Nature Conservancy.

Guided tours are given on Tuesdays and Thursdays 3–5 P.M. The public is welcome to tour the grounds on their own at other times.

Salt River Bay

A wide estuary on the northern coast of St. Croix, Salt River Bay National Historic Park and Ecological Preserve (340/773-1460, www.nps.gov/sari) is a site of both natural and historical significance. Archeological studies have shown that the pottery-making Igneri people settled at Salt River Bay as early as A.D. 50, attracted by its protected waters, fertile fishing grounds, and nearby sources of freshwater. By 700 A.D. the Taino people arrived at Salt River. They absorbed the remaining Igneri and lived there for centuries. In 1923 archeologists found evidence of a large ceremonial ball court on Salt River Bay's western shore, proof of the settlement's size and importance to the Taino people. Petroglyphs, stone belts, and zemis associated with the ball court remain in the possession of the National Museum in Copenhagen.

In the early 1400s the warlike Kalinago people arrived in St. Croix, quickly conquering and enslaving the Tainos. When Christopher Columbus sent a longboat ashore at Salt River Bay in search of water on November 17, 1493—on his second voyage—the party encountered several Kalinago in a canoe. The two parties fought, with both sides suffering casualties in the first recorded instance of Native American resistance to European encroachment. Columbus named the site Cape of Arrows.

Salt River Bay was the site of successive fledgling European settlements during the early years of colonization on St. Croix. Between 1641 and 1655, the English, Dutch, French, and Knights of Malta (through a lease from the French) sited settlements on the bay's western shore. Remains of an unusual triangular earthwork fort called Fort Flamandor or Fort Sale, started by the English in 1641 and finished by the Dutch in 1642, sit on the western point of the bay.

In addition to its historical importance,

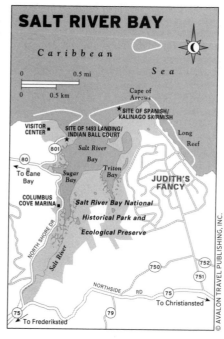

Salt River Bay is a dynamic coastal habitat that plays a critical role in the area's marine environment. Extensive mangrove forests that line the estuary act as a buffer between the sea and the land, providing a sheltered home for juvenile fish and filtering runoff from the land. Just past the mouth of the bay the sea floor falls away, creating the deep Virgin Islands Basin and its coral-covered walls.

The National Park Service operates a visitors center on the western shore of the bay. Pick up the free Park Service guide to Salt River Bay, which includes a good map showing the location of ruins and walking trails. To reach the Cape of Arrows, on the eastern side of the bay, take Rte. 75 west from Christiansted and then turn north onto Rte. 751. You will have to pass through a security gate to enter the residential community of Judith's Fancy. A number of tracks on the eastern shore take you through the mangrove forest and to the top of the point overlooking the site of the 1493 skirmish.

To explore the western shore, follow Rte. 75 west from Christiansted and turn north onto Rte. 80, also called North Shore Drive. Turn onto narrow Rte. 801 to reach a small beach and parking lot. This is where the Park Service visitors center is located, and the area of the Taino ball court and the European forts.

If you want to explore Salt River Bay in greater detail, sign up for a kayak tour with **Caribbean Adventure Tours** (Columbus Cove, 340/778-1522, U.S. toll free 800/532-3483, www.stcroixkayak.com), which offers 2.5-hour historical, ecological, and moonlight tours for $45. **Virgin Kayak Co.** (Cane Bay, 340/778-0071) also offers guided half-day kayak tours of the bay for $45.

Ras Lumumba Corriette of **Ay-Ay Eco Hikes and Tours** (340/772-4079 or 340/277-0410) offers an excellent hike along the eastern shore of Salt River Bay, which focuses on the ecological importance of the area.

【 The Wall

St. Croix's greatest underwater sight is the Wall, a massive ledge that runs parallel to the island's north shore for seven miles between Christiansted and Ham's Bluff on the northwest coast. From the shore, the sea floor slopes gradually to about 30 feet before plunging to depths of 3,200 feet.

The Wall teems with marinelife: extensive hard and soft coral, turtles, eagle rays, barracuda, damsel fish, butterfly fish, cleaner wrasses, gobies, squirrelfish, and more. Since the wall faces deep, open water, large pelagic species like snappers, jacks, and sharks can be seen here too.

There are more than 20 different established Wall dive sites, but the easiest and best place to start is **Cane Bay,** a sandy beach about halfway between Christiansted and the northwest point of the island. No dive boat is necessary here (although some operators use small dinghies) because you can easily swim the 300 feet offshore to where the Wall begins. Snorkelers can explore the shallow parts of the Wall, but divers get the best views of its intricate holes, passages, and the awesome precipice below.

If one Wall dive is not enough for you, try the **Salt River Canyon** dives, at the mouth of Salt River Bay. Here, healthy coral gardens border the east and west sides of the large undersea canyon. For experienced divers, **Vertigo,** at Annaly Bay, is the holy grail of St. Croix diving. Here the Wall slopes back under itself, creating an overhang that puts divers in the middle of wide, dark ocean. This is a challenging, dangerous dive, and not all dive shops will take you there.

Beaches

Wide, sandy **Cane Bay** is a destination for water sports enthusiasts with a penchant for good times. After a morning or afternoon out exploring the celebrated Cane Bay Wall, divers and snorkelers share stories over a cold one at one of the friendly beach bars nearby. If you feel more like taking it easy, the palm-lined beach has plenty of shade, sand, and space to relax.

Davis Bay, the setting of Carambola Beach Resort, is a lovely beach. Nonguests are welcome. Walk to the far western end for the best snorkeling and easiest entry into the water.

A remote, rocky bay on the northwest coast of St. Croix, **Annaly Bay** has a sandy beach, good snorkeling, and neat tidepools. There are no facilities here, but the setting and seclusion make roughing it worthwhile.

To hike into Annaly Bay, drive into Carambola Resort and ask at the guard gate to be pointed toward the trail to Annaly. It is about an hour of moderate to difficult hiking from there. You can also reach the bay via the Scenic Route, an unpaved and often very rough road. The best way to get here, though, is to come with a guide. **Ay-Ay Eco Hikes and Tours** (340/772-4079 or 340/277-0410) offers a guided hike to Annaly, and **Tan-Tan Tours** (340/773-7041 or 340/473-6446) does open-air, off-road jeep tours.

WEST ISLAND

From the broad plain in the south to the rainforest in the north, no part of St. Croix offers as much diversity and richness as the west island. Museums here pay tribute to the island's colorful and brutal past, while other attractions showcase its rich natural resources.

C Whim Plantation Museum

The Whim Plantation Museum (52 Estate Whim, 340/772-0598, fax 340/772-9446, www.stcroixlandmarks.com) is the best place to learn about St. Croix's Danish plantation era. In high season (November–April) the museum is open 10 A.M.–4 P.M. Mon.–Sat.; at other times it opens 10 A.M.–3 P.M. Monday, Wednesday, Friday, and Saturday. Admission is $8 for adults, $5 for seniors and students, and $4 for children 6–12. Children under 6 get in free.

The elegant 18th-century Whim great house is the centerpiece of the museum. Guided tours of the house, which has been furnished with period pieces, are included with admission. A self-guided tour of the grounds takes you to the only fully restored windmill on the island, a sugar factory, watch house, cookhouse, and more.

Whim was first surveyed between 1733 and 1735, when Danish authorities divided the island into estates and began encouraging set-

tlers to establish plantations on the island. By 1754, sugar cultivation began on the Whim estate, fueled by the labor of enslaved Africans. In 1810, a peak year for sugar production on the island, there were 105 slaves at Whim and 130 acres under cultivation. Sugar continued to be produced until 1920, when the estate turned to livestock. This was short-lived; in 1932, the federal government bought the plantation as part of a Depression-era homestead program.

In 1954, 11 acres at Whim, including the great house, was deeded to the St. Croix Landmarks Society for preservation and education. Over the years, the Society has collected sugar mill artifacts from area estates. The surrounding area is now residential.

The museum shop sells reproduction Danish colonial furniture, as well as books, crafts, and gifts. A library and archives on-site has an excellent collection of material about St. Croix and the Virgin Islands, including extensive genealogical resources.

Lawaetz Family Museum

Carl Lawaetz left Denmark to seek his fortune in St. Croix in the early 1890s, where he found work on one of the island plantations. In 1896 he bought the run-down sugar factory, land, and estate house at Little LaGrange, north of Frederiksted. Five years later, he married, and the estate soon became home to Carl and Marie's growing family. The Lawaetz name is closely associated with the St. Croix cattle industry and its specially bred Senepol cattle.

Carl and Marie's home is now a museum, turned over to the St. Croix Landmarks Society in 1996, on the centennial of Carl Lawaetz's purchase of the estate. Visitors to the Carl and Marie Lawaetz Family Museum (Mahogany Rd., 340/772-1539, www.stcroixlandmarks.com, 10:30 A.M.–3:30 P.M. Tues., Thurs., and Sat., adults $8, seniors $5, children 6–12 $4, under six free) receive a 30-minute guided tour of the house and grounds, during which they are given a glimpse at life on St. Croix in the early 20th century. After the tour, visitors can stroll the gardens or walk along one of the trails that traverse the grounds.

ST. CROIX

St. George Village Botanical Garden

Tropical flora combines with history at the St. George Village Botanical Garden (127 Estate St. George, 340/692-2874, www.sgvbg.org, adults $6, children $1). The gardens are open daily 9 A.M.–5 P.M. in high season (Nov.–April) and 9 A.M.–4 P.M. Tues.–Sat. at other times. Set on the site of Taino Indian and Danish settlements, the 16-acre garden contains a botanical collection of more than 1,500 native and exotic species, including fruit trees, orchids, medicinal herbs, cactus, and flowering shrubs and trees. A short self-guided tour takes visitors through sugar mill ruins, gardens, orchards, and a tropical forest. There is a gift shop and office in the Great Hall at the entrance to the gardens. Plants are on sale at the nursery on Tuesdays and Fridays 9–11 A.M.

The gardens are a peaceful place for a stroll, especially for families or visitors who won't have time to do hiking elsewhere on the island. Every July the gardens come alive for the annual Mango Melee, a celebration of the juicy fruit featuring food, music, educational presentations, garden tours, and mangos galore.

Caldonia Rainforest

No, this is not a real rainforest (there's not enough rain), but that's what everyone on St. Croix calls the damp northwestern corner of the island, so don't quibble. This is the most mountainous and thickly forested part of St. Croix—a land of running streams, damp air, and huge trees. It is a world apart from the arid east end, or the gentle rolling hills of the south. To explore the rainforest by car, take Route 76, Mahogany Road, which winds through dense forest. You can also take Route 765, Annaly Road, to Route 58, Creque Dam Road, and follow that west to the coast. You will need four-wheel drive to explore Route 78, Scenic Drive, which heads east towards Route 69.

A recommended pit stop is **The Mount Pellier Domino Club** (Rt. 76, 340/772-9914). The casual bar is famous for three things: beer-drinking pigs, potent mamajuana (spiced rum), and some excellent, down-home hospitality from

hosts Norma and George. The pigs switched to nonalcoholic brew a few years ago, but it is still fun to watch them crack open a can and chug its contents down. The bar here is almost always crowded, often by locals discussing politics and news. As the name suggests, there is sometimes a spirited domino game in progress, too.

Another interesting rainforest stop is **St. Croix LEAP**, or Life Environmental Arts Project, (Mahogany Rd., 340/772-0421, 8 A.M.–5 P.M. Mon.–Sat., free) a woodworking shop located deep within the rainforest. Started years ago by the late master woodworker Fletch Evans Pence, LEAP is now operated by "Cheech," a 30-year island resident who harvests mahogany trees and transforms them into works of art. Cutting boards, sculptures, and coffee tables are for sale.

Nestled among the northern foothills of the rainforest is **Estate Mount Washington**, sugar estate ruins about 1.5 miles off Rte. 63 in the island's northwest corner. Look for the yellow sign at the turnoff. Estate Mount Washington began as a cotton plantation in 1750 but turned to sugar production in 1779. The current owners have preserved the ruins while planting groves of avocado and other trees on the grounds. The ruins are open during daylight hours.

Sprat Hall (Rt. 63, 340/772-0305) is a bed-and-breakfast, but nonguests can get a tour of the historic great house for $5. Another good rainforest stop is the campground at **Mount Victory Camps** (Creque Dam Rd., 340/772-1651), where you can see red-legged tortoises, sample organic bush tea, and meet interesting people.

Cruzan Rum Distillery

You can witness rum production from fermentation to bottling at the Cruzan Rum Distillery (No. 3 Estate Diamond, 340/692-2280, 9 A.M.–11:30 A.M. and 1–4:15 P.M. Mon.–Fri., adults $4, under 18 $1). The half-hour tour takes you past massive vats of fermenting liquid and through the warehouse where Cruzan rum is aged in wooden barrels. A complimentary rum punch is included in your tour.

Rum has been produced at Cruzan's Estate Diamond factory since 1760. Today, the molasses used in the rum production is imported from Central or South America, and most of the rum leaves the island in huge containers. It arrives in Florida, where it is bottled and then sold around the world. About 15 percent of the rum produced on St. Croix is bottled there and stays in the Caribbean.

Sandy Point National Wildlife Refuge

The U.S. Fish and Wildlife Service owns the 380-acre area around Sandy Point, at the far southwestern tip of St. Croix. The beach is the single most important nesting site for leatherback turtles in the Virgin Islands—an estimated 150 animals nest here on an average year. At least 100 species of birds have been spotted in the refuge, including endangered brown pelicans, peregrine falcons, black-bellied plovers, and roseate terns.

Sandy Point is remote and has been the site of violent and petty crime in the past. From September to April the refuge is open to the public on weekends only (10 A.M.–4 P.M. Sat.–Sun.), when the Fish and Wildlife Service post officers there to ensure safety of visitors and of the endangered animals that live there. The refuge is closed during the summer turtle nesting season.

Beaches

Besides Sandy Point, the best beaches on the west coast are at Sprat Bay, north of Frederiksted, and Sandcastle on the Beach, south of Frederiksted.

EAST ISLAND

Arid and relatively undeveloped, eastern St. Croix looks and feels different from the rest of the island. Unlike western St. Croix, which is dominated by rainforests in the north and the flat plain in the south, the eastern end of the island is dry and scrubby. Socially, it is a land of ostentatious homes, quiet drives, and

ST. CROIX

© SUSANNA HENIGHAN

windmill ruins at Sprat Hall on the west coast of St. Croix

American snowbirds. There is very little of the cultural richness so evident in the island's two towns or western suburbs.

Nonetheless, there are several very good reasons to head east. East St. Croix has some of the island's most remote and least developed beaches, as well as its best public beach and park, ideal for picnics and family outings. The landscape itself is captivating—especially in contrast to the rest of the island. Windswept Point Udall is the easternmost point in the United States.

The east end is easy to navigate. Rte. 82 heading east out of Christiansted follows the coast, taking you past a string of beaches, resorts, and restaurants, and eventually to Point Udall, the easternmost point in the United States. Along the way, you pass Cramer Park, a popular beach, picnic site, and the starting point of hikes to Jack and Isaac Bays.

Rt. 60 follows the southern coast, past the island's most elite estates, the Carina Bay Casino and the wide open plain surrounding Great Pond Bay, an important wetland. Pressing on, you enter St. Croix's cattle country, home to the hearty Senepol breed.

Base Array Telescope

At 82 feet wide and 10 stories high, the radio telescope that sits just across the road from Cramer Park stands out from its surroundings. The telescope is part of the national **Very Long Baseline Array** (340/773-0196, www.vlba. nrao.edu), a system of 10 identical radio telescopes located across the continental United States and Hawaii. Funded by the National Science Foundation, the 10 telescopes intercept radio waves to look deep into the universe. They are controlled at the National Radio Astronomy Observatory in New Mexico. Group tours are available by prior appointment only.

Point Udall

Up until 1999, Point Udall, named for Stewart Udall, secretary of the interior 1961–1969, was simply a remote lookout point on the far eastern end of St. Croix. But when millennium fever struck, the local government

paved the road to Point Udall and built a monument in recognition of the fact that, as the easternmost point on U.S. soil, Point Udall would be first in the U.S. to welcome the new millennium.

After the excitement of the millennium, Point Udall returned to being a remote, windswept place, although with the added bonus of a nicely paved road and interesting monument. It is a nice drive out here, through wild, scrubby landscape, and the view of wide open ocean is captivating.

Jack and Isaac Bay Preserve

St. Croix's best secluded beaches are located side by side in the 300-acre Jack and Isaac Bay Preserve (340/773-5575, www.nature. org) on the southeastern end of the island. These pristine, quiet beaches are part of a coastal wildlife reserve managed by the Nature Conservancy and protected by local law. Goat Hill rises more than 600 feet above the bays, providing awesome views of St. Croix, Buck Island, and Point Udall. Hiking trails at the reserve cut through a dry, open landscape dominated by guinea grass, wild frangipani, and manjack trees. The beaches are important nesting sites for green, hawksbill, and leatherback turtles.

Jack Bay, a broad crescent of white sand shaded by sea grape trees, is the farther west of the two bays. Isaac Bay is longer, straighter, and equally inviting. Many people like to bathe in the nude here, although the practice is illegal in the U.S. Virgin Islands. There are no facilities here, so bring plenty of water and don't forget to carry your trash out with you.

Hiking is the only way to access Jack and Isaac Bays. The best (but longest) way is to park at Cramer Park and follow the dirt road immediately east of the gravel driveway leading to the Very Long Baseline Array Telescope. It's a half-mile hike up to the saddle of Goat Hill, where you can turn right to hike the mile down to the beaches or turn left to hike a half mile to the top of Goat Hill. There are trail markers after you enter the reserve along the saddle of the hill.

You will almost always have Jack and Isaac Bays to yourself.

The other way to get to the preserve is to hike through East End Bay from Point Udall. Look for the track, which has now been blocked by large boulders to prevent people from driving down. Parking is limited at this entrance.

Beaches

The northeastern coast of St. Croix is a series of crescent bays, many of them fringed by sandy beaches. Most of these are developed, and beach amenities are reserved for hotel guests or paying day-trippers. Generally, visitors to these beaches are asked not to picnic.

Developed beaches include Beauregard Bay, better known as the **Buccaneer** after the luxury resort built around it, where nonguests must pay $6 for beach access. Other developed beaches are **Tamarind Beach,** next to Green Cay Marina, which is rocky and tends to be rough, and **Chenay Bay,** a long, protected crescent of honey-colored sand. Swimming at Chenay is good because there aren't many offshore rocks and you can snorkel along

the eastern end of the bay. On the south coast, **Turner Hole** at Divi Carina Bay Resort is a long, straight stretch of sand with good swimming. Snorkels and kayaks are available for rent at each of these beaches; Divi also has small sailboats.

There are also undeveloped beaches on the east end. **Shoys Beach** is a quiet, protected, honey-colored beach without facilities about a mile east of Christiansted. To get there, follow signs to The Buccaneer, but turn right immediately before passing through the Buccaneer guard gate. You will pass another guard, who will probably ask your name and can give you directions to the beach. The parking area is about half a mile down paved roads and past exclusive homes. The beach here tends to be a bit rocky, but the water is calm and clear.

Cramer's Park, near the island's eastern tip, is a popular public park with picnic tables, bathrooms, shelters, and plenty of parking. Crucians flock here on holidays and weekends, many of them setting up camp, especially at Easter. After the exclusivity of many of the east end beaches, the public nature of Cramer Park is a relief. This is the sort of place where you will see families celebrating a child's birthday, courting couples, and beachgoers just like yourself. It is not necessarily a quiet retreat, although you may well have it to yourself, especially on weekdays.

HOVENSA

Hess Oil established an oil refinery on the south shore of St. Croix in 1966. Then, as today, the refinery processed crude oil from Venezuela for export to the United States. In 1998, a corporate restructuring led to a new name for the facility, HOVENSA.

The HOVENSA plant has a processing capacity of 495,000 barrels per day, making it one of the largest oil refineries in the world. Both gasoline and heating oil are produced there. In 2002, a coker unit was added, which is used to manufacture gas and heating oil from lower cost, heavier crude oil. Nearly 1,000 islanders are employed at the HOVENSA plant.

ST. CROIX

Sports and Recreation

St. Croix's scenery is lovely to look at, but even nicer when you experience it firsthand. Outdoor pursuits like hiking, horseback riding, snorkeling and diving bring you up close to St. Croix's unique environment.

If you're interested in combining recreation with education, contact the **St. Croix Environmental Association** (Gallows Bay, 340/773-1989, fax 340/773-7545, www.seastx.org) before you come. SEA is the island's leading voice for environmental protection, but it also organizes a smorgasbord of educational outings for residents and visitors, ranging from stargazing to kayak trips. These are often excellent opportunities to see sites that are off the beaten track, and to learn about environmental issues of the day. Most activities are free for Association members; visitors are asked to pay $10–20, depending on the activity. It is worthwhile checking the calendar of events before you arrive and reserving a spot on any trips that catch your eye, as many activities fill up quickly.

WATER SPORTS
Diving

St. Croix offers the best and most diverse diving in the Virgin Islands. Its main attraction is The Wall, a deep undersea ledge that runs parallel to the island's northwestern shore, providing divers with a remarkable number of interesting, exciting, and rewarding dives. But what sets St. Croix apart most of all is the diversity of diving; in addition to Wall dives, there are reef dives, wreck dives, and a world-class pier dive. As dive operators like to say, St. Croix is the only island in the Virgins where you can dive a wreck, a reef, a wall, and a pier in one day.

St. Croix's dive sites are located along the northwestern and western shore—draw a line from Frederiksted to Christiansted along the shore, and you have defined the diving territory. Wall dives are located along the north coast, while the best wreck, reef, and pier dives are on the western shore. As a rule, west coast dives are calmer—they are in the lee of the island—and are the best choice when the sea is rough.

The lone exception to all this categorization is Buck Island, a 180-acre island surrounded by an extensive reef system off the northeastern coast of St. Croix. While snorkeling is the main attraction at Buck Island (only one dive shop, Anchor Dive Center, offers Buck Island dive trips), diving here can be rewarding.

Standout dives on St. Croix include the **Cane Bay Wall,** a beach dive, which is the perfect starting point for exploring the north shore Wall. **Salt River Canyon East and West** are two more outstanding Wall dives. For wreck diving, try **Butler Bay,** where five different wrecks have been intentionally sunk between 1984 and 1999 for the benefit of divers. Two of the most unusual dive sites on St. Croix are the old and new **Frederiksted Piers.** These shallow, protected dive sites bring you up close to some of the sea's wackiest creatures: seahorses, bat fish, octopi, eels, sponges, and anemones. The pier is especially neat at night.

Dive shops on St. Croix tend to specialize in the dives closest to them. Christiansted and Salt River Bay shops take divers to the Salt River Canyon or reef dives along the Christiansted Harbor. Cane Bay shops head to the north shore Wall, while west coast shops specialize in the pier, wreck, and reef dives on that side of the island. When choosing a dive operator, consider proximity; the longer you have to travel to get to a site, the less time you will have to explore it.

Expect to pay $75–90 for a two-tank dive on St. Croix. All dive shops offer a wide range of refresher and certification courses, including some you can start online before you arrive. A full certification course, which includes classroom sessions and confined and open-water dives, costs between $300 and $500; many shops charge more for an accelerated, one-on-one course.

In Christiansted, your first choice should be

DIVERSE VIRGIN

St. Croix dive operators have joined to create the Diverse Virgin program (www.diverse-virgin.com), which promotes scuba diving on St. Croix and supports conservation efforts around the island. Through Diverse Virgin, visitors have the option of buying a package of 6-14 dives, which can be redeemed with the seven participating Diverse Virgin members.

Pricewise, it's a good deal when compared to diving à la carte. The Diverse Virgin package rate is about $34 per tank dive; you will pay $60-70 for a single one-tank dive at most dive shops. The package rates are comparable to package rates offered by individual dive shops, but Diverse Virgin gives you the opportunity to enjoy package rates while diving with a different dive shop every day.

The bottom line is that if you want to do a lot of diving, and you like the idea of using a different dive shop every time (that's the rule),

then you should take advantage of the Diverse Virgin packages. One important catch is that you must buy your Diverse Virgin package before you arrive on island. Call any of the following participating dive operators to do so.

Scuba Shack (340/772-3483, 888/789-3483, www.stcroixscubashack.com)

Scuba West (340/772-3701, 800/352-0107, www.divescubawest.com)

St. Croix Ultimate Bluewater Adventures (340/773-5994, 877/567-1367, www.stcroix-scuba.com)

Anchor Dive Center (340/778-1522, 800/532-3483, www.anchordivestcroix.com)

Cane Bay Dive Shop (340/773-9913, 800/338-3843, www.canebayscuba.com)

Dive Experience (340/773-3307, 800/235-9047, www.divexp.com)

N2theBlue (340/713-1475, 866/712-2583, www.n2blue.com)

ST. CROIX

St. Croix Ultimate Bluewater Adventures, (14 Caravelle Arcade, 340/773-5994, U.S. toll free 877/567-1367, www.stcroixscuba.com) which goes by the convenient acronym SCUBA. Ed and Molly Buckley came to the island to work for an airline decades ago, but now they run one of the most popular dive shops on island. Their boats leave from the Christiansted waterfront with no more than 14 people.

Another choice is **Dive Experience,** (1111 Strand St., Christiansted, 340/773-3307, U.S. toll free 800/235-9047, www.divexp.com), operated by divemaster Michelle Pugh.

Cane Bay Dive Shop (340/773-9913, U.S. toll free 800/338-3843, www.canebay-scuba.com) has locations in Christiansted and Frederiksted, but their main base is at Cane Bay. For personalized service, try **N2 The Blue Diving Adventures** (La Vallee, 340/713-1475, U.S. toll free 866/712-2583, www.n2blue.com), which takes no more than six passengers per trip. It specializes in Wall dives, especially Rust op Twist, Gentle Winds, and the Salt River Canyon dives.

Headquartered inside Salt River Bay National Park, **Anchor Dive Center** (Columbus Cove, 340/778-1522, U.S. toll free 800/532-3483, www.anchordivestcroix.com) also has locations at Divi Carina Bay Resort on the south shore and Carambola Resort at Davis Bay. The Salt River Canyon dives are the specialty here; Anchor is the only company licensed to lead dive trips to Buck Island.

West coast dive shops include **Scuba Shack** (72B La Grange, 340/772-3438, U.S. toll free 888/789-3438, www.stcroixscubashack.com), just north of Frederiksted, next to Changes in L'Attitude. **Scuba West** (Strand St. 340/772-3701, U.S. toll free 800/352-0107, www.divescubawest.com) is located downtown, right across the road from the pier.

Snorkeling

The first and best place for snorkeling on St. Croix is at Buck Island, where the shallow, protected reef provides a lot to look at. (See *Buck Island,* under *Sights*). Other excellent snorkel sites around the island include Cane

Bay, North Star, and Davis Bay, where you can view healthy reefs and the undersea Wall. Cane Bay and Davis Bay are both accessible from the beach; you will need to catch a ride with a dive boat to visit North Star. Gentle Winds, just west of Salt River Canyon, is another good snorkel site accessible only by boat.

Snorkel equipment is available from any of the dive shops listed above. Water sports centers at Carambola Resort, Divi Carina Bay, Protestant Cay, and the Buccaneer also rent gear for exploring shallow reefs around the resorts.

Kayaking

The best place to kayak on St. Croix is Salt River Bay, a quiet estuary protected from waves and currents. Just put in your kayak and start exploring. Go at early morning or late afternoon for exceptional bird-watching. You can explore the expansive bay on your own or with a guide. A guide will give you added safety and be able to explain the history and ecology of the area. Expect to pay $45 for a 2.5-hour guided tour, per person, and $25 per hour for a two-person kayak rental.

There are two kayak tour and rental companies that specialize in Salt River Bay. **Caribbean Adventure Tours** (Columbus Cove, 340/778-1522, U.S. toll free 800/523-3483, www.stcroixkayak.com) offers three different 2.5-hour trips a day, including an historical tour, an ecological tour, and a moonlight tour. **Virgin Kayak Co.** (Cane Bay, 340/778-0071) offers a tour that focuses on the Taino settlement of Salt River Bay.

Fishing

There is a fertile deep-sea fishing ground a short sail away from St. Croix, where anglers can troll for mahimahi, marlin, tuna, and wahoo. Expect to pay about $500 for a half-day charter and $800 for a full day. Fishing rates are always quoted per charter, not per person.

Capt. Carl Holley (340/277-4042, www.fishwithcarl.com) can take up to six people out on his 36-foot *Mocko Jumbie*. Carl gladly crafts sportfishing charters for experienced or novice anglers and welcomes children, too.

Or fish in luxury with **Fantasy Sportfishing** (59 King's Wharf, 340/773-2628, www.milemarkwatersports.com), an offshoot of Mile-Mark Watersports, which uses a well-equipped 38-foot Bertram.

SAILING
Yachting Facilities

It is a day's sail to St. Croix from the other Virgin Islands, but well worth the journey. The seaward approach to Christiansted harbor is one of the most picturesque in the Caribbean. If you are sailing from the BVI, be sure to visit **Customs and Immigration** (Gallows Bay, 340/778-0216, 8 A.M.–4 P.M.) first. The best chandlery is **St. Croix Marine** (Gallows Bay, 340/dddd, 340/773-0289, 7:30 A.M.–5 P.M.). This full-service boatyard and marina is just east of the Customs dock. It can accommodate boats up to 200 feet, with up to 10-foot drafts. Gallows Bay is convenient to restaurants, services, and grocery stores.

Also near Christiansted are **Jones Maritime Company** (1215 King Cross Street, Christiansted, 340/773-4709, U.S. toll free 866/609-2930, www.jonesmaritime.com), which has 15 slips and all services except fuel. **Silver Bay Dock** (Christiansted, 340/778-9650) can accommodate boats up to 40 feet long.

East of Christiansted, there's **Green Cay Marina,** (340/773-1453) located opposite Green Cay, a small offshore nature preserve. It is well protected and has 140 slips, a hotel, restaurant, fuel, laundry, electricity, showers, a pump-out station, and ice. It monitors Channel 16 and can accommodate boats with depths up to 10 feet.

West of Christiansted, **Salt River Marina** (Salt River Bay, Channel 16) is a small marina within the protected Salt River Bay Historic Park and Ecological Preserve. Boats with more than six-foot drafts should not attempt to sail in here. Marina facilities include fuel, water, electricity, ice, and laundry. There is a restaurant and bar ashore.

Anchorages

The area in the lee of Protestant Cay in **Christiansted Harbor** is the best anchorage there, but it is often crowded. The harbor is also busy with seaplane traffic. Instead, visiting yachts should anchor east of Protestant Cay or in Gallows Bay.

Frederiksted is an open, exposed harbor protected from wind, but it is not safe during a storm. Visiting yachts are asked to anchor north of the cruise ship pier. You can also sail farther north and anchor near any of the west coast beaches north of town.

Yacht Clubs

The **St. Croix Yacht Club** (Teague Bay, Channel 16) is on the east end of St. Croix. There are moorings for visiting yachts. This is a good place to meet other sailors and learn about upcoming regattas. There is a bar and restaurant, showers, and garbage disposal.

LAND PURSUITS

St. Croix's relatively flat topography combined with its large size make the island a natural setting for a wide range of land pursuits. St. Croix is the first choice for golfers in the Virgin Islands, and its winding back roads are ideal for biking.

Golf

With its flat valleys and dramatic views, St. Croix is a natural setting for world-class golf. The leading golf course is the 18-hole **Carambola Golf and Country Club** (River Rd., 340/778-5638, fax 340/779-3700, www.golfvi.com), designed in 1966 by Robert Trent Jones Sr. and built by Laurance Rockefeller. Carambola hosts the annual Konica USVI Golf Classic for ladies and features rolling terrain with excellent views. Greens fees range $95–104, depending on season. Cart rental is $25.

The other principal golf course on St. Croix is at **The Buccaneer** (340/712-2144, www.thebuccaneer.com) east of Christiansted. The par 70, 18-hole course was designed by Bob Joyce in 1973. It boasts nice sea views, a putting green, chipping area, and practice nets. Greens fees are between $60 and $100, depending on season.

The Reef Golf Course (Teague Bay, 340/

773-8844) is a nine-hole course and driving range. The greens fee is $10 for nine holes; golf cart rentals start at $8. At the driving range you will pay $4 for 50 balls.

Tennis

There are public tennis courts at D.C. Canegata Ballpark outside of Christiansted. **The Buccaneer** (Gallows Bay, 340/773-3036, www.thebuccaneer.com) has eight courts and has been cited as one of the best tennis facilities in the Caribbean by *Tennis Magazine*. The rate is $16 per court per hour ($20 for one of two lighted courts). Lessons are available. There are also tennis courts at **Divi Carina Bay Resort** (Estate Turner Hole, 340/773-9700) and **The Reef** (Teague Bay, 340/773-8844), where the cost is $5 per person, per hour.

Hiking

There are not any formal hiking trails on St. Croix, but the diverse terrain makes exploring on foot interesting and rewarding. The **St. Croix Hiking Association** (340/642-4089 or

hiking at Salt River Bay

horseback riding through the rainforest

COURTESY OF U.S. VIRGIN ISLANDS DEPARTMENT OF TOURISM

340/778-2076, odavis@uvi.edu) organizes frequent hikes led by naturalist and writer Olasee Davis. Announcements of these hikes are often published in the *St. Croix Avis* and *Virgin Islands Daily News*.

You can also call Ras Lumumba Corriette of **Ay-Ay Eco Hikes and Tours** (340/277-0410 or 340/772-4079), who leads hikes through St. Croix's most beautiful natural areas, including Jack and Isaac Bays, Annaly Bay, Salt River Bay, Maroon Ridge, and Mount Eagle. Fees range $40–50, depending on the length of the hike.

Biking

When the cruise ships stopped coming to St. Croix, the island's best and only bike shop catering to visitors closed down. This is unfortunate, because St. Croix has some of the best biking in the Virgin Islands. Its rolling hills, quiet back roads, and impressive scenery all lend to the appeal.

Many bikers prefer the northwest part of the island. Coastal Rte. 63 is relatively quiet, and the roads that branch off it are great for exploring. The far eastern end of St. Croix is equally nice; the road to Point Udall is never busy, and the views here are spectacular.

Currently, you can rent bikes at **Endurance Sports** (Sunny Isle Shopping Center, 340/719-1990), located within a GNC store. Rates are $35 per day or $100 per week. The water sports center at **Divi Carina Bay Resort** (Estate Turner Hole, 340/773-9700) also rents mountain bikes for $8 an hour or $20 a day.

Horseback Riding

Paul Wojciechowski and Jill Hurd lead rainforest, beach, ruins, and nature trips on friendly and willing horses at **Paul and Jill's Equestrian Stables** (Creque Dam Rd., 340/772-2880 or 340/772-2627, www.paulandjills.com). Rides cost $60 per person and leave in the morning or afternoon; advance reservations are recommended, especially during high season.

Entertainment and Events

St. Croix's greatest strength is its diversity, and this diversity is well manifested in the range of cultural events, entertainment, and nightlife on the island. On any given weekend, you may be able to choose from an arts festival, community theater, or blistering nightclub. Some entertainment events are geared to tourists, but most are meant for the enjoyment of local residents, too. Getting out is a great way to get a feel for the pulse of this happening island.

Check *St. Croix This Week* for a rundown of live music, festivals, fairs, theater, and more. Also check the *St. Croix Avis'* entertainment column on Friday.

NIGHTLIFE
Christiansted
The Moonraker (43A Queen Cross St., 340/713-8025) draws a diverse late-night crowd, and its air-conditioned dance floor is often jammed. This is the place to come for a good mix of disco, R&B, calypso, and soca music. The scene heats up well past 11 P.M.

Young Continentals frequent **Club 54** (54B Company St., 340/773-8002), which gets crowded after 11 P.M. when waiters and bartenders from island restaurants get off work. **The Mix Lounge** (King Cross St., 340/773-5762) aims for an older, more sophisticated crowd with more than 25 different martinis and live jazz and blues.

The **Fort Christian Brew Pub** (Waterfront, 340/713-9820) is the only microbrewery on the island, and the best place for draft beer. The downstairs bar draws a young crowd during happy hour. It is especially popular among young Continentals.

Outside town, the **Cormorant Beach Club** (Estate Princess, 340/778-8920) has live music on weekends and lots of drink specials and activities during the week. It is especially popular among gay revelers.

Frederiksted
The most popular gathering place in Frederik-

sted is **Blue Moon Café** (17 Strand St., 340/772-2222), a jazz club especially popular on Friday nights. The club underwent renovations in 2005.

Pier 69 (69 King St., 340/772-0069) attracts a trendy, young crowd for drinks and late-night dancing.

East Island
Divi Carina Bay Casino (Southshore Rd., 340/773-7529, www.carinabay.com) is St. Croix's first and only casino (for now). Located across the street from its partner resort, Divi has video poker, slot machines, live poker, table games, bingo, and live entertainment. The casino draws a diverse crowd; lots of Crucians come here, especially on weekends when the live music heats up.

EVENTS
Jump-Ups
Four times a year, Christiansted retailers throw a block party. These "Jump-Ups" (Jump-Up is slang for a party, especially one that involves dancing) happen in July, October, January, and April. If you are on island for one, don't miss it. The heart of downtown is closed to traffic, local bands set up on street corners, and retailers often offer significant discounts. Mocko Jumbies perform in the streets, face painters delight children, vendors sell street food and beer, and everyone seems to have an excellent time. Jump-Ups generally last 6–9 P.M., but many revelers don't go home. Christiansted bars and nightclubs are especially hopping well into the night on a Jump-Up.

Agriculture Fair
St. Croix celebrates its agricultural heritage at the annual Agriculture Fair, usually held in late February. The three-day event is like a traditional American county fair, but with a distinctly Caribbean twist. Come here to buy, or just admire, local fruits and vegetables like

papayas, carambolas, cassava, pumpkin, and bananas. This is also a great place to try local food, take in local music, or watch cultural demonstrations, such as dancing and traditional games.

The Ag Fair, as it is called, is held on the Department of Agriculture's Fair Grounds at Estate Lower Love, in central St. Croix. The fair normally runs for three days, opening on a Friday and closing on a Sunday. Admission is $5 for adults, $2 for children. For information, or to confirm the dates, contact the Department of Agriculture (340/778-0997).

Taste of St. Croix

Diners get to sample a buffet of mammoth proportions at the annual Taste of St. Croix (www.tasteofstcroix.com), a food- and wine-tasting event held every April. Nearly every major restaurant on St. Croix takes part, preparing appetizers, main dishes, desserts, salads, and cocktails. Tickets to this event tend to sell out very quickly; buy them online to avoid disappointment. Proceeds benefit the St. Croix Foundation, which supports a number of charitable and economic development projects on the island.

St. Croix Half Ironman

Hundreds of athletes converge on St. Croix every May for the St. Croix Half Ironman (340/773-4470, fax 340/773-7400, www.stcroixtriathlon.com), where they battle the heat, humidity, hills, and headwinds over a 70-mile course. The race includes a 2-km (1.24-mile) swim in Christiansted Harbor, a 90-km (56-mile) bike race through the St. Croix countryside, and a 21-km (13.1-mile) run around Christiansted. The race is nicknamed "Beauty and the Beast" by those who know: beauty for the unbeatable views along the way, beast for the tough 600-foot climb 21 miles into the bike segment.

The best athletes finish the 70.3-mile course in just over four hours, and top finishers qualify for the 70.3 Ironman World Championships. There is also a Sprint Triathlon that features a 750-meter swim, eight-mile bike, and four-mile run.

Race Week is a fun time to visit St. Croix.

There are more than the usual number of parties and events; there is always a Christiansted Jump-Up a few days before the race. Spectators are encouraged to line the racecourse and cheer on athletes; people line up early at "Hot Corner" at Strand Street and Strand Lane in Christiansted, and at the top of the Beast, where they cheer on flagging bikers.

Emancipation Day

St. Croix was the setting of the momentous events that led to Emancipation in the Danish West Indies in 1848, and every July islanders celebrate and remember this historic milestone. Events include panel discussions, performances, donkey and horse races, and culminate with a remembrance ceremony and re-enactment on Emancipation Day, July 3, in Frederiksted. Check local papers and *St. Croix This Week* for schedule details.

Mango Melee

Mangoes begin to ripen in late May and early June, and by July these silky sweet fruits are for sale by the bucket at roadside stands and supermarkets. St. Croix celebrates the mango at the annual Mango Melee, held in early July at the St. George Village Botanical Gardens (340/692-2874). There are mango displays, mango desserts, mango preserves, mango demonstrations, mango seed crafts, and plenty of opportunities to taste the unadulterated fruits. In addition to mangoes, vendors sell local food, drinks, arts, and crafts.

Crab Races

Tito and Sue put on entertaining hermit crab races at Christiansted watering holes twice a week. Pay $2 to pick out a crab from the bucket (or bring your own), and then watch to see which crab claws past the finish line first. Sponsors of the winning crabs get a prize. The crab races are held at the Fort Christian Brew Pub on Mondays and Stixx on Fridays. Hotel on the Cay puts on crab races of its own on Wednesday nights. Races begin around 5 P.M. This is a good event for kids, but adults like it just as much.

Crab races in Christiansted are a popular family activity.

ARTS

St. Croix's rich history and diverse community engenders a robust amount of arts events. *St. Croix This Week* lists upcoming events. Also check *The St. Croix Avis* for listings, or check out its entertainment column every Friday.

Caribbean Community Theatre

Caribbean Community Theatre (No. 18 Orange Grove, 340/773-7171, www.geocities.com/cctofstcroix) puts on five plays between October and May, and two each summer. The theater is located behind Pueblo at the Orange Grove Shopping Center.

Island Center

St. Croix's premier venue for live music and performances is Island Center (Rt. 79, 340/778-5271), near the hospital. This is where you may be able to catch performances by leading reggae, calypso, and jazz musicians, as well as shows by the Heritage Dancers.

Sunset Jazz

On the third Friday of every month, the Frederiksted Economic Development Association hosts Sunset Jazz, a free, open-air jazz concert held on the Frederiksted waterfront. Music starts around 6 P.M. and runs until 9 P.M. Bring a blanket or chairs. This is a family-friendly event.

Art Thursday

Christiansted's art galleries have collaborated to organize Art Thursday, a monthly event when galleries stay open late for gallery walks. Restaurants and other retail shops get into the mix by opening late and offering specials. Art Thursday takes place on the first Thursday of the month 5–9 P.M.

ST. CROIX

Shopping

Christiansted

There are a multitude of inviting shops in Christiansted. In fact, while Christiansted's shopping may not compete with that on St. Thomas in terms of sheer volume, it is the hands-down winner when it comes to the offbeat, unique, and original. The town's shops are located on Company Street, King Street, and the alleys that run between these thoroughfares.

St. Croix is famous for the Crucian bracelet, a silver or gold bracelet featuring a range of unique clasps. All downtown jewelers have their own style of bracelet, and if you look, you will soon notice that most Crucians sport at least one or two on each wrist. Dozens of shops sell Crucian bracelets, and more than a few claim to be the originator of the concept. Some of the most popular of these are **Sonya's** (1 Company Street, 340/773-8924), **Crucian Gold** (Waterfront, 340/773-5241), and **ib designs** (Company and Queen Streets, 340/773-4322).

Another notable shop is **Memories of St. Croix,** (16A Church St., 340/713-8444) a retail co-operative showcasing the work of some of St. Croix's most talented artisans. It sells a wide variety of things, ranging from local music to hand-hewn sandals. This is also the only place in town where you can pick up Kings Caribbean Coffee.

Like its sister store at the Whim Plantation near Frederiksted, the **St. Croix Landmarks Society Museum Store** (Apothecary Hall, 340/713-8102) has one of the best selections of books in town, as well as reproduction Danish colonial furniture, prints, note cards, and more. The National Park Service shop in the Scale House (340/774-1460) sells books, maps, and children's educational toys and games.

Sportswear, swimsuits, and shoes can be found at **The Centipede Outdoor Store** (Caravelle Arcade, 340/773-4482), while the town's dive shops are the best sources of underwater gear, including snorkels and masks.

Frederiksted

There are a handful of shops along Strand Street in Frederiksted, selling T-shirts and other souvenirs. For Rastafarian-inspired clothing and arts, stop at **UCA Kitchen** (King St.).

Outside of town, **The Garden Gate Gift Shop** (St. George, 340/692-2874) at the St. George Village Botanic Garden has a nice selection of books, prints, and botanical-inspired gifts. The shop at **Whim Museum** (Rte. 70, 340/772-0598) is the best on St. Croix, with a wide selection of books, decorative goods, T-shirts, postcards, prints, and West Indian–style furniture.

Accommodations

St. Croix has some of the most affordable hotel rooms in the Virgin Islands, many of which come with nice beachfront views, comfortable amenities, and great hospitality. The island also has luxury resorts, campgrounds, and superb bed-and-breakfasts. A number of hotels, especially the largest ones, offer packages that include airfare and lots of nice extras.

Some of the best budget accommodations are in Christiansted, where you are within walking distance of shopping, nightlife, dining, and a great beach a short ferry trip away. Beachfront hotels, resorts, and cottages are found along the north coast and around Frederiksted. Out east, you can stay at a large full-service resort and casino.

St. Croix has two openly gay-friendly hotels (Sand Castle and Cormorant), and many more that provide an equally warm, but more discreet, welcome to gay and lesbian travelers. The island also has some distinctive accommodations; nowhere else in the Virgin Islands can you stay in a working cattle farm, rainforest camp, or 18th-century great house.

Villas

Villas are private houses for rent, usually by the week. St. Croix villas are mostly located on the east end of the island, in the upscale residential neighborhoods that define that area.

The best way to arrange a villa rental is through a rental agency, which will help identify a villa that suits your needs. Reputable rental agencies include **CPMI Vacation Rentals** (King's Wharf, 340/778-8782, U.S. toll free 800/496-7379, www.enjoystcroix.com); **Vacation St. Croix** (340/778-0361, U.S. toll free 877/788-0361, www.vacationstcroix.com); and **Island Villas** (340/773-8821, U.S. toll free 800/626-4512, www.stcroixislandvillas.com).

CHRISTIANSTED
Under $125

The **◖ Pink Fancy** (27 Prince St., 340/773-6448, U.S. toll free 800/524-2045, fax 340/773-6448, www.pinkfancy.com, $85–150) is a small, modern hotel set in an 18th-century Danish town house. Built in 1780, the building served for many years as a private club for wealthy planters. It is on the National Historic

Trust's register of buildings. In 1948 Jane Gottlieb turned the property into a hotel, and it has been used for that purpose ever since. Current owners David and Motansem took over in 1999. David was the head concierge at the Ritz-Carlton in New York before they moved to St. Croix, so he knows what he's doing.

The hotel's 12 rooms are tastefully decorated and furnished in a style that blends Danish colonial with urban chic. Rooms have kitchenettes, cable TV, air-conditioning, phones, and data ports. The Pink Fancy is about two blocks from the heart of Christiansted's historic district, but don't be surprised if you choose to pass your day at the hotel's inviting pool, sundeck, and courtyard.

The 39-room **King Christian Hotel** (340/773-6336, U.S. toll free 800/524-2012, www.kingchristian.com, $100–135 winter, $95–120 summer) faces the Christiansted wharf and is centrally located in the middle of the town's historic district. Guests choose between standard and superior rooms; superior rooms have balconies and waterfront views and can sleep up to four people. All rooms have air-conditioning, phones, TV, refrigerators, and coffeemakers. There is a pool on the property.

The **Danish Manor Hotel** (2 Company Street, 340/773-1377, U.S. toll free 800/524-2069, fax 340/773-1913, www.danish-manor.com, $90 winter, $80 summer) is set about two blocks from the waterfront in the middle of the town's shopping district. Its 25 rooms are typical motel style; each has two double beds, cable TV, air-conditioning, and a small refrigerator. The rooms overlook a slightly overgrown courtyard.

Named for the first boat to provide scheduled day trips to Buck Island, **☾ Club Comanche** (1 Strand St., 340/773-0210, U.S. toll free 800/524-2066, $100–200 winter, $65–200 summer) has been housing guests to St. Croix continuously since 1948. This 30-room landmark hotel has been eclipsed by newer hotels in terms of modernity, but owner Mary Boehm soldiers on, providing some of the best hospitality around. Rooms range from loft-style suites to small motel-style rooms without a

view. There is a saltwater pool (better for you, Mary says), and all rooms have air-conditioning, televisions, and refrigerators. This is a great choice for budget travelers. Special discounts and group rates are available.

It would be hard to imagine a better arrangement than the one enjoyed by guests at **Hotel on the Cay** (Protestant Cay, 340/773-2035, U.S. toll free 800/524-2035, www.hotelonthecay.com, $120 winter, $90 summer). The beach is right outside their doors while bustling Christiansted is a 90-second ferry ride away. Rooms at the hotel, which is located on the tiny islet in the middle of Christiansted harbor, have excellent views, as well as comforts like coffeemakers, toaster ovens, and cable TV. The beach on the cay is small but nice.

$125-175

Hotel Caravelle (44 Queen Cross St., 340/773-0687, fax 340/778-7004, www.hotelcaravelle.com, $139–169 winter, $115–135 summer) is a small, popular hotel facing the waterfront. Many of its 33 rooms have harbor views, and there is a pool, sundeck, and free Internet access for guests. All rooms have air-conditioning, refrigerators, and cable TV. The staff members are friendly and efficient, and management is serious about high-quality innkeeping.

FREDERIKSTED
Under $125

The 40-room **Frederiksted Hotel** (442 Strand St., tel./fax 340/772-0500, U.S. toll free 800/595-9519, www.frederikstedhotel.com, $100–110 winter, $90–100 summer) has seen better days, but it is a clean, comfortable choice for budget travelers. Rooms have a/c, cable TV, microwaves, and refrigerators.

$125-175

Sand Castle on the Beach (127 Smithfield, 340/772-1205, U.S. toll free 800/524-2018, fax 340/772-1757, www.sandcastleonthebeach.com, $130–300 winter, $80–200 summer), the best-known gay hotel on St. Croix, welcomes straight people as well. Its 23 rooms vary from standard hotel-style studios to expansive beachfront villas. All rooms have a/c, fans, cable TV, VCR, kitchenettes, and coolers. Complimentary breakfast is provided at the adjoining beach bar and restaurant.

Right next door to the Sand Castle is **Cottages By the Sea** (127A Smithfield, 340/772-0495, U.S. toll free 800/323-7252, fax 340/772-1753, www.caribbeancottages.com, $125–155 winter, $105–135 summer), a complex of 16 brightly painted cottages. Some have beach views; all are steps away from the sand. Each cottage has cable TV, a full kitchen, a/c and fans, and patios; they sleep between two and six people.

NORTH SHORE
$175-225

(Hibiscus Beach Resort (4131 La Grande Princess, 340/773-4042, U.S. toll free 800/442-0121, fax 340/773-7668, www.1hibiscus.com, $190–200 winter, $140–150 summer) is a friendly, beachfront hotel just east of Christiansted. Under new management since June 2005, Hibiscus's 36 rooms have a/c, coffee-

Sandy Point Wildlife Refuge is a major turtle nesting beach.

makers, refrigerators, microwaves, and cable TV. There is a pool, but it doesn't get much use; the beach here is good. The on-site restaurant is justly popular.

Right next door, the **Cormorant Beach Club and Hotel** (4126 La Grande Princess, 340/778-8920, U.S. toll free 800/548-4460, fax 340/778-9218, www.cormorantbeach-club.com, $180–265 winter, $130–225 summer) is a gay-owned and gay-friendly hotel whose 40 beachfront rooms are set amid coconut palms. Rooms are tastefully decorated and come equipped with a/c, coffeemakers, tennis courts, a beachfront restaurant, and frequent live entertainment.

$225-300

Expect to be pampered at the intimate **(Villa Greenleaf** (Estate Rattan, 340/719-1958, U.S. toll free 888/282-1001, fax 340/772-5425, www.villagreenleaf.com, $265–285 winter, $165–185 summer), a bed-and-breakfast overlooking Salt River Bay. Guests are treated to gourmet breakfasts, evening cocktails, and the hospitality and helpful assistance of hostess Connie Wolveris. Rooms are luxurious and modern. There is a pool, entertainment center, and the largest kapok tree on St. Croix on the grounds.

Carambola Beach Resort (Davis Bay, 340/778-3800, U.S. toll free 888/503-8760, fax 340/778-1682, www.carambolabeach.com, $180–209 summer, $209–240 winter) is a perfect getaway. Tucked away at lovely Davis Bay, 151-room Carambola was built by Laurance Rockefeller in 1986. The red-roofed resort has elegant rooms finished with rich mahogany, featuring a/c, screened-in porches, rocking chair, satellite TV, coffeemaker, refrigerator, hair dryer, iron, and king-size bed. The resort has two restaurants, an on-site dive shop, Internet access, fitness center, and a freshwater pool.

WEST ISLAND
Under $125

Tucked away in the rainforest, **(Mount Victory Camp** (Creque Dam Road, 340/772-1651, U.S. toll free 866/772-1651, www.mtvictorycamp.com, $75–85 winter, $65–75 summer) is a unique outdoor retreat. Bruce and Mathilde Wilson have constructed five hardwood bungalows on the hillside below their garden and home. Each is equipped with beds, a cold-water sink, two-burner gas stove, dishes, and a dining table. Screens keep unwanted critters out at night. All campers share the tidy bathhouse and solar-heated showers. Campers fall asleep to the sounds of tree frogs and wake to birdsongs.

Bruce and Mathilde host weekly pig roasts every Sunday during the high season, often with entertainment by a local scratch band, which attract a great mix of islanders, tourists, and stateside transplants. The camp is also a great place to meet environmentally minded island residents and become acquainted with the environmental issues of the day.

$125-175

Guests at **Sprat Hall Plantation** (Rt. 63, Frederiksted, 340/772-0305, U.S. toll-free 800/843-3584, fax 340/772-3010, $135–150) sleep in a 350-year-old plantation great house. Built around 1650 by a French settler and later used as a great house during the plantation era, Sprat Hall has been an inn for more than 50 years. Joyce Hurd ran the inn alongside her husband, Jim, until his death in 2003. Today, Joyce is assisted by her daughter.

The two bedrooms in the great house are furnished with antique Danish colonial furniture, while the four modern units next door are typical of island hotel rooms. There are sugar mill ruins on the property, and a nice beach is right across the road. Breakfast is served on the veranda. Children and smokers are not allowed to stay in the great house but are welcome in the other units.

EAST ISLAND
Under $125

Longford Hideaway (Longford Estate, 340/773-5912, fax 340/773-2386, www.longford-hideaway.com, $90 summer, $110 winter) is a fully equipped one-bedroom cottage set on a working cattle farm. Guests at the hideaway will be welcomed by the whole farm family—Velaria and Chicco Gasperi, their children, grandchildren, resident dogs, cats, chickens, and, of course, the Senepol cattle. The neat cottage has a full kitchen, air-conditioning, pool, porch, and TV. Guests can walk on trails around the farm and along the southern coast.

$175-225

Nearly all 46 rooms at **Tamarind Reef Hotel** (5001 Tamarind Reef, 340/773-4455, U.S. toll free 800/619-0014, fax 340/773-3989, $195–245 winter, $176–192 summer) have ocean views. The two-story hotel is right next door to Green Cay Marina and the Tamarind Reef Beach. Rooms have air-conditioning, cable TV, coffeemakers, refrigerators, hair dryer, and iron. Suites have a kitchenette and dining area for four.

Divi Carina Bay Resort (Turner Hole, 340/773-9700, U.S. toll free 877/773-9700, fax 340/773-6802, www.divicarina.com, $279–368 winter, $151–198 summer) is the only large-scale accommodation on St. Croix's beautiful southeast shore. The 53-room beachfront resort is across the street from the casino that shares its name, but guests here don't necessarily have to be interested in gambling. Rooms sport a bright, modern décor, and all have balconies or patios overlooking the beach. Amenities include in-room refrigerators, coffeemakers, microwaves, cable TV, and data ports, as well as a pool, water sports center, two restaurants, fitness center, and tennis courts.

Over $300

If luxury and exclusivity are what you want, **The Buccaneer** (Gallows Bay, 340/712-2100, U.S. toll free 800/255-3881, www.thebucaneer.com, $295–840 winter, $240–580) will provide them. The 138-room resort, which includes an 18-hole golf course, eight tennis courts, and three restaurants, set the standard for luxury on St. Croix when it opened in 1947 and continues to do so today. Rooms are well appointed, with window seats, generous balconies, and all the amenities you would expect from a classy resort. Unique among large

ST. CROIX

resorts these days, The Buccaneer has been owned and operated by the same family since it was established.

Accommodations at **Chenay Bay Beach Resort** (340/773-2918, fax 340/773-6665, www.chenaybaybeachclub.com, $275–590

winter, $190–375 summer) are in one- and two-bedroom Caribbean-style cottages. Each air-conditioned cottage is equipped with a kitchenette, cable TV, and private porch. The beach is a long crescent with clear, calm water. This is a good choice for families.

Food

ST. CROIX

CHRISTIANSTED
Downtown

Christiansted's restaurants have some of the most creative and eclectic menus in the Virgin Islands. While there are a number of casual choices for lunch and breakfast, Christiansted eateries are decidedly upscale at dinnertime.

Located a block east of Fort Christensvaern, **Savant** (Hospital St., 340/713-8666, 6–10 P.M. Mon.–Sat., $18–34) serves a sophisticated menu that fuses Asian, Mexican, and Caribbean cuisine. You can dine inside in air-conditioning, or outside on the back patio.

(Bacchus (Queen Cross St., 340/692-992, 6–10 P.M. Tues.–Sat., $20–35) is a world-class restaurant serving American and French cuisine inside an old town house in historic Christiansted. Chef Frank Pugliese's specialties include hand-cut steaks, local lobster, duck confit, rack of lamb, and oysters Rockefeller. Bacchus is noted for its extensive wine list, the best on the island. Diners can finish off their meal with French press coffee enjoyed over a game of billards in the poolroom.

A St. Croix landmark, **Club Comanche** (1 Strand St., 340/773-0210, $15–35) has an atmosphere of old-fashioned elegance. A long-serving staff serves lunch and dinner of classic seafood, meat, and poultry dishes, often with an Indian influence. The susu chicken curry is a favorite.

A long-time favorite for fans of truly fine food, **Kendricks** (Company St., 340/773-9199, 6–9:30 P.M. Mon.–Sat., $17–31) features the sophisticated cuisine of chef and owner Dave Kendrick. Kendrick's features classic cuisine like pork loin, duck, lamb, and fresh local fish.

When it is really hot, take shelter at **The Bombay Club** (5-A King Street, 340/773-1838, 11:30 A.M.–4 P.M. Mon.–Fri., 6–10 P.M. daily, $16–25). No gentle breezes or seaside ambience here, but there are plenty of private niches and the a/c is always on. Daily specials usually feature fresh seafood, salads, and pasta.

Indian specialties including curry, roti, and doubles are the main attraction at family-owned **Singh's Fast Food** (23B King Street, 340/773-7357). Not far away, **Paulina's Bar and Restaurant** (15 King Street, 340/713-8585) specializes in Puerto Rican cuisine.

For local Crucian fare, **Zeny's Restaurant** and **Zeny's II** (3940 Queen Cross St., 340/719-0181) is famous for its fried chicken, Spanish rice, and the best mofongo on St. Croix.

For sandwiches, look no farther than **Turtles Deli** (55 Company St., 340/772-3676, 8:30 A.M.–3 P.M. Mon.–Sat., $8–12). The long-time Frederiksted favorite now has a Christiansted location, too. Turtles' sandwiches are the best on the island. Favorites include the chicken curry sandwich and the Reuben. The deli also sells homemade bread by the loaf, sandwich meat and cheese, and coffee.

Paradise Café (Queen Cross St., 773-2985, 7:30 A.M.–9:30 P.M. Mon.–Sat., $6–15) is a classic American diner transported to the Caribbean. And, like a diner, it is a good choice if you're on a budget or if you want a generous American-style meal and friendly, efficient service.

For a casual breakfast, lunch, or afternoon snack, try **The Avocado Pit** (59 Kings Wharf, 340/773-9849, 6:30 A.M.–5:30 P.M., $5–12), a small café in the center of Christiansted's historic district. Breakfast is served all day; at lunch try one of the freshly made wraps or a hot dog. This is a nice place for an afternoon ice cream treat.

Outside of Town

Italian for "everything good," **Tuttu Bene** (Gallows Bay, 340/773-5229, 6–10 P.M. nightly, $19–27) is the gold standard of Italian eating on St. Croix. Specialties include veal saltimbocca, spaghetti Bolognese, and osso bucco. Old hands should note that Tuttu Bene moved from its Company Street location to a shopping plaza near Gallows Bay, just east of Christiansted.

The **Morning Glory Café** (Gallows Bay, 340/773-6620, 6:30 A.M.–6 P.M. Mon.–Fri., 7 A.M.–3 P.M. Sat., $6–10) is a popular morning pit stop for east end residents, especially Continentals. In addition to coffee, the café serves a full breakfast menu of omelettes, eggs, breakfast sandwiches, and French toast, as well as lunchtime sandwiches.

Located in the shipyard at St. Croix Marine, **The Golden Rail** (Gallows Bay, 340/719-1989, $8–16) attracts yachters and other marine-minded customers. Landlubbers come for the all-day bar menu, with budget-priced burgers, grilled cheese, and chicken wings. The restaurant's barbecued ribs are some of the best on the island.

It may not have atmosphere, but **Ice Cream Decadence** (East End Road, 340/773-4320, 11:30 A.M.–6:30 P.M. Wed.–Sat., 2–6:30 P.M. Sun.) has the best ice cream on St. Croix. Located across the road from the D.C. Canegata Ballpark just east of town, Decadence makes flavors like mango, coconut, and soursop, as well as all the old standards. This business supplies most of the major restaurants, too.

Markets

Schooner Bay Marketplace (Gallows Bay, 340/773-3232) is St. Croix's gourmet market with fresh produce, a large deli, and ready-made meals. There is a large **Pueblo** (340/773-0118) grocery store on Rte. 75, near the Orange Grove stoplight. A little farther west, on Rte. 75, is **Food Town,** (LaGrande Princess, 340/692-9990) the best all-purpose supermarket on St. Croix.

FREDERIKSTED

Probably the most romantic place to eat on St. Croix, **⊂ Le St. Tropez** (227 King St., 340/772-3000, $15–30) is an upscale French restaurant in the heart of Frederiksted. Owners André and Daniéle Ducrot serve authentic French and Mediterranean dishes, such as *scampi niçoises* and *coq au vin*. Set in an old Victorian home, Le St. Tropez seats diners at one of its 15 patio tables. The sound of classic jazz sets an appropriate backdrop. Lunch ($10–15) is served Monday through Friday. Dinner is served Tuesday through Saturday. Reservations are a good idea, especially during the high season.

For vegetarian food, try **UCA Kitchen Daily Itals** (King St., 340/772-5063, 11:30 A.M.–7 P.M. Mon.–Fri., 12:30–7 P.M.Sat., $5–10) located in a broad, low building just off Buddhoe Park behind the Customs Building. In addition to daily specials, it serves a range of vegetarian soups and sandwiches. This is a great place to meet some of the island's Rastafarians. The **SICA Health Food Store and Restaurant** (King St., 340/772-9500, 9 A.M.–4:30 P.M. Mon.–Sat., $3–5), serves tofu sandwiches, veggie burgers, and natural fruit juices. This is also a good source of hard-to-find herbs, spices, and natural foods.

For sandwiches, choose the delightful **Turtles Deli** (Strand St., 340/772-3676, 8:30 A.M.–3 P.M. Mon.–Fri.).

South of Frederiksted, the **Beachside Café,** (127 Smithfield, 340/772-1205, Thurs.–Mon., $12–25), at the Sandcastle hotel, serves salads, sandwiches, and burgers at lunch and more upscale fare at dinner. Like at all the eateries along the west coast, the sunsets here are spectacular. The restaurant is right on the beach.

If you're looking for a good cup of coffee, the friendly staff of **Tropical Java** (11–12 Strand St., 340/773-5282, 8 A.M.–3 P.M. Mon.–Fri., 8 A.M.–1 P.M. Sun.) will be happy to oblige.

They also serve fresh pastries, bagels, and biscotti. There is a used book exchange here.

North of Frederiksted, **Changes in L'Attitude** (Rt. 63, 340/772-3090, 11:30 A.M.–9 P.M. Mon.–Fri., 11:30 A.M.–10 P.M., $8–24) is a casual beachfront eatery with a lively bar, especially on Sunday afternoons. Come here to watch the sunset.

NORTH SHORE

Casual is the name of the game at **Off the Wall Beach Bar and Restaurant** (Cane Bay, 340/778-4771, $9–26, 8 A.M.–10 P.M.), a shore-side restaurant with nice views of Cane Bay. Chefs serve a hearty breakfast 8–11 A.M.; after that, choose from the diverse menu of burgers, pizza, quesadillas, fish and chips, and barbecue.

◖ H2O (Hibiscus Beach Resort, 340/773-4042, 7:30 A.M.–9 P.M.) is a very popular restaurant near Christiansted. The dining room is set on the white sandy beach at Pelican Cove, and the menu is nicely varied, with a good mix of down-home favorites and gourmet choices.

WEST ISLAND

About a mile east of Frederiksted on the Queen Mary Highway, **PaQuitos** (340/772-1669, 11 A.M.–6 P.M. Tues.–Sat., $7–10) is a good place to sample local cuisine. The food is Crucian with Puerto Rican influences. The beans and rice are delicious and make a good meal if you're on a budget.

For excellent local food in a homey, welcoming setting, try **◖ Villa Morales** (Estate Whim, 340/772-0556, 10 A.M.–10 P.M. Thurs.–Sat., $16–35). This family-run restaurant serves traditional Crucian dishes, many with a Spanish accent. Chef Angela Morales prepares dishes like conch in butter sauce, roast pork, grilled fish, and lobster. This is a casual restaurant that attracts a large local clientele.

Armstrong's Homemade Ice Cream (Queen Mary Highway, 340/772-1919, 7 A.M.–7 P.M. Mon.–Sat., 11 A.M.–7 P.M. Sun., $4–8) is a favorite stop for locals. Ice cream cones start at $2. It also serves hearty American-style

breakfasts and lunch sandwiches. The grill closes at 2:30 P.M. daily.

Near the turnoff to Creque Dam Road, **The Sunset Grill** (Rt. 63, 340/772-5855, 11:30 A.M.–9 P.M., $9–27) serves both an all-day bar menu and daily sandwich, salad, and dinner specials. Dining is on either the open-air patio or on the beach with the sand between your toes. Both afford excellent views. This is the site of the monthly full-moon "Lunasea" bash, complete with live music and a beach barbecue.

EAST ISLAND

One of the only casual restaurants on the east end, **Cheeseburgers in Paradise** (Estate Southgate, 340/773-1119, 11 A.M.–10 P.M. daily, $5–12) serves burgers of every stripe, as well as burritos and daily specials. This roadside joint is a popular stop for east enders on their way home or for families looking for an affordable, kid-friendly place to eat.

The **Just-n-Case Deli** (No. 14 Teague Bay, 340/778-7330, 8:30 A.M.–6:30 P.M. Tues.–Sat., $6–11) is especially popular for takeout, but you can eat in, too. It serves hearty breakfasts, as well as soup, hot and cold sandwiches, pizza, and steak platters. There is a small grocery (7 A.M.–7 P.M. daily) here, too.

Chef Diane Marie Scheuber serves handmade pasta, homemade bread, generous salads, and fresh meat and fish at the **◖ Southshore Café** (Petronella Dairy, 340/773-9311, 6–8:30 P.M. Wed.–Sun., $17–27). Set in an old dairy farm, the Southshore Café has nice views of Great Pond and the south shore. The atmosphere is relaxing and classy, with a little twist of funk.

For a quick bite, the counter at **Smokey's Service Station** (Estate Solitude, 340/773-8382, $4–8) is a perfect pit stop. Located at the last gas station as you head east on Rte. 82, Smokey's serves hot breakfasts, sandwiches, and rotis, as well as coffee and sweets.

St. Croix's organic farmers market is **Southgate Farms** (340/514-4873, 3–6 P.M. Wed. and Fri., 9 A.M.–noon Sat.), located directly across Rte. 82 from Cheeseburgers in Paradise. The farmstand sells local organic fruits, vegetables, and eggs raised on the five-acre Southgate Farm. Many of the best restaurants get produce here. Ask for a tour, and they will show you where they grow their bananas, papayas, vegetables, and herbs. In summer, it is open only on Saturdays.

Practicalities

INFORMATION AND SERVICES
Tourist Offices

The **U.S. Virgin Islands Department of Tourism's** offices in Christiansted (Company St., 340/773-0495, 8:30 A.M.–4:30 P.M. Mon.–Fri.) and Frederiksted (Customs House, 340/772-0357, 8:30 A.M.–4:30 P.M. Mon.–Fri.) stock brochures and maps of St. Croix. The Frederiksted bureau is not always open when advertised; count yourself lucky if you find it open.

For information on the island's three national parks—Christiansted, Salt River Bay, and Buck Island—go to the National Park shop in the Old Scale House by the waterfront. The park rangers and other staff on duty there are helpful and stock a wide variety of useful brochures behind the counter—just ask.

Maps and Charts

Cartographer's Limited (340/777-6219) publishes a free, pocket-sized map of St. Croix that is widely available and will meet the needs of most visitors. Roads and major attractions are clearly marked on the map. **St. Croix This Week,** the free monthly tourist magazine, publishes an island map that also shows the locations of most hotels and restaurants, which can be helpful.

Detailed topographical maps are available from the **National Park Service** shop in Christiansted. Nautical charts can be found at **St. Croix Marine** (Gallows Bay, 340/773-0289).

Libraries

In Christiansted, the **Florence Williams Public Library** (King St., 340/713-5715, 9 A.M.–5 P.M. Mon.–Sat.) has a good collection of books and magazines and Internet access for a small fee.

Frederiksted's **Althalie Peterson Library** (Strand St., 340/772-0315), located in the historic Bell house, also has Internet access and a nice collection of books.

Media

The *St. Croix Avis* is the island's leading newspaper, although the St. Thomas–based *Virgin Islands Daily News* also covers St. Croix happenings, with a bit more polish. The *Avis* comes out every day but Monday; the Daily News takes Sundays off.

St. Croix–based WSVI, an ABC affiliate, broadcasts local news, complete with a weather forecast, weekdays at 7 P.M. on channel 8. St. Thomas–based TV 2 does the same on channel 2. Tune in to 95.1 FM (Isle 95) for music and news.

Emergencies

The Juan Louis Hospital (Rte. 79, 340/778-1634) in Kingshill is a modern, full-service facility, with complete emergency services. The Virgin Islands Police Department (340/778-2211) has stations around the island. Call 911 in an emergency. V.I. Search and Rescue (340/773-7150) responds to reports of missing persons and vessels at sea.

Banks

Several U.S. and Canadian banks operate on St. Croix. Both **Banco Popular de Puerto Rico** and **First Bank VI** have branches and ATMs at Orange Grove and Sunny Isle.

Most establishments welcome credit cards. Personal checks are generally not accepted.

Post Offices

The U.S. Postal Service operates on St. Croix, and rates are the same as in the continental

ST. CROIX

United States. Post offices are located in downtown Christiansted (100 Church St., 340/773-3586), outside Christiansted (103-104 Richmond, 340/773-1505), Gallows Bay (No. 118 Estate Welcome, 340/773-4538), Frederiksted (No. 1 Mars Hill, 340/772-0040), Kingshill (No. 2 Estate LaReine, 340/778-0199), and at Sunny Isle Shopping Center (340/778-6805).

Communications

In Christiasted, the best place to check your email is **Strand Street Station Internet Café** (1102 Strand St., 340/719-6245, 8 A.M.–6 P.M.). You will pay $4 for 15 minutes. Staff here can also help you with copies, faxes, calls, and photo processing.

In Frederiksted, you can get on the Internet at the strangely named **Awakening Community Efforts** (Market Street, 9:30 A.M.–5 P.M. Mon.–Thurs., 9:30 A.M.–6 P.M. Fri., 10 A.M.–5 P.M. Sat.) a small red and white building a few steps off Strand Street. The rate is $3 for 15 minutes.

Customs and Immigration

You must clear customs when you leave St. Croix. Departing passengers will be asked to fill out a customs declaration form (members of a family residing together may make a joint declaration), and your bags are subject to search. U.S. Customs officers are on duty at the airport and at their offices at Five Corners on Rte. 75 (340/773-5650).

U.S. Immigration and Naturalization officers are stationed at Henry E. Rohlsen Airport (340/778-1419). The INS department's administration offices are located at Sunny Isle Shopping Center (340/778-6559).

Launderettes

La Reine Laundry (Barren Spot, 340/778-2801, 5:30 A.M.–11 P.M. Mon.–Thurs., 4 A.M.–11 P.M. Fri.–Sun.) is a large launderette on Centerline Road, where you will find super-sized washers and plenty of dryers.

Another large, full-service laundry is **S&S Laundry** (Grove Place, 340/692-1010, 6 A.M.–

9 P.M. Mon.–Thurs., 5:30 A.M.–10 P.M. Fri.–Sun.). A single wash will cost about $1.50.

GETTING THERE
By Air

St. Croix's Henry E. Rohlsen Airport (STX) is located on the island's southwest coast, nine miles south of Christiansted and six miles southeast of Frederiksted. The terminal is open from 5:30 A.M. to 11 P.M. daily; the 10,000-foot runway remains open 24 hours a day. Taxis meet all scheduled flights; car rental counters are open during business hours, and sometimes later. Arrangements can be made for late arrivals.

From the U.S. mainland and Canada: There is limited nonstop service to St. Croix from the U.S. mainland. Delta Airlines (www.delta.com) has nonstop flights from Atlanta on Wednesdays and Saturdays, American Airlines (340/778-2000, www.aa.com) has a nonstop flight from Miami daily, and U.S. Airways (www.usairways.com) has a nonstop flight from Charlotte, N.C., on Saturdays. Otherwise, visitors will change planes in San Juan. American, Continental (340/693-3139, www.continental.com), and U.S. Airways have code share arrangements with commuter airlines that enable passengers to book with a single airline and check luggage all the way to St. Croix. American Airlines works with American Eagle. Continental works with Cape Air (340/774-2616, U.S. toll free 800/352-0714, www.flycapeair.com), and U.S. Airways code shares with Caribbean Sun Airline (www.flysca.com).

From Puerto Rico and Vieques: Commuter airlines American Eagle, Cape Air, and Caribbean Sun provide regular scheduled service between San Juan International Airport and St. Croix's Rohlsen Airport. In addition, Seaborne Airlines (34 Strand St., Christiansted, 340/773-6442, U.S. toll free 888/359-8687, www.seaborneairlines.com) provides seaplane service from Old San Juan Harbour to Christiansted Harbor, via St. Thomas.

Vieques Air Link (787/741-3266, www.vieques-island.com) has two scheduled flights per day between Vieques and St. Croix.

From St. Thomas: Seaborne Airlines (34 Strand St., Christiansted, 340/773-6442, U.S. toll free 888/359-8687, www.seaborneairlines.com) has up to 15 flights daily between St. Thomas and St. Croix, leaving from the seaplane terminals on the Christiansted and Charlotte Amalie waterfronts. Nothing beats the convenience of the seaplane—there are no airport hassles—but beware the baggage restrictions; you will be charged 50 cents for every pound over 30.

From the Eastern Caribbean: Leeward Islands Air Transport, or LIAT, (340/778-9930, www.liatairline.com) flies to St. Croix from Caribbean destinations including Antigua and Barbados.

By Sea

By Ferry: Virgin Islands Fast Ferry (Gallows Bay, 340/719-0099, U.S. toll free 877/733-9425, www.virginislandsfastferry.com, adult $77 RT, children 3–12 $65 RT, Fri.–Mon., Wed.) is expected to resume service from Charlotte Amalie, St. Thomas, to Christiansted aboard a high-speed catamaran after a hiatus during the 2005-2006 winter travel season. The trip takes 75 minutes.

By Cruise Ship: The number of cruise ships visiting St. Croix dwindled to nearly nothing in 2004, when most of the major cruise lines pulled out of the island, citing increasing crime. Islanders did not buy that story, feeling instead that the territory's tourism brokers had failed to adequately represent the island in the competitive field of cruise ship destinations. Whatever the reason, there are few ships visiting the island right now.

GETTING AROUND
Taxis

Taxis are widely available on St. Croix. Taxi stands are located on King Street in Christiansted, near Government House, and on Market Street. In Frederiksted, there is a taxi stand near Fort Frederik. If you need a pick-up try **Antilles Taxi Service** (Christiansted, 340/773-5020 or 340/514-4680), **Frederiksted Taxi Service** (Frederiksted, 340/772-4775), or the

St. Croix Taxi Association (Henry E. Rohlsen Airport, 340/778-1088).

Taxi rates are set by the government's Taxi Commission (340/773-8294), which also fields complaints on taxi service and can help trace lost luggage. The rate for one or two people from the airport to Christiansted is $13 per person, from the airport to Frederiksted is $10 per person, and from Christiansted to Frederiksted is $20 per person. Check *St. Croix This Week* for current rates. Luggage is charged at $1 for each bag in excess of one. For oversized luggage, agree on a price ahead of time. A premium of between $1 and $1.50 is charged on trips between midnight and 6 A.M. The minimum fare in town is $5.

Buses

VITRAN buses operate between 5:30 A.M. and 9:30 P.M. Mon.–Saturday. The bus route begins at Tide Village east of Christiansted and ends at Fort Frederik, following Centerline Road. The fare is $1 for adults, and 25 cents for transfers. Adults over 55 pay 55 cents. Exact change is required. For schedule information, call 340/773-0898 or 340/773-1290, but remember that the only thing certain about VITRAN is that it will not run on schedule. Look for the VITRAN signs for pick-up locations.

Informal, open-air taxis, called the "dollar bus," run frequently between Frederiksted and Christiansted along Centerline Road, stopping at Sunny Isle Shopping Center. Although there is no official schedule or rules, these are a pretty reliable way to get around during daylight hours. The fare is $2 per person. At night, stick to official taxis.

Car Rentals

Reserve your rental car early for the best rates. Expect to pay between $45 and $50 per day, although you can sometimes find a better rate if you book early or for an extended period. National rental chains including **Hertz** (340/778-1402, www.rentacarstcroix.com), **Budget** (888/264-8894, www.budget.com), and **Avis** (340/778-9355, www.avis.com) have counters at the Henry

ST. CROIX

E. Rohlsen Airport and at resorts and other locations throughout the island. Avis has the only car rental counter at the seaplane terminal in Christiansted. All three offer online booking and reservations.

Independent rental agencies include **Centerline Car Rental** (LaReine, 340/778-0450, U.S. toll free 888/288-8755, www.centerlinecarrentals.com); **Judi of St. Croix** (4017 Herman Hill, 340/773-2123, U.S. toll free 877/903-2123, www.judiofcroix.com); **Olympic-Ace Rent-a-Car** (1103 Richmond, 340/773-8000, U.S. toll free 888/878-4227, www.stcroixcarrentals.com); and **Skyline Rentals** (LaReine, 340/719-5990, U.S. toll free 877/719-5990).

ST. JOHN

For many travelers, St. John is as near to perfection as a Caribbean island can be. More than 60 percent of the 20-square-mile island is national park, so its beaches, vistas, underwater coral gardens, and quiet hiking paths are quiet and unspoiled. For outdoor enthusiasts, there is no better place to explore a tropical wilderness. St. John may be small, but its bays, hills, and reefs hold a seemingly infinite array of sights and sounds; as you peel off the layers, you will be surprised, enchanted, and inspired.

St. John complements its natural beauty with two laid-back hamlets, Cruz Bay and Coral Bay. These small towns have pretty much everything a visitor needs to feel at home: gourmet coffee, trendy restaurants, cold beer, and Internet access, for start-ers. While Cruz Bay often vibrates with the day-to-day comings and goings of car barges, passenger ferries, trucks, cars, and gangs of tourists, Coral Bay is a sleepy row of bars, restaurants, and shops.

St. John's perfection has consequences. So many people have come here and loved it that real estate agents, development companies, and construction firms are trying to build on every piece of the island's undeveloped, privately held land. In some parts of the island, the sound of waves crashing is drowned out by the scream of air brakes, ringing of hammers, and hum of construction generators. Equally problematic, the influx of wealthy snowbirds has created a social divide between native St. Johnians and their American guests.

© SUSANNA HENIGHAN

HIGHLIGHTS

《 Trunk Bay: With fine white sand, lots of shade, and good snorkeling, this is the most beautiful beach on St. John (page 111).

《 Waterlemon Cay: The colorful reef around this offshore cay teems with life, making this a snorkeler's paradise (page 113).

《 Coral Bay: Unwind with a cold beer and dance under the stars to live music in this funky, laid-back village on the east end (page 115).

《 Petroglyphs: These mysterious stone carvings may have been made by some of the island's first residents, but no one knows for sure. Stop by and ponder their origins while hiking at Reef Bay (page 119).

《 Ram's Head Trail: Hold on to your hat at this remote headland, where the sound of waves crashing and wind blowing will fill your ears. The view is spectacular here at the island's southernmost point (page 122).

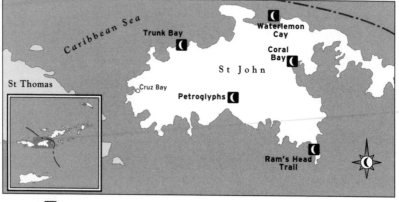

LOOK FOR 《 TO FIND RECOMMENDED SIGHTS, ACTIVITIES, DINING, AND LODGING.

PLANNING YOUR TIME

It is safe to assume that no matter how much time you spend on St. John, it won't be enough. It is a tired joke that most of the Continentals living here came down for vacation and never left. It's hackneyed, but there is definitely a kernel of truth to the belief: St. John is just that enchanting.

It is also safe to assume that even if you squeeze in journeys to every one of St. John's beaches, trails, and vistas, you will have only scratched the surface of what the island has to offer. Trails and bays are dynamic, weather conditions change, and your own ability to see details increases with time and experience. Even people who live here have not finished "doing" St. John.

St. John is an island packed with exceptional natural beauty, but there are a few standout sights. The **Petroglyphs,** stone carvings left by pre-Columbian Taino Indians, are found along the popular Reef Bay Trail. Snorkelers should take the sojourn to **Waterlemon Cay,** a tiny spit of land off the coast of St. John where you can gaze upon a rich undersea landscape of hard and soft corals, sea cushions, and multicolored fish. The most popular beach on St. John is also its most beautiful; you will want to avoid coming to **Trunk Bay** at the peak of the day, but no trip to St. John is complete unless you spend some time there. For solitude, head to **Ram's Head,** a dramatic headland bombarded by strong winds and the sound of pounding

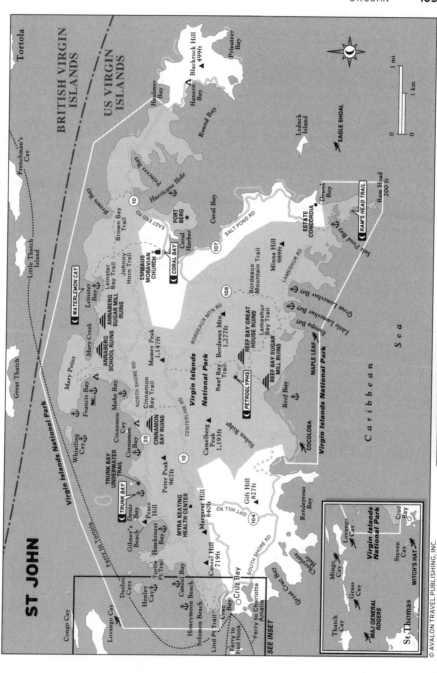

ST. JOHN

ST JOHN

Tortola

Frenchman's Cay

Little Thatch Island

Great Thatch

BRITISH VIRGIN ISLANDS

US VIRGIN ISLANDS

Virgin Islands National Park

Congo Cay

Durloe Cays

Henley Cay

Lovango Cay

Honeymoon Beach
Solomon Beach
Caneel Bay
Turtle Pt Trail
Lind Pt Trail
Cruz Bay
Ferry to Red Hook
Ferry to Charlotte Amalia

SEE INSET

Hawksnest Bay
Gibney's Beach
Denis Bay
Peace Hill
Trunk Bay
TRUNK BAY UNDERWATER TRAIL
Peter Peak 967ft

Whistling Cay
Mary Point
Francis Bay
Cinnamon Cay
Cinnamon Bay
WATERLEMON CAY
Leinster Bay
Mary Creek
ANNABERG SCHOOL RUINS
ANNABERG SUGAR MILL RUINS

Mary Point

Maho Bay
Cinnamon Bay Trail
NORTH SHORE RD
CINNAMON BAY RUINS
Maney Peak 1,147ft

Leinster Bay Trail
Johnny Horn Trail
Brown Bay Trail
EAST END RD

Hurricane Hole
Princess Bay
Brown's Bay
10

FORT BERG
EMMAUS MORAVIAN CHURCH
CORAL BAY
Coral Harbor

Blackrock Hill 499ft
Hansen Bay
Round Bay
Haulover Bay
Privateer Bay

Leduck Island

EAGLE SHOAL

Ram Head 200 ft
Drunk Bay
RAM'S HEAD TRAIL
ESTATE CONCORDIA
Salt Pond Bay
Salt Pond Rd
107
SALT POND RD
Coral Bay
LAMESHUR RD
Minna Hill 989ft
Bordeaux Mountain Trail
BORDEAUX MTN RD
Bordeaux Mtn 1,277ft
108
Reef Bay

Myra Keating Health Center
Margaret Hill 840ft
Caneel Hill 719ft
CENTERLINE RD
10
20

Camelberg Peak 1,193ft
Sieben Ridge
REEF BAY GREAT HOUSE RUINS
Lameshur Bay Trail
REEF BAY SUGAR MILL RUINS
PETROGLYPHS
Reef Bay
Little Lameshur Bay
Great Lameshur Bay
Europa Bay
MAPLE LEAF
COCOLOBA

Virgin Islands National Park

Gift Hill 827ft
GIFT HILL RD
SOUTH SHORE RD
104
Cruz Bay
Rendezvous Bay

Caribbean Sea

Chocolate Hole
Great Cruz Bay

Inset (St. Thomas):

ST. JOHN

Thatch Cay
Grass Cay
Mingo Cay
Steven Cay
Lovango Cay
Congo Cay
Cruz Bay

Virgin Islands National Park

MAJ GENERAL ROGERS
WITCH'S HAT

St Thomas

© AVALON TRAVEL PUBLISHING, INC.

1 mi
1 km
0

surf. When you've had enough of quiet, it is time to head down to one of St. John's watering holes, either in bustling Cruz Bay or laid-back **Coral Bay,** on the east end of the island.

Plenty of people make St. John into a day trip; they arrive by ferry from St. Thomas or Tortola, take an island tour, and spend a few hours on one of its more accessible beaches. The frequency of ferries makes this easy, and there are few better ways to spend a day. If this is all you have time for, don't miss it.

DRIVING TOUR

Most people use four-wheel drive vehicles— Jeeps, Suzuki Sidekicks, and the like—to get around St. John. In fact, that is all the St. John rental companies have. While you can get around with a car, you will have to stick to the nicely paved roads.

A good driving tour starts and ends at Cruz Bay. Depending on how frequently you stop along the way, this tour can take anywhere from two hours to all day. Leave Cruz Bay on Northshore Road (Rte. 20). In less than a mile, you will enter the Virgin Islands National Park. Northshore Road passes several fantastic overlooks and some of the best beaches on St. John, including Hawksnest Beach, **Trunk Bay,** and Cinnamon Bay. If you want to stretch your legs, stop at Peace Hill for great views, or Cinnamon Bay's Self-Guided Loop for a glimpse into the island's history.

Six miles into your drive you come to the Annaberg traffic triangle. Bear right and you will go to the Annaberg Sugar Plantation Ruins and **Waterlemon Cay.** Bear left and you head to Francis Bay and Maho Bay Camps. After exploring either or both of these detours, take a sharp left onto on a steep, winding road that connects to Centerline Road. (There will be signs pointing you to Coral Bay.)

Turn left onto Centerline Road (Rte. 10), pausing if you like for a cold drink or ice cream from the food bus parked at the intersection. Centerline Road follows the spine of St. John. It is windy and relatively highly trafficked, so slow down and be careful. Stop at Yucca Point, where you can look out at a fantastic panorama of Coral Bay and the British Virgin Islands.

Turn around at Yucca Point and head back to Cruz Bay along Centerline Road. If you have time and energy you can drive on down to **Coral Bay** and poke around before heading back to town.

Take note that there are two gas stations in Cruz Bay and one in Coral Bay. It's a good idea to fuel up before starting any driving tour.

Sights

St. John is shaped like an elongated, lacyedged cookie, out of which someone has taken a bite. Cruz Bay, on the far western end of the island, is where ferries and boats from neighboring islands arrive. Many of the best and most popular beaches are along the north coast of the island, accessible by Northshore Road (Rte. 20). Coral Bay (where the bite was taken) is a small settlement along a wide, horseshoeshaped bay on the far eastern end of the island. Centerline Road (Rte. 10) connects Cruz Bay and Coral Bay.

The south side of St. John is accessible only by four-wheel-drive vehicle or on foot. Dirt tracks lead to remote, pebbly beaches with good snorkeling and no crowds.

CRUZ BAY

Named by the Spanish, Cruz Bay is St. John's first and only real town. The heart of Cruz Bay lies within about six square blocks immediately adjacent to the **Franklin A. Powell, Sr., Park,** which faces the passenger ferry terminal. This is a good place to people-watch.

Cruz Bay's streets are lined with quaint shops, open-air bars, and stylish courtyard restaurants. The town is steadily expanding, with the construction of upscale shopping centers, condominiums, and homes around the outskirts of the original village.

For decades, the pace was slow and the attitude was casual in Cruz Bay. While some of this low-key ambience remains, old Cruz Bay is quickly being replaced by another sort of town, one where SUVs rule the road, parking is a nightmare, and people are in a hurry.

For visitors, Cruz Bay is a necessary part of any journey to St. John. This is where the passenger and car ferries arrive and depart and where the greatest number of restaurants and shops are found. It is where to come if you want to mail a letter, check your email, or buy a cup of coffee. It is also home to St. John's most happening nightlife and the visitors center for the Virgin Islands National Park,

the best starting point for any tour of the island. Two excellent beaches are a short hike away from the town center.

Logistically speaking, a car is a liability in central Cruz Bay. Parking is atrocious (there are plans for a high-rise parking lot near the waterfront), and the maze of one-way streets is confusing. Walking is the best way to get around, but beware the narrow sidewalks, hills, and hot sun.

Finding your way around can be challenging, as there are no road names in town. Directions are often given in relation to community hubs, like Mongoose Junction, the Post Office, and the churches. Pick up one of the glossy hand-drawn *St. John Guidebook* maps, the best tool for finding your way around Cruz Bay.

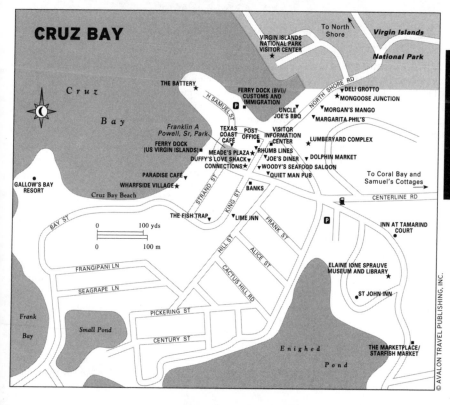

ST. JOHN

© AVALON TRAVEL PUBLISHING, INC.

© SUSANNA HENIGHAN

Cruz Bay, St. John

ST. JOHN

Virgin Islands National Park Visitor Center

The Virgin Islands National Park Visitor Center (Waterfront, 340/776-6201, 8 A.M.–4 P.M.) should be the first stop of any visit to St. John. Its exhibit offers a good introduction to the history and natural features of St. John, and park rangers can tell you about any scheduled hikes, snorkel trips, or other events inside the park. Sign up for these early; they often fill up.

The Battery

Built on the finger of land jutting out in the center of Cruz Bay, The Battery was and is the headquarters of island administration. The present building sits atop the foundation of Christian's Fort, built in 1734 in response to an islandwide slave revolt a year earlier. Note that the cannons face landward—colonial authorities feared another slave revolt more than an attack from the sea.

In 1825 Christian's Fort was expanded to include a prison, courthouse, dungeon, and "justice post," where slaves were beaten, sometimes to death, for breaking the restrictive slave code. The additions were supposed to improve life for slaves on the island since they allowed punishment to be prescribed and delivered by state authorities rather than individual overseers, some of them known for extreme brutality.

Today, the Battery contains government offices, as well as the governor's accommodations when he visits St. John. There are plans to convert part of it into a museum.

Elaine Ione Sprauve Museum and Library

A small, somewhat muddled exhibit exists in the basement of the Elaine Ione Sprauve Museum and Library (9 A.M.–5 P.M. Mon.–Fri., free), the island's only library. Displays touch (lightly) on the nature, history, and culture of the island. You will see things like the skeleton of a blowfish and a locally made doily. Most impressive are the photographs showing St. John locales and people from 1896 until the 1970s. Take note of the two-man police force of 1916, and Cruz Bay when it was mostly pasture. As you leave the quiet of the library and return to the bustling Cruz Bay of today, you will envy those who knew it in the past. There are plans to relocate this exhibit to the Battery when restoration of that building is complete.

Beaches

The beach at Cruz Bay is too crowded and built up for swimming. The nearest nice beaches are a one-mile hike from town. **Solomon Beach** is a secluded, white-sand beach with good snorkeling; it's known as the unofficial nudist beach on St. John (nude bathing is illegal in the U.S. Virgin Islands). **Honeymoon Beach** is a slightly larger, equally charming, white-sand beach just beyond Solomon where people tend to keep their clothes on. The rocky headland between the two is good for snorkeling. You will almost always have both these beaches to yourself, unless you have the bad luck of choosing to visit at the same time day-sail operators drop in with a boatload of tourists.

Both Solomon and Honeymoon Beaches are accessible by foot or boat only. To get there on land, take the Lind Bay Trail, which begins behind the National Park visitors center in Cruz Bay. It is .9 mile to Solomon Beach and .1 mile farther to Honeymoon.

NORTH SHORE

As you head north out of Cruz Bay, you leave behind the bustle of town and in less than 0.5 mile enter the Virgin Islands National Park. Immediately, the air feels cooler and the landscape more lush, and it is quiet. This is quintessential St. John: powder white beaches, pristine coral reefs, hiking trails, and awesome overlooks. No trip to St. John is complete without traversing this part of the island.

You can drive along most of the North Shore. Route 20, known better as Northshore Road, extends from Cruz Bay to Annaberg, passing six excellent beaches along the way. After that, you can continue on foot, hiking to remote bays and beaches on the northwestern shore.

Caneel Bay

Best known now as the setting for St. John's most famous resort, Caneel Bay is a picturesque, straight bay on the western side of Hawksnest Point. During the colonial period, this area was known as Klein Caneel Bay, or Little Cinnamon Bay. Ruins of the Duurloo great house have been preserved and are open to the public. The house served as the headquarters for white plantation owners during the 1733 slave rebellion and was never taken by the Africans.

To visit, drive into the resort (you may be asked to give your name at the guard gate), and park in the visitor lot. You can explore the ruins, shop or dine at the resort, or go to Caneel Bay beach (right in front of the registration desk). As the most popular of the resort's seven beaches, Caneel Bay is usually pretty crowded. There is a platform a short swim offshore for diving, and decent snorkeling to the right of the pier. If you want to explore any of the resort's other beaches, check in at the front desk first.

Hawksnest Bay

Hawksnest Bay is a deep bay home to several excellent beaches. The most prominent is **Hawksnest Beach,** a sloping crescent of sand sandwiched between rock promontories. Sea grape trees provide shade, especially on the western end of the sand. This is the beach closest to town that you can drive to, making it popular with families and children from Cruz Bay. You will find some of the best and newest facilities here—changing rooms, bathrooms, shelters, and grills.

East of Hawksnest is **Gibney's Beach,** also called Oppenheimer Beach or Little Hawksnest Beach. The history of this bit of shoreline is involved. Beatniks Robert and Nancy Gibney bought 40 acres of land here in 1950, four years after they first visited St. John on their honeymoon. In 1957, the Gibneys sold a small piece of beachfront land to J. Robert Oppenheimer, inventor of the atom bomb. When Oppenheimer's daughter died, she left the land and house to "the children of St. John." Meanwhile, in 2000, two-thirds of the original Gibney property was sold to the park; the remaining third is still private property. The upshot of all this: the yellow building you can see on the shoreline (the

ST. JOHN

ST. JOHN

THE 1733 SLAVE REBELLION

In 1733, there were 1,295 adults living on St. John; 1,087 of them were slaves, many who had only recently arrived from Africa. The island was in the throes of a very hard year. There had been drought, a hurricane, and a plague of insects, and starvation was a very real problem, especially for slaves.

With such dire living conditions on the plantations, an increasing number of slaves were running away. Maroon camps popped up in remote parts of the island – Ram's Head was the site of a large one. To address planters' fears of more runaways, the Danish governor issued a new slave code in September that prescribed brutal punishment for runaways and cash incentives for slaves who informed on a maroon.

It was all more than some of the slaves – especially those recently arrived from Africa – could take. At night, the sound of drumbeats could be heard around the island, as slaves at different plantations planned and prepared for what came next.

The St. John slave rebellion began in the early morning of November 23, 1733, when a dozen slaves entered Fort Berg in Coral Bay, carrying cane knives and cutlasses hidden in bundles of wood. The rebels killed all but one of the Danish soldiers – the one who survived hid beneath a bed – and fired the fort's gun three times to signal to slaves that the planned rebellion was now under way. In the

BLOW FOR BLOW.

The rebellion was many planters' worst fear and many Africans' greatest aspiration.

© COURTESY OF LIBRARY OF CONGRESS/H.L. STEPHENS

old Oppenheimer house) is maintained by the V.I. government and can be rented for community functions. To access the beach, take the second driveway on your left after you pass Hawksbill Beach (be sure to park so that your car is completely off the road). Since the Oppenheimer bequest is not actually part of the park (it belongs to the children of St. John, remember), it is a popular place to bring dogs and horses, which are not allowed on park beaches.

Peace Hill

At the top of the headland between Hawksnest and Trunk Bays is Peace Hill, a grassy knoll and windmill ruin with beautiful views of the British Virgin Islands and the north shore of St. John. The land was donated to the national park in the 1950s by Col. Wadsworth, who wished that "Peace Hill be perpetually dedicated as a place where people might meditate and find inner peace, in the hope that in some way this might contribute to world peace." In 1953 Wadsworth commissioned a statue of Jesus, which he named "Christ of the Caribbean." The statue gradually deteriorated and was eventually knocked down by Hurricane Marilyn in 1995. The Park Service put up a plaque in its place.

days that followed, two bands of rebels circled the island, looting and burning many plantations. Some whites were killed, others were spared, and many were able to escape by sea to outlying cays, either by their own initiative or because of warning and assistance from "loyal" slaves. Able-bodied white men, as well as a significant number of loyal slaves, set up camp at the Duurloo Plantation at Klein Caneel Bay, which remained their encampment for the duration of the rebellion.

The standoff continued for six months. Attempts by the local militia, the free black corps, and British army companies from Tortola and St. Kitts failed to round up the remaining African rebels. Meanwhile, the Africans, who had set up camps at Leinster Bay, Maho Bay, and Catherineberg, were running out of weapons and gunpowder. Their leaders, including King Bolombo and Prince Aquashi, quarreled over which of them would rule the island after their rebellion succeeded. This power struggle distracted them from organizing any significant offensive against the remaining whites. In retrospect, many historians say that if the Africans had continued their attack on St. John's whites, the rebels may have found themselves in control of the whole island.

In the end, the rebellion failed. In May 1734 a company of more than 200 French soldiers came to the Danes' rescue. They spent a whole month scouring every part of the island, capturing several Africans and finding many more who had committed suicide. Five months after the French left, 14 remaining rebels were captured after being tricked into returning to their old plantation. Their leader was beheaded. Four more died in prison, four were sentenced to be worked to death building St. Croix's new forts, and the rest were tortured to death.

When it had all ended, less than one-quarter of the island's 208 whites had been killed. Danish authorities determined that 146 slaves, or 14 percent of the slave population, had taken part in the rebellion. All these were killed – in battle, by their own hand, or by torture and execution. Of the island's 92 plantations, 48 had been damaged.

St. John's planters rebuilt following the rebellion, and four years after the revolt was put down, the island's population exceeded its 1733 level. But relations between slave and master on St. John were never the same.

Peace Hill is at the end of a short trail that departs from a parking area just off Northshore Road. There is a steep, unmaintained foot trail to **Denis Bay** about 50 yards up the Peace Hill trail on the right as you hike in. Be aware that the home at the eastern end of Denis Bay is private property.

Jumbie Beach

This small sandy beach is said to be haunted by the ghosts of slaves who were abused and killed by a brutal overseer at the nearby Denis Plantation. Needless to say, this beach is not usually crowded. There is a shallow reef (be careful not to get too close) and some nice shade. Access is via stairs and a short path from Northshore Road. Parking is limited to three spaces on the right-hand side of the road about 10 yards from the trailhead.

◖ Trunk Bay

Trunk Bay is St. John's most magnificent beach, and by extension, its most popular. The bay is a vision of fluffy white sand, sea grape trees, and coconut palms. Trunk Cay, just offshore, is a tiny island of rocky cliffs, tufted by hearty palm trees. The National Park Service maintains an underwater snorkel trail alongside the cay, which is good for beginners. The extensive facilities—lifeguards, bathrooms, showers, a snack bar, gift shop, and telephones—are open daily from 7:30 A.M.–4:30 P.M.

Park rangers lead a weekly snorkel tour of Trunk Bay for experienced snorkelers every Tuesday. The group usually meets at the Trunk Bay lifeguard station at 9:30 A.M., but call the NPS Visitor Center (340/776-6201) to confirm.

Trunk Bay is the only beach on St. John that you must pay to enter. The National Park Service collects $4 per person (under 17 free) 9 A.M.–4 P.M. If you save your entry ticket, you won't have to pay at the Annaberg Ruins (or vice versa) on the same day.

Trunk Bay is often mobbed, because it is the most popular stop for organized day trips from St. Thomas and the cruise ships. To avoid the crowds come early or late, but do come—this is what Caribbean beach dreams are made of.

Cinnamon Bay

At the other side of the steep switchbacks that carry you up and over Peter Ridge is Cinnamon Bay, another standout spot in the National Park. In addition to an excellent beach, there are extensive ruins, a short hike, and some of St. John's best conditions for water sports.

Early archaeologists identified Cinnamon Bay as the site of a Taino village, and recent excavations have uncovered evidence that the area was a site of social and spiritual significance for these early people. Digs discovered religious zemis, remnants of a chief's house, and evidence of religious celebrations and sacrifices.

Colonial settlement at Cinnamon Bay dates back to 1680, when a small-scale cotton plantation was established. During the 1733 slave rebellion the plantation buildings were looted and burned. Following the rebellion, the plantation was rebuilt and expanded to include a sugar factory. In the early 20th century a mechanized bay rum distillery was built on-site, and Cinnamon Bay was the leader in producing this refreshing tonic.

You can explore the **Cinnamon Bay Ruins** by taking the self-guided half-mile walk that begins about 200 feet east of the entrance to the campground and beach. The walk takes you through the ruins of the sugar factory and bay rum still, and then loops through the nearby forest, with markers that identify common trees, animals, and insects.

Park rangers lead a weekly nature and culture walk through the ruins every Monday 9:30–10:30 A.M. The hike begins at the benches next to the gift shop on the beach. Call the NPS visitors center (340/776-6201) to confirm that the hike is on.

You will often find waves at **Cinnamon Bay Beach** a long, winding beach popular with surfers, boogie boarders, and windsurfers.

Maho Bay

Maho Bay is a long, well-protected beach popular with families. When all the other beaches on the north shore are pounded by waves, Maho will be calm. Northshore Road (Rt. 20) runs parallel to the beach, and the road and beach are separated by just a few yards of sand in places. There are picnic tables and bathrooms that are rarely open. Parking can be tricky; make sure your car is all the way off the road. **Little Maho Bay** is a small, sandy, not-quite-so-calm beach on the other side of Maho Bay point. Land access is through Maho Bay Camps.

There is a water sports shop near the beach, and nonguests are welcome to use the beach. Just park up by the dining pavilion and take the stairs down. (It's a long way down!) You can also scramble along a goat trail from the eastern end of big Maho Bay beach.

Francis Pond and Bay

This crescent bay on the western side of Mary Point is a great place for a peaceful swim and home to the best bird-watching on St. John. The water at **Francis Bay Beach** is invariably calm—most days it is like a pond. For this reason it is a favored anchorage for sailboats and a good place for children. It is almost always quiet. There are picnic tables and pit toilets.

There is a small area of coral reef at the western end (nearest Maho) that is good for beginning snorkelers. Strong swimmers can snorkel out from the eastern end of the beach, where a narrow reef begins about halfway to the point. You can also launch here for a kayak trip to Whistling Cay.

Francis Bay Pond is a salt pond and mangrove area behind the beach, and a great place for bird-watching. The Francis Bay Trail passes through dry forest and great house ruins before bringing you to the salt pond, where a boardwalk has been built to enable bird-watching. The trail ends at the beach. Don't forget the bug spray and binoculars.

Park Service rangers host a weekly bird-watching walk at Francis Bay on Sunday mornings 7:30–9 A.M. It meets at the Francis Bay trailhead; call the NPS Visitor Center (340/776-6201) to confirm and to arrange taxi service if necessary.

◖ Waterlemon Cay

Some of St. John's best snorkeling is around Waterlemon Cay, an offshore islet with a hard-packed sand beach on one end. There is an informal snorkel trail around the island (start by the sand and head in a clockwise direction) where you will see a wide variety of hard and soft coral, plus fish, squid, and turtles.

Hike to Waterlemon Cay along the Leinster Bay Trail, just past the Annaberg Sugar Mill ruins. The beach at Leinster Bay itself is not outstanding—the sand is coarse and yellow—but the sea grass and coral offshore make a good place to spot fish, turtles, and sea stars.

Waterlemon is an easy half-mile walk from the Annaberg Sugar Mill ruins parking lot. The trail follows the coastline. Don't try to drive it. To get to Waterlemon Cay continue walking around to the extreme east of the bay and swim across to the cay.

Annaberg School Ruins

The 1840s saw the construction of the first government schools in the then-Danish West Indies. Governor-General Peter von Scholten saw universal compulsory education as a means of amelioration and a way to prepare the colony for the eventual elimination of slavery. Government

ST. JOHN

There are arts and cultural demonstrations weekly at the Annaberg Sugar Plantation.

MAKING SUGAR

A lot of work went into producing sugar on a 17th and 18th century sugar plantation in the Virgin Islands.

The process began with the clearing of huge swaths of land on which cane would be planted. Slaves would use machetes to clear the brush, let the cut brush dry out, and then burn the dried brush. Heavy rocks also had to be cleared from the land, and on hilly islands like St. John and Tortola, terraces were cut into the hills to provide space to grow the cane.

Once the land was cleared, cane was planted. Sugarcane takes between 12 and 15 months to mature, and during this time slaves were put to work weeding and fertilizing the crops and building the sugar works.

When the time came for harvest and production, the plantation worked 24 hours a day. The cane was cut and carried to the sugar factory, where it had to be crushed within 24 hours of its cutting. Cane was crushed by running the long canes through wheels, which crushed the cane and extracted juice, which ran into a reservoir beneath the wheels. Cane crushers were powered either by wind or animal. In flat islands like St. Croix, windmills were common, but on hilly islands, where you were less assured of a good, steady breeze, animals were relied upon.

Once the cane juice was gathered, it was poured into a series of "coppers" – large round bowls placed over fires. The fires were carefully regulated so the cane juice never boiled but was hot enough to slowly evaporate until a thick molasses was all that was left. A skilled slave, called the boilerman, kept close watch over the molasses. When he declared it was time to "strike" the sugar, the molasses was quickly removed from the heat and placed in a cooling pan, where it would stay until crystals began to form.

At this stage the sugar was transferred to pyramid-shaped bags that hung from the ceiling of the curing house. Any remaining liquid ran out, leaving a pure block of sugar.

COURTESY OF LIBRARY OF CONGRESS

Crucians work in a cane field in 1941, much as they had for two hundred years.

schools were first built in St. Croix, and in 1844 funds were made available for the construction of two schools on St. John. One was situated at Bethany, near Cruz Bay, and the other was near Annaberg, on the north shore of the island.

The ruins of the Annaberg School are located a short distance from the road to the Annaberg Sugar Mill. Steps have been built so you can better view the ruins, and there is a small display describing the history of the school and efforts to preserve it.

Annaberg Sugar Mill Ruins

The ruins of the Annaberg Sugar Mill are the best place to learn about the colonial-era life of both planters and slaves on St. John. The ruins, located at the far northeastern end of the Northshore Road, include a windmill, sugar factory, mill round, and slave quarters. The National Park Service organizes cultural demonstrations here four days a week, when local artisans and bakers display traditional basket-making and bread-baking, among other things. There is a small garden with local vegetables and herbs. A short self-guided hike takes visitors through the process of sugar production at an 18th- and 19th-century sugar factory.

Annaberg (Anna's Hill) was named after the daughter of the plantation's absentee owner, Christopher Gottschalk. Like all plantations on the island, the 518-acre Annaberg Plantation produced sugar, rum, and molasses. The windmill was the tallest of the five windmills on St. John, and the adjoining sugar factory was one of the largest on the island. Many of the remaining buildings were built in the early 1800s, but several date back to the 1700s.

Annaberg is one of two attractions in the National Park you must pay to enter; admission is $4 for adults. Children under 17 are free. The ticket gate is usually open 9 A.M.–4 P.M. If you save your receipt, you can enter Trunk Bay free on the same day. When the ticket booth is closed, you can still come in and walk around during daylight hours. Cultural demonstrations take place 10 A.M.–2 P.M. Tuesday–Friday. Call the NPS Visitor Center (340/776-6201) to find out what kind of demonstration is scheduled during your visit.

◖ CORAL BAY

Technically, the term Coral Bay refers to the expansive, broad bay that stretches from Sabbat Point in the west to Long Point in the east. It encompasses Round Bay, Hurricane Hole, and Coral Harbor, plus dozens more creeks, bays, and points.

For most people, however, Coral Bay is better known as the sprawling, laid-back hamlet that lines the shore here. This village is the last frontier of St. John and one of its most unique places. It takes some 45 minutes to drive here from Cruz Bay, and by the time you make the dramatic descent into the town, you feel as if you have left the rest of the world far behind.

For many decades, this part of St. John was practically undeveloped. The tight-knit local community that lived here for generations had closer ties with nearby Tortola, which was only a short sail away, than they did with Cruz Bay. But as St. John was discovered in the middle part of the 20th century, so was Coral Bay. The area's breathtaking views of the British Virgins and enchanting sense of isolation attracted successive waves of American and European transplants. The first were free spirits who built small homes or lived aboard their sailboats, but recent arrivals are not so modest. These days, luxurious homes peer down from the hillsides around Coral Bay and upscale markets, restaurants, and boutiques are opening to cater to the changing clientele.

Despite the changes, however, Coral Bay is still the most laid-back part of St. John, and the best place to feel the magical calm that is St. John's greatest attraction.

The area got its name from the Dutch word *kraal,* which means corral, an indication of the importance of cattle and livestock in the bay's early history. Coral Bay did not always play second fiddle to Cruz Bay. When the Danish settled St. John in the early 1700s, they took note of Coral Bay's large natural harbor and established their capital and only fortification

ST. JOHN

WILL YOU MARRY ME?

Late ethnologist J. C. Trevor spent several months in Coral Bay, St. John, in 1935 and recorded his observations of traditional Virgin Islands culture in his unpublished doctoral thesis. In this excerpt, reprinted in *St. John Backtime* by Ruth Hull Low and Rafael Valls, Trevor describes the marriage tradition:

"If you want to marry a girl on St. John," said a young man who lived there, "you will ax her to be in love with you; if she say 'yes,' you will tell her that you are going to write her father; if she decide for you to write to him, you will write to him axing to marry his daughter; if he say 'no,' and the girl loves you, you could run away." This last means leaving the island, in which case the father will be "vexed" with both parties. ... the father will "write you back if he wants you," and the boy and girl are then engaged. ... for the wedding feast on St. John in 1935-36 a marriage might involve the expenditure of from 15-30 dollars, since a couple of goats, a whole demijohn of white rum and a quantity of cakes were provided for the guests. A license from the Police Officer cost 40 cents, but no fee is paid to the Moravian Church should either party be a member of it. If the ceremony is a civil one, the Police officer charges a dollar...

On both St. John and Tortola between two and four in the afternoon is the usual time to be married. ... In any case a feast will be held for them about seven in the evening. Between twenty and a hundred persons usually attend a wedding feast and bring gifts for the newly wedded couple. Glasses, cups and saucers, chickens, "a little lamp," and a pair of pillowcases were given as examples of wedding presents.

there. The Danish West India and Guinea Company secured the choicest property on the island for its plantation: Carolina, a wide, flat plain facing Coral Harbor. A few decades later, it was in Coral Bay that the slave revolt of 1733 began when a dozen slaves attacked the Danish fort atop Fort Berg Hill overlooking the bay.

Orientation

Route 107 follows a north-south path along the western coast of Coral Bay, ending just past Salt Pond Bay. Route 10, also called the East End Road, follows the eastern coast of the bay through some of St. John's most remote territory and then through some of its most expensive private real estate. The two roads meet up at the head of Coral Harbor, which can be thought of as the center of Coral Bay. Most bars, restaurants, and shops are within a mile of this crossroads, on either Rte. 107 or Rte. 10,

but development is spreading outward along these routes.

It is fun to explore Coral Bay by car, and even more fun to explore by boat. Trying to get around here on foot would be frustrating and slow-going. Plan a few hours if you want to see the whole bay, more if you want to refresh yourself at one of the nearby beaches or restaurants.

Emmaus Moravian Church

The handsome church that overlooks Coral Bay was built by German Moravian missionaries who arrived in the Danish West Indies in 1732 to minister to the slaves. The Emmaus manse was built around 1750, and the original church was constructed in 1782. Both were rebuilt after a destructive hurricane in 1916. The masonry foundation, which survived the storm, was built of rubble, ballast brick, and coral. The one-story church holds a

© SUSANNA HENIGHAN

Emmaus Moravian Church in Coral Bay

belfry attached to the west end. The property on which the church sits was once owned by the Danish Governor, Thomas de Malleville, who deeded it to the Moravians in 1782 after he converted to the faith.

This is still an active congregation (340/ 776-6713).

Fort Berg

The ruins of the Danish fort that served as the site of the opening scene of the 1733 slave revolt sit atop Fort Berg (Fort Hill), the sugarloaf that juts out between Coral Harbor and Hurricane Hole.

The fort was constructed in 1717, the same year Danish settlement of St. John began in earnest. In 1760, four bastions and a gun deck were added to the fort. During the Napoleonic Wars the fort and adjacent battery were occupied by the British in 1801, and again from 1807 to 1815.

The ruins, and the hill on which they stand, are on private property. Get permission before setting out to find them. Once a year, around November 23, the date of the start of the 1733

rebellion, locals commemorate the slave revolt by hiking to the hilltop and holding a ceremony of remembrance. An announcement of this event is published in the local newspapers.

Beaches

The beaches in this part of St. John are modest compared to others on the island. **Haulover Bay** is rocky and rough but can be good for snorkeling. **Hansen Bay,** home of Vie's Campground, is a mixture of sand and rocks and has some very good snorkeling.

SOUTH SHORE

The south coast of St. John is remote and largely unspoiled. The paved road ends just past Salt Pond Bay—beyond that you need four-wheel-drive or your feet to get there. Some of the best snorkeling is at the south shore beaches, as well as some excellent hikes.

Salt Pond Bay

For many St. John residents, Salt Pond Bay is a favorite beach, if for no other reason than that it tends to be uncrowded, even on weekends. This is partly due to the bay's remote location near the end of Rte. 107, and partly due to the 10-minute hike to the beach.

Salt Pond's wide, white beach is speckled by small pebbles. It offers some shade, several picnic tables, and pit toilets. The hikes to Ram's Head Point and Drunk Bay begin at the eastern end of the beach. There is good snorkeling around the two sets of jagged rocks that break the surface in the middle of the bay.

Lameshur Bay

Some of St. John's best snorkeling is found around Great Lameshur Bay and Little Lameshur Bay—side-by-side bays along the island's south coast. Great Lameshur is scattered with rock and coral; the best snorkeling is on its eastern side. The remains of *Tektite,* an underwater living habitat for aquanauts built in the late 1960s, lie submerged under 50 feet of water here. Little Lameshur has a sand and rubble beach. There is good snorkeling just off the western end of the beach. If you are lucky to visit on a calm day, follow the western

shoreline as far as Europa Bay for some exquisite snorkeling.

If you have a four-wheel-drive vehicle you can drive to Lameshur Bay by following Rte. 107 and continuing after the road narrows and becomes dirt. You can also hike in from both the Reef Bay and Bordeaux Mountain Trails.

Reef Bay

This broad, wooded bay was the site of one of the most productive sugar plantations on St. John. Par Force, as the estate was called, was owned by the Rif family. The name Reef Bay is a corruption of this name; it has nothing to do with coral.

There are sugar mill ruins at the edge of the bay, which are marked by NPS signs explaining the sugar production process. The old sugar factory here is also home to a rare species of bats—look up when you step inside.

Most people get to Reef Bay by hiking (the only other alternative is by boat). On the trail down, you pass several other sugar mill ruins

© SUSANNA HENIGHAN

The Reef Bay petroglyphs have intrigued people for centuries.

and the foundation of an old worker's cottage. The Reef Bay Great House is a short detour off the Lameshur Bay Trail. The old great house is one of the largest on St. John, but it's in disrepair, and the National Park Service does not encourage visits here.

◖ Petroglyphs

Stone carvings along the Reef Bay Trail are a reminder of St. John's rich history, although their origin is something of a mystery.

The most widely accepted explanation of the carvings' origin is that they were made by Taino Indians who lived on St. John beginning around 200 A.D. Petroglyphs like these have been found at other former Taino settlements in Puerto Rico, Hispaniola, and other islands in the Caribbean. It is also believed that many of the petroglyphs are representations of bats, animals of significance to the Tainos.

But there are other theories. One is that Africans carved the petroglyphs during a pre-Columbian journey to the Caribbean and Central America. This stems from similarities between the St. John petroglyphs and an Ashanti symbol that means "accept God". It has also been argued that the symbols resemble a script used by peoples of southeast Libya.

The petroglyphs make a nice pit stop along the Reef Bay Trail. When there has been recent rain, there is a waterfall here. At other times, the pool will remain, but there won't be any running water. The petroglyphs are cut into the rock above the main pool; splash a little water on them and you'll see them better.

Entertainment and Events

People don't come to St. John for the party, but they'll find one once they're here. Nightlife here is relaxed but fun, and the island's annual events calendar includes live music festivals, sporting events, and a Carnival. Pick up the local papers for entertainment listings, or call the entertainment hotline (340/714-7074) for a rundown on upcoming events.

NIGHTLIFE

Nightlife on St. John is laid-back and fun. After a day in the wild of the national park, many people head to bars in Cruz Bay and Coral Bay for some companionship, music, and a chance to share stories of the day.

Cruz Bay

Cruz Bay is lively at night, especially on the weekends. Happy hour starts early at **Woody's Seafood Saloon** (Cruz Bay, 340/779-4625) where beers are just a buck 3–5 P.M. daily. The 20-something crowd that loves this place often spills out onto the sidewalk. Many people here are getting warmed up for a long night out.

The Woody's crowd heads to **Duffy's Love Shack,** (Cruz Bay, 340/776-6065, 11:30 A.M.– 2 A.M. daily) just around the corner, a little later. Duffy's is reminiscent of Swiss Family Robinson—there are rope bridges and lots of decks, and a tree is growing straight through the building. The dance floor here gets going around 10:30 P.M., but doesn't usually get hot until around midnight. Duffy's is known for its ridiculous tropical concoctions, some of which are served in fishbowls.

A more mature crowd heads to the **Quiet Mon Pub** (Cruz Bay, 340/779-4799), the best spot for people-watching in town. This is also the place for draft beer.

For a different kind of entertainment, try video poker and off-track betting at **Captain's Cabin** (Wharfside Village, 340/693-8210, open 1 P.M. until late).

Coral Bay

By and large, nightlife in Coral Bay is mellower than Cruz Bay. **Skinny Legs** (340/779-4982) and **Island Blues** (340/776-6800) often have live music (blues, bluegrass, and reggae are especially popular). **Shipwreck**

Landing (Rt. 107, 340/693-5640) is a popular place for drinking.

EVENTS

The biggest event on St. John is the annual July 4 Carnival, but the island throws some other parties, too.

8 Tuff Miles

Runners brave St. John's hills in the annual 8 Tuff Miles (www.8tuffmiles.com) road race. The route from Cruz Bay to Coral Bay, along Centerline Road, climbs 1,400 feet in less than six miles. This race takes place in late February.

A few weeks later, the island holds a St. Patrick's Day parade through Cruz Bay: "8 tuff minutes for the rest of us."

St. John Blues Festival

For four days in late March, St. John sings the blues. The St. John Blues Festival (www.st-johnbluesfestival.com) is held in bars in Cruz Bay and Coral Bay; it finishes with an all-day blues concert on the field at Coral Bay.

St. John Carnival

Carnival on St. John starts in mid-June and lasts through July 4, when a small but energetic parade winds through Cruz Bay. The Carnival Village is erected in the parking lot next to the Customs and Immigration building on the waterfront. There is lots of live music, a food fair, and much more.

Love City Triathlon

Athletes swim 0.5 mile, bike 14 miles, and run four miles in the **Love City Triathlon** (340/779-4214). Love City is St. John's nickname, redolent of the hippie-style love many residents embrace. The triathlon, which takes place every September, usually attracts athletes from the U.S. and British Virgin Islands, plus Puerto Rico.

Shopping

St. John has an increasing number of small, unique boutiques catering to the upscale and funky tastes of its visitors. Shoppers won't find acres of gold jewelry, as on St. Thomas, but will find some of the most upscale and trendy shopping in the Virgin Islands.

Cruz Bay

The best place for shopping on St. John is in Cruz Bay. A dedicated shopper could spend a day exploring here: start at Mongoose Junction north of the ferry dock and make your way to Wharfside Village on the south end. At Mongoose Junction, **The Body Deli** (340/776-0454) sells natural soaps, body washes, and creams. **Hurricane Alley** (340/776-6548) sells island-style beach and resort wear, while **Caravan Gallery** (340/779-4566) has the most distinctive jewelry on the island.

In other parts of Cruz Bay, **St. John Spice** (Wharfside Village, 340/693-7046) has local spices plus pottery and crafts. **Love City Surf Shack** (Raintree Court, 340/693-7357) has swimsuits, beachwear, and surf gear. For books, maps, and children's toys, your best choice is the **National Park Service Visitor Center;** or try newly-opened **Book and Bean** (340/779-2665) in the Marketplace.

Coral Bay

As in all things, Coral Bay's shopping is offbeat and unique. It is also growing. The opening of the Coccoloba Shopping Center has doubled shopping outlets in this far-flung community for better or for worse. Take, for example, the roadside tent selling nothing but bikinis.

The original Coral Bay shopping complex is at Skinny Legs, just east of the main Coral Bay crossroads of Routes 107 and 10. Here **Mumbo Jumbo** (340/779-4277) sells island clothes, handbags, sunglasses, and footwear. Other shops here sell local art. A great stop for everyone, especially families, is the **Tall Ship Trading Company** (340/776-6816), next to Shipwreck Landing along Route 107. Here you can watch an old-fashioned silkscreen T-shirt press in operation and choose from the latest designs for yourself.

The North Shore

For brand-name resort wear, check out the boutiques at Caneel Bay (or, likewise, the Westin Resort). The most interesting shop on St. John is at **Maho Bay Camps** (340/776-6226, www.maho.org), right next door to the campground restaurant. Here, artists convert discarded glass and plastic into works of art. Most evenings you can watch a master glassblower at work, and there are frequent classes and detailed demonstrations. Check out its website for a schedule.

Sports and Recreation

Recreation on St. John generally has one aim: to bring you closer to the exquisite natural beauty of the island. Hiking and snorkeling are the most popular pursuits because they are rewarding, easy, and require little gear. For people seeking something a little more involved, there are also opportunities for biking, kayaking, scuba diving, windsurfing, and sailing.

For some of the most rewarding activities, check with the **Friends of the Virgin Islands National Park** (340/779-4940, www.friends-vinp.org), which organizes guided hikes, workshops, arts and crafts lessons, and other fun educational activities. Past workshops have showcased traditional island cooking, how to take better nature photographs, and stargazing. The Friends accept donations in support of their conservation work.

HIKING

There are more than 28 miles of hiking trails on St. John, ranging from easy 15-minute rambles to challenging all-day outings. Trails wind through moist tropical forest and scrubby woods, passing Danish plantation ruins and quiet bays. Despite the development occurring on St. John, hiking remains the only way to reach some of the island's most remote, and most beautiful, places. If you're feeling a little crowded walking around Cruz Bay or on the beach at Trunk Bay, go for a hike and you will quickly regain the sense of quiet that makes St. John so appealing.

Official National Park trails are detailed on a free NPS trail guide, which includes brief descriptions of each trail and a somewhat hard-to-read map. The guide is available at the Cruz Bay Visitor Center; don't hike without it. If you plan to do a lot of hiking, try to find a copy of the *Trail Bandit Guide,* a pocket-sized map of hiking trails, including unofficial paths. The guide includes a clearly labeled, full-color map, trail descriptions, and GPS waypoint locations. I found mine at Miss Lucy's near Salt Pond Bay. Try online map sources too, such as www.vitrader.com.

Don't be fooled by the fact that most hikes on St. John are short; hiking in the island's tropical climate is grueling. Bring twice the water you think you will need, and cover up from the sun and insects. The best time to hike is in the early morning or late afternoon, but beware that darkness comes quickly this close to the equator. In the winter it is dark at 6 P.M., in the summer at 7 P.M.

There are more than 30 official and unofficial trails on St. John, plus secondary spurs. The hikes detailed below are some of the best.

Lind Point Trail

A relatively easy and very rewarding hike, the Lind Point Trail (1.1 miles) connects the National Park Service Visitor Center with Honeymoon Beach at Caneel Bay. There is an upper and lower track; the upper trail climbs more than 150 feet to Lind Point, with nice views of

ST. JOHN

Cruz Bay and Pillsbury Sound, before heading back down toward the beaches. The lower trail goes straight to the bay. In both cases, a side trail branches off to Solomon Beach, while the main track continues on to Honeymoon Beach, one of Caneel Bay Resort's seven beaches. Nonguests are welcome at the beach. You can either hike back the way you came, or continue on to Caneel Bay Resort and catch a taxi back to town.

Turtle Point Trail

This 0.5-mile hike is fully contained within the grounds of Caneel Bay Resort. Nonguests must check in at the resort front desk, where you will be given a map and instructions on where to meet the shuttle that will take you to the trailhead. The trail circles Hawksnest Point, where there are convenient benches and beautiful views, and ends at Turtle Bay Beach.

Cinnamon Bay Self-Guided Loop

This is an easy 0.5-mile walk, but plan on about an hour if you want to absorb all the information along the way. The trail starts among the ruins of the old sugar factory across the road from the entrance to Cinnamon Bay Campground. It continues through the woods behind the ruins; markers identify prominent trees, animals, and insects. The hike ends by the ruins of the estate house.

Cinnamon Bay Trail

Don't confuse this trail with the self-guided loop. The Cinnamon Bay Trail is a 1.1 mile-uphill trail that begins about 100 yards east of the campground entrance and follows an old Danish road all the way to Centerline Road. Of course, if you start at Centerline Road it is all downhill. The trail passes through land that would have been cultivated with sugarcane during the plantation era; it is now all secondary forest.

Francis Bay Trail

This is a good hike for bird-watchers. The beginning of this 0.5-mile trail is well marked on the west end of the Mary Creek paved road. It passes through dry forest, past estate house ruins, and through a mangrove forest and salt pond. The trail ends at Francis Bay Beach.

Leinster Bay and Johnny Horn Trails

This 2.6-mile trail, often considered two separate trails, connects the Emmaus Moravian Church in Coral Bay with Annaberg on the north coast. From Annaberg, the trail follows the shoreline of Leinster Bay for 0.8 mile before striking out over Leinster and Base Hills. It finishes at the driveway of the Moravian Church.

◖ Ram's Head Trail

This 1.2-mile hike takes you to the windswept end of Ram's Head, the southernmost point of St. John. First, you follow the wide, sunny 0.25-mile path down to Salt Pond Beach. The Ram's Head trail starts at the eastern end of the beach, climbing through dry, scrubby woods before reaching a rocky bay. The final ascent is up 200 feet to Ram's Head—the views and general atmosphere are spectacular. The 0.25-mile trail to Drunk Bay veers off near the beginning of this hike. Drunk Bay is excellent for beachcombing.

Yawzi Point Trail

This 0.5-mile, easy hike follows the headland that separates Little Lameshur and Great Lameshur Bays. People suffering from yaws, a tropical skin disease, were sent to a quarantine camp here in the 18th and 19th centuries. The trail cuts through a dry forest before reaching the point. You will need a four-wheel-drive vehicle to drive to the trailhead, unless you hike in from Bordeaux Mountain or the Reef Bay trail.

Reef Bay Trail

The most popular hike on St. John is the 2.1-mile Reef Bay Trail, which descends from Centerline Road to the shore at Reef Bay. The trail passes through both moist and dry tropical forests and the remains of four different sugar factories, including the extensive Reef Bay ruins. The hike descends 600 feet from start to finish. Plan on two hours to hike down; three to hike up.

Several markers along the way identify significant plants, trees, and landmarks. You may see white-tailed deer along the trail. Introduced on St. Thomas and St. John as game for planters, the deer swam to St. John and have flourished. They are not fearful of people.

The 0.25-mile spur trail to the **Reef Bay Petroglyphs** branches off 1.6 miles down. Just past the petroglyph trail is the beginning of the Lameshur Bay Trail. It's a 1.5-mile hike to that bay. The Reef Bay Great House Ruins are a short distance up this trail. If you keep going straight, you come to the Reef Bay Sugar Ruins and a short spur trail to Little Reef Bay, where you can swim.

The National Park Service leads guided hikes down the Reef Bay Trail several days a week. On these hikes a ranger leads about 30 people down the trail, stopping regularly to describe the natural and historical landmarks along the way. This is a great opportunity to learn about the island, but the biggest perk of the outing is that you don't have to hike back up. The Park Service arranges a boat to pick you up at the end of the trail and sail back to Cruz Bay. The hike costs $20 per person. Sign up early, preferably before you arrive on St. John, because it is almost always full.

SNORKELING

Snorkeling is probably the most popular activity on St. John, and for good reason. It requires minimal equipment and allows you to explore the underwater cornucopia of fish, coral, shellfish, turtles, and other marine creatures that live in the waters around St. John. Because of strict rules governing fishing, anchoring, and pollution in national park waters, the snorkeling around St. John is excellent.

You can snorkel anywhere. Most people gravitate toward coral reefs, but snorkeling over sea grass or in the mangroves can be just as interesting. The National Park Service publishes a brochure, *Where's the Best Snorkeling?* that gives detailed descriptions of snorkeling at the major beaches on St. John.

ST. JOHN

Hawksnest Beach is one of many good snorkeling beaches on St. John.

SNORKEL SAFETY

Before you start snorkeling, be sure to take some basic health and safety precautions.

1. Don't enter the water where there are a lot of sea urchins, sharp coral, or wave action.

2. Protect yourself from the sun; while snorkeling, your back and legs are subject to terrible sunburns. Wear a T-shirt and shorts or wetsuit. A bathing cap is a good idea for bald heads. If you are only using sunscreen, apply it at least 15 minutes before you go in the water and reapply frequently.

3. Be sure to tell someone where you are going and when you will be back. Always snorkel with a buddy, and agree ahead of time how far you will separate from each other in the water.

4. Ask about currents before you go in the water. If you do get caught in a current, do not fight it. Swim across it until you can get out or are washed toward the shore.

Coral Reef Sites

On the north shore, the **Trunk Bay Underwater Trail** is a good reef for beginners. Signs along the sea floor identify types of coral and fish, and lifeguards are on duty for safety. **Jumbie Beach** has a shallow, maze-like reef along the eastern (right-hand) side, where you may see lobsters and nurse sharks. **Waterlemon Cay,** accessible via Leinster Bay, has excellent coral reef snorkeling.

When the north shore is too rough for snorkeling, try south shore bays, which are normally calm. On the south shore, **Salt Pond Bay** has good reef snorkeling around the two jagged rocks that break the surface of the bay. There is also good snorkeling on the eastern shoreline (nearest Ram's Head), which gets better the farther out you go. At **Great Lameshur Bay,** the snorkeling is best along the eastern shore. You may see the sunken foundation remains of *Tektite,* an underwater habitat for aquanauts from 1969 to 1970. **Little Lameshur Bay** has snorkeling for beginners just off the western end of

the beach. If it is calm, strong swimmers can explore the western shoreline, which features deep cliffs, canyons, and schools of fish.

Sea Grass Sites

Maho Bay has offshore sea grass beds that provide food for green turtles, especially in the early morning and late afternoon. **Brown Bay,** accessible only on foot, has a sea grass bed just offshore. Although not part of the national park, **Chocolate Hole** has a thick sea grass bed where you can see juvenile fish, rays, conch, and sometimes turtles. Chocolate Hole was named for the color of the rocks along the shore. It is located on Route 104, on the southern coast.

Mangrove Sites

Mangroves are not as flashy as reefs or sea grass, but they provide a fascinating glimpse into an important marine habitat. Mangroves are where juvenile fish, lobsters, and crabs live until they get big enough to fend for themselves in the great big ocean. Mangroves are often referred to as the nursery of the ocean. The best place for mangrove snorkeling is **Princess Bay** along Rte. 10 (East End Road). Get as close to the knobby trees as you can, and look carefully for the marinelife. It is shallow, and fins will disturb the sea bottom; it is best not to wear them.

Snorkel Equipment

If snorkeling appeals to you at all, it is a good idea to rent snorkel gear for the duration of your stay. It is cheaper than renting it by the day or hour, and that way you will always have gear on hand. Check first to see if where you are staying has or rents snorkel equipment; most hotels do. You can also rent snorkel gear from any water sports operation on the island. In Coral Bay, **Crabby's Watersports** (Coccoloba Shopping Center, 340/714-2415) rents a full set of snorkel gear for $10 a day or $50 a week. In Cruz Bay, **Low Key Watersports** (Wharfside Village, 340/693-8999) rents gear for $7 a day and $35 a week. Water sports shops at Trunk Bay, Cinnamon Bay, and Little Maho Bay also rent gear.

KAYAKING

Kayaking is a good way to get from bay to bay or out to the small cays around St. John, where you can picnic or just enjoy a day on a desert island. How easy or hard it is to kayak around St. John depends a lot on the weather and sea conditions; calm weather means easy kayaking, so check the marine forecast or a water sports center before planning a trip. The most popular area for kayaking is off St. John's north shore, where you can paddle up to beaches or out to offshore islets, like Whistling Cay, Waterlemon Cay, or the Durloe Cays. A kayak is the ideal means to explore the creeks and bays that make up Coral Bay or reach the remote east end of the island.

On the north shore, kayak rentals are available at **Cinnamon Bay Watersports** (Cinnamon Bay, 340/776-6330 or 340/693-5902) and at **Maho Bay Watersports,** (Little Maho Bay, 340/776-6240, 9 A.M.–4 P.M.). For exploring around Coral Bay, **Crabby's Watersports** (Coccoloba Shopping Center, 340/714-2415) rents single and two-seater kayaks. Expect to pay $50–75 for a full-day kayak rental.

For a little bit more than you would spend for a kayak rental, you can go on a kayak trip with a guide. **Arawak Expeditions** (340/693-8312, www.arawakexp.com) offers guided kayak tours to Henley and Lovango Cays, leaving from Cruz Bay. Half-day tours cost $50; full-day tours are $90, including lunch.

SAILING

There are a number of day-sail operators who offer sailing trips around St. John and to the nearby British Virgin Islands. Choices typically include half-day snorkel trips around St. John; full-day expeditions to Jost Van Dyke, Norman Island, or Virgin Gorda in the British Virgins; or sunset sails around St. John. Many trips include extras like free drinks and lunch. Rates range from $40 to $60 for half-day sails, and from $60 to $130 for a full-day sail.

The easiest way to book a day sail is through one of the clearinghouse activity desks around St. John. These desks will match you with the kind of day sail you want and make the reservation for you. You can make arrangements in person or on the phone. Desks include **St. John Adventures Unlimited** (Gallow's Point and Cruz Bay, 340/693-7730, www.st-johnadventures.com) and **Connections** (Coral Bay and Cruz Bay, 340/776-6922).

Anchorages

If you need to clear U.S. Customs and Immigration, use one of the private moorings (in Cruz Bay) or anchor out of the way of the commercial traffic. Once you clear customs, you will want to find somewhere else to use as your home base. It is a good idea to stop at the National Park Service Visitor Center on the waterfront to check on any new marine regulations. NPS also publishes a free guide for mariners.

There are National Park Service moorings at **Caneel Bay, Hawksnest Bay, Cinnamon Bay, Maho Bay, Francis Bay, Leinster Bay, Salt Pond Bay, Great Lameshur Bay,** and **Little Lameshur Bay.** Each bay has its own specific anchoring regulations; check with the National Park Service guide before dropping anchor.

At Coral Bay, don't pick up any of the private moorings; instead, drop your anchor. There is a dinghy dock in front of Skinny Legs.

DIVING

St. John has a half dozen good dive sites off its southeastern shore, as well as two good sites just off Cruz Bay. The string of cays between St. John and St. Thomas—from Carval Rick to Thatch Cay—are also popular with divers. The **Maj. Gen. Rogers,** a 1940 army freighter, was sunk in 1972 to become an artificial reef. The excellent reef around **Grass Cay** and **Mingo Cay** are good for beginning divers. There is a dizzying array of sealife at **Witch's Hat** on the southern tip of Steven's Cay, just off Cruz Bay.

South shore dives include **Cocoloba,** an easy, sandy, reef dive, and **Maple Leaf,** a large offshore reef east of Reef Bay. The most famous east end dive site is **Eagle Shoal,** between Ram's Head and Leduck Island. The

ST. JOHN

shoal, known for its massive underwater cave, has been the site of underwater weddings. Access to Eagle Shoal is limited due to its exposure to southeasterly swells.

Low Key Watersports (Cruz Bay, 340/693-8999) offers daily dive trips as well as certification courses. Capt. Bob Carney leads dive trips with **Paradise Watersports** (Caneel Bay Resort, 340/779-4999, www.paradisevi.com), which specializes in small groups. **Cruz Bay Watersports** (Cruz Bay and the Westin Resort, 340/693-8720) departs from the National Park dock in Cruz Bay. Its office is located below Chilly Billy's in the Lumberyard Complex.

OTHER LAND PURSUITS
Tennis
There are two public tennis courts in Cruz Bay, next to the Department of Motor Vehicles. Tennis classes and pro shop services are available at the **Westin** (340/693-8000) and **Caneel Bay Resort** (340/776-6111).

Miniature Golf
If you grow weary of sandy beaches and turquoise waters, escape to **Pastory Gardens** (Rt. 10, 340/777-3147, 11 A.M.–midnight), an 18-hole miniature golf course outside Cruz Bay. The course winds through gardens and features mildly educational displays at each hole.

Biking
St. John's hills make biking a challenging pursuit. If you want to accept the challenge, contact **Arawak Expeditions** (340/693-8312, www.arawakexp.com), which provides guides and routes tailored for beginning, intermediate, or advanced bikers. Rates are $50 for a half day or $90 for a full day.

Gyms
Gym in Paradise (The Marketplace, 340/776-0600, 7 A.M.–9 P.M. Mon.–Sat., 7 A.M.–noon Sun.) has visitor memberships.

There are yoga classes every morning at Maho Bay Camps (340/776-6240).

Accommodations

St. John's accommodations run the gamut from luxurious resorts to bare-bones campsites. Because of the great variety, they are presented here according to three categories: resorts and inns, campgrounds, and villas.

VILLAS
The fastest-growing sector of St. John's accommodation market is villas, private homes rented out for a week or more at a time. Many are owned by snowbirds, who rent the house out while they are not using it. Others were constructed specifically for vacation rentals. Villas come in a wide variety of styles and sizes, but most can easily sleep four or more people. Villa rental rates vary widely but generally start around $1,800 per week in the winter and top out at over $10,000. Most villas rent for between $2,500 and $4,500 per week. The best way to book a villa is to contact a villa

rental agency. These agencies represent villas, make reservations, and, in many cases, manage the properties for the owners.

Carefree Getaways (340/779-4070, U.S. toll free 888/643-6002, www.carefreegetaways.com) specializes in villas south of Cruz Bay, in Chocolate Hole, Rendezvous Bay, and Gift Hill. **Windspree Vacation Homes** (Coral Bay, 340/693-5423, fax 340/693-5623, www.windspree.com) represents several dozen villas around Coral Bay and the east end. **Catered To Inc.** (Marketplace, Cruz Bay, 340/776-6642, U.S. toll free 800/424-6641, fax 340/693-8191, www.cateredto.com) represents two dozen villas in the Cruz Bay and North Shore areas. **Virgin Islands Vacations and Villas** (Boulon Center, Cruz Bay, 340/779-4250, fax 703/940-4571, www.vivacations.com) has a wide selection of villas all over the island.

RESORTS AND INNS
Under $125

The three one-bedroom cottages at **Samuel's Cottages** (Rt. 10, tel./fax 340/776-6643, www.samuelcottages.com, $100) are cute, clean, and provide a good home base for exploring Cruz Bay and the rest of St. John. Each peach-colored cottage has a full kitchen, cable TV, and phone and can sleep up to five people. The views are of Cruz Bay and Enighed Pond. Be aware that the road traffic and general noisiness of Cruz Bay mean that this is not necessarily a quiet retreat. The cottages generally rent by the week ($600 for seven nights); if you are staying for three nights or less, the rate is $125 per night. Kids under 13 stay free.

The **Inn at Tamarind Court** (340/776-6378, U.S. toll free 800/221-1637, www.tamarindcourt.com, $75–240 winter, $60–170 summer) is a 20-room hotel about three blocks from the heart of Cruz Bay. Rooms range from an apartment that can sleep four people to single economy rooms with a shared bath. All rooms are clean, air-conditioned, and comfortable. The restaurant on-site serves breakfast, lunch, and dinner; guests get a free continental breakfast.

$125-175

The 11-room **St. John Inn** (Enighed, 340/693-8688, U.S. toll free 800/666-7688, fax 340/693-9900, www.stjohninn.com, $140–165 winter, $75–120 summer) is another choice for travelers with more modest budgets. Rooms have a/c, cable TV, phone, refrigerator, coffeemaker, and microwave. Guests can also use the inn's outdoor grill or relax around its teeny pool. The Inn overlooks Enighed Pond.

$175-225

If you want to stay right in the heart of Cruz Bay, try **Suite Dreams** (340/714-3235 or 340/693-8545, www.suitedreamsstjohn.com, $200 winter, $145 summer), two apartments just up the hill from the Lumberyard Complex. These comfortable suites come with full kitchens and excellent views of Cruz Bay and the harbor.

$225-300

Garden by the Sea (Turner Bay, 340/779-4731, www.gardenbythesea.com, $215–240 winter, $125–140 summer) is a charming bed-and-breakfast on the point between Turner and Frank Bays, just outside of Cruz Bay. The house has an elegant cottage feel; rooms are equipped with private baths and air-conditioning, but no phones or television. Full breakfast is served on the wide deck.

Estate Lindholm (Lindholm, 340/776-6121, U.S. toll free 800/322-6335, www.estatelindholm.com, $290–340 winter, $140–190 summer) is a family-run bed-and-breakfast overlooking Cruz Bay. Its 10 rooms come with air-conditioning, cable TV, refrigerators, microwaves, and coffeemakers. A free continental breakfast is served daily.

Over $300

About halfway down the East End Road, past Coral Bay, are the beach houses at █ **Estate Zootenvaal** (Hurricane Hole, 340/776-6321, $275–550 winter, $250–500 summer). The setting is serene—the sound of the gentle surf is about the only noise around—and the cottages elegant yet unpretentious. Accommodations include one-bedroom and two-bedroom cottages, each with a full kitchen and large screened-in porch.

Set along the outskirts of Cruz Bay, **Gallow's Point Resort** (Gallow's Bay, 340/776-6434, U.S. toll free 800/323-7229, fax 340/776-6520, www.gallowspointresort.com, $435–575 winter, $225–375 summer) is a series of individual condominiums, each with four one-bedroom suites. The suites come with full kitchens, a/c, fans, cable TV, and phones. A pool and restaurant are on-site, and Cruz Bay is a short, downhill walk away.

One of the two large resorts on St. John, **The Westin** (Great Cruz Bay, 340/693-8000, U.S. toll free 888/627-7206, www.westinresortstjohn.com, $659–1189 winter, $389–919 summer) sprawls along the beach at Great Cruz Bay. Guests have no real reason to leave the resort; it has a beach, water sports, shopping, a pool, three restaurants, spa, gym, and

ST. JOHN

tennis courts on the grounds. The 282 rooms come with all the amenities you would expect, plus free Starbucks coffee, Nintendo game systems, and two voicemail boxes. Across the street are the Westin Villas, many of which are time-shares.

For decades, **Caneel Bay Resort** (Caneel Bay, 340/776-6111, fax 340/693-8280, www.caneelbay.com, $450–1350 winter, $350–875) has set the standard for barefoot elegance in the Caribbean. Laurance Rockefeller created Caneel Bay in the 1950s as a resort for guests wanting to stay within the boundaries of the new national park. Today, Caneel Bay still attracts guests looking for a luxurious vacation that emphasizes natural beauty and a peaceful setting. The resort's 166 rooms are nestled discreetly into the surroundings. Each guest room is tastefully decorated and comes equipped with a coffeemaker and mini-bar, but no telephones or televisions.

Resort amenities include a pool, seven beaches, tennis courts, free continental breakfast and afternoon tea, evening turn-down service and use of sunfish sailboats and kayaks.

CAMPGROUNDS

Camping is the best way to immerse yourself in the natural beauty of St. John, and the best choice for visitors who don't want to shell out big bucks for a hotel room. Campsites on the island range from bare tent sites to completely equipped eco-cottages. Take note that NPS rules forbid camping anywhere but on established, commercial campsites.

Under $125

【 Maho Bay Camps (340/776-6240, U.S. toll free 800/392-9004, fax 340/776-6504, www.maho.org, $125 winter, $75 summer) sets the standard for Caribbean camping and eco-friendly development. Accommodations are "tent-cottages," built out of wood, canvas, and mesh screening on 16-foot elevated square platforms. The cottages are set among the trees and connected by broad wooden walkways with names like Mongoose Highway and Sandy Landing. Little Maho

Bay, a quiet, protected beach, is at the foot of the camp's hill (a few steps or long hike, depending on which cottage you are in). Each cottage is furnished with two twin beds, a sleeper couch, a two-burner propane stove, a cooler, dishes, fresh linens, towels, a porch, clothesline, lights, fan, and electrical outlets. There are toilets and cold-water showers in the camp's communal bathhouses.

If you want, Maho can be much more than just a place to stay. The camp restaurant serves moderately priced breakfasts and dinners, and its sunset happy hour is especially popular. There's a full-blown activities desk on-site that coordinates Maho's own activities and hooks guests up with outside activity providers. There are art classes, daily yoga sessions, a water sports center, and regular shuttles to town.

Guests who want to be close to nature but prefer a few more creature comforts can choose **Harmony Studios** ($200–225 winter, $120–145 summer), also under Maho ownership and management. The studios employ the latest in sustainable building technology—recycled building materials, solar power, minimal water usage—but provide a level of comfort equivalent to a traditional resort.

Maho Bay opened in 1976 with just 18 cottages; today there are 114, plus the studios, and in winter there is a waiting list. The camp's success speaks to the vision of owner and developer Stanley Selengut, as well as the undeniable pleasure of accommodations nestled so closely to the bosom of St. John.

Get here while you can. Maho's 35-year lease is due to expire in 2011 and will not be renewed. Doomsayers say that a gated community will go up in its place. Others contend hopefully that the camping tradition will continue, but under different management. Whatever happens, the Virgin Islands will lose one of its jewels when Maho closes its doors.

The other big campground on St. John is **Cinnamon Bay Campground** (Cinnamon Bay, 340/776-6330, fax 340/776-6458, www.cinnamonbay.com). Cinnamon Bay has cottages ($110–140 winter, $70–90 summer), prepared tents ($80 winter, $58 summer), and bare sites

($27). Like Maho Bay, Cinnamon Bay is popular, especially with return guests.

The cottages, some of which are beachfront, are fully screened, with electric lights, a terrace, four twin beds, linens, ceiling fans, charcoal grill, propane stove, ice chest, and cooking and eating utensils. The prepared tents sit on raised platforms. Each comes with four twin beds, a propane stove, lantern, ice chest, linens, and cooking and eating utensils. The bare sites fit one large tent or two small ones. A picnic table and charcoal grill are provided.

Cold-water showers and lavatories for all guests are in shared bathhouses. There are group campsites. There is a restaurant on-site that serves three meals a day, and a small store with basic food and supplies (at exorbitant prices).

If you thumb your nose at the relative luxury of St. John's most popular campgrounds, or are just in search of a good place to pitch your tent, consider **Vie's Campground** (Hansen Bay, 340/693-5003, $25–35). Vie, who also runs the popular roadside food stand just over the hill, provides her campers with pit toilets, tanks of rainwater, grills, and a shoreside location. You can bring your own tent ($25) or use one of hers ($35). The campground is remote; no buses and few cars head down this way.

$125-175

The environmentally friendly design of popular Maho Bay Camps was improved upon at Maho's sister resort, **C Estate Concordia** (Concordia, 340/776-6240, U.S. toll free 800/392-9004, fax 340/776-6504, www.maho.org) at the far southeastern tip of the island. Concordia has two kinds of accommodation, 18 eco-tents ($145 winter, $95 summer) and nine studios ($135–210). The eco-tents, which can sleep up to six people, are constructed with recycled material and employ modern eco-friendly technology to keep their environmental footprint minimal. Four are accessible to disabled travelers. The studios, which were half-built condominiums when developer Stanley Selengut bought the estate, are more traditional villa-style accommodations, but they have been retrofitted, where possible, with environmentally friendly appliances and furniture.

Guests at Concordia enjoy a few luxuries absent at Maho Bay Camps. Each unit has a private bath with solar-heated shower, and there is a pool on the property. They also have spectacular views of Salt Pond Bay and Ram's Head. There are plans for more units, including luxury eco-friendly villas, as well as a restaurant and amphitheater.

ST. JOHN

Food

St. John is known for its elegant restaurants, which combine sophisticated cuisine with stunning settings. For upscale dining, there is no better island in the Virgin archipelago. For more casual fare, the selection is limited to a few beachfront snack bars and barbecue joints.

CRUZ BAY
Casual Dining

For cheap eats, you can't do better than **Joe's Diner** (340/776-6888, 6 A.M.–6 P.M. Mon.–Sat., $3–9), an open-air lunch counter around the corner from the post office. Joe's Diner opens early for the breakfast crowd, serving johnnycakes, pâtés (fried meat-stuffed bread),

and eggs. The rest of the day you can choose from sandwiches, burgers, and fried chicken.

You will smell **C Uncle Joe's BBQ** (Waterfront, 340/693-8806, 6–9 P.M. daily, 11 A.M.–2 P.M. Sat., $6–12) before you see this tiny barbecue stand that teems with people, even during the week. Joe grills chicken, ribs, and steak and serves them with sides like rice and peas, coleslaw, and macaroni salad. You'll be hard-pressed to find a more filling and better-tasting meal for under $10.

At lunchtime, St. Johnians head to **Dolphin Market** (Centerline Road, 11 A.M.–1 P.M. Mon.–Fri., $5–10), where the takeout deli serves generous plates of local dishes like grilled fish, barbecued chicken, and stewed ox-tail. Side dishes include boiled plantain, sweet potatoes, macaroni pie, and rice and peas. Forget about the Caribbean-style fare of Cruz Bay's more genteel eateries, this is your best bet for real local food. Get here early (around noon) for the best choices. This place serves takeout only.

Delis and Coffee Shops

All the sandwiches at **Deli Grotto** (Mongoose Junction, 340/777-3061, 7 A.M.–6 P.M. Mon.–Sat., 8 A.M.–3 P.M. Sun., $4–9) weigh in at under $8, making it a good place for a low-key and affordable meal. Breakfast here is a real attraction, with breakfast sandwiches, omelettes, pancakes, French toast, and oatmeal. And don't forget the smoothies, coffee, tea, and chai. Dine in air-conditioning or outside on the patio.

On the road to the Westin, **Simple Feast** (South Shore Rd., 340/714-7989, 7 A.M.–7 P.M. daily) is a small grocery with a nice deli in the back. It also serves carryout dinners, salads, and desserts.

Paradise Café (Wharfside Village, 340/779-4810, 6:30 A.M.–9 P.M.) is a booth with nearby tables in the middle of the Cruz Bay shopping district. Light breakfasts and lunches are available, as well as smoothies, baked goods, and cold drinks.

Sit-Down Restaurants

Located in a courtyard in the heart of Cruz Bay, **Rhumb Lines** (Mead's Plaza, 340/776-0303, 11 A.M.–2 P.M. and 5:30–10 P.M. Wed.–Mon., $15–23) serves Pacific Rim cuisine with a Caribbean touch. Entrées include dishes like pad Thai, fresh grilled seafood, and mojo pork, or try a few of the "pupu portions" of tempura shrimp, spring rolls, dumplings, and samosas.

If you get a hankering for Chinese food, the **China Shack** (The Marketplace, 340/715-4998, 11 A.M.–3 P.M. Mon.–Fri. and 4:30–9 P.M. nightly, $8–20) will fix you up. The menu is standard Chinese takeout, with vegetarian, beef, seafood, and chicken entrées. They deliver to locales around Cruz Bay for $5, if you order at least $25 of food.

A long-standing island favorite, **The Fish Trap** (Raintree Court, 340/693-9994, www.thefishtrap.com, 4:30–9:30 P.M. Tues.–Sun., $10–44) serves shrimp, scallops, and fresh fish, as well as pasta, steaks, and burgers.

Texan Jean Jewell brings the taste of the American southwest to St. John at **Texas Coast Café** (Cruz Bay, 340/776-6908, 8 A.M.–9 P.M. daily). At breakfast, the menu features breakfast burritos, huevos rancheros, and biscuits and gravy; the rest of the day you can dine on chicken-fried steak, taco salad, and burritos.

Polli's Mexican Restaurant (Northshore Road, 340/775-4550, 11 A.M.–9:30 P.M. Mon.–Sat., $10–25) serves Mexican burritos and taco salads, as well as down-home cooking like barbecue, meatloaf, and fried chicken. There is a fish fry every Friday night.

On the waterfront across from the National Park Service headquarters, **Margarita Phil's** (340/693-8400, noon–9:30 P.M. Tues.–Sat., $14–20) specializes in quesadillas, burritos, and sizzling fajitas, as well as fresh seafood. Chef Phil Hoffman also serves up some killer frozen drinks.

The leader in Caribbean cuisine is **Morgan's Mango** (340/693-8141, 5:30–10 P.M., $9–30), a cute, inviting restaurant on the waterfront about halfway to Mongoose Junction. Dishes on the menu are labeled according to their island of origin and include Cuban, Jamaican, Haitian, and Virgin Island specialties. There is also a vegetarian plate. Live music is on tap Tuesday and Thursday nights.

Tucked away on a side street in Cruz Bay, **Lime Inn** (Lemon Tree Mall, 340/779-4199, 11:30 A.M.–3 P.M. Mon.–Fri., 5:30–10 P.M. nightly, $8–12 lunch, $18–24 dinner) is a favorite among locals and longtime visitors. The courtyard dining room is decorated with plants and a waterfall. At lunch, choose from gourmet salads, pasta, and seafood specials. The dinner menu features fresh seafood, steaks, pasta specials, and more. Wednesday night brings an all-you-can-eat shrimp fest.

The view and the varied menu are the main reasons to come to **Pastory Gardens** (340/777-3147, 11 A.M.–midnight, $8–25), an open-air restaurant about a mile outside of Cruz Bay along Centerline Road. You can choose from the casual bar menu (no fewer than five burger variations), a raft of different salads, or elegant dinner entrées. This is a nice place to watch the sunset, and you can stretch your legs after eating with a game of mini-golf.

Greek for "an agreeable and leisurely passing of time," **Asolare** (Caneel Hill, 340/779-4747, 5:30–10 P.M., $33–40) serves gourmet meals from its dining room overlooking Cruz Bay. The creative menu features lamb, lobster, pork tenderloin, and fresh fish.

At **La Tapa** (Cruz Bay, 340/693-7755, $23–42), chef Alexandra Ewald serves Mediterranean cuisine, with an emphasis on fresh seafood. Diners can choose entrée-sized "large plates" or sample several "small plates." Specialties include Prince Edward Island mussels and paella.

Markets

For grocery shopping, try **Starfish Market** (The Marketplace, 340/779-4949, 7:30 A.M.–9 P.M.), a full-service grocery store just outside of Cruz Bay. In town, **Dolphin Market** (340/776-5322, 7:30 A.M.–11 P.M.) is your best bet. Prices are high; consider bringing food from St. Thomas if you're on a budget.

NORTH SHORE

There are not many eateries inside the National Park boundaries. There are plenty of picnic tables, though. If you don't pack your own food, here are your choices.

While geared mostly to guests and staff at nearby Maho Bay Camps, **Pavilion Restaurant** (Maho Bay Camps, 340/776-6226, 7:30–9:30 A.M., 5:30–7:30 P.M. daily, $13–18) is open to the public for breakfast and dinner daily. There are no waiters; order and pay for your food at the counter and wait for your name to be called at the window. At breakfast you can get muffins, cereal, and fruit, or more substantial omelettes, pancakes, and French toast. For dinner, each evening has its own theme, ranging from Italian to West Indian. Call ahead to find out the fla-

vor for the day. Sunsets are spectacular here, and happy hour drinks come with free popcorn. The camp's shop sells sandwiches, ice cream, drinks, and other picnic supplies.

There is a casual restaurant at Cinnamon Bay. **T'ree Lizards** (Cinnamon Bay Campground, 340/776-6330, $14–24) serves breakfast, lunch, and dinner daily. T'ree Lizards mostly attracts Cinnamon Bay campers, but others may find it to be a convenient and relatively affordable place to eat, especially at lunch. The lunch menu features sandwiches; for dinner, choose grilled chicken, steak, or nightly specials.

No restaurant can claim a better view than **C Chateau Bordeaux** (Bordeaux Mountain, 340/776-6611, 5:30–10 P.M. daily, $28–38). Located atop Bordeaux Mountain between Cruz Bay and Coral Bay, this cottage restaurant serves some of the most elegant cuisine on St. John. The intimate dining room overlooks Coral Bay. If you're here for a full moon, don't miss the opportunity to watch the moon rise over Coral Bay. The menu here is classy and sophisticated; try the Caribbean lobster crepe or Chilean sea bass.

CORAL BAY

M&M Donkey Diner (East End Rd., 340/693-5240, 8 A.M.–noon Wed.–Sat., 8 A.M.–1 P.M. Sun., 4–8 P.M. Fri.) is the place to come for breakfast. Islanders swear by the café's pancakes, eggs, and French toast. M&M also does pizza on Friday nights—another very popular event.

Calling itself "a pretty OK place," **Skinny Legs** (Emmaus, 340/779-4982, 11 A.M.–9 P.M.) embodies the spirit of Coral Bay when it was just a remote and unpretentious community of free spirits, salty dogs, and welcoming locals. This is the place for burgers, sandwiches, and salads, but don't ask for fries—they don't serve them. This is the first choice for Coral Bay's live-aboard sailors, who anchor out in the Bay and dinghy up to Skinny Legs' dock.

C Sweet Plantains (340/777-4653, 6–9 P.M., $18–25) delivers an imaginative menu with fresh flavors and style. The menu was crafted by owners Rose and Prince Adams,

ST. JOHN

who are very much present in the kitchen and behind the bar. Entrées include braised short ribs, fresh fish, roti, and fantastic West Indian and East Asian curries. Many meals come with the namesake sweet plantains.

Outside Coral Bay

Set on a quiet bay a few miles south of Coral Bay, **[Miss Lucy's** (Friis Bay, 340/693-5244, $7–30) is one of the best places to go for a plate of authentic local food. Miss Lucy serves fried or grilled fish, local style, with side dishes like plantain, peas and rice, and potato stuffing. The best thing about Miss Lucy's is that if you or your companion doesn't want local food, she has international favorites too. On full moons, Miss Lucy's throws a special party complete with a traditional Caribbean pig roast.

Vie's Snack Shack (340/693-5033, $4–8) is the only place to get food and drink after you leave Coral Bay proper and head out onto St. John's eastern tip. Stop by for a hot dog, johnnycake, or some of Vie's famous conch fritters.

Markets

For food shopping, choose between **Love City Mini-Mart** (7 A.M.–9:30 P.M. daily), a small but well-stocked grocery just past the gas station in Coral Bay, and **Lily's Gourmet Market,** (340/777-3335), an upscale market in the Coccoloba Shopping Center just past Island Blues. As with all shopping on St. John, expect to pay premium prices at both establishments.

Practicalities

INFORMATION AND SERVICES
Tourist Offices

The Department of Tourism claims to have a visitor information center (340/776-6450) in Cruz Bay, next to the post office. The building and sign are there, but from what I can tell, this office is almost never open. Far more reliable is the Virgin Islands National Park's **Cruz Bay Visitor Center** (340/776-6201, 8 A.M.–4:30 P.M. daily). Rangers here can provide you with an excellent free map, brochures on hiking and snorkeling, and the best selection of books about the history, culture, and natural resources of the island. This is also where you can find out about upcoming Park Service hikes, lectures, and demonstrations, as well as pick up a calendar of events sponsored by the Friends of the Park organization. There is also an exhibit about the park, public restrooms, and a picnic table.

The visitors center is located in an elegant, high-ceilinged building on the far shore of the existing car ferry and cargo port at Cruz Bay, opposite the customs and immigration buildings.

Maps and Charts

The best map of St. John is published by the National Park Service. The full-color foldout map shows roads, hiking trails, beaches, and park facilities and offers a short introduction to the history and natural features of the island. It is available free from the NPS Visitor Center.

Widely available, the free *St. John Guidebook* map is useful for finding restaurants and stores, many of which are marked on the map. It is also especially good for finding your way around Cruz Bay.

The St. John map inside the pocket road map available at car rental agencies is about the size of a postage stamp, but it can be helpful in a pinch.

If you require nautical charts, you will have to buy them on St. Thomas before you come over to St. John. The National Park Service publishes a guide for mariners that details rules on anchoring, mooring, vessel size, and safety. The guide also has a map that shows the locations of NPS moorings, but it should not be used for navigation.

Libraries

The Elaine Ione Sprauve Library (340/776-6359, 9 A.M.–5 P.M. Mon.–Fri.) has a good collection of fiction and nonfiction, magazines, and newspapers. When it is working, you can log onto the Internet for $2 per hour.

Media

St. John events and happenings are covered in the St. Thomas–based *Virgin Island Daily News,* which you will find for sale at stores around the island. For more detail, and the best listings of local events, pick up the two St. John papers.

St. John Tradewinds ($.75, www.stjohntradewindsnews.com) is a weekly paper published every Monday. *St. John Sun Times* (free) is published monthly. Both are a good source of information on events, live music, and the issue du jour.

Emergencies

There is no hospital on St. John; emergency medical care must be obtained off-island on St. Thomas or Puerto Rico. Doctors and nurses at the **Myra Keating Health Center** (340/693-8900) at Susannaberg provide routine medical care.

Cruz Bay Family Practice (Cruz Bay, 340/776-6789) is another choice if you need to see a doctor.

The **Chelsea Drug Store** (The Marketplace, Cruz Bay, 340/776-4888) is open 9 A.M.–7 P.M. Mon.–Fri., 9 A.M.–6:30 P.M. Sat., and 9 A.M.–4:30 P.M. Sunday. Or try **St. John Drug Center** (Cruz Bay, 9 A.M.–6 P.M. Mon.–Sat.) at the Boulon Center.

Police can be reached by calling 340/693-8880, 340/776-6262, or 911.

Banks

There are two banks on St. John, which are located right across the street from each other in Cruz Bay, near Connections. Both have ATMs that accept major U.S. debit and credit cards.

Most businesses on St. John accept credit cards and travelers checks. Personal checks are not accepted; cash is preferred by some smaller outfits.

Post Offices and Communications

St. John's lone post office is located in Cruz Bay, near the waterfront. Postal rates are the same as in the continental United States.

One hates to imagine the consequences if **Connections** (Cruz Bay, 340/776-6922, 8:30 A.M.–5:30 P.M. Mon.–Fri., 8:30 A.M.–1 P.M. Sat., or Coral Bay, 340/779-4994, 9:30 A.M.–5:30 P.M. Mon.–Fri., 9:30 A.M.–1:30 P.M. Sat.) suddenly ceased to exist. These guys can help you mail letters and packages, make phone calls, send faxes, check your email, make copies, notarize documents, and wire money. They can also answer questions, book excursions, and provide tourist information. There is a bulletin board with help wanted, for rent, and for sale postings, as well as the best-stocked gallery of handbills for places to stay on the island. It is probably the most highly trafficked spot in town for locals, many of whom get their mail here. You'll pay $4 for 15 minutes on the Internet.

Surf Da Web (Cruz Bay, 340/693-9152, 9 A.M.–6 P.M. Mon.–Sat.), at the Marketplace, also has Internet access.

In Coral Bay, **Keep Me Posted** (Coccoloba Shopping Center, 8 A.M.–6 P.M. Mon.–Fri., 8 A.M.–2 P.M. Sat.) has cheap Internet access: $2 gets you 15 minutes. It also provides mail forwarding, faxing, and local and long-distance phone calls.

Photography

Film, photo processing, and digital image printing are all available at **Cruz Bay Photo** (Wharfside Village, 340/779-4313).

Launderettes

St. John's "Laundry Row" is located along the South Shore Road, between the Texaco Station and the Tamarind Court Inn. Try **Santos Laundromat** (340/693-7733). A wash will cost about $3.

GETTING THERE

There is no airport on St. John; the only way to get here is by boat.

From St. Thomas

Transportation Services (340/776-6282) and **Varlack Ventures** (340/776-6412) operate ferries between Red Hook, St. Thomas, and Cruz Bay. Ferries depart Red Hook at 6:30 A.M., 7:30 A.M., and then hourly 8 A.M.–midnight. Return ferries leave Cruz Bay every hour 6 A.M.–11 P.M. The fare for the 20-minute ride is $3 one-way for adults and $1 one-way for children under 12.

From Charlotte Amalie, ferries leave hourly 9 A.M.–11 A.M., hourly 1 P.M.–4 P.M., and at 4:30 P.M. Fare for the 45-minute trip is $7 one-way for adults.

Caneel Bay and the Westin provide private ferries that bring guests directly to the resort.

From the British Virgin Islands

Inter-Island Boat Services (Tortola, 284/495-4166, and Cruz Bay, 340/776-6597) provides ferry service from West End, Tortola, to Cruz Bay for $45 round-trip.

GETTING AROUND
Taxis

Taxis are widely available on St. John, especially in Cruz Bay and at the popular north shore beaches. When you disembark the St. Thomas ferry in Cruz Bay you will be bombarded by taxi drivers offering to take you where you need to go. Taxi rates are set by the government. From Cruz Bay to Trunk Bay you will pay $5.50 per person; from Cruz Bay to Maho Bay it's $11 per person; and from Cruz Bay to Salt Pond Bay the rate is $15 per person.

If you need to call for a taxi, try **C&C Taxi Service** (340/693-8164) or **St. John Taxi Services** (340/693-7530). To complain about a taxi, contact the Taxi Commission at 340/774-3130. This agency can also help trace lost or missing luggage.

COURTESY OF U.S. VIRGIN ISLANDS DEPARTMENT OF TOURISM

ST. JOHN

the Cruz Bay ferry dock

Rental Cars

Rental vehicles are a popular way to get around St. John. This is the kind of place where you want the wind in your hair and the freedom to go wherever you want.

Rental companies based on St. John only rent four-wheel-drive sport utility vehicles. This means that you will pay more for a rental on St. John ($60–65 per day is the going rate), but you will also be able to explore areas inaccessible to cars and low-riding vehicles. It is a good idea to reserve your car well ahead of time, since rentals get booked up, especially in the winter season.

Hertz (Cruz Bay, 340/693-7580, www .hertz.com) is the only major rental car company with an office on St. John. Independent rental companies include **Best Rent A Car** (Enighed, 340/693-8177); **Courtesy Car Rental** (Enighed, 340/776-6650); **Delbert Hill Jeep Rental** (Cruz Bay, 340/776-6637); **O'Conner Car Rental** (Cruz Bay, 340/776-6343); and **Sun and Sand Car Rental** (Cruz Bay, 340/776-6374).

An alternative for the budget traveler is to rent a car on St. Thomas, where rates tend to be lower, and bring it to St. John on one of the car barges that sail from Red Hook, St. Thomas, to St. John. This practice is frowned upon by St. John car rental companies, for obvious reasons, and can pose a real hassle if you have the bad luck to require mechanical help, since you will probably have to get it back to St. Thomas yourself before the rental company will be able to help you. Call **Republic Barge Service** (340/779-4000) for a schedule and rates for its car ferry.

Buses

One of the best things about St. John is its bus, which runs hourly from Cruz Bay to Coral Bay and Salt Pond Bay, along Centerline Road. It costs just $1 no matter how far you go along this route. The bus picks up passengers in Cruz Bay at the passenger ferry dock and stops along the way at the orange and brown VITRAN bus signs. It turns around in Coral Bay at the base of Fort Berg hill and turns around again at the parking lot for Salt Pond Bay. Call 340/774-0165 for a schedule.

ST. JOHN

TORTOLA

Tortola is the hub of the British Virgin Islands: home to its quaint capital, modern airport, magnificent beaches, and the most wide-ranging array of activities, accommodations, and restaurants in the territory. The island's spine runs east to west, punctuated by ridges that descend to the Atlantic Ocean to the north and the Caribbean Sea to the south. Between these ridges are bays, some edged by sandy beaches and seaside communities. High hills and steep, windy roads make exploring exciting (or terrifying, depending on your perspective) and the views that greet you from the top will take your breath away. At its longest point, Tortola is 12 miles long; at its widest it is three miles across. Its southern shore, washed by the Caribbean Sea, is generally calm and home to marinas and the largest settlements. The north shore has the best beaches and, in season, the best waves.

Tortola is an island of contrasts—a place where chickens and goats share the roadways with the latest model cars and trucks. Of all the British Virgin Islands it is the most developed—three-quarters of the territory's 23,000 people live here—and as such it is the island most acquainted with the scourges of development: crime, traffic jams, and environmental damage. But despite the inroads of change, Tortola is still by and large a sleepy, green jewel willing to content itself with the daily rhythms of life.

Though it is touched in places by large-scale development, Tortola remains a rustic island. For visitors, it offers a comfortable balance between creature comforts (grocery

© SUSANNA HENIGHAN

HIGHLIGHTS

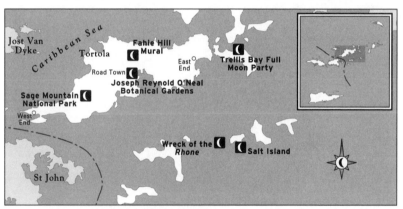

◖ Joseph Reynold O'Neal Botanical Gardens: A four-acre oasis in the heart of Road Town, these botanical gardens are a living museum of colorful and unusual tropical plants and animals (page 145).

◖ Fahie Hill Mural: An ode to Tortola's past, this colorful mural painted on a roadside retaining wall depicts islanders' way of life after Emancipation but before widespread development (page 146).

◖ Sage Mountain National Park: Cool, moist, and remote, Tortola's Sage Mountain is the highest point in the Virgin Islands and a hiker's dream (page 147).

◖ Salt Island: Take a trip back in time at Salt Island, where the small settlement seems to be from a different era. Hike around the salt pond where islanders still harvest salt annually (page 158).

◖ Wreck of the *Rhone:* It's believed by some to be the best wreck dive in the Caribbean. Swim past portholes, cabins, and the propeller of the RMS *Rhone*, sharing the experience with a dizzying variety of fish (page 160).

◖ Trellis Bay Full Moon Party: This funky full moon celebration on Beef Island features traditional music, arts, and Aragorn Dick-Read's flaming fireballs (page 163).

LOOK FOR ◖ TO FIND RECOMMENDED SIGHTS, ACTIVITIES, DINING, AND LODGING.

stores, nice restaurants, hospital, and modern shops) and the unusual and obscure (dirt roads, goats and chickens, quiet mountain peaks, and dusty mom-and-pop shops). Tortola has a more "regular-people" feel than Virgin Gorda and St. John—there are accommodations and attractions for nearly every budget—but it still maintains a level of refinement hard to find on St. Thomas.

Tortola is an island that caters to a wide range of tastes and interests. It is an ideal jumping off point for water-based pursuits: sailing, diving, snorkeling, and windsurfing are the most popular. Its marinas are home to the Virgin Islands' largest fleet of charter yachts. Landlubbers will find two excellent national parks, several historical attractions, and dozens of quiet, undisturbed beaches. Meals can be had from jerk chicken stands in the island capital or under the stars at a fine restaurant.

PLANNING YOUR TIME

You could visit all of Tortola's major attractions in a day, but why would you want to?

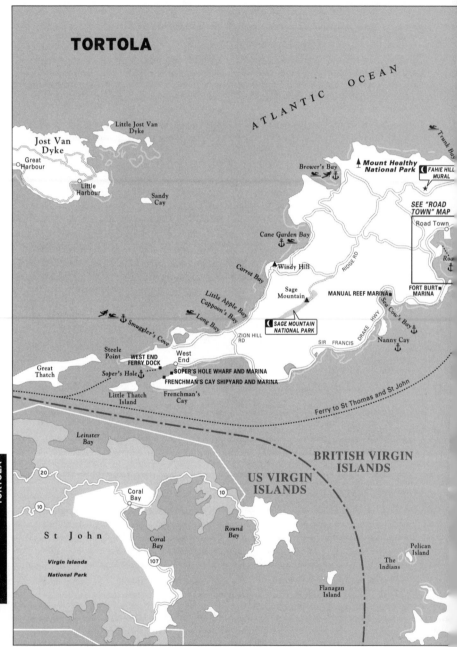

TORTOLA

ATLANTIC OCEAN

Jost Van Dyke

Little Jost Van Dyke

Great Harbour

Little Harbour

Sandy Cay

Trunk Bay

Mount Healthy National Park

Brewer's Bay

FAHIE HILL MURAL

SEE "ROAD TOWN" MAP

Road Town

Cane Garden Bay

Carrot Bay

Windy Hill

RIDGE RD

Roa

Sage Mountain

MANUAL REEF MARINA

FORT BURT MARINA

Little Apple Bay

Cappoon's Bay

Long Bay

SAGE MOUNTAIN NATIONAL PARK

Sea Cow's Bay

Smuggler's Cove

ZION HILL RD

Steele Point

West End

SIR FRANCIS DRAKE HWY

Nanny Cay

Great Thatch

WEST END FERRY DOCK

Soper's Hole

SOPER'S HOLE WHARF AND MARINA

FRENCHMAN'S CAY SHIPYARD AND MARINA

Little Thatch Island

Frenchman's Cay

Ferry to St Thomas and St John

Leinster Bay

BRITISH VIRGIN ISLANDS

US VIRGIN ISLANDS

20

10

Coral Bay

10

St John

Coral Bay

Round Bay

Pelican Island

The Indians

107

Virgin Islands National Park

Flanagan Island

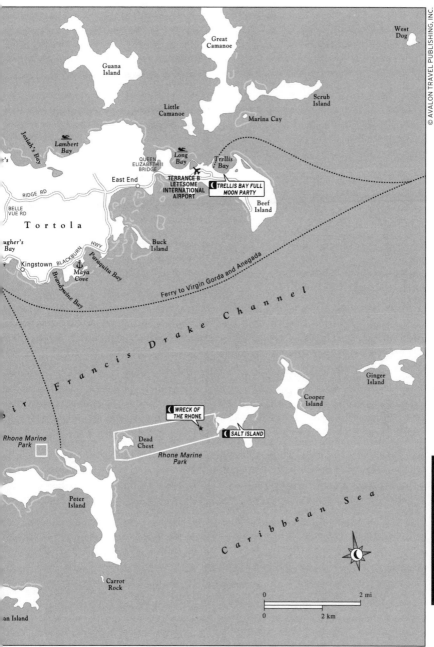

© AVALON TRAVEL PUBLISHING, INC.

West Dog

Great Camanoe

Guana Island

Scrub Island

Little Camanoe

Marina Cay

Josiah's Bay

Lambert Bay

Long Bay

Trellis Bay

's

QUEEN ELIZABETH II BRIDGE

East End

TERRANCE B LETTSOME INTERNATIONAL AIRPORT

TRELLIS BAY FULL MOON PARTY

RIDGE RD

BELLE VUE RD

Beef Island

T o r t o l a

Buck Island

ugher's Bay

HWY

Kingstown

BLACKBURN

Maya Cove

Paraquita Bay

Brambwine Bay

Ferry to Virgin Gorda and Anegada

S i r   F r a n c i s   D r a k e   C h a n n e l

Ginger Island

Cooper Island

WRECK OF THE RHONE

SALT ISLAND

Rhone Marine Park

Dead Chest

Rhone Marine Park

Peter Island

C a r i b b e a n   S e a

Carrot Rock

an Island

0   2 mi

0   2 km

TORTOLA

People don't exhaust themselves with that kind of frenzied activity here, and you would be silly to buck the trend. The whole point of vacationing in a place like Tortola is to slow down.

Ten days is enough time to explore Tortola, figuring in a few do-nothing days spent on the beach and one or two day trips to surrounding islands. Look for accommodations outside of Road Town—the capital city offers little in the way of ambience. If your first priority is the beach and your second is the beach bar, you will be happiest at Cane Garden Bay, the island's premier beach with the widest array of accommodations, restaurants, and entertainment choices. The only downside—and it can be significant depending on your disposition—are the throngs of cruise ship visitors that descend on the bay many days from October to March.

If you prefer to make a quieter beach your home base, look for places to stay near Apple Bay, Brewer's Bay, or Josiah's Bay—all nice beaches that lean on the quiet side. Remember that accommodations away from the beach can be a good value, and hillside rooms generally have better views and more breeze than those directly on the water. Nowhere on Tortola is more than 10 minutes from a beach.

Whatever your interests, there are a few things you should try not to miss during a trip to Tortola. Road Town's narrow, winding Main Street is a diamond in the rough, where modern office buildings rub shoulders with centuries-old traditional island homes and buildings. A walk down Main Street can culminate in a visit to the town's **J. R. O'Neal Botanical Gardens,** an oasis of tranquility where you can see tropical flowers, trees, and animals.

Hire a rental car for at least a day to drive along the Ridge Road, a narrow paved road that teeters along Tortola's backbone. Your tour should take you to **Sage Mountain National Park,** home to the Virgin Islands' highest peak. It's also the only place on the island where you will see forests untouched since the time of Columbus. For a glimpse into more modern history, visit the **Fahie Hill mural,** a series of colorful paintings depicting life in the islands before tourism and development changed them for good.

If your vacation coincides with a full moon, you should head to Trellis Bay for a low-key **Full Moon Party,** where you will find stilt-walking mocko jumbies, traditional music, and real great balls of fire.

Because Tortola is the transportation hub of the British Virgin Islands, it is easy to make day trips to any of the neighboring islands. Ferries run daily to St. Thomas, St. John, Jost Van Dyke, Virgin Gorda, and Peter Island, and there is ferry service three days a week to Anegada. If you are staying for more than a few days, it is well worth the time and expense to see at least one other island. Snorkelers and divers should not miss a chance to explore the **Wreck of the Rhone;** while you are there, stop at **Salt Island** for a look at one of the only remaining traditional island settlements in the Virgin Islands.

DRIVING TOUR

Tortola is well suited to driving tours, but you should be sure your wheels can handle steep hills before taking off. The driving tour described here will take at least three hours and can take all day if you make frequent stops or detours.

Head east from Road Town along the Blackburn Highway, continue through East End, and cross the bridge to Beef Island, where you can check out Trellis Bay and Long Bay. Stop at D' Best Cup on Trellis Bay for a coffee or ice cream.

Retrace your steps back to Tortola and into East End. Take Little Dix Road (just before the police station) through the residential community. Be sure to drive slowly and look out for goats, children, potholes, and speed bumps. At the top of the steep Lambert Hill, turn right onto a new concrete road that follows the ridge. Look to your left for nice views of East End and the Sir Francis Drake Channel.

The road passes apartment buildings before plunging steeply to a four-way intersection. Turn right for a detour to Josiah's Bay, or continue straight on the Ridge Road.

Follow the Ridge Road for the next five

miles or so as it climbs gradually past the communities of Hope Hill, Bellevue, Great Mountain, and Meyers, among others. Pull off the road onto the grass verge (where there is one!) if you want to take photographs along the way. Roll your windows down and feel the cool mountaintop breezes. Look on your left for the **Fahie Hill Mural.** To park, pull off the road in a straight section and look out for traffic.

Shortly after you pass Skyworld Restaurant, the road descends, and you will come to a stop sign. Turn left to return to Road Town, or turn right to continue the tour along the Ridge Road. About 50 yards from the stop sign is Rudy's Bar and another crossroads. Stop for a drink and enjoy the breeze up here. When you're done, turn right and head down Soldier's Hill into Cane Garden Bay. Myette's or Stanley's make good lunchtime pit stops. Stretch your legs at the Callwood Rum Distillery.

Now you will follow the coastal road through Cane Garden Bay, up to Ballast Bay, and down Windy Hill, a series of steep switchbacks that take you to Carrot Bay. Stay on the coastal road as it passes through Apple Bay. If you arrive before 2 P.M., Islands Café is a good place for lunch.

Turn left onto Zion Hill Road, right next to Nan's Gallery. This is a great place to pick up a unique gift for the folks back home. Zion Hill is a short climb, and the road puts you out next to Big Ben's Gas Station on Drakes Highway. You can turn right to take a detour to West End and Frenchman's Cay, where you will find several different restaurants and bars, or turn left and follow Drakes Highway all the way back to Road Town.

Sights

ROAD TOWN

The capital of the British Virgin Islands, Road Town sprawls along the shore of Road Harbour, its namesake, a deepwater port on the south-central Caribbean coast of Tortola. (Road was once a common word for a harbor. Early writings refer to this area of Tortola simply as "The Road.") Steep hillsides rush down to the shore on all sides, creating what looks like a giant amphitheater, with Road Town as the stage.

For most of its history, Road Town ended at the seaward-facing side of Main Street; the sea lapped against the backyards of homes on the southern side of the narrow old street. In the 1960s a private developer filled in what has become known as Wickham's Cay I and II (named after an islet consumed by the landfill), creating dozens of acres of new real estate for commercial development. Today, this new part of town is the commercial and administrative center of Road Town. Additional landfill was completed in 2005 next to the Road Town ferry terminal; the new land is reportedly to be used for a boardwalk, park, and expanded ferry facility.

Road Town is like an adolescent who has reached the awkward stage. Planning here has been haphazard, the effects being poor traffic design, lack of parking, and spotty sidewalks. A recent effort to build more sidewalks, plant trees, and create crosswalks has made it a little easier to get around on foot, but it is still hard going for pedestrians.

Road Town possesses little of the old-world charm that exists in other port towns in the Virgin Islands. After all, it operated in the shadow of ports like Charlotte Amalie and Christiansted during the plantation era. A townwide fire in 1853 that destroyed nearly every building did not help things.

Despite its flaws, Road Town has a certain appeal, embodied by its ramshackle appearance, roaming chickens, and the constant ebb and flow of people.

Road Town's main thoroughfare is Waterfront Drive, which follows the waterfront as far as the Crafts Alive shopping area before

TORTOLA AND THE TURTLE DOVE MYTH

It is said that Tortola was named by Christopher Columbus, who christened the island Land of the Turtle Dove after the birds he saw here. This story, while quaint, is untrue.

In truth, Columbus named Tortola *Santa Ana*, a moniker that did not stick.

It was Dutch settlers who gave the island the name that stayed. These early settlers were reminded of Tholen, a small island off the western coast of the Netherlands. They called it *Tor Tholen* (New Tholen) after this island. When English settlers came, the Dutch name was anglicized to today's Tortola.

Turtle doves, properly called *Zenaida* doves, do live on Tortola, as they do on many other islands in the Caribbean. Reddish brown with light brown heads, turtle doves are best identified by the iridescent purple on their necks and white-tipped tail feathers.

turning inland. Waterfront Drive ends at Road Town's main roundabout, where the town's central arteries meet, and runs roughly parallel to Main Street.

The best bet for parking in Road Town is at the public lot next to the Road Town ferry terminal.

Road Town is generally safe, even at night, although some areas are known for the criminal activity that tends to take place in them. Scatliffe Alley, a narrow road that runs from the Sunday Morning Well to the Fire and Rescue Station, is best avoided.

Main Street

There is no better place to soak up Road Town's charm, such as it is, than on narrow and winding Main Street, home to historic buildings, museums, boutiques, and cafés. It is a wonderful place for an early morning or late afternoon stroll and has the best shopping on Tortola.

Explore Main Street on foot; it simply is not practical or pleasant to navigate it in a car. The

sights presented here can easily be turned into a walking tour that begins at Old Government House, on the western end of Main Street, and concludes at the Legislative Council chambers in the center of town. From there you can easily find the J. R. O'Neal Botanical Gardens about two blocks away. Plan on at least one hour to do this one-mile walk, more if you spend a lot of time in the shops and museums.

Old Government House Museum, (284/ 494-4091, www.oghmuseum.org, 9 A.M.–2 P.M. Mon.–Sat., $3 adults, children under 10 free) on the hill behind the Governor's Office at the western end of Main Street, is a study of the island's colonial past and present. The white, Spanish-inspired home was built in the late 1920s after the original Government House was destroyed in a powerful 1924 hurricane. The building served as the home of the island's British governor until the mid-1990s, when it was decided it was no longer up to the task. While in use, it was often referred to as Olympus by islanders because of its position overlooking Road Town and, presumably, because of the superior attitude of those who inhabited it.

After years of debate over the future of the building—and a very real proposal to tear it down—Government House underwent modest restoration and reopened as a museum in 2003. A new residence for the governor was built next to the old one. You can see the tennis court as you walk up to the museum entrance.

The museum's exhibits include historical paraphernalia, such as a guest book signed by Queen Elizabeth II, and the plumed pith helmet worn by governors at parades and ceremonial occasions up until 2000. The dining and sitting rooms of the museum are set up as they would have been during earlier days. Upstairs is a library that contains an ad hoc but rich selection of books and articles about the British Virgin Islands. There are nice views of Road Harbor from the museum's second-floor veranda. The museum's shop sells books, crafts, and gifts.

Across from the downtown ferry jetty is the **Sir Olva Georges Plaza,** named for the first British Virgin Islander to be knighted by the Queen. Sir Georges lived on Main

Old Government House, built in the 1920s, is now a museum.

Street in a home that has now been converted into a trendy restaurant. Before reclamation changed the shoreline, Sir Olva Georges Plaza served as the main jetty and market square for Tortola. During slavery, it was the site of slave auctions. After emancipation, the square retained its prominence as a center for trade and commerce. A 1920s visitor described the weekly market held there:

> The sellers mostly squatted on the ground with their produce in front of them in calabashes, in trays, or displayed on old sacking. Everyone appeared radiant as the sun and the sea, exchanging greetings of the marketplace, chattering and gesticulating whether anyone attended or no. ... A row of brown sloops from the islands lay moored alongside the white glare of the wharf, their sails furled, lazily rocking in the blue-lit waters.

Today, the plaza is a quiet place to sit, rest, and watch the comings and goings of Road Town life. It comes to life for occasional events and performances, especially at Christmastime.

Across Main Street from Sir Olva Georges Plaza is the **Old Administration Building,** which today houses the Road Town Post Office and several other government offices. It was from this building that the British Virgin Islands were administered for many years, until the mammoth Central Administration Building was completed in 1993 and most offices moved there.

The Virgin Islands Folk Museum (98 Main Street, 284/494-3701 ext. 5005, 8:30 A.M.–4:30 P.M. Mon.–Fri., free)is up a short flight of stairs in a traditional home built by shipwright Joseph Wilfred Penn in 1911. The three-room museum houses a small collection of pre-Columbian and plantation-era artifacts, an exhibit of traditional architecture, and crockery salvaged from the wreck of the RMS *Rhone,* which sank off Salt Island in 1867. There is no razzle-dazzle to the exhibits, but if you are truly interested in the BVI's history the Folk Museum

TORTOLA

THE HANGING OF ARTHUR HODGE

For a brief moment in the spring of 1811, events that took place on Tortola held all the West Indies and much of Great Britain transfixed. The event in question was the trial and execution of an influential and wealthy planter, Arthur Hodge, on charges that he murdered a slave.

The evidence was strong. Two witnesses at the trial, which ran for 22 consecutive hours in Road Town's tiny courthouse on March 29, 1811, described the events that led to the slave's death in 1808. They said Hodge ordered Prosper to be flogged for over an hour on two consecutive days after he was unable to pay Hodge the six shillings the planter demanded for a mango Prosper had picked up from the ground. His skin in shreds, Prosper languished in the estate's sick house for five days before crawling to his own cabin. He died days later, alone, and was buried in a pit behind his cabin.

The jury of 13 white men took three hours to return its guilty verdict. While a majority of the jurors recommended mercy, the Governor of the Leeward Islands, Hugh Elliot, who had traveled to Tortola to observe the trial, refused the plea. Hodge was hung on May 8 in the yard behind the prison. It was the first time a white person in the British colonies had been convicted and executed for killing a slave.

Days before the trial began, Gov. Elliot wrote to his wife in England: "The eyes of all the West Indies are turned towards this cause and it will create a no less general sensation in Great Britain."

Elliot's prediction was not overstated. In July, reports of the trial appeared in *The Times, The Globe,* and two leading magazines. The transcript of the trial, taken by Road Town merchant Abraham Belisario, was published in London in September and in the United States the next year. The *Annual Register* included the Hodge trial in its list of significant events of 1811, and the trial was often referenced even years later in the debate that led to the eventual abolition of slavery in the British colonies in 1833.

is a valuable resource. A small shop in the rear sells modern-day arts and crafts, books, and T-shirts.

The long, low **Old Customs House,** home to several boutiques and a plant store, marks the division between Lower Main Street and Upper Main Street, where the street makes a sharp left turn and heads farther inland. The corner is known locally as Fonseca Corner, named after a prominent Road Town family that lived there.

The picturesque **St. George's Anglican Church** (170 Main Street, 284/493-3894) is one of the oldest houses of worship on Tortola. All the early church records were lost in 1819 when a hurricane destroyed the building. Following Emancipation, the church served as a school and community center for the residents of Road Town.

A few steps farther up Main Street is the **Road Town Methodist Church** (186 Main Street, 284/494-2198) centerpiece of the other long-standing denomination of the British Virgin Islands. The first Methodist missionary came to Tortola in 1789 and quickly converted thousands of slaves to the faith. In 1796, the church had 3,168 members in the British Virgins, more than any other Methodist mission in the West Indies. It remains the single largest denomination in the BVI. Today's Road Town Methodist Church was built in 1926 after the original structure was destroyed by hurricane in 1924.

Sandwiched between the two churches is the **Old Prison,** with high white walls and a broad red double door. The prison was in use continuously from the late 17th century until the mid-1990s, when a new prison, financed by the British government, opened on Tortola's remote northeastern corner. In the early 2000s plans were made to convert the old prison into a museum; minor repair work was carried out and exhibit space was built. But after a small prison riot broke out at the new prison in 2004, authorities decided to ease overcrowding there by moving a handful of low-security prisoners back to the old prison.

Across Main Street from the Methodist Church is a large, pink concrete structure known as **The Fireproof Building,** which now houses a craft shop. The building got its name in 1853 when it was one of the only buildings to remain standing after rioters set fire to Road Town in protest of an increase in the cattle tax. The unrest eventually spread throughout the countryside as residents lit fire to many of the remaining plantations and estate homes.

It was near here that hangings took place in the territory, the most famous of which occurred in 1811 when Arthur Hodge, a wealthy planter, was hanged for the murder of his slave. The last execution to take place here is a distant memory, and in 1999 the UK government forced the territory to take capital punishment off its books—which it did, but over loud local protests.

Sunday Morning Well

Located two blocks past the intersection of Joe's Hill Road and Main Street is the Sunday Morning Well, the place where some historians believe Emancipation was announced on August 1, 1834. Others say it was read in churches around the territory. The Sunday Morning Well is the site of an annual emancipation remembrance ceremony that takes place during the August Festival. Today there is a sheltered seating area and fountain. It's a popular place for residents to gather for discussions on island politics and happenings.

Legislative Council Chambers

The white, colonial-style, two-story building next to the Sunday Morning Well is the Legislative Council Chambers and courthouse. The 13 members of the Legislative Council meet downstairs to pass laws and approve the annual budget. High Court convenes upstairs most days. Busts of the first four elected members of the Legislative Council sit in front of the building.

© SUSANNA HENIGHAN

The O'Neal Botanical Gardens are an oasis of calm in the middle of Road Town.

Joseph Reynold O'Neal Botanical Gardens

A short foot trail loops around the four-acre Joseph Reynold O'Neal Botanical Gardens (Botanic Station, 284/494-4557, 8 A.M.–4 P.M., $3 adults, $2 children under 10), an oasis of quiet in bustling Road Town. The gardens were opened in 1986 on part of what was once the island's 60-acre agricultural station, the rest of which has been consumed by schools, roads, and commercial development.

Named for the founder and first chairman of the BVI National Parks Trust, the gardens are the place to come to get acquainted with the rich variety of tropical plants and animals that live in the BVI. The gardens include an orchid house, fern collection, and a garden of local medicinal herbs. You will also find a wide range of fruit trees, such as mango, passion fruit, and breadfruit. Look out as well for the gardens' collection of palm trees, including the native tyre palm, traditionally used to make brooms.

Ask at the ticket booth for a printed walking

TORTOLA

guide to the gardens, which provides detailed information about many of the species you see. Look around Fishlock Hall, the one-room wooden building at the center of the gardens, for staff who can answer any other questions you may have.

The gardens are a popular venue for weddings. Call the **BVI National Parks Trust** (284/494-2069, www.bvinationalparkstrust. org) for the fees.

Planter's Burial Ground

During the plantation era, a formal burial was a privilege granted only to the white planter class. One of the sites of these burials was the Planter's Burial Ground at Johnson's Ghut, a valley lying to the east of Road Town. A low wall and fence keep wandering livestock from damaging the gravestones. You can open the gate and walk among the gravestones, which remember former governors, governor's wives, and planters. The burial ground has been the subject of study by Caribbean Volunteer Expeditions (www.cvexp.org), which has cataloged the gravestone information and done simple maintenance work.

To find the burial ground, take the first left immediately after the Riteway Supermarket in Pasea. Follow this road until it forks; take the left-hand fork to the burial ground, which is right next to the island's animal shelter.

RIDGE ROAD

As you climb up any of the steep roads that rise spectacularly to the top of Tortola's spine, the air gets cooler, the breeze intensifies, and the views become more and more fantastical. Once at the top, the narrow Ridge Road winds past hillside communities and cool roadside bars. This is what Tortola residents refer to as "up country," and in many ways it is truly the most rural part of the island.

The Ridge Road extends seven miles along Tortola's backbone. A half dozen roads climb from sea level on both the north and south shores of the island to meet the road.

If you are going to explore in a car, it is best to start in either Carrot Bay or East End. From Carrot Bay, follow the Windy Hill road up until you reach a four-way stop. Turn right: this is the western end of the Ridge Road. From East End, follow Little Dixs Road (next to the East End police station) until you reach a four-way stop. If you turn left, you are at the eastern end of the Ridge Road.

The Ridge Road is also nice to explore on foot, but few people do it. Traffic is not too heavy, the breezes are cool, and you will have time to savor the views along the way. For the least uphill climbing, walk from west to east.

◖ Fahie Hill Mural

In 2001 a local artist, Reuben Vanterpool, decided to turn a retaining wall in his Fahie Hill community into a gallery of its history; he sketched a series of scenes on the wall and, with the help of other artists, painted them in vivid colors. The result was the Fahie Hill Mural, an excellent depiction of life on Tortola after Emancipation but before widespread development.

Panels show how islanders raised and gathered their food: they depict young men fishing, older men watering cattle, and the whole family working together to terrace land for crops. One panel illustrates women baking bread in traditional Dutch brick ovens.

Other panels show the schoolhouse where children once studied, a sugar factory at harvest time, and men working at the nearby rum distillery. The mural also shows how islanders had fun: One panel depicts a fungi band at work, and another shows traditional dancing.

The mural is located along the Ridge Road between Great Mountain Road and Johnson's Ghut Road.

Mount Healthy National Park

A well-preserved 18th-century windmill is the main attraction at Mount Healthy National Park (284/494-3904, www.bvinationalparkstrust.org, free), a one-acre park perched atop a foothill overlooking Brewer's Bay on the north shore. Built around the turn of the 19th century, the Mount Healthy windmill provided power to crush sugarcane grown on the surrounding plantation owned by Tortola's wealthiest planter, Bezaliel Hodge. All other plantations on Tortola used an animal round—a simple mill operated by mules, horses, or oxen—to power their cane-crushing machine rather than windmills, which were expensive to build and required 360-degree exposure to winds to be worthwhile.

In addition to the main windmill ruins, you can see other remnants of the Mount Healthy sugar ruins at the park. There is also a short trail that circles the edge of the park and a picnic table.

(Sage Mountain National Park

Hikers at Sage Mountain National Park (284/494-2069, www.bvinationalparkstrust. org, free) can climb to the highest point in the U.S. and British Virgin Islands, 1,716 feet above sea level. The 92-acre park located in west-central Tortola is also home to forest untouched for over 500 years.

The National Parks Trust has erected dozens of signs that identify trees and plants along the trails, including the West Indian mahogany, elephant-ear vine, and bulletwood tree. Visitors will hear the sounds of resident birds and bo-peeps, one of the most common kinds of tree frogs.

The entrance to Sage Mountain National Park is located about 0.3 mile from the parking lot, at the end of a wide trail that cuts through private property. Once inside the park, you can choose to follow the North Trail, which descends slightly before passing through some of the oldest and most lush parts of the forest; the South Trail, which cuts through drier forest; or the Central Trail, which follows the spine of the ridge. All three trails meet at a giant old fig tree at the western end of the park. Other trails track eastward from the park entrance and climb past impressive lookouts to the highest point in the park.

Shelters have been built at several spots along the trails, and there is a picnic table on the North Trail just past the park entrance. Brochures, which include a map of the park, are usually available at the park entrance, and there is a map on display at the parking lot.

Sage Mountain is almost always cool and damp; the air here can be a real relief on hot days. Wear sturdy shoes and plan to spend about two hours here if you want to see most of the park.

CANE GARDEN BAY

The north shore of Tortola is a series of scalloped bays ringed by powder white sand. The most popular of these is Cane Garden Bay, a traditional island village fringed by a picture-perfect beach.

Cane Garden Bay lies near the center of Tortola's north coast. The eastern end of the beach is the most developed: you will find a half dozen beach bars, a water sports center, and several inns here. The western end of the beach is much quieter. This is a popular anchorage for yachts, so a swimming area has been cordoned off all along the beach for safety. A narrow paved street runs parallel to the beach. Along it are small traditional West Indian houses. Large modern homes are quickly appearing on the hillsides above Cane Garden Bay.

Following the north shore east from Cane Garden Bay, you will find a series of increasingly peaceful and private beaches.

Callwood Rum Distillery

The Callwood family runs the only rum distillery still operating in the British Virgin Islands about 100 yards from the beach at Cane Garden Bay. Located on what was once better known as Estate Arundel, the Callwood Rum Distillery (284/495-9383, 8 A.M.–5 P.M. Mon.–Sat., free) still produces rum much the same way it was done 300 years ago—the biggest concession to modernity is that instead of animal power they use a small diesel engine to crush the sugarcane. Inside, things appear to have changed even less. Wooden barrels filled with aging rum line the walls, and demijohns of rum are lined along the floor. The air is musty and the light is dim. It doesn't take much imagination to picture this place in the days of planters and pirates.

Admission to the distillery is free, but you should definitely splurge on the $1 tour,

Brewmaster Kervin Joseph shows off the fruits of his labor.

© SUSANNA HENIGHAN

which involves an explanation of the process of rum production. If you want to take pictures, you will have to pay $2 or buy at least one bottle of rum.

Beaches

If you've ever seen a brochure promoting the British Virgin Islands, chances are you have seen a photo of **Cane Garden Bay Beach,** a crescent of white sand along the northern coast of Tortola. By far the most developed beach in the British Virgin Islands, Cane Garden Bay is home to a half dozen beachfront restaurants, several shops, and numerous guesthouses. Water sports equipment, personal watercraft, motorboats, and snorkeling equipment are all available for rent at Cane Garden Bay.

Most development at Cane Garden Bay is concentrated on the eastern end of the beach, allowing visitors to choose between a quiet or more rambunctious beach experience. Regardless, the beach does get too crowded for most tastes when large cruise ships call on Tortola. On these days, hundreds of cruise ship passengers descend on the beach between 10 A.M. and 4 P.M. Many land-based guests try to avoid the beach at these times. (Cruise ship schedules are printed in the local papers. Cruise ship visits tend to begin in October, peak in December and January, and taper off substantially by April.) When the surf is up, keep an eye out for surfers who seek waves off "The Point" on the far eastern tip of the Bay.

Quiet and undeveloped, **Brewer's Bay** is the reward for people brave enough to drive down one of the two steep roads that plummet from Tortola's Ridge Road to the beach. Beachfront development has been limited to a campground, and a grove of coconut and sea grape trees provides plenty of shade. There is good snorkeling along the rocks at the western edge of the bay, and the waters in the bay are invariably calm, even in rough weather. A snack bar at the west end of the beach sells casual beach fare.

Two of the nicest beaches on Tortola are the hardest to get to. **Rogues Bay** and **Trunk Bay** on the north-central coast are totally undeveloped. There is no public road or footpath to either. Boaters can anchor offshore and swim or dinghy in for a perfect day alone on the beach, but heavy swells often make this impossible. Hikers should ask for permission and directions from landowners if they want to make the trek from the road.

EAST ISLAND

The Blackburn Highway follows the southern coast of Tortola east of Road Town, up and down through a series of small bays, to East End, the second most populated area of Tortola. Josiah's Bay beach, just over the hill from East End, is popular among surfers. Beyond East End, a bridge connects Tortola to Beef Island, home to the territory's airport and the site of a proposed new resort.

St. Philips Anglican Church

The ruins of St. Philips Anglican Church are the most visible remains of the Kingstown settlement of free Africans. The village was established as a settlement for Africans liberated

TORTOLA

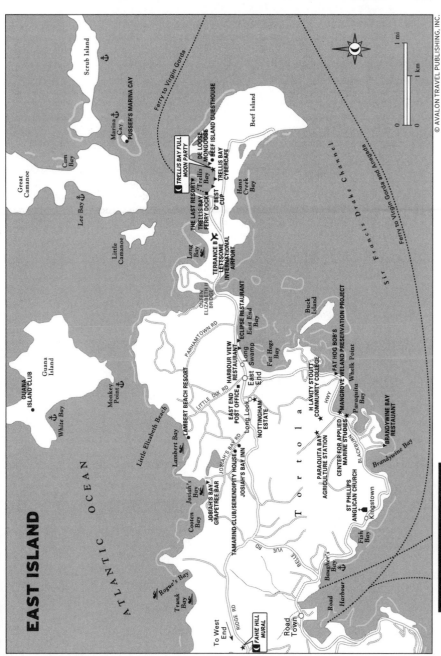

EAST ISLAND

© AVALON TRAVEL PUBLISHING, INC.

Scrub Island

PUSSER'S MARINA CAY

Marina Cay

Cam Bay

Great Camanoe

Lee Bay

Little Camanoe

Beef Island

Ferry to Virgin Gorda

TRELLIS BAY FULL MOON PARTY

THE LAST RESORT

TRELLIS BAY / TRELLIS BAY FERRY DOCK

DE LOOSE MONGOOSE

BEEF ISLAND GUESTHOUSE

TRELLIS BAY CYBERCAFE

D' BEST CUP

Trellis Bay

Hans Creek Bay

Long Bay

TERRANCE B LETTSOME INTERNATIONAL AIRPORT

Sir Francis Drake Channel

Ferry to Virgin Gorda and Anegada

QUEEN ELIZABETH II BRIDGE

PARHAMTOWN RD

ECLIPSE RESTAURANT

Long Swamp

East End Bay

Fat Hogs Bay

Buck Island

GUANA ISLAND CLUB

Guana Island

White Bay

Monkey Point

LAMBERT BEACH RESORT

HARBOUR VIEW RESTAURANT

LITTLE DIX RD

EAST END POST OFFICE

East End

Long Look

NOTTINGHAM ESTATE

H LAVITY STOUT COMMUNITY COLLEGE

FAT HOG BOB'S

MANGROVE WELAND PRESERVATION PROJECT

Whelk Point

Paraquita Bay

BRANDYWINE BAY RESTAURANT

Brandywine Bay

ATLANTIC OCEAN

Little Elizabeth Beach

Lambert Bay

JOSIAH'S BAY RD

Josiah's Bay

Cooten Bay

JOSIAH'S BAY GRAPETREE BAR

TAMARIND CLUB/SERENDIPITY HOUSE

JOSIAH'S BAY INN

PARAQUITA BAY AGRICULTURE STATION

CENTER FOR APPLIED MARINE STUDIES

BLACKBURN HWY

ST PHILLIPS ANGLICAN CHURCH

Kingstown

Fish Bay

T o r t o l a

Rogue's Bay

Trunk Bay

BELLE VUE RD

RIDGE RD

To West End

FAHIE HILL MURAL

Road Town

Road Harbour

Baugher's Bay

N

1 mi

1 km

0

0

from slaving vessels after Britain outlawed the slave trade in 1808. In 1831, the King gave land grants to the settlers, and within a year some 100 cottages were erected to house 300 people.

The church was built between 1831 and 1834 by settlers and served as a house of worship and school. The ruins are the property of the Anglican Church, and some basic steps have been taken to prevent the building from collapsing. Visitors can pull off the road and look more closely at the ruins.

Paraquita Bay Agricultural Station

The Department of Agriculture leases garden plots to local farmers in Paraquita Bay, one of the largest areas of undeveloped flat land on Tortola. Farmers raise livestock or produce crops including sugarcane, bananas, mangos, tomatoes, and okra. Narrow paths between the plots make the area ideal for walking, and the station is an excellent place to see unusual fruits and vegetables. If you go in the early morning or late afternoon, you are likely to meet some of the farmers, who can answer your questions or sell you whatever's in season.

Centre for Applied Marine Studies

Across the Blackburne Highway from the Agricultural Station is the Centre for Applied Marine Studies at H. Lavity Stoutt Community College (284/494-4994. www.hslcc.edu.vg, 8:30 A.M.–5:30 P.M., free), a two-year college named for the first chief minister of the British Virgin Islands. Students at the Marine Centre study navigation, sailing, outboard engine mechanics, marine biology, hospitality, and maritime history. A sculpture outside the building depicts a traditional Tortola sloop, and an exhibit on the second floor of the Marine Centre details attempts to preserve these vessels. Also on display are artifacts from the 1867 wreck of the *RMS Rhone* off Salt Island.

A partially completed boardwalk winds through the mangroves in front of the Marine Studies Centre, part of the college's **Mangrove Wetland Preservation Project.** A visitors center was hurriedly built in 2005 for the visit of Princess Anne, who dedicated the building. At some point in the future, you will find information about the importance of mangroves here; the project awaits funding to be completed.

Nottingham Estate

Tucked into densely populated East End is the community of Long Look, known to some as Nottingham Estate after its plantation-era owners, Samuel and Mary Nottingham. The Nottinghams were part of the small Quaker community that thrived in the British Virgin Islands in the 18th century. When the Nottinghams decided to abandon Tortola in 1778 they took the unprecedented step of not only freeing their 25 slaves but deeding them their 50-acre estate as well.

Later reports suggest that the freed slaves and their descendants maintained comfortable and happy lives at Nottingham Estate. Their success was cited by one American abolitionist as evidence that the end of slavery need not lead to social instability. Quaker Joseph John Gurney wrote to Henry Clay of Kentucky about visiting the residents of Nottingham Estate in 1839. "Their land is on the brow of a mountain, and a considerable part of it is well cultivated with yams, and other vegetables. We held a religious meeting with them, in the largest of their cottages, and were entirely satisfied with their respectable appearance and orderly behavior," he reported.

Today, plots in the Estate are still occupied only by people who can prove they descended from the Nottingham's original 25 freed slaves. Unfortunately for visitors, there are no markers or signs to indicate the exact boundaries of the estate. To find it, turn off the Blackburn Highway onto Long Look Road. Follow this road until you reach a crossroads, where you will see All Eyes On Me Department Store and Carolina's Beauty Supply. Look up: the hillside in front of you is Nottingham Estate.

Beef Island

Many a traveler flying to the British Virgin Islands has been perplexed to see that Beef Island, not Tortola, is their final destina-

CARIBBEAN FRIENDS

In 1727 an important new group of settlers began to arrive in the British Virgin Islands: Quakers. The Quakers fled England some years before to escape religious persecution and settled throughout the West Indies. Tortola's Quakers first settled in Anguilla but sought permission to leave that island after a major drought made survival difficult.

The Quakers eventually settled throughout the present-day British Virgin Islands. The largest group lived at Fat Hog's Bay, Tortola, but smaller Quaker settlements were found in Road Harbour, Virgin Gorda, and Jost Van Dyke. One of the first lieutenant governors of the Virgin Islands was John Pickering, a Quaker, who was later stripped of the post when he refused to bear arms.

Several other Quakers are still remembered today as well. William Thornton, who owned an estate in present-day Sea Cow's Bay, won the contest to design the U.S. Capitol Building in Washington, D.C. Another Quaker, Dr. William Coakley Lettsome, who was born on Little Jost Van Dyke, went on to found the London Medical Society. And Samuel and Mary Nottingham, both Quakers, made history when they freed all their slaves in 1776 and gave them the estate land to live on.

The Quaker era did not last long, however. The faith was unpopular with many planters, since Quakers were expected to live upright and moral lives. It ran counter to the West Indian planter lifestyle and philosophy. As the Tortola meeting reported to London in 1750: "The love that had kept them in fear of the Lord appears to be much abated and the too eager pursuit after the things of the World that choke and hinder the growth of Truth, too much sought after."

The last meeting took place in 1762, although individual Quakers remained. The ruins of the Quaker burial ground and meeting house at Fat Hog's Bay remain, although they are overgrown and deteriorating. In 2005, the land on which they sit was acquired by the government.

tion. The reason is simple: Beef Island, which is connected to the southeastern coast of Tortola by a two-lane bridge, is home to the Terrance B. Lettsome International Airport, the port of entry for many visitors to the British Virgin Islands.

Beef Island got its name from the cattle that were raised there during the plantation period. There is a popular legend about a widow who lived on Beef Island, raising cattle, during the age of piracy. It is said that she became fed up losing livestock at the hands of pirates, who used the waters around Beef Island for a rendezvous point. One day she invited the whole pirate gang to dinner and poisoned them with rum tainted with juice from the toxic manchineel fruit. The island's pirate legacy lives on in name: Bellamy Cay, just off the coast, is named for Black Sam Bellamy, a pirate said to have used the cay as his base while prowling the northern Caribbean in the early 1700s.

Beaches

Though technically on Beef Island, **Long Bay** is easily accessible from Tortola and is one of the most popular beaches among residents of the East End. Long Bay is protected from heavy surf, and its length will satisfy those who enjoy meditative strolls along the sand. There is nice beachcombing at the far eastern end, but no permanent restaurants or bathroom facilities. In 2005, the government bought nearly 100 acres of land around the beach to protect it from development.

Kayaks and other water sports equipment are available for rent at **Lambert Beach,** also known as Elizabeth Beach, the location of a resort of the same name. Food and drinks are for sale from the hotel restaurant, and there is plenty of shade under the sea grape trees that run along the beach. Big waves are possible if the north swell is up and there is an undertow, so check conditions before diving in. Drownings have been known to occur here.

TORTOLA

East of Lambert is **Little Elizabeth Beach,** a quiet, sunny beach well off the beaten track. Find it by heading east past the turnoff to Lambert Beach Resort and looking for a narrow, paved road on your left near a cattle trough. Follow the road down (four-wheel-drive is recommended) to the beach. You can also walk.

One of two surfing beaches on Tortola, **Josiah's Bay** is a long, straight stretch of sand on the northeastern coast. A casual beach bar sells food and drinks at the eastern end, and there is often an informal game of beach volleyball under way. You can also rent surfboards and boogie boards.

OFF THE EAST END

A number of small cays and islands are easily accessible from the east end of Tortola. Several are clustered around Trellis Bay; others are a short sail away.

Marina Cay

This seven-acre island is about 10 minutes by ferry from Beef Island, near Tortola's east end. Home to a resort, restaurant, and dive shop, Marina Cay was immortalized in Robb White's 1953 memoir *Our Virgin Island.* The book describes White and his wife Rhodie's two-year sojourn on the island in the late 1930s. The book was made into the movie *Our Virgin Island* in 1958, which starred Sidney Poitier and John Cassavetes and was filmed on Marina Cay and Long Bay, Beef Island.

The one-room house that Robb and Rhodie built largely by hand atop the island still stands; its present owners have converted it into a happy hour bar.

Marina Cay's other claim to fame is that it moonlights as the Republic of Cuervo, so-called independent nation of the tequila brand. The effect of this is that the island is used frequently in Jose Cuervo promotions and is sometimes closed to the public when the Cuervo folks come to town.

A free ferry (284/494-2174) to Marina Cay leaves Trellis Bay, Beef Island, every hour on the half hour from 10:30 A.M. to 12:30 P.M. and every hour on the hour from 3 P.M. to 7 P.M.

Bellamy Cay

This tiny spit of land in the middle of Trellis Bay is barely big enough for the intimate restaurant built on it. Named for a famous pirate, Sam Bellamy, this little cay has attracted quite a following over the years, thanks to its famous restaurant, The Last Resort.

Guana Island

Named for a rock outcropping that looks like an iguana head, 850-acre Guana Island lies off Tortola's northeastern tip, a short sail from Trellis Bay. In the 18th century, Quakers settled the island, building sugar mills and houses and cultivating sugar, cotton, and other crops. Following the end of slavery, Guana was mostly undeveloped until 1935, when Beth and Louis Bigelow bought the island and built a small clubhouse on the saddle of the main ridge. The Bigelows invited intellectuals and artists to Guana, which was known as a rustic retreat with spectacular natural beauty and good conversation. In 1975, Henry and Gloria Jarecki bought Guana and expanded the guest facilities to accommodate up to 32 people. They also hired a naturalist and began a project to reintroduce native animal species to the island. Every summer, Guana Island hosts research scientists who stay on the island, perform research on environmental topics, and then present their findings at a community science symposium.

Unfortunately for those without deep pockets, Guana does not welcome non-resort guests to come ashore, although you can anchor out, snorkel, and swim onto the beaches, which are, by law, public.

WEST ISLAND

Heading west from Road Town, Drake's Highway runs parallel to the Sir Francis Drake Channel, its namesake, all the way to the western tip of Tortola. The road passes through Sea Cow's Bay, a community that borders a wide bay once home to manatees. After that, the road passes through a series of more sparsely populated bays until reaching the end of the island.

Two cays lie just offshore Tortola; both are

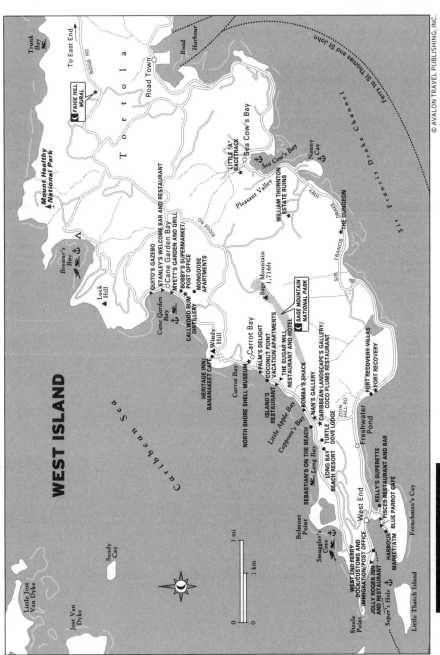

© AVALON TRAVEL PUBLISHING, INC.

WEST ISLAND

Caribbean Sea

Little Jost Van Dyke

Jost Van Dyke

Sandy Cay

Trunk Bay

To East End

RIDGE RD

Tortola

Road Town

Road Harbour

Ferry to St. Thomas and St. John

Sir Francis Drake Channel

FAHIE HILL MURAL

Mount Healthy National Park

Brewer's Bay

Luck Hill

Sea Cow's Bay

LITTLE 'A' RACETRACK

Nanny Cay

Pleasant Valley

WILLIAM THORNTON ESTATE RUINS

HWY

SIR FRANCIS

THE DUNGEON

QUITO'S GAZEBO
STANLEY'S WELCOME BAR AND RESTAURANT
Cane Garden Bay
MYETT'S GARDEN AND GRILL
BOBBY'S SUPERMARKET/
POST OFFICE
MONGOOSE APARTMENTS

RIDGE RD

CALLWOOD RUM DISTILLERY

Windy Hill

Sage Mountain 1,716ft

SAGE MOUNTAIN NATIONAL PARK

HERITAGE INN/
BANANAKEET CAFE

Carrot Bay

PALM'S DELIGHT

COCONUT POINT VACATION APARTMENTS

THE SUGAR MILL RESTAURANT AND HOTEL

NORTH SHORE SHELL MUSEUM

ISLAND'S RESTAURANT

Little Apple Bay

BOMBA'S SHACK

COCO PLUMS RESTAURANT

FORT RECOVERY VILLAS
FORT RECOVERY

SIR FRANCIS

NAN'S GALLERY

CARIBBEAN LANDSCAPE'S GALLERY

ZION HILL RD

Cappoon's Bay

SEBASTIAN'S ON THE BEACH

Long Bay

TURTLE DOVE LODGE

LONG BAY BEACH RESORT

Freshwater Pond

West End

KELLY'S SUPERETTE

PISCES RESTAURANT AND BAR
BLUE PARROT CAFE

Belmont Point

Smuggler's Cove

WEST END FERRY DOCK/CUSTOMS AND IMMIGRATION/POST OFFICE

JOLLY ROGER INN AND RESTAURANT

HARBOUR MARKET/ATM

Frenchman's Cay

Steele Point

Sopers Hole

Little Thatch Island

0 1 mi

0 1 km

TORTOLA

© SUSANNA HENIGHAN

western Tortola

connected to the main island by bridges. Nanny Cay lies about halfway between Road Town and West End and is home to a large marina, hotel, and two restaurants. Frenchman's Cay lies near the western tip and houses a marina, several shops, a hotel, and a small community. Soper's Hole, officially the name of the body of water between Tortola and Frenchman's Cay, now refers to a waterfront complex of bright Caribbean-style buildings on the western end of the cay.

On the north shore, western Tortola is a series of lovely bays, from Smuggler's Cove, a remote and protected crescent of sand, to Carrot Bay, a traditional village where many islanders still make their living from the sea and the land.

William Thornton Estate Ruins

Located in aptly named Pleasant Valley, just west of Sea Cow's Bay, are the ruins of an estate house where William Thornton drew the design of the U.S. capitol building. Thornton, a Quaker, was living at his Pleasant Valley plantation in March 1792 when then-Secretary of State Thomas Jefferson advertised a contest to design the U.S. capitol building and president's home, which would be built in the new city of Washington.

By the time Thornton learned of the contest and sailed to Philadelphia with his design, the contest was closed. But the commissioners, who had not been impressed by any of the other designs, waived the deadline and accepted his entry. Thornton won $500 in gold and a plot in the new city.

Little remains of the Thornton estate, which is privately owned and used as a storage facility for a local water company. A few crumbling walls are visible through the trees.

To find the Thornton Estate, turn off Drake's Highway at the abandoned gas station-turned-junkyard in Pleasant Valley, also called Palistina, and pass the Cable and Wireless complex. The road crosses a small stream and turns to the right before passing the estate ruins on the right.

The Dungeon

The ruins of Fort Purcell, just east of Pockwood Pond along Drake's Highway, are more commonly known as The Dungeon because of a below-ground magazine that looks more sinister than it probably ever was.

First built in the 17th century by Dutch settlers, Fort Purcell was expanded and strengthened by the British in the mid-18th century. Located on about five acres of land, the fort complex was dozens of buildings, including water catchments and storage facilities. It was named for an influential governor, James Purcell, who oversaw construction of a number of the fortifications that once ringed Tortola and the other British Virgin Islands.

The ruins are badly overgrown, and there is no sign marking their location from the road; look for a dirt access road on the hillward side of the highway between Havers and Pockwood Pond. You can park along the highway and walk in, but be careful crossing the road.

Fort Recovery
The remains of **Tower Fort** on the southwestern coast are better known by the name of the adjacent resort, Fort Recovery. The Tower Fort is believed to be the oldest building still standing in the British Virgin Islands, built in the 17th century by early settlers.

Zion Hill Methodist Church
The West End Methodist Chapel was first built in the early 1800s and was located on top of Zion Hill, with views looking north to Jost Van Dyke and south to St. John. In 1834, Emancipation was proclaimed from the altar. The chapel was destroyed or damaged in successive hurricanes, and in 1926 it was rebuilt at the foot of Zion Hill, where it would be less exposed to high winds. The church served not only as a place of worship but a school as well.

In 2002, a new, larger church was built next door, but the old chapel, where the territory's first chief minister, H. Lavity Stoutt, was educated, remains.

North Shore Shell Museum
Carrot Bay's North Shore Shell Museum (284/495-4714, 8 A.M.–8 P.M. daily, free) is more folk art gallery than shell museum. Proprietor Egbert Donovan combines hand-painted signs and collected shells for his funky island-style museum. Handmade musical instruments are also on display.

Beaches
A humble place, **Apple Bay,** also called Cappoon's Bay, may not rate among the top beaches in the British Virgin Islands, but it is not without charm. Surfers flock here during the winter months when the surf is up. Beachgoers can buy food and drink from two different seaside restaurants, recline in the sun or shade, and spend a day watching pelicans dive for food.

A long, straight stretch of sand set next to a picturesque sugarloaf mountain, **Long Bay** is a good beach for walking, sunning, and beachcombing. A buffer of rocks just offshore makes swimming difficult in most places. The best swimming area is located near the western end of the beach, opposite a low rock bluff. The far western end of the beach is excellent for beachcombing. Food, drink, and restroom facilities are available at Long Bay Beach Resort's beachfront restaurant.

Residents of Tortola are thankful that **Smuggler's Cove** is accessible only by a long and painfully bumpy road; otherwise, they say, it would become too popular. Their devotion is not hard to understand. Smuggler's Cove is a small crescent of sand at the northwestern tip of Tortola, sandwiched between two sugarloaf hills, with a reef to snorkel on and plenty of sea grape trees to shelter under. The cove is protected from high surf, making it a good choice for small children and uncertain swimmers. On most days, vendors sell cold drinks and snacks near the entrance of the beach. A beach bar near the center of the beach sells food.

SIR FRANCIS DRAKE CHANNEL
The south shore of Tortola faces the Sir Francis Drake Channel, the wide, deep thoroughfare used by European explorers, early settlers, and today's cruise ships. The string of islands on the opposite side of this channel are ideal for

TORTOLA

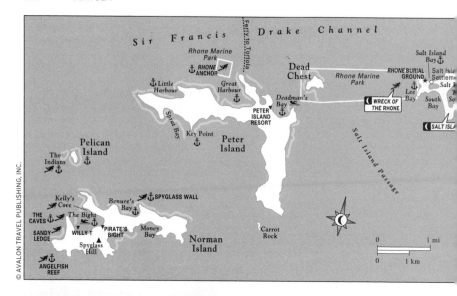

Sir Francis Drake, the namesake of the channel that runs between Tortola and its outer islands

day trips from Tortola or can make up part of a charter yacht sail through the islands.

Norman Island

Long associated with pirate treasure, Norman Island is a one-square-mile island about six miles from Road Town, Tortola. It is claimed that the island was the inspiration for Robert Louis Stevenson's 1883 novel, *Treasure Island*. True or no (Stevenson never traveled here, but may have seen a map of the island), it is easy enough to be convinced that Stevenson's imagined island was much like Norman Island. In more modern times, a legend flourished that a local fisherman found pirate booty in one of the underwater caves on Norman Island.

The Bight is Norman Island's largest bay and most popular anchorage. There are two bars and restaurants here, and it is a short dinghy trip to some excellent snorkeling. Those seeking solitude may prefer anchoring at Benure's or Money Bay instead.

New York businessman Dr. Henry Jarecki, who also owns Guana Island, bought Norman Island in 1999 and has applied for permission to develop an upscale resort there. If his plans

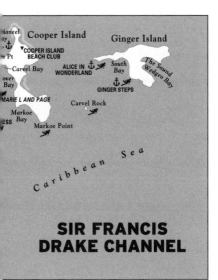

are approved, the whole character of the island will change, and probably not for the better.

Norman Island has some great snorkeling and is one of the most popular destinations for day-sail snorkeling trips in the British Virgins. **The Caves,** to the west of the Bight, are one of the only places where you can see darkness-dwelling coral and fish in the middle of the day. Bring an underwater flashlight if you want to plumb the full 70-foot length of the largest of the caves. At **Kelly's Cove,** east of the Bight, is a shallow, diverse reef great for beginning snorkelers. **The Indians,** near neighboring Pelican Rock, is considered one of the best reef dives in the BVI, but it is rewarding for snorkelers, too. Other good snorkel sites are **Angelfish Reef, Spyglass Wall,** and **Sandy Ledge,** all a short dinghy trip from the Bight. There are no dive shops on Norman Island, but Tortola-based dive and day-sail operators come here nearly every day. Rendezvous dives are also possible.

At least until the bulldozers move in, Norman Island has some excellent hiking trails. Old service roads and numerous footpaths cross the island in practically every direction. There are not trail markers, nor a trail map, but ask at Pirate's Bight for some quick directions. Trails depart from the restaurant to Spyglass Hill, where there is a rudimentary helicopter landing pad and excellent views in all directions. You can also hike along both the eastern and western shores of the Bight or out along the spine of the island to Benure's Bay and Money Bay.

If you take more than a stroll, be sure to be prepared. This is real backcountry exploration, and there will be no food or water along the way. Take a means of communication, if you can, and be sure to finish well before darkness falls.

There is no regular ferry service to Norman Island, and most people get there on a charter yacht or day sail. You could also make Norman Island one of your stops if you rent a powerboat for the day. If you're really hard up for a ride out there, call up either Pirate's Bight or the Willy T to find out if you could hitch a ride over on the staff boat—usually the answer will be yes if you are planning to eat a meal at the respective establishment while you're there. For special events, there is sometimes a ferry.

Peter Island

Home to one of the Virgin Islands' most famous luxury resorts, Peter Island is a tiny universe unto itself. Resort guests can spend their days on Deadman's Beach, one of the prettiest in the Virgin Islands, or take advantage of the world-class spa and water sports facilities. For day-trippers, the greatest attraction, aside from the beach and spa, is the Loop, a hiking trail that cuts through miles of untouched forest on the 1,800-acre island. Many people also make a special trip to Peter Island to eat at its award-winning restaurants.

Peter Island has a unique history. In the late 1600s a group of slave traders from Brandenburg, Germany, settled the island, intending to establish a large settlement. They got as far as building several forts before the Danes chased them out. Peter Island was cultivated during the plantation era, and remains of an island church, homes, and burial ground have been found there. In 1855 a coaling station

TORTOLA

was opened on Peter Island, where steam ships could load up. The Peter Island coaling station was an alternative to one on St. Thomas, which was closed regularly due to yellow fever outbreaks on that island.

In the 1930s, British diplomat John Brudnell-Bruce moved his family to Peter Island, where they lived for several decades. In 1950, Brudnell-Bruce was one of the four men elected to the first Legislative Council of the British Virgin Islands.

In the late 1960s, a Norwegian millionaire, Peter Smedwig, became smitten with Peter Island, bought it, and had a fleet of luxury A-frame chalets shipped there from Norway. He built a small clubhouse and opened the first guesthouse on the island. In the late 1970s, U.S. entrepreneurs linked to the Amway Corporation bought Peter Island and have continued to expand and upgrade the resort.

Guests at Peter Island resort ride the **Peter Island Ferry** (Baugher's Bay, 284/495-2000) free, as do people with dinner reservations at Tradewinds Restaurant. Everyone else pays $14

one-way. The ferry, which also carries resort staff departs Tortola at 7 A.M., 8:30 A.M., 10 A.M. noon, 2 P.M., 3:30 P.M., 5:30 P.M., 6:30 P.M. 8 P.M., and 10:30 P.M.

Private yachts are welcome at Peter Island. There are anchorages at the extreme southeast corner of Deadman's Bay, Little Harbour, Great Harbour, and Key Point.

Dead Chest

The sheer rock face of Dead Chest island is said to be the final resting place of the 16 mutineers immortalized in the old sea song line: "16 men on a dead man's chest. Yo ho ho and a bottle of rum." Others say that the 16 men left here by the pirate Blackbeard tried to swim to nearby Peter Island but drowned, washing ashore on what is now Deadman's Bay. For now, the impenetrable rocky face of Dead Chest isn't betraying the truth.

◖ Salt Island

Before refrigeration, islanders relied on salt to preserve meat. Many islands in the Virgin

The settlement at Salt Island is mostly deserted.

THE WRECK OF THE RMS *RHONE*

On Oct. 29, 1867, the RMS *Rhone* was at anchor in Great Harbour, Peter Island. The 310-foot *Rhone* had left St. Thomas, her usual port of call, days earlier due to a yellow-fever outbreak there and was taking on passengers and cargo for a journey to Europe. A member of the Royal Mail Steam Packet Company, the *Rhone* transported mail, passengers, and goods between England and its colonies in the West Indies and South America.

During the morning, Captain Robert Wooley noticed that the barometer was falling but thought it was too late in the season for a hurricane. He decided that the *Rhone,* which had weathered terrible gales in the open sea, would remain at anchor off Peter Island for the incoming weather. It was a deadly decision. At about 11 A.M. the barometer fell dangerously low, and the hurricane began in earnest. The *Rhone* was knocked about but remained whole and upright. Capt. Wooley became worried, however. When there was a lull in the storm about an hour later, he decided to flee for the open ocean. Unable to free the ship's 3,0000-pound anchor, the crew cut the chain, and the *Rhone* steamed out of Peter Island, through the Salt Island Passage, toward the open sea.

As it turned out, the lull was the passage of the eye, and as the *Rhone* rounded Dead Chest and headed out to sea, it was battered by full-force hurricane winds. The ship was blown backwards onto Salt Island's Black Rock and split in half. Cool ocean water ran into the ship's overheated boiler, causing a massive explosion. The ship sank in minutes.

Only six people survived – five crew members and one passenger who clung to debris for six hours before washing ashore. Witnesses reported seeing Capt. Wooley washed onto a skylight before being thrown overboard into the roiling sea. He was never seen again. Residents of Salt Island did what they could to collect the bodies of those who perished – a dozen or so are buried on the west end of the Salt Island settlement. The burial ground is the only memorial in the BVI to the more than 150 souls lost on board the *Rhone* – except of course the wreck itself. Sadly, many people think that if the *Rhone* had remained at anchor off Peter Island, it would have fared far better, since the hills of the island would have shielded it from the worst of the winds.

In the years following the wreck, treasure-seekers gathered nearly everything of value from the wreck. An 1870 article in the Port-of-Spain, Trinidad, *Gazette* recounts a party held by visiting divers who took cases of champagne, beer, brandy, lemonade, and soda water from the wreckage: "The liquors were as good as they were the first day and it is nearly three years since they have been down; the champagne was first rate, as cool as possible." Some *Rhone* artifacts were deposited with the Virgin Islands Folk Museum (Main Street, tel. 284/494-3701 ext. 5005, 8:30 A.M.-4:30 P.M. Mon.-Fri.,) and the Marine Studies Centre (H. Lavity Stoutt Community College, Paraquita Bay, tel. 284/494-4994), where they are on display.

have salt ponds where crystal salt was collected, but no island had a larger or more productive pond than Salt Island, a small T-shaped island about five miles from Tortola. For centuries the small settlement on Salt Island thrived on the island's salt industry.

Salt is harvested in the early spring, at the end of the dry season. Traditionally, the Salt Island harvest was a time of great festivity. Residents from nearby islands would travel there to watch as a government agent supervised the "breaking of the pond" and lent a hand. After it was harvested from the pond, the salt was dried in a special salt house. Up to 1,000 pounds of salt were harvested annually from Salt Island. Today, islanders still harvest salt, but on a much smaller scale. Most of it is finely ground and mixed with local seasonings to make "seasoning salt" for fish and meat.

Few, if any, people still live on Salt Island year-round, although some Salt Islanders who live on Tortola come back regularly. The settlement along the north coast is a cluster of simple homes, set amid coconut palms. There are no restaurants, snack bars, or stores, and no electricity or public water. In fact, this is the best place to glimpse life as it was throughout the Virgin Islands before tourism and development changed them so dramatically.

There is no ferry service to Salt Island, so if you want to come you will have to sail yourself. Strangely, even though Salt Island is unique among the BVI's outlying cays, it is off the radar of most visitors and likewise is not featured on any regular day-sail itineraries. This is all the more reason to go.

Sailors can anchor at Salt Island Bay or moor at Lee Bay. Both are exposed, however, and are considered day-use only. When you go ashore, look around the settlement for signs of life. If someone happens to be home, be sure to extend them the courtesy of a greeting and explanation of what you intend to do. They may even agree to show you around. Hiking trails circle the pond, or you can trek over to South Bay in the west or The Sound in the east. Don't disturb the salt pond or take any salt unless you have permission.

◖ Wreck of the *Rhone*

The Wreck of the RMS *Rhone* is the preeminent dive site in the British Virgin Islands and one of its most visited attractions. The 310-foot twin-masted steamer, which sank during a ferocious hurricane in 1867, lies in three sections west of Salt Island and has beckoned underwater explorers for decades. In 1977 it was the primary filming location for the film *The Deep*, starring Nick Nolte and Jacqueline Bisset.

Lying in between 65 and 80 feet of water, the bow is the deepest, largest, and most intact section of the *Rhone*. Here divers can enter the interior of the vessel and will find the mast and crow's nest still attached to the ship. The midsection, lying in about 60 feet of water, is dominated by a series of support beams—all that remains of the ship's deck. The stern, the shallowest part of the wreck, can be explored by snorkelers as well as divers. It features the ship's large rudder and 15-foot propeller.

Divers should not try to explore the whole wreck in one dive. It is too deep, and there is too much to see. The best way to explore the ship is to start with a dive on the deepest section, the bow, and follow that with another dive on the stern and midsection. If you really want to get to know this wreck, you will need to plan more than two dives, however, including one at night, when it comes alive with unusual and colorful sea life.

Visibility around the wreck is usually good—between 60 and 100 feet. The bow and midsection are sometimes susceptible to currents. For ease and safety, always go diving with a local dive company, since staff will be familiar with local conditions and dangers.

Local dive boats visit the *Rhone* every day of the year. In fact, many days it seems like a whole fleet make the journey. For the best experience, choose a dive boat that specializes in small groups and avoid the busiest times, 9 A.M.–noon and 2–4 P.M.

Cooper Island

Located about four miles from Tortola, Cooper Island got its name from the skilled coopers who practiced their trade there during the plantation era. About 1.5 miles long and 0.5 mile wide, Cooper Island is undeveloped except for a small hotel and clutch of vacation homes at Manchioneel Bay on the north end of the island.

No less than nine dive sites form a ring around Cooper Island. **Cistern Point,** at the southern tip of Manchioneel Bay, is one of the most popular since it is shallow, easy, and equally good for snorkeling. There are three nice wrecks around Cooper Island, all sunk intentionally by the BVI Dive Association. The ***Inganess Bay*** lies in about 50 feet of water halfway between Salt and Cooper Islands. The ***Marie L*** and ***Pat*** lie side by side off Hallovers Bay on Cooper Island's western shore. Other good dives around Cooper Island include **Carvel Rock,** between Ginger and Cooper, and **Markhoe Point,** an isolated and geologically interesting dive on the extreme southern tip of Cooper Island.

There is no public ferry service to Cooper Island, although visitors on private boats are welcome. Some day-sail operations include Cooper Island in their itinerary; dive shops also take visitors to its most popular dive spots. Cooper Island maintains overnight moorings at Manchioneel Bay for visiting yachts.

Ginger Island

Uninhabited and undeveloped, Ginger Island lies between Salt Island and Round Rock. The island is shaped like a two-pronged pitchfork. There are sheer cliffs on the north and south sides, plus protected Wedgeo Bay in the center, between the pitchfork prongs.

There are some excellent diving and snorkeling sites around Ginger Island. In South Bay you will find **Alice in Wonderland,** one of the best deep-water reef dives in the territory. Staghorn coral here grow to heights of 15 feet and more. You are likely to encounter pelagic species like rays, sharks, and barracuda at **Ginger Steps,** another deep coral site in South Bay. The north shore of Ginger Island, near Grapetree Landing, is a long, healthy, and shallow reef, good for either diving or snorkeling.

Entertainment and Events

NIGHTLIFE
Road Town
The Bat Cave (Baugher's Bay, 284/494-4880) has dance music and the in-crowd on Friday and Saturday nights. **Stone's** (Long Bush, 284/494-6776) has Caribbean dance hall and soca music for a late-night crowd. Also in Long Bush, follow your ears to the upbeat sound of Dominicano music, which flows from several bars popular with immigrants from the Dominican Republic. Other popular bars are **Le Cabanon** (Waterfront Drive, 284/494-8660) and **The Treehouse** (Inner Harbour Marina, 284/494-6749).

Cane Garden Bay
The most famous of Tortola's musicians, Quito Rhymer, performs several nights a week at his **Gazebo** (284/495-4837). Quito plays acoustic on Tuesdays and Thursdays, while on weekends he plugs in with his band, The Edge. The sound is an upbeat combination of reggae and calypso. The crowd here tends to be an equal mix of tourists and island residents, and this is a good place for dancing.

Other bars in Cane Garden Bay provide entertainment regularly. **Myett's** (284/495-9649) has live music Fridays through Mondays, and there is often live music at **Big Banana** (284/495-4606). Pick up the latest copy of the free *Limin' Times* for a full rundown of upcoming events.

East Island
Besides whatever's happening at Trellis Bay, check out **Bing's Drop Inn** (East End, 284/495-2627) which has DJ music nightly except Mondays. Check **Fat Hog Bob's** (Fat Hog's Bay, 284/495-1010) for its weekly live music schedule. **The Last Resort** (284/495-2520) on Bellamy Cay off Trellis Bay puts on a cabaret show on weekends.

West Island
If you don't want to check out Bomba's Shack, in Apple Bay, **Sebastian's** (284/495-4212) has live fungi music Sunday nights.

In Carrot Bay, check out **Clem's** (284/495-4350)for steel pan music. **The North Shore Shell Museum** (284/495-4714) has fungi music nightly except Sundays.

Over at West End, the best place for entertainment is **The Jolly Roger** (284/495-4559), which has live local music on weekends and sometimes brings in acts from the U.S.

EVENTS
The best source of up-to-date information on events and entertainment is the **Limin' Times,** published every Thursday and

© AVALON TRAVEL PUBLISHING, INC.

HUNTUMS GHUT

To Great Mountain

HUNTUM'S GHUT RD

JOHN'S HOLE

PASEA ESTATE

RITE WAY FOOD M

LOWER ESTATE RD

JOSEPH REYNOLD O'NEAL BOTANICAL GARDENS

POLICE STATION

STATION AVE

JAMES WALTER FRANCIS DR

Moorings

WICKHA CAY

LOWER ESTATE

MULTI-PURPOSE COMPLEX

AO Shirley Recreation Grounds

Marina

BVI HIGH SCHOOL

SUNDAY MORNING WELL

LEGISLATIVE COUNCIL CHAMBERS

Village Cay Marina

WICKHAM'S CAY 1

DAREOS

FISHLOCK RD

LONG BUSH RD

Softball Field

IMMIGRATION HEADQUARTERS

MAIN ST

PUBLIC LIBRARY

BOBBY'S SUPERMARKET

VILLAGE CAY RESORT

JOE'S HILL RD

To Joe's Hill

FLEMING ST

A&L INN

FIREPROOF BUILDING

LA DOLCE VITA

BVI TOURIST BOARD

BANK OF NOVA SCOTIA

BANCO POPULAR

FIRSTBANK

FIRST CARIBBEAN INTERNATIONAL BA

METHODIST CHURCH

ST GEORGE'S ANGLICAN CHURCH

OLD PRISON

COURTYARD COFFEESHOP

CENTRAL ADMINISTRATION COMPLEX

MID-TOWN RESTAURANT

ROAD TOWN BAKERY

OLD CUSTOMS HOUSE

MARIA'S BY THE SEA

VIRGIN ISLANDS FOLK MUSEUM

CRAFTS ALIVE

ROTI PALACE

LE CABANON

OLD ADMINISTRATION COMPLEX

CAPRICIO DI MARE

SIR OLVA GEORGES PLAZA

THE DOVE

MAIN ST

VISITOR INFORMATION CENTER/ FERRY DOCK/ CUSTOMS AND IMMIGRATION

PEEBLE'S HOSPITAL

WATERFRONT DR

OLD GOVERNMENT HOUSE MUSEUM

McNAMARA

ROAD TOWN

TORTOLA

HOTEL CASTLE MARIA

FORT BURT RESTAURANT

To West End

CRANDALLS PASTRY PLUS

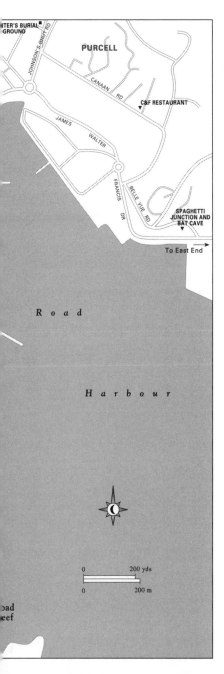

available free from many hotels, grocery stores, and restaurants.

◖ Trellis Bay Full Moon Party

Beef Island's Trellis Bay is an artsy and hip place to be every day of the year, but on full moons its funky atmosphere boils over at the Full Moon Party, a joint production of Aragorn's Studio and the Trellis Bay Cybercafé. The parties may share a name with Bomba's Full Moon Parties on the west end of the island, but the similarities end there. Trellis Bay's fetes feature local musicians, a top-notch barbecue buffet, stilt walkers, and local artist Aragorn Dick-Read's flaming fireballs.

The parties are a good place to sample Tortola's traditional music form, scratch-band music called *fungi.* Entertainment also often includes *mocko jumbies,* colorful stilt-walking characters that perform impressive moves at heights of up to 10 feet.

Aragorn's fireballs are a story unto themselves. Spherical metal sculptures about five feet in diameter, the fireballs are stuffed with flammable material, fastened on stands over the water, and lit afire. The effect is mesmerizing; flames dance over the crystal water, allowing glimpses at the balls' intricate carved designs.

The fireballs have a checkered past. Aragorn engaged in a very public dispute with the island's Conservation and Fisheries Department in 2004 and 2005 over whether he had the required permission to station them on the seabed. (Local law states that landownership ends at the high water mark; the seabed is controlled by the government). At the height of the dispute, the fireballs were confiscated and locked up at the East End Police Station. The matter seems to have been resolved for the time being.

If your visit to Tortola does not include a full moon, check out what else is happening at Trellis Bay. The businesses there have plans to expand their entertainment offerings in the near future. The Bay also throws a great New Year's Eve bash.

Bomba's Full Moon Party

Bomba's Surfside Shack (Apple Bay, 284/495-4148) is legendary in the Virgin Islands for its

TORTOLA

© SUSANNA HENIGHAN

Fireballs are the center of attention at the Trellis Bay Full Moon Parties.

raucous Full Moon Parties and risqué shack decor. Ladies' underwear hangs from the rafters, often shed after imbibing Bomba's potent rum punch or his even more potent mushroom tea, brewed from locally grown hallucinogenic mushrooms.

The tea is served at midnight during the full moon parties, which inevitably draw a huge crowd, even in the dead of summer. Bomba's full moons feature live bands, dancing, and, sometimes, attractions like wet T-shirt contests.

If you want a Shack experience that is a bit more tame, try it out on a Sunday or Wednesday night when there is live music and more mellow company. Or stop by any afternoon to benefit from the pieces of wisdom previous partygoers have scrawled on the shack's walls over the years.

August Festival

Tortola's biggest party of the year commemorates the end of slavery on August 1, 1833. The August Festival actually starts in late July with the opening of the Festival Village and lasts through the first week of August. There is entertainment nightly in the Village, where you can sample authentic local food like goat water (goat soup), stewed conch, roti, and pâtés (fried meat-stuffed bread). Entertainers from all over the Caribbean perform, including some well-known reggae and soca artists. A favorite night is the calypso competition, when local singers perform calypsos touching on island politics, culture, and current events.

The centerpiece of the August Festival is the parade, held the first Monday of August. Beginning around noon (never mind any schedule that says it will start any sooner), colorful troops, dancers, and floats parade down Waterfront Drive to the Festival Village. If you plan to attend, it is wise to bring chairs and scope out a shady spot early.

Other popular festival events are the horse races, the Miss BVI pageant, water sports events, food fair, and Carrot Bay Fiesta, a mini-festival that takes place on the Thursday, Friday, and Saturday after the Festival parade.

The **BVI Tourist Board** (284/494-3134, www.bvitourism.com) posts up-to-date information about the Festival schedule on its website.

BVI Music Fest

Held over Memorial Day weekend, the BVI Music Fest (www.bvimusicfest.net) brings popular reggae, R&B, and calypso acts to Cane Garden Bay. The three-day event usually boasts at least one big-name act. Past headliners have been Jimmy Cliff and Maxi Priest. Admission is $10 a night or $25 for the whole weekend. For the least hassle, book ahead for a room in Cane Garden Bay—traffic into and out of the Bay can be nasty during the Fest.

Performing Arts Series

H. Lavity Stoutt Community College presents a Performing Arts Series (284/494-4994, www.hlscc.edu.vg) every year with classical and jazz performers. Concerts take place from September to May at the Atrium at the College's Paraquita Bay campus.

TORTOLA

Shopping

Main Street

The best place to shop in Road Town is along Main Street, which has the greatest concentration of shops and a pleasant atmosphere. Most shops are open by 10 A.M. and close around 5 P.M. Many are closed on Sundays. Some of the best Main Street shops are **Kaunda's Kysy Tropix** (87 Main Street, 284/494-6737), which sells local and international music; **Latitude 18** (Fonseca Corner, 284/494-3811), which sells beachwear; and **The Gallery** (102 Main Street), which features framed and matted watercolors and photos of the BVI.

Another good place to browse is **Little Denmark** (147 Main Street, 284/494-2455), which has an intriguing mix of goods including Cuban cigars, jewelry, luggage, and kitchenware. For jewelry, try **The Jewelry Box** (101 Main Street, 284/494-7278). You will be hard-pressed to leave **Sunny Caribbe Spice Shop and Art Gallery** (121 Main Street, 284/494-2178) empty-handed. Here you will find a wide array of spices, sauces, relishes, and body products, as well as Caribbean postcards, prints, and crafts.

The best place for books is **Serendipity Books** (151 Main Street, 284/494-5865). **Esme's Shop** (Sir Olva Georges Plaza, 284/494-3961) sells newspapers and magazines.

Around Road Town

Across from Main Street, facing the waterfront, is **Crafts Alive,** an open-air market of brightly painted Caribbean-style houses. Space is rented to local artisans, but, sadly, the local art is overshadowed by cheap tourist goods—T-shirts, bags, and hats. But if you look hard, you can also find locally made hot sauce and preserves, crafts produced by senior citizens, and locally produced soaps. There are benches and, during the season, live music, making this a pleasant place to relax.

Other shops of note include **Cantik** (Inner Harbour Marina, 284/494-7927), which sells imported and stylish gifts and home decor. Hard to find, **The Ark** (Wickham's Cay II, 284/494-9151) has a wide range of housewares and gifts imported from Indonesia at its store, located next to Tico beverage supply, just off the four-lane highway east of town. Near the roundabout, **Hiho** (284/494-7694) has surfing, windsurfing, and other water sports gear, as well as trendy bathing suits and beachwear.

Cane Garden Bay

The best shopping in Cane Garden Bay is at **Olivia's Corner Store** (Myett's, 284/495-9649), which has crafts, island beachwear, local music, books, and more. Petite **Popo's Art Gallery** (284/495-0265), run by Paulette Maduro, has touristy trinkets as well as genuine Haitian paintings and sculptures. You'll find Popo's near the turnoff to the Callwood Rum Distillery at the west end of the bay.

Main Street in Road Town is the best place to shop.

East Island

Trellis Bay is the best place for shopping in the east. **Aragorn's Studio** (284/495-1849) has unique local arts, Carib crafts, pottery, and silk-screened T-shirts of Aragorn Dick-Read's woodcut prints. At the other end of the bay, **Flukes** (284/495-2043) has cheerful local art produced by Roger F. Ellis.

At the airport, you will find shops selling local crafts, T-shirts, and postcards.

West Island

Located in the heart of Apple Bay, **Nan's Gallery** is a roadside stand specializing in handpainted calabash gourds. Proprietors Nan Thomas and Benito Potter harvest the gourds, sand them, polish them, and paint them with colorful designs. They also sell handpainted bowls and watercolors. The gallery is open daily from mid-September to early June.

Also in Apple Bay, **Caribbean Landscapes Art Gallery** (10 A.M.–10 P.M. Mon.–Sat.) showcases the work of artist David Thrasher, as well as other painters and photographers. Stop here for one of Thrasher's unique hand-drawn maps of the west end of Tortola. The gallery is located at the rear of Coco Plums Restaurant.

At Nanny Cay, **Arawak Gifts** sells clothing, jewelry, and beachwear, while **Bamboushay** (284/494-0393) has locally made pottery and other arts.

Soper's Hole has several nice shops, including **Latitude 18** (284/495-4347), which sells island-style clothing and footwear. **Samarkand Jewellers** (284/495-4137) and **Zenaida's** (284/495-4867) are good places for unique jewelry.

Sports and Recreation

Tortola is a land of plenty for sailors and water sports enthusiasts. This is ground zero for the territory's charter yacht industry, one of the largest in the Caribbean. The island also hosts the largest annual windsurfing race in the region, has the best surfing in the entire Virgin Islands, and is an excellent home base for anyone wanting to scuba dive on the reefs and wrecks that lie all around the BVI.

Praises of Tortola's land-based pursuits are not as commonly sung, but they should be. There is good hiking in the island's largest national park, exciting bicycling, and opportunities for tennis and horseback riding.

SAILING

If the British Virgin Islands are the sailing capital of the Caribbean, Tortola is the epicenter of the city. The island is home to nearly all the BVI's 800-plus charter yachts, dozens of daysail operators, sailing schools, two yacht clubs, and a growing community of enthusiastic sailors. While Tortola may lag behind the rest of the world in many things, don't be surprised to find the latest sailing technology, services, and equipment here.

Charters

So far, Tortola's greatest gift to the world is the charter yacht vacation. Ginny and Charlie Cary cooked up the idea of renting sailboats to tourists back in the 1960s. They started their company, The Moorings, with just six yachts. Today, the Moorings has 900 yachts at 41 bases around the world, and its success has spawned a thriving charter yacht industry in the BVI.

This is good news for sailors since it means choices: choices between motor or sailing yacht, between monohull or catamaran, between bareboat or crewed, and between large or small charter companies. It also means that sailors are bound to find like-minded people at watering holes and restaurants all around the BVI. (See the sidebar *Setting Sail* in the *Essentials* chapter for a complete listing of charter boat companies.)

Tortola has a sizeable number of private

GLI-GLI, THE CARIB CANOE

In 1997 British Virgin Islands artist Aragorn Dick-Read and Jacob Fredericks, a member of Dominica's Kalinago (Carib Indian) community, led an expedition from Dominica to the Oronoco river delta of Guyana in South America. Their means of transport was the *Gli-Gli*, a traditional Carib dugout canoe.

Their journey retraced that of the Kalinagos' ancestors, who settled the Caribbean island chain centuries before. The canoe stopped at islands along the way to meet school groups, talk to reporters, and spread the message that the Kalinago and their traditions were still alive. The voyage ended in the heart of the Kalinago community of Guyana, where the Dominican Indians were welcomed.

The *Gli-Gli* lives at anchor in Trellis Bay. Ask at Aragorn's Studio (tel. 284/495-1849) to look through a scrapbook of newspaper clippings from the trip and see parts of a documentary about the journey. Aragorn also offers occasional day sails on the *Gli-Gli*.

crewed charter yachts—yachts with their own dedicated crews, personalities and services. The **Charter Yacht Society of the BVI** (Columbus Centre, 284/494-6017, www.bvicrewedyachts.com) maintains a database and provides booking services for more than 50 crewed yachts operating in the BVI.

Day Sails

For visitors who have chosen land-based accommodation rather than a charter yacht, a day sail is often the easiest and best way to see what this sailing fuss is all about.

Day-sail operators usually take guests to a handful of popular sites: Norman Island, the Baths, and Jost Van Dyke are the most common. Each operator fosters a different kind of atmosphere aboard, ranging from party-hearty to family-oriented. If you have a large group, many operators will offer a private charter where you get to choose your destinations. Most operators offer both half- and full-day trips. Full-day sails range $75–110 per person, while half-day sails run $50–75. Most serve lunch onboard. This is one aspect of your vacation that you should plan in advance; many day-sail companies book up, especially in high season.

Patouche Charters (Penn's Marina, Road Harbour, 284/494-6300) wins the prize for friendliest crew and is an especially good choice if there are inexperienced snorkelers in your group. Favorite stops include Norman Island and the Indians.

White Squall II (Village Cay Marina, 284/494-2564, fax 284/495-9753) is an 80-foot traditional schooner that takes day sailors to the Baths, Norman Island and Cooper Island. It tends to book large groups.

Other good choices in the Road Town area are **No Problem** (Village Cay Marina, 284/499-1987), which also offers luxury one- to three-night cruises, and **Promenade Cruises** (Village Cay Marina, 284/499-2756), which has scuba equipment onboard for certified divers.

In West End, try **Aristocat Charters** (Soper's Hole, tel./fax 284/495-4087, cellular 284/499-1249) or **Kuralu** (tel./fax 284/495-4381), both of which specialize in trips to Jost Van Dyke.

Boat Rentals

A boat gives you the freedom to travel easily and quickly from one island to another, and a motorboat means you can do it quickly. Renting a boat is a good way for experienced boaters to chart their own course for a day or more. It's not cheap, though; powerboats go for $200 and up for a day's rental, excluding fuel. Expect to pay twice that, at least, if you need a skipper.

In the Road Town area, **Sunshine Pleasure Boats** (Inner Harbour Marina, 284/494-8813) rents boats in a variety of sizes for $250–450.

In Cane Garden Bay, Glen Henley rents small powerboats at his **Cane Garden Bay Pleasure Boats and Waterports** (284/495-9660) for $175–400 a day.

TORTOLA

At Nanny Cay, **Island Time** (Nanny Cay Marina, 284/495-9993, www.island-timeltd.com) rents 22-foot Contenders for $250 a day and 15-foot inflatables for $125, while **Virgin Traders** (Nanny Cay Marina, 284/495-2526, www.virgintraders.com) rents 40- to 60-foot luxury motor yachts.

Sailing Schools

While many charter yacht companies offer special sailing school packages, if you want to gain sailing certification while you're on vacation, serious students should go directly to a sailing school. These schools offer a variety of courses, from land-based courses for beginners to week-long charters designed to teach intermediate or advanced skills. Expect to pay $800 for a short learn-to-sail land-based course, and $1,600 and up for longer boat-based courses.

One of the best sailing schools is **Sistership Sailing School** (tel./fax 284/495-1002, www.sailsistership.com), which specializes in courses for women, couples, and families. Captain Pat Nolan earns high marks for her patience and knowledge.

Rob Swain Sailing School (284/495-9376, U.S. toll free 800/948-7245, www.swainsailing.com) offers U.S. sailing certificates and courses from basic keelboat sailing to advanced cruising.

Another choice is **Full Sail Sailing School** (284/494-0512, fax 284/494-0588, U.S. 518/587-7452, www.fullsailbvi.com).

Yachting Facilities

Road Harbour is home to a half dozen different marinas and yachting facilities. If you are clearing customs and immigration, anchor off the main government dock and dinghy ashore; the dock itself is crowded with ferry traffic and exposed to an uncomfortable surge. **Village Cay** (Wickham's Cay, 284/494-2771) is a 100-slip marina that can accommodate boats up to 150 feet in length. It is home to a popular restaurant, bar, and hotel. Services include a spa, laundry, showers, phone service, and cable TV. It is also convenient to all of Road Town's services, including travel agencies, courier services, book-

stores, and grocery stores. Right next to Village Cay is **Inner Harbour Marina** (Channel 16) equally convenient to Road Town. Services here include water and electricity.

On the eastern end of the harbor you will find the bases of **The Moorings** and **Footloose Charters,** both of which can be used for transitory yachts, provisioning, refueling, and more.

Fort Burt Marina in Road Reef on the western end of Road Harbour has recently upgraded slips and is near to a marine supply retailer.

One of the newest marinas on Tortola **Manual Reef Marina** (Sea Cow's Bay, 284/495-2066) offers electricity, water, showers, and yacht management. The BVI Watersports Centre on the premises offers sailing instruction.

Nanny Cay Marina (Nanny Cay, 284/494-2512) is a full-service boatyard and marina with a 40-room hotel, two restaurants, chandlery, spa, Internet access, and much more.

On the west end, **Soper's Hole Wharf and Marina** (Frenchman's Cay, 284/495-4589) has 50 slips, a small hotel, and services. It also has moorings. Also at Soper's Hole, **Frenchman's Cay Shipyard and Marina** (284/495-4353) has dockage for ships up to 150 feet, a chandlery, and repairs. It specializes in wooden yachts, multihulls, and teak decking.

Hodge's Creek Marina (Maya Cove, 284/494-5000) is one of the largest marinas on the east end of Tortola. The base of Sunsail charters, this is a busy marine hub. Call ahead to see if there is space for you.

In East End Bay, **Penn's Landing Marina** (East End, 284/495-1134) and **Harbour View Marina** (East End, 284/495-0165) provide services and overnight accommodation.

Anchorages

Probably the favorite anchorage on Tortola **Cane Garden Bay** is usually comfortable for overnight use. Be sure to stay out of the swimming area. There is a dinghy dock on the eastern end of the bay, near Quito's Gazebo.

On the west end, **Soper's Hole** has moorings for visiting yachts.

A nice anchorage on the east end is **Buck**

Island, off Maya Cove. Anchor on the southwestern shore in 7–10 feet of water. Also on the east, **Trellis Bay,** Beef Island, is a great stop for yachters. Check on the latest regulations in the area, however, as the presence of the international airport has rendered some parts of the harbor off-limits.

Yacht Clubs
Both the **Royal BVI Yacht Club** (Road Reef, 284/494-3286, www.rbviyc.net) and the **"Loyal" West End Yacht Club** (Soper's Hole, www.weyc.net) put on a series of regattas every year. Hang out among the yacht crowd long enough and you are bound to be invited along if there's a regatta coming up.

Some of the West End Yacht Club's most popular local racers are the Firecracker Regatta held every July 4, the Anegada Dark and Stormy in March, and the Sweethearts of the Caribbean in February.

The Royal BVI Yacht Club puts on the Road Tortola Race every November, the Virgins Cup (where the skipper must be a woman) in October, and the Anegada Pursuit Race in July.

BVI Spring Regatta
The **BVI Spring Regatta** (www.bvispringregatta.org), part of the Caribbean Ocean Racing Triangle, is one of the premier regattas in the Caribbean, often attracting entries from Europe, North America, and all over the Caribbean. In recent years organizers have tacked a Sailing Festival on to the beginning of the regatta to attract less-experienced sailors who want to make the regatta into a vacation.

The Spring Regatta takes place in early April and is based at Nanny Cay Marina. The regatta village, a grassy area with bars, restaurants, seating, and music, draws a diverse crowd of racers, residents, and landlubbers who come out to soak in the yachty atmosphere.

WATER SPORTS
Snorkeling
While the British Virgin Islands' most impressive snorkeling is generally found around outer islands or on submerged rocks in between islands, you should not write Tortola off completely. There are several nice snorkel sites easily accessible from the beach.

The best snorkeling around Tortola is found at Marina Cay, a small island just off the coast of Beef Island. Smuggler's Cove on the west end has a shallow offshore reef best explored in calm weather. Other good snorkel sites are Gun Point, at the western point of Smuggler's Cove, and at both the western and eastern points of Brewer's Bay.

Snorkel equipment can be rented from any of the dive operators listed under *Diving.* Or try **BVI Yacht Charters** (Road Town, 284/494-4289) or **Cane Garden Bay Pleasure Boats** (284/495-9660), which rent mask, snorkel, and fins for about $10 a day.

Diving
There are more than 60 popular dive sites in the British Virgin Islands, and dive operators on Tortola lead trips to many of them every day. Most famous is the RMS *Rhone,* the remains of which lie submerged between Salt and Peter Islands. Other popular sites include the Indians off Norman Island, the Dogs between Virgin Gorda and Tortola, and Blonde Rock between Salt Island and Dead Chest. Weather conditions will dictate the best sites on any given day.

There are more than a dozen Tortola-based dive operators, and the competitive nature of the industry means that only the best survive.

In the Road Town area, try **Aquaventure Scuba Services,** (Wickham's Cay I, 284/494-4320, fax 284/494-5608, www.aquaventure-bvi.com) which specializes in small groups and boasts about the rich and famous they have taken out to dive.

With locations at Nanny Cay and Soper's Hole, **Blue Water Divers** (Nanny Cay Marina, 284/494-2847, fax 284/494-0198, Soper's Hole Marina 284/495-1200, www.bluewater-diverbvi.com) dive off a catamaran or motor boat. It offers only one trip a day, leaving at 9 A.M. and often returning after 1 P.M. It offers a complete array of certification courses.

On the East End, try **Sail Caribbean Divers**

TORTOLA

(Hodge's Creek Marina, 284/495-1675, fax 284/495-3244, www.sailcaribbeandivers.com), which offers daily pick-ups from Marina Cay, Cooper Island, and Norman Island, or **UBS Dive Center,** (Harbour View Marina, 284/494-0024, fax 284/494-0623, www.scubabvi.com).

In Cane Garden Bay, **We Be Divin'** (284/499-2835, fax 284/494-5172) rents equipment and leads guided trips to nearby dive sites. It offers a $25 "try dive" for beginners.

On Marina Cay, Virgin Gorda–based **Dive BVI** (284/495-9363, www.divebvi.com) offers dive trips for no more than six people at a time.

Dolphin Swimming

Much to the chagrin of many Tortola residents, a Mexico-based company established a "swim with the dolphins" facility on Tortola in 2003. **Dolphin Discovery** (Prospect Reef Resort, 284/494-7675, www.dolphindiscovery.com) did not lead to the immediate and wholesale demise of BVI's reputation for responsible nature-based tourism, as some had warned. But neither did it meet great success; business has been slower than proponents expected. One reason for this, no doubt, is the steep price tag: it costs upwards of $125 for a brief dolphin "encounter", which includes about 20 minutes of being pulled, pushed, and prodded by the trained animals. Many of the facility's customers are from cruise ships that visit Tortola.

Dolphin Discovery has tried to smooth over the bad feelings left from its arrival by inviting school groups and families to come watch shows free on special occasions. But there is still little enthusiasm in the community about the facility or what it does, and for pretty good reason.

Surfing

Tortola has the best and most reliable surfing of any of the Virgin Islands. On weekends surfers from St. John and St. Thomas often sojourn to Tortola in search of waves. The surf is generally up during the winter, from December through March, when cold fronts come off the East Coast of North America and create swells along Tortola's Atlantic shore. September and

October can be good months as well, but they are less reliable.

The best surfing beaches are Apple Bay on the west end, Josiah's Bay in the east, and Cane Garden Bay. Apple Bay sees reliable two- to four-foot waves during the season and is probably the most heavily surfed location on Tortola. Josiah's Bay is popular among longboarders and is considered "on" when it has one- to three-foot waves. Josiah's is known for its dangerous riptide, so be careful in rougher conditions.

"The Point" at the far eastern end of Cane Garden Bay is mythic among surfers. When it's on, Cane Garden Bay delivers six- to seven-foot waves that last up to 200 yards. Cane Garden Bay is on only about a dozen days a year; when it is, word spreads quickly among all who surf.

Surfers also sometimes paddle to Cooten Bay, west of Josiah's Bay, for a change of scenery and nice meaty waves.

Windsurfing and Kayaking

Windsurfing, a cross between sailing and surfing, is exhilarating and physically challenging. When conditions are right, windsurfers skim across the water at speeds rivaling those of a speedboat. Beginners can get a taste of this sport with lessons, while experienced windsurfers will find plenty of gear to rent and a community of kindred spirits.

Some of the world's best windsurfers descend on the BVI every July for the **Highland Spring HIHO** (www.go-hiho.com), a weeklong windsurfing race that takes competitors throughout the British Virgin Islands.

When there's no wind, water sports enthusiasts often turn to kayaks for a little excitement. Seaworthy one- and two-person kayaks are a good way to explore coastal areas, especially on the southern shore of Tortola and other protected areas.

Kayaking can be hard work, especially if there is strong wind, current, waves, or all of the above. But it is a great way to maneuver around mangroves, rocky shores, and other hard-to-reach areas.

Gear and Lessons

There are three major players in the water sports industry on Tortola. Expect to pay about $25–35 to rent gear for the day, and $150–200 to rent it for the week. Most operators will deliver gear to you or your boat if you are renting it for more than a few days.

HIHO (Road Town, 284/494-7694, www.go-hiho.com), an apparel and gear shop run by local Andy Morrell, stages the **Red Stripe Surf Series,** a surfing competition held annually from early December until March, and the **Highland Spring HIHO,** the annual windsurfing race.

HIHO also rents surfboards and windsurfing equipment by the day and by the week; two hours of instruction in either sport runs between $75 and $95.

Island Surf and Sail (Nanny Cay Marina, 284/494-0123, www.surfandsailbvi.com) is a welcoming water sports mecca where the staff are enthusiastic about just about any water-based pursuit. If they don't offer a specific service, owner Owen Walters will hook you up with someone who does. Island Surf and Sail specializes in windsurfing and surf equipment rentals and lessons. It also has a half-pipe for skateboarders, kayaks, and kiteboard equipment rentals.

You can rent a range of gear or take windsurfing lessons at **Boardsailing BVI** (Trellis Bay, 284/495-2447, fax 284/495-1626, www.windsurfing.vi, 7 A.M.–6 P.M.). A two-hour beginner's lesson costs $75, and success is guaranteed—if you can't windsurf by the end of your lesson, you don't pay. Boardsailing BVI also offers advanced lessons and rents a range of small sailing dinghies ($25/hour) and kayaks ($15/hour).

Nanny Cay–based **Caribbean Fly Fishing** (Nanny Cay Marina, 284/494-4797, www.caribflyfishing.com) leads fly-fishing trips around Tortola. Rates are $450 for a half-day trip and $850 for a full day. Anglers pursue tarpon, permits, and bonefish in the 28-foot *After You.*

LAND PURSUITS
Hiking

The only formal hiking trails on Tortola are found at **Sage Mountain National Park** off the Ridge Road. But there are a number of other places where you can hike, either on less-traveled roads or private paths.

Some of the best hiking is found at **Belmont Estate,** an exclusive residential area at the western tip of Tortola. A network of lightly trafficked gravel roads connect Long Bay, Smuggler's Cove, Steele Point, and West End. For a nice hike, follow the paved road that climbs Belmont Hill just before the West End ferry terminal parking area. After cresting the hill, the road turns to gravel and you are greeted with views of Smuggler's Cove and Long Bay. Turn left at the bottom of the hill and follow it to Smuggler's Cove beach. You can hike back the way you came or follow the road heading west from Smuggler's Cove, which passes Steele Point before dropping you out next to the Jolly Roger Inn. The whole loop will take about 90 minutes.

Horseback Riding

There is one horseback riding outfit on Tortola. **Shadow Stables** (Todman Estate, 284/494-2262) lets you choose between a two-hour rainforest ride through Sage Mountain or a three-hour ride to Brewer's Bay beach. The fee is $100 per hour per person.

Tennis

There are no public tennis courts on Tortola, but you can pay to use courts at many of the larger resorts. Expect to pay between $5 and $15 per hour. In the west, there are courts at **Long Bay Beach Resort** (284/495-4252) and **Nanny Cay** (284/494-2512). Out east, try **Lambert Beach Resort** (284/495-2877); near Road Town, the **Cutting Edge Fitness Centre** (284/495-9570) has several courts.

The **Tortola Sports Club** (Pasea Estate, 284/494-3457) has four tennis courts and two squash courts. Visitors can purchase temporary membership to the club, which puts on the BVI Tennis Open every June.

Biking

Biking is an increasingly popular sport on Tortola, and it is not unusual to see bikers out in the early morning or late afternoon, especially along Drake's Highway, the flat road that connects West End and Road Town. If you want a challenge, there is no shortage of hills to choose from. Two of the best are the fearsome "East End Wall", a steep road between Greenland and Lambert in East End, and Trellfall, which climbs to Sage Mountain from the westernmost end of Sea Cow's Bay. Once you get there, the ride along the Ridge Road is pleasant and relatively flat.

The **BVI Bicycling Federation** (www.bvicycling.com) puts on a series of bike races, including the Jason Bally Memorial in October, which often attracts racers from around the Caribbean. Serious bikers are welcome to join in for a race, and many races feature a novice/fun class for less-seasoned riders.

Bikes and related equipment can be rented from **Last Stop Sports** (Purcell, 284/494-1120, 8:30 A.M.–5 P.M. Mon.–Fri., 10 A.M.–4 P.M. Sat.) for $25–30 a day.

Golf

There are plans for a full 18-hole golf course on Beef Island, but for now the only golf opportunities on Tortola are nine-hole pitch-and-putt courses at **Long Bay Resort** (West End, 284/495-4252) and **Prospect Reef Resort** (Road Town, 284/494-3311).

If you want to practice your swing in a laid-back environment, try **Captain Mulligan's** (Nanny Cay, 284/495-4414, noon–dusk) where you can drive golf balls into the ocean and watch them float back in to shore. Captain Mulligan's also has a playground for kids, a bar, and a restaurant. It is a popular happy-hour stop for expats and often throws weekend barbecue and Thai food parties.

Spectator Sports

Sports including cricket, basketball, and softball are played in the BVI. The best way to find out what sporting events are upcoming is to consult the *Limin' Times,* a free weekly entertainment guide that includes a sports calendar.

Men's and women's fast-pitch softball is played at the Old Recreation Grounds next to the BVI High School in Road Town. The season usually begins in March and wraps up in July. Games are played on Friday, Saturday, and Sunday nights.

Basketball is played in the Multi-Purpose Complex on Botanic Station Road in Road Town. The season usually opens in May and concludes in July. Admission is $5 for adults.

Cricket is played on the Greenland field in East End, and pick-up games take place sometimes on the open space next to the cruise ship pier at the waterfront.

Horse racing is very popular among islanders, and there is always a crowd for the races at the Little "A" Racetrack in Sea Cow's Bay. Races are held about seven times a year on Sunday afternoons, except for the annual Festival races held on the second Tuesday in August and the Boxing Day Races in December. Admission is $5 for adults.

The Horseowners' Association, which manages the races, hangs a banner across the road at Sea Cow's Bay to advertise upcoming races.

Accommodations

Tortola has casual inns, budget campgrounds, and luxury hotels. Quoted room rates do not include a 7 percent hotel tax. In addition, most accommodations add a 10–15 percent service charge to bills.

Villas

Tortola, like other Virgin Islands, is well endowed with a variety of private villas. While most of these are luxurious (and expensive), some can fit more modest budgets, especially during summer. Winter rates generally range $1,200–4,000 a week for one- to two-bedroom homes. In summer, rates drop to as low as $700 a week.

Private villas are completely equipped homes: they have full kitchens, several bedrooms, entertainment centers, and water sports gear. Many have a private pool. Villas are a great choice for families or large groups, or for visitors who want independence and privacy.

The easiest way to find a private villa is to use a villa rental agency. These agencies represent dozens of villas, making it easy to find one that fits your needs. The best villa rental agencies on Tortola are **Areana Villas** (P.O. Box 263, Road Town, Torotola, 284/494-5864, www.areanavillas.com) and **Purple Pineapple Rental Management** (284/495-3100, fax 305/723-0855, www.purplepineapple.com).

ROAD TOWN

Stay in Road Town only if you are traveling for business or need a convenient hotel before or after your Road Town–based yacht charter. The town atmosphere is simply not the best Tortola has to offer.

Under $125

Hotel Castle Maria (Macnamara, 284/494-2553, fax 284/494-2111, $90 winter, $70 summer) is a 30-room hotel in a shady residential neighborhood outside Road Town, but it's within walking distance of shops and marinas. The hotel facilities here are adequate,

Road Town from above

but nothing more. The rooms are small and the decor is shabby, but the neighborhood is pleasant and quiet (with the exception of the roosters). The Hotel Castle Maria is a good alternative if you need to stay near town but don't want to shell out big bucks for a fancy hotel. It has the dubious distinction of doubling as the immigration detention facility when authorities run out of space at the prison.

Located on one of Road Town's busiest commercial streets, the **A&L Inn** (Flemming Street, 284/494-6343, fax 284/494-6656, $75–100 winter, $70–90 summer) is a good choice if you need affordable but comfortable accommodation in the capital. The inn's 14 a/c rooms are clean; some have kitchenettes.

Maria's By the Sea (Waterfront Drive, 284/494-2595, fax 284/494-2420, www.mariasbythesea.com, $110–250 winter, $95–210 summer) has ocean views but no beach. There is a pool, restaurant, and conference room, and the 38 air-conditioned rooms come with

© SUSANNA HENIGHAN

TORTOLA

telephones and TV. There is one handicapped accessible room here.

$125-175

Located at Road Town's largest marina, **Village Cay Hotel** (284/494-2771, fax 284/494-2773, www.villagecay.com, $150–190 winter, $115–150 summer) is convenient for yachters and businesspeople. The 19 air-conditioned rooms come with TV and phone, and the best have nice views of Road Harbour. A popular restaurant and bar are downstairs, and the hotel is within walking distance of dozens of other places to eat.

CANE GARDEN BAY
Under $125

Brewer's Bay Campground (284/494-3463, $40) has a dozen prepared and bare campsites nestled under the palms at beautiful Brewer's Bay beach. Prepared sites come with a platform tent, beds, bedding, a two-burner propane stove, cooler, table, chairs, and cooking equipment. You must provide your own ice and drinking water. Bare sites, which come with a table, chairs and a place to pitch your tent, are available for $15 per night. Shared bathrooms are at a concrete bathhouse, with utility sink, toilets, and showers.

The greatest attraction here is being able to sleep just a few steps away from Brewer's Bay beach, one of the best and least disturbed beaches on Tortola. The campground facilities are a little run-down, and its unsophisticated approach to guest services may be charming or frustrating, depending on your perspective. Nevertheless, the campground often fills up in the winter months.

Consider logistics if you stay here; Brewer's Bay has no grocery store and few restaurants, and taxis charge upwards of $20 for a one-way trip to town. Walking to the nearest market in Cane Garden Bay will easily take several hours. It is a good idea to either stock up on groceries before you come or plan to rent a car.

Columbus Sunset Apartments (284/495-4751, fax 284/495-9114, $80 winter, $60

summer) is a good choice for budget-minded travelers who want to be close to the beach. The two-story concrete hotel is located just across the road from the sand at Cane Garden Bay. The 10 one- and two-bedroom apartments have full kitchens and private baths.

$125-175

(Mongoose Apartments (284/495-4421, fax 284/495-9721, www.mongooseapartments.com, $165 winter, $105 summer) is a brightly painted and well-managed inn located a short walk from Cane Garden Bay Beach. The six one-bedroom apartments include full kitchens, outdoor grills, a/c in the bedrooms, TVs, and sleeping accommodation for up to four people. A phone is available in the office, and guests may use the inn's beach chairs, snorkels, floats, and kayaks free. Hosts Elroy and Sandra Henley will happily help you arrange activities during your stay, and don't miss the wall of newspaper clippings recounting Elroy's success as a minor league baseball star in Chattanooga, Tennessee, in the late 1970s. There are no dramatic ocean views here, but the inn's location nestled among coconut and banana trees is so charming you probably won't mind.

If you prefer to be in the thick of things, try **Elm Beach Suites** (284/494-2888, U.S. toll free 800/878-6359, $140 winter, $105 summer). Elm's five one-bedroom apartments come with kitchens, cable TV, and a/c in the bedrooms. A pull-out couch means each suite can accommodate up to four people. The suites are sandwiched between three different bars and restaurants; they can be quite noisy.

$175-225

The Lighthouse Villas, (284/494-5482, fax 284/495-9101, www.travel-watch.com/lighthouse, $165–255 winter, $95–160 summer) is located a few (steep) steps above the beach at Cane Garden Bay. The three-story concrete building rises above the surrounding buildings, giving guests lovely views of the bay. The best views are from the two penthouse suites on the third floor. The one-

and two-bedroom villas are neat, clean, and homey, with full kitchens, private balconies, phones, cable TV, and a/c. Guests share a hot tub. Stays of at least a week preferred; for short-term rates, add 10 percent. There is no service charge.

Steps away from the beach, the **Cane Garden Bay Cottages** (284/495-9649, fax 284/495-9579, www.virginislandsholidays.com, $180 winter, $120 summer) are two cute cottages surrounded by coconut trees. Each cottage is divided into two one-bedroom units, each with a small kitchen, sitting area, screened-in dining room, and porch. Larger groups may rent both sides of a cottage. There is a/c in the bedrooms.

EAST ISLAND
Under $125
Located on Trellis Bay, **◖ The Beef Island Guesthouse** (284/495-2303, fax 284/495-1611, $115 winter, $90 summer) is homey, comfortable, and well run. The guesthouse's four rooms boast comfortable beds, ceiling fans, and private baths. There is a shared living room, full kitchen, and screened-in porch. Amenities include satellite TV, high-speed Internet, and continental breakfast.

The guesthouse is set right on Trellis Bay, where you can swim or relax in a hammock. There is a restaurant and beach bar next door. The guesthouse is the only place to stay within walking distance of the airport and is a popular choice for people who need a room the day before or after their sailing charter.

The white, concrete **Josiah's Bay Inn** (tel./fax 284/495-2818, $80 winter, $65 summer) is a 10-minute walk to Josiah's Bay beach, popular among surfers and sunbathers. The one- to four-bedroom apartments are plain but clean and come equipped with full kitchens.

Another choice in the Josiah's Bay area is **Serendipity House** (284/495-1488, fax 284/494-5774, www.serhouse.com, $75–150). The house has one- to five-bedroom suites, including full kitchens, TV, telephone, and a shared pool. The beach is a 10-minute walk down shady Josiah's Bay Road.

$125-175
The Tamarind Club (284/495-3477, fax 284/495-2795, www.tamarindclub.com, $110–140 winter, $90–120 summer) is a small inn set amid flamboyant trees on the road to Josiah's Bay beach. Under new ownership since late 2004, the Club has undergone a series of improvements to spruce up rooms and the adjoining bar and restaurant. The Club's nine rooms face either the pool or the garden and come equipped with air-conditioning, phone, and television (no cable, but plenty of videos). There is a continental breakfast for guests.

$175-225
White stucco cottages line lovely Lambert Beach at **Lambert Beach Resort** (284/495-2877, fax 284/495-2876, www.lambertbeachresort.com, $185–285 winter, $100–170 summer) on the northeastern coast of Tortola. The 38-room hotel features a pool, tennis courts, restaurant, and water sports equipment rental. Accommodation ranges from modest yet comfortable garden rooms to two-bedroom beachfront villas. Various meal plans are available for $14–70 per day.

Pusser's Marina Cay (Marina Cay, 284/494-2174, www.pussers.com/outposts/marina-cay, $195 winter, $135 summer) consists of a beachfront restaurant and a handful of hilltop villas and smaller double rooms. Rooms have private balconies and refrigerators and enjoy views of Trellis Bay, while villas gaze out toward the open ocean.

Over $300
The **◖ Guana Island Club** (Guana Island, 284/495-9786, U.S. 914/964-6050, U.S. toll free 800/544-8262, fax 284/495-2900, www.guana.com, $785 winter, $650 summer) is one of the best private island retreats in the BVI. Guest accommodations are in private stone and masonry cottages along the ridge with commanding views of the beaches and bays below. There is also one private beach cottage on North Beach. Three meals daily, plus afternoon tea and evening cocktails, are served in the clubhouse, where there is also a

TORTOLA

comfortable library and sitting room. Many of the tropical fruits, vegetables, and herbs served in the dining room are grown in Guana's own garden near White Bay.

Guests can spend their days hiking some of the 22 marked and maintained trails, at any of the island's seven beaches, or just relaxing on their balcony with a book. In addition, guests have access to kayaks, snorkel equipment, sailboards, and small sailboats for exploring the ocean. There is also tennis, croquet, volleyball, ping-pong, waterskiing, and badminton. Visitors seeking total privacy can book the whole island for between $12,500 and $21,500 per night, depending on the number of guests.

WEST ISLAND
Under $125

Budget travelers should look to **The Jolly Roger Inn** (284/495-4559, fax 284/495-4184, www.jollyrogerbvi.com, $55–85 winter, $40–70 summer), whose five rooms overlook Soper's Hole on Tortola's western tip. For these prices don't expect any frills such as telephones, TV, or kitchenettes, but you can count on clean, comfortable rooms. You can choose from a private or shared bath. The inn is a short walk from the West End ferry dock and taxi stand and is convenient if you have to catch an early-morning ferry. There is a car rental agency and restaurant downstairs.

$125-175

Its spectacular view of western Tortola and the U.S. Virgin Islands is the **Heritage Inn's** most outstanding attraction. The Inn (284/494-5842, fax 284/495-4100, www.heritagevillas-bvi.com, $165 winter, $110 summer) is located atop Windy Hill overlooking Carrot Bay and points farther west. Its nine modern rooms are equipped with phones, TVs, full kitchens, private balconies, and a/c in the bedrooms. For guests uninterested in leaving the property, there is a pool and a restaurant. Beaches are about 10 minutes away in either direction by car. Both one- and two-bedroom rooms are available.

⟨ Coconut Point Vacation Apartments (284/495-4892, www.go-bvi.com/coconut_

point, $175 winter, $100 summer) is a small complex of five well-equipped villas located in Carrot Bay, a seaside community of farmers and fishermen. Coconut Point's one- and two-bedroom apartments feature full kitchens, cable TV, phones, private balconies, outdoor grills, and a/c. A small wading pool will keep you cool in a pinch, but if you want a beach you will have to walk about 15 minutes to Apple Bay. Another excellent choice in Carrot Bay is **Sugar Apple Villa** (284/494-1946, www.sugarapplevillas.net, $150-$220), a cozy, comfortable, and well-maintained guest house that sleeps up to six people. Surrounded by a lush garden, the villa is a short stroll to the ocean. Hostess Cheryl Smith overlooks no detail.

$175-225

At the end of a winding, narrow road that climbs to the top of Long Bay Hill on the western end of Tortola sits the rustic **⟨ Turtle Dove Lodge** (284/495-4430, fax 284/495-4070, www.bviwelcome.com/turtledl, $190-250 winter, $160–200 summer). The Lodge consists of three one-bedroom cottages surrounded by lush tropical gardens. The private decks are eye-level with the local frigate birds and provide nice views of Little Apple Bay and Long Bay some 250 feet below. Proprietress Carol Vanterpool has decorated the lodge with her own artwork and photography. The cottages are comfortable but not luxurious. Each has a queen-size bed, kitchen, private bath, Internet access, and dining area. There is no a/c, TV, or in-room phone.

Sebastian's on the Beach (Apple Bay, 284/495-4003, U.S. toll-free 800/336-4870, fax 284/495-4466, www.sebastiansvillas.com, $135–230 winter, $85–140 summer)is a 26-room hotel facing picturesque Apple Bay, a favorite for surfers. In addition to beachfront and garden rooms, Sebastian's has several new luxury villas at the west end of the beach. Sebastian's is set amid the welcoming community of Apple Bay, and outgoing guests can look forward to making friends at the weekly Friday night fish fry.

$225-300

Perched above one of the most picturesque beaches on Tortola, **Long Bay Beach Resort** (284/495-4252 or 954/481-8787, U.S./Canada toll-free 800/858-4618, U.K./Europe 0870/160-1645, fax 954/481-1661, U.K./Europe fax 1870/160-9651, www.eliteislandresorts.com, $300 winter, $155 summer) is the island's largest hotel. Open since 1963, it is one of Tortola's oldest resorts, too, although you wouldn't guess it from the modern facilities. Its 153 rooms range from small one-bedroom beachside cabanas to spacious two-bedroom villas on the hillside above. The resort also manages a half dozen privately owned estate homes, which boast the best views of the mile-long beach below. All rooms have a/c, TV, phone, and refrigerator, and many have full kitchens. Resort amenities include a pool, three restaurants, a nine-hole pitch-and-putt golf course, tennis courts, spa, gym, dive shop, car rental agencies, and water sports equipment rental.

Fort Recovery Villas, (284/495-4467, toll-free 800/367-8455, fax 284/495-4036, www.fortrecovery.com, $250 winter, $160 summer) a complex of one- to four-bedroom beachfront villas, lies in the shadow of a 17th-century Dutch fort. Billing itself as "a Bit of Britain in the Sun," Fort Recovery sees a largely European clientele, many of whom take advantage of its attractively priced package deals. The rooms, which are small but comfortable, face the private beach. Amenities include a pool, continental breakfast, yoga classes, Internet access, and a library.

Over $300

The Sugar Mill (284/495-4355, fax 284/495-4696, www.sugarmillhotel.com, $325–355 winter, $240–280 summer) is as good as a luxury Caribbean hideaway can get. The hotel is set amid almond, breadfruit, and mango trees, and many of its 23 air-conditioned rooms have superb ocean views. Accommodations range from well-appointed hotel-style rooms to one- and two-bedroom luxury villas. There is a pool on the property, but most guests prefer to bathe at the idyllic beach right across the road. Ruins of a 360-year-old sugar mill have been incorporated into the hotel's award-winning restaurant, which is one of the best places to eat on Tortola. Given that, the hotel's $65-per-day meal plan is worth considering. Children under 11 are not allowed during the winter months, and the hotel closes every August and September.

With views of St. John and Soper's Hole, **Casa Flamboyant** (284/495-3251, www.casa-flamboyantbvi.com, $280 summer, $450 winter) consists of two upscale villas with unique flair. Constructed of tropical hardwood and surrounded by fruit trees, flowering flamboyant trees, and lovely landscaping, the villas are a relaxing and quiet retreat. Modern amenities, such as state-of-the-art kitchen appliances, air-conditioning, and high-speed Internet access make the accommodations comfortable. The villas, which sleep up to six people each, are thoughtfully stocked with a reading library, local music collection, and beach toys. You will need a rental car to get to nearby beaches and attractions.

SIR FRANCIS DRAKE CHANNEL
$125-200

Cooper Island Beach Club (284/494-3111, U.K. 020/8758-4775, U.S. 413/863-3162, U.S. toll free 800/542-4624, www.cooper-island.com, $195 winter, $105 summer) is a comfortable and idyllic 12-room retreat. Rarely has a private island experience been so cheap. Don't expect frills—there are no room phones, TVs, electrical outlets, or a/c—but do expect a warm welcome, comfortable rooms, and a genuinely relaxed setting. Rooms are equipped with full kitchens, and they are all just steps away from the beach. The trade winds, helped along with ceiling fans, will keep you cool. Hotel guests can request provisioning for your kitchen, bring groceries over from Tortola, or eat in the restaurant. Days here are spent sunbathing, swimming, reading, or exploring the island trails and reefs.

Cooper Island Hideaways (513/232-4126, www.cooperisland.com, $220 winter, $130 summer) operates two villas at Manchioneel

Bay. The Beach House can sleep two people, while the Hideaway sleeps up to six. Both are equipped with full kitchens, balconies, and solar-powered lights, fans, and appliances.

Over $300

Peter Island Resort (284/495-2000, U.S. 770/476-9988, U.S. toll free 800/346-4451, fax 770/476-4979, www.peterisland.com, $560 summer, $1,015 winter) often finds itself near the top of "best-of" Caribbean resort lists, winning points for its spectacular setting, luxury accom-

modations, and world-class dining and spa. The 52 guest accommodations include beachfront, ocean-view, and garden-view rooms, plus a few luxury villas. Room rates include three meals daily (but not drinks) at the seaside **Deadman's Beach Bar and Grill** and the formal restaurant **Tradewinds.** Both welcome non-resort guests.

Peter Island's spa, opened in 2004, is an attraction in itself, with hydrotherapy tubs, private steam rooms, private whirlpools, spa lounge, meditation area, indoor treatment suites, and movement classes.

Food

You won't find the same sophisticated dining on Tortola that exists on the U.S. Virgin Islands, but you will still find good food. In addition to a handful of truly gourmet restaurants, Tortola has a number of homey beachfront eateries and a whole range of local food choices.

ROAD TOWN

Road Town has the greatest variety of food choices, especially at lunchtime.

Main Street

Located in a refurbished traditional Caribbean home, **The Dove Restaurant** (67 Main Street, 284/494-0313, 6:30–10 P.M. Tues.–Sun., $15–35) is an oasis of urban-style sophistication in the heart of Road Town. Its upscale clientele come for specialties like the honey and sesame Peking duck and peppercorn-crusted tuna. The Dove has one of the best wine lists on the island.

For authentic Indian roti, there is nowhere better than the **(Roti Palace** (94 Main Street, 284/494-4196, $8–16). Up a narrow flight of stairs next to Samarkand Jewellers, the Roti Palace serves nothing but rotis, the Indian-style wraps filled with curried meat and vegetables. Homey and welcoming, the Roti Palace overlooks Main Street and Road Town harbor. This is real home-style cooking. Call ahead to make a reservation.

Steps away from the Road Town ferry dock, **Capricio di Mare** (Waterfront Drive, 284/494-5369, 8 A.M.–9 P.M. Mon.–Sat., $4–14) is one of the best casual restaurants on the island. For breakfast try the croissant French toast, fruit, and a cappuccino. The lunch and dinner menu features salads, pastas, pizzas, and focaccia sandwiches. There is covered sidewalk dining and a few small tables inside. Takeout is popular here, too.

For Tortola's take on the greasy spoon, visit **Mid-Town Restaurant** (132 Main Street, 284/494-2764, 7 A.M.–10 P.M., $4–10). Located at the midpoint of Main Street, this aptly named restaurant has a genuine lunch counter as well as about a dozen tables. In addition to local daily specials, such as boiled fish, oxtail soup, and stewed mutton (goat meat), you can get sandwiches and fries. Full American-style breakfasts are available.

Sample the work of H. Lavity Stoutt Community College's culinary students at the **Road Town Bakery** (123 Main Street, 284/494-0222, 7 A.M.–7 P.M. Mon.–Fri., 7:30 A.M.–3 P.M. Sat., $2–8) one of three hands-on culinary training centers on Tortola. Don't worry about the quality of the students' work; the bakery produces top-notch pastries, cakes, and breads, as well as one of the most popular lunch menus in Road Town. In addition to a daily lunch special, you can choose from salads, sandwiches, and quiche.

Coffee lovers, take heart. Good coffee has arrived on Tortola in the form of the **Courtyard Coffeeshop** (145 Main Street, 284/494-3280, 7:30 A.M.–5:30 P.M. Mon.–Fri., 7:30 A.M.–1:30 P.M. Sat., $2–5), a charming oasis of calm in the middle of Road Town. In addition to fine hot and cold coffee and coffee drinks, you will find fresh fruit juices, teas, toasted sandwiches, and pastries. Take food out or dine in the rear fan-cooled courtyard.

Waterfront Drive and Wickham's Cay

For a cooling treat, try **La Dolce Vita** (Waterfront Drive, 284/494-8770, 10 A.M.–9 P.M. Mon.–Thurs., 10 A.M.–10 P.M. Fri.–Sat., 10:30 A.M.–9:30 P.M. Sun., $2–4) for homemade Italian ice cream. No kidding, this is the real thing. Try some of the unique flavors like soursop, cantaloupe, and ginger. It also serves soy ice cream, frozen yogurt, milk shakes, and banana splits.

Located in the Mill Mall across from the government administration building, **Nature's Way** (284/494-6393, 8:30 A.M.–5 P.M. Mon.–Fri., $4–10) serves vegetarian food. Owned by Seventh-Day Adventists, this popular lunch spot is also a good source for hard-to-find vegetarian and health food products. Try Joan's Delight, a filling veggie sandwich on whole wheat bread.

Village Cay Marina's **Dockmasters Deli** (284/494-2771 ext. 4, 10 A.M.–4 P.M. Mon.–Fri., $6–9) serves sandwiches during the week.

Outside of Town

Overlooking the western shore of Road Harbor, **Fort Burt Restaurant** (284/494-2587, 7 A.M.–10 P.M., $7–28) is built over the remains of a 17th-century fort. One of three hands-on training facilities for the community college's culinary arts program, Fort Burt serves an eclectic gourmet menu. Lunch features sandwiches, seafood, and soup. At dinner, try the lamb chops or cashew-encrusted tuna.

In the shadow of Fort Burt, across from Road Reef marina, **Crandalls Pastry Plus** (284/494-5156, 5 A.M.–4 P.M. Mon.–Fri., $3–8) is a popular early-morning breakfast stop for commuters on their way into Road Town. It serves fried johnnycakes, fried fish, and pâtés (fried bread stuffed with seasoned beef, chicken, or seafood). This is also a good place to try local "bush tea", a sweetened tea made from herbs including lemongrass and mint.

Tucked away at the end of a narrow alley in Purcell, a residential community just east of Road Town, is **C&F Restaurant** (284/494-4941, 6:30–10 P.M., Wed.–Mon., $12–25) the best West Indian restaurant on the island. Chef Clarence serves fresh fish, steak, lobster, barbecue, and curries. That may sound familiar, but it all just tastes better here. Red-checkered tablecloths and a jumbled decor gives the restaurant a homey feel. Takeout is popular, since one dinner plate can easily serve two people.

You will find a diverse mix of patrons at **Spaghetti Junction** (Beach Club Terrace, Baugher's Bay, 284/494-4880, 11 A.M.–10 P.M., Mon.–Sat., $10–35), a popular restaurant and bar (a.k.a. The Bat Cave) about a mile east of Road Town. When Spaghetti Junction's waterfront home burned down in 2004, it relocated to the Beach Club Terrace in Baugher's Bay. The result is that you can choose Spaghetti Junction's Italian and bar fare or the Beach Club's local West Indian specialties. At night, this is a popular bar, club, and hangout for the island's 30-something crowd.

Located at CSY Marina east of Road Town, **Chillin Café** (Baugher's Bay, 284/494-9236, 11 A.M.–10 P.M., $8–25) has a big-screen TV indoors and a lovely view of Road Harbor outside. Choose from Caribbean favorites or European and American standards. This is a nice happy hour spot.

Street vendors

With no McDonald's or KFC, Tortola's version of fast food are the itinerant food vendors who grill meat over charcoal fires, often on weekend nights. One of the best is **Dareo's** (Lower Estate Road, $3–12), which sets up next to the softball field behind the BVI High School after dark on Friday and Saturday nights. Dareo serves barbecue and jerk chicken, jerk pork, and soups. Dinner plates come with sides such as macaroni and cheese, peas and rice, salad, coleslaw, and baked potato pie.

Another good food vendor is **J. Blakx** (Fishlock Road, 284/496-7157, $5–12), which sets up across from the Road Town Fire and Rescue Station. J. Blakx sells barbecued chicken, ribs, and side dishes.

Two favorite late-night food spots are **Neto's** and **Panchi's,** which sell fried chicken and french fries out of mobile buses. Both set up near the Road Town roundabout: Neto operates out of an old school bus, and Panchi out of a green van.

Markets

There are three major grocery stores in Road Town, plus a number of wholesale distributors and smaller markets. This is also the venue for a weekly Saturday morning farmers market, your best opportunity to find local fruits and vegetables and meet the people who grow them.

Grocery stores include **Bobby's Supermarket** (284/495-2140) on Wickham's Cay, which is open every day until midnight. The other big grocery store is **Riteway Food Markets** (284/494-2263) with shops at Road Reef, Flemming Street, and Pasea Estate.

The weekly **farmers market** is held 4:30–7:30 A.M. Saturdays (yes, it really does start that early). The market takes place in the shadows of the RFG Plaza near the Road Town roundabout. Vendors sell locally grown fruit and vegetables, as well as hot sauces, preserves, tarts, and breakfast.

RIDGE ROAD

Good food meets a one-of-a-kind view at **Skyworld Restaurant** (Meyers, 284/494-3567, 10 A.M.–11 P.M., $7–30). Lunch is casual wraps, burgers, and salads, while dinner is classy gourmet meals. There is also a gift shop that sells Sunny Caribbe spices and other knickknacks. Climb a short flight of stairs to the upstairs lookout while you wait for your food to arrive. On a clear day, you can see as far as St. Croix in the south and Anegada in the north.

CANE GARDEN BAY

(Myett's Garden and Grill (284/495-9649, 11 A.M.–9:30 P.M. year-round, 7 A.M.–9:30 P.M. in winter, $10–30) is a pleasant oasis at the western end of Cane Garden Bay. Its dining area, built amid lush gardens, is a cool retreat from the heat of the beach, just steps away. Lunch here is a casual affair of wraps, salads, rotis, and burgers. For dinner, things get more sophisticated with seafood pasta, roasted duck, and fresh lobster, plus a loaded grill menu.

In 2004 Quito Rhymer tore down his old, wooden beach gazebo and built a mammoth concrete one in its place. The transformation sacrificed the restaurant and bar's casual atmosphere but made more space for restaurant seating. **Quito's** (284/495-4837, noon–late, $8–25) has a widely varied menu, ranging from casual food like rotis and burgers to upscale entrées like yellowfin tuna and prime rib. He serves a fish fry on Wednesday nights.

Rhymer's (284/495-4639, fax 284/495-4820, $3–20) serves some of the cheapest sandwiches and snacks on the beach. The restaurant is part of a larger complex, which includes a gift shop, small grocery, laundry, and a few hotel rooms.

Stanley's Welcome Bar and Restaurant (284/495-9424, 10 A.M.–late, $5–20) claims to be the burger joint Jimmy Buffett had in mind when he penned the song "Cheeseburger in Paradise." This claim is not unique to Stanley's, but neither is it too hard to imagine: the atmosphere at Stanley's seems to come right out of a Buffett song. In addition to burgers and wings, Stanley's serves more upscale fare like grilled fresh mahimahi, lobster, and grouper.

Markets

Grocery shopping prospects for Cane Garden Bay visitors got considerably better in 2004 when **Bobby's Supermarket** (284/495-2140) opened a store in Cane Garden Bay. The centrally located market is well stocked with fresh produce, meats, cheeses and all manner of staples. For a more colorful shopping experience, try **Columbus Sunset Bar** (284/495-4751) at the western end of the bay.

EAST ISLAND

Italian chef Davide Pugliese personally describes the specials of the evening at (**Brandywine Bay Restaurant** (284/495-2301, fax 284/495-1203, www.brandywine-bay.com, 6:30–9:30 P.M. Mon.–Sat. $20–40), one of the finest restaurants on Tortola. The menu here fuses classic Tuscan traditions with Caribbean ingredients and style. For starters try fresh mozzarella cheese (made on the premises) or a plate of homemade lamb ravioli. Davide's signature dish is his roasted duck in mango sauce, but the menu includes beef, ostrich, fresh seafood, and vegetarian entrées.

If you arrive before dark, enjoy a cocktail while you watch the sun set over the Sir Francis Drake Channel. Brandywine Bay is an intimate restaurant with limited seating, so make your reservation well in advance, especially during high season. The restaurant is closed from August to October every year.

Bring your appetite to **Fat Hog Bob's** (Fat Hog's Bay, 284/495-1010, 7 A.M.–late, $8–32), where they serve "hog-sized" portions of ribs, chicken, burgers, lobster, and other filling foods. For lighter eaters, try the pasta, soups, and Caesar salad. The setting is one of the best; the porch seating puts you right next to the water's edge. You can get beer on tap here, and the massive television at the bar is often tuned to sports.

Uncommonly sophisticated, **Eclipse Restaurant** (Penn's Marina, 284/495-1646, www.eclipse-restaurant.com, 11 A.M.–10 P.M. Mon.–Fri., 4 P.M.–10 P.M. Sat.–Sun., $8–32)serves upscale dishes in a casual seaside environment. There is an Asian flair to many of the dishes here. Chef and owner B.J. Turnbull writes a cooking column in the local newspaper. You can make a whole meal out of a few items from the creative "grazing" menu, such as cracked calamari, fresh mussels, or coconut shrimp, or choose a main course of filet mignon, shrimp tempura, or lobster ravioli. Reservations are a good idea.

Set under flamboyant trees in Josiah's Bay, **The Tamarind Club** (284/495-2477, 7:30 A.M.–10 P.M. daily, $8–30) serves "global cuisine" at its refurbished restaurant. Soufflés, pastas, grilled seafood, sandwiches, and tamarind rack of lamb are some of the specialties. The Club also serves a daily bar menu of burgers, curry chicken, and the like from 3 P.M. onward.

Casual is the name of the game at **Josiah's Bay Grapetree Bar and Restaurant** (284/495-2818, 11 A.M.–4 P.M., $5–10), where you can grab a burger, sandwich, or barbecue chicken plate, not to mention a whole array of cold drinks. Open for lunch most days, Grapetree serves dinner by reservation only.

Beef Island

The (**Trellis Bay Cybercafé** (Trellis Bay, 284/495-2447, 9 A.M.–6 P.M., $5–12) attracts windsurfers, artists, and those hungry for the fruit juice smoothies and Caribbean-inspired lunch and breakfast dishes on offer. Breakfast is served all day, and lunch includes sandwiches, rotis, and seafood dishes. Try the appropriately named "awesome sandwich" of mahimahi, vegetables, and tasty sauce on whole wheat. The atmosphere is low-key; you serve yourself from drink coolers around the porch, and seating ranges from picnic tables to comfy couches. The food here is consistently good, and there's an Internet café on the premises.

Gourmet coffee, coffee drinks, smoothies, ice cream, and sandwiches are served at **D' Best Cup** (Trellis Bay, 6:30 A.M.–6 P.M., $3–7). The coffee here is excellent, and you can enjoy it seated on the inviting and shady patio.

De Loose Mongoose (Trellis Bay, 284/495-2303, 8:30 A.M.–10 P.M. Tues.–Sun., $5–25) serves casual fare on the water's edge. Try their rotis, burgers, or fish and chips for a substantial lunch. For dinner, favorites include burritos, steak, and grilled fish. Dining is inside a screened-in porch (a plus when mosquitoes are out) or out front at a picnic table. De Loose Mongoose does a great Sunday night barbecue.

TORTOLA

Off the East End

At **The Last Resort** (Bellamy Cay, 284/495-2520, www.lastresortbvi.com, $16–30, 6:30–9:30 P.M. daily) restaurant staff entertain during dinner with a comedy and music routine. Founder Tony Snell is now enjoying his retirement in the United Kingdom, but his daughter has carried on the tradition of a fun-loving atmosphere and high-quality food. Gourmet fish, meat, and vegetarian dishes are on offer at this welcoming place. Use the hotline phone at the Trellis Bay dock to summon a free ferry to the island.

WEST ISLAND
Carrot Bay

Don't be turned off by the somewhat ramshackle appearance of **◖ Palm's Delight** (Carrot Bay, 284/495-4863, 6:30–9 P.M., $8–16), a real gem among restaurants on Tortola. This is simply the best place on the island for local food. Specialties include fried and steamed fish, shrimp, rotis, and a special chicken dish made with Stone's Gingerwine. Try its generous portions of peas and rice, fried plantain, coleslaw, and vegetables, or ask for fungi, dumplings, and ground provisions. On weekends or in season, come early so you don't have to wait for a table.

Bananakeet Café (Windy Hill, 284/494-5842, 11:30 A.M.–9 P.M., $12–25) is a good pit stop if you're touring around the island—the view is unrivaled. On top of that, you can take a dip in the pool to cool off. For lunch try the chicken curry pita or lobster quesadillas. At dinner, specialties include fish grilled in banana leaves, sesame salmon, and rack of lamb. With a dramatic sunset view, this is an excellent happy hour (4–6 P.M.) choice.

Apple Bay

Probably the best restaurant on Tortola, **◖ The Sugar Mill Restaurant** (Great Apple Bay, 284/495-4355, 7–9 P.M., $12–30) fuses traditional gourmet fare with Caribbean ingredients and style. The service here is second to none. Run by food writers Jeff and Jinx Morgan, the Sugar Mill changes its menu nightly based on what's fresh and in season. Come early for a sunset cocktail on the patio. Dinner is served in a restored 18th-century sugar factory; Caribbean artwork adorns the walls.

The Sugar Mill goes casual for lunch at its seaside **Islands Restaurant** (Great Apple Bay, 284/495-4355, noon–2 P.M., $7–15), where you can watch the pelicans dive for food while you enjoy yours. In addition to its regular menu of sandwiches and salads, Islands has daily soup, seafood, and pasta specials. After you eat, relax on the beach next door. This is a great place to while away a few hours.

Hip and funky, **Coco Plums Restaurant** (Little Apple Bay, 284/495-4672, 7:30 A.M.–10 P.M. Sun.–Fri., 6–10 p.m. Sat., $8–17) serves bistro-style cuisine in a welcoming atmosphere. Set amidst the cozy village of Little Apple Bay, Coco Plums has indoor and patio seating. It serves sandwiches, pasta, fresh seafood, pizza, and upscale entrées like grilled steak and lobster. You can't get food like this at these prices anywhere else on Tortola.

Soper's Hole

If you're catching an early ferry from West End, try **Zelma's Courtesy** (284/495-4211, 6 A.M.–4 P.M., $2–8) for breakfast. Zelma's, located right across the road from the dock, serves fresh johnnycakes, pâtés (fried stuffed bread), fried fish, and bush tea. Or try hot "dumb bread" (so called because it is unleavened and does not rise) with cheese.

Appropriately, the skull and crossbones fly over the **Jolly Roger** (284/495-4559, 8 A.M.–midnight, www.jollyrogerbvi.com, $8–25), a bar and restaurant as popular with locals as it is with tourists. Choose to dine upstairs by the bar or downstairs by the waterfront. Regular menu items include barbecue, rotis, pizzas, and salads, while the daily specials always feature fresh seafood, pasta, and more, often with an Asian flair. This is a good place for hearty breakfasts, too, and is within walking distance from the West End ferry dock.

Pisces Restaurant and Bar (284/495-3154, 7:30 A.M.–10 P.M., $4–18) is a friendly and casual café serving three meals a day. Located right next to Soper's Hole Marina, Pisces serves hearty American-style breakfasts, casual lunch, and dinners with a touch of class. There is also Internet access here, and Pisces is a wi-fi hot spot.

Located within the brightly painted Soper's Hole shopping complex, **Blue Parrot Café** (284/495-4811, 8 A.M.–noon, $3–20) serves coffee and coffee drinks, sandwiches made from fresh homemade bread, and light breakfast dishes like yogurt, fruit, cereal, and pastries. You can eat inside the comfortable air-conditioning, or outside on the cobblestone patio.

The deli at **Harbour Market** (284/495-4541, 8 A.M.–6 P.M., $5–7), a high-end grocery store at Soper's Hole Marina, makes good sandwiches.

Markets
The best grocery stores in the western area are found on Frenchman's Cay. **Kelly's Superette** (284/495-4303) has a good selection of canned goods, frozen meats, and vegetables. Upscale **Harbour Market** (284/495-4541) is a full-service grocery at Soper's Hole.

SIR FRANCIS DRAKE CHANNEL
At Norman Island you can choose between dining on land or the sea. **Pirate's Bight** (284/496-7827, channels 16 and 69, www.normanislandpirates.com, $4–12 lunch, $14–35

dinner) sits square in the middle of the Bight, in front of the dinghy dock and just a few yards away from a peaceful, sandy beach. There are hammocks, beach chairs, and porch swings where you can sip a piña colada and while away an afternoon. At 4 P.M. the bartender explodes a mini-cannon signaling the beginning of happy hour. A good deal of happiness ensues. Lunch is a relatively casual affair of burgers, rotis, and sandwiches. At dinner expect delectable fresh lobster, seafood, and expertly grilled steak.

If you would rather dine on the water, then your choice is the **Willy T** (284/494-7138, channel 16 or 74, www.williamthornton.com, $7–12 lunch, $18–24 dinner), one of the BVI's most celebrated watering holes. A 93-foot schooner, the *William Thornton* (its proper name) has been serving cold beer, belly shots, and the shotski since 1989. It specializes in booze of all kinds (no blended drinks, however) and serves lunch and dinner, too. This is not the sort of place to come for peace and quiet—one of the favorite activities is jumping from the aft deck in the buff—but it is surely the place to come to find the party.

At Manchioneel Bay, Cooper Island, the **Cooper Island Beach Club** (284/494-3111) serves a diverse lunch menu of sandwiches and salads ($5–15) and elegant dinners of fresh seafood, lobster, steak, and chicken ($15–22).

Practicalities

INFORMATION AND SERVICES
Tourist Offices
For reliable tourist information, call or visit the **BVI Tourist Board Waterfront Office** (Road Town ferry dock, 284/494-7260, 8:30 A.M.–4:30 P.M.). Other Tourist Board information booths are located at the airport and the cruise ship dock.

Maps and Charts
Free pocket maps published by American Express are available from car rental agencies, tourist information booths, and many businesses. This map will be adequate for most people. There is also a good map printed in the middle of the free *Welcome Magazine*. For a more detailed map, visit the **Survey Department** (Waterfront Drive, 284/494-3459, 8:30 A.M.–3 P.M. Mon.–Fri.) for the official "tourist" map ($12).

Imray-Iolaire charts are available from **Golden Hind Yacht Services** (Wickham's Cay II, 284/494-2756) and **Island Marine Outfitters** (Road Reef Plaza, 284/494-2251).

Libraries and Bookstores

The Road Town Public Library (Flemming Street, 284/494-3428, 8:30 A.M.–7 P.M. Mon.–Fri., 9 A.M.–1 P.M. Sat.) has adult, children's, and reference sections, as well as a West Indian collection. It offers free public Internet access. A small public library is also open in East End.

The best bookstore on the island is **Serendipity Books** (Main Street, 284/494-5865), which has books by West Indian and BVI authors, as well as an extensive children's collection. You can also try **Books Etc.** (Mill Mall, 284/494-6611), which sells current newspapers, magazines, and a wide selection of self-help and Christian titles.

Media

There are three newspapers published on Tortola. *The BVI Beacon* comes out on Thursdays; the *BVI StandPoint* is published twice weekly, on Tuesdays and Fridays; and *The Island Sun* comes out Fridays. All three can be obtained from supermarkets and a number of smaller stores around the island.

Major U.S. newspapers are available (for a small fortune) at supermarkets in Road Town, while British papers can be found at **Best of British** (Mill Mall, 284/494-3462).

ZBVI Radio (780 AM) broadcasts local and international news, including the BBC world roundup, daily at 7 A.M., noon, and 5:45 P.M. For music, try ZROD (103.7 FM) or ZVCR (106.9 FM)

Emergencies

The British Virgin Islands' only hospital is located in Road Town. **Peebles Hospital** (Main Street, 284/494-3497) is named for the British governor who saw to its construction more than 80 years ago. A new wing that opened in 2005 doubled the size of the hospital and made room for more services. The hospital

provides 24-hour emergency, diagnostic, surgical, and obstetric services, as well as regular dialysis and laboratory service. Dial **999** in an emergency. There is no decompression chamber, and many advanced services are not available. Air ambulance service is provided by **Island Helicopters** (284/499-2663).

There are also a number of private medical clinics. **B&F** (Mill Mall, 284/494-2196, 7 A.M.–5 P.M.) is open seven days a week and has its own pharmacy. Also try **Eureka Medical Clinic** (284/494-2346, 8:30 A.M.–6 P.M. Mon.–Fri., 8:30 A.M.–1 P.M. Sat.). The pharmacy at **Qwomar Trading** (Blackburn Highway, 284/494-1902) is open seven days a week near the Port Purcell roundabout.

Banks

There are four commercial banks in the British Virgin Islands, all of which have offices and ATMs in the heart of Road Town. Puerto Rico–based **Banco Popular** (Main Admin Drive, 284/494-2117) is located across from the government administration complex. **First Caribbean International Bank** (Admin Drive, 284/494-2171) is located next to the Palm Grove, also near the administration building. **Scotiabank** (284/494-2526) and **FirstBank** (284/494-2662) are practically next door to each other behind Village Cay.

There are ATMs at Soper's Hole Marina, Paraquita Bay, Pasea Estate (next to Riteway Food Market), and in East End.

Banks generally open at 9 A.M. and close as early at 2 P.M. Mon.–Fri., although some stay open later on Friday. None of the banks are open on Saturday.

Post Offices

The island's main post office is located on Main Street, opposite Sir Olva Georges Plaza in the Old Administration Building (8:30 A.M.–4:30 P.M. Mon.–Fri., 9 A.M.–noon Sat.). You can buy money orders, mail letters and packages, and buy collectable stamp sets.

Other post offices are located at the West End ferry dock, East End (next to the police station), Carrot Bay, Cane Garden Bay (next to the school), and at the Terrance B. Lettsome International Airport.

Major international air courier companies operate on Tortola.

Launderettes

There are laundries in nearly every community on Tortola, so ask around to find the one closest to where you are staying. Nearly all provide drop-off service or let you do your own wash. In Road Town, try **Freeman's Launder Centre** (284/494-2285, 8 A.M.–5 P.M.) in the Palm Grove shopping center, which also provides dry cleaning. If you have a car, it is worth the drive to air-conditioned **Speed Clean** (284/494-9428, 6 A.M.–midnight) in Baugher's Bay, which has plenty of machines and hot water and is open late.

Immigration and Customs

Immigration and Customs officers are stationed at Tortola's official ports of entry: the West End ferry dock, Road Town ferry dock, and the T. B. Lettsome International Airport. As long as you are on a scheduled ferry or plane, there will be an officer on duty to check your passport and clear your goods. If you plan to arrive on a private boat or plane outside of normal working hours, call ahead for instructions.

If you plan to stay more than 30 days, you will have to visit the **Immigration Department** (284/494-3471, 8:30 A.M.–4:30 P.M. Mon.–Fri.) for an entry permit renewal. The **Customs Headquarters** (284/494-3475) are upstairs in the Richard Stout Building in Road Town.

Fax and Internet

There are no dedicated Internet cafés on Tortola, but shopkeepers around the island have responded to the demand for Internet service. In Road Town, try **Bits and Pieces** (Mill Mall, 284/494-5954, fax 284/494-7055, 8:30 A.M.–5 P.M. Mon.–Fri.), which has high-speed Internet service for $5 for 30 minutes, as well as fax and phone calls. **Infinite Solutions** (Palm Grove, 284/494-5030, 8:30 A.M.–5 P.M., Mon.–Fri.) charges $6 per 30 minutes for In-

ternet use. The **Road Town Library** (Flemming Street, 284/494-3428, 8:30 A.M.–7 P.M. Mon.–Fri., 9 A.M.–1 P.M. Sat.) has free public Internet access (half hour time limit), although it is sometimes very slow.

At West End, **Pisces Restaurant** (Soper's Hole Marina, 284/495-3154, 7:30 A.M.–10 P.M.) charges $5 per 30 minutes and is also a wi-fi hotspot. At the East End, try **Trellis Bay Cyber Café** (Beef Island, 284/495-2447), which charges $10 for 30 minutes. In Cane Garden Bay, try **Myett's** for Internet and fax service.

GETTING THERE
By Air

There are no nonstop flights from the U.S. mainland to Tortola. U.S. and Canadian travelers destined for Tortola arrive via San Juan, Puerto Rico, or St. Thomas, U.S. Virgin Islands. American Airlines, Cape Air, and Caribbean Sun are the main airlines providing scheduled service between the Terrance B. Lettsome International Airport and San Juan. Visitors from Europe usually fly to Antigua and connect to the BVI on Caribbean Star or LIAT.

Other travelers choose to fly into St. Thomas and catch a ferry to Tortola. This is often a good choice if you are on a budget, since tickets from the U.S. mainland to St. Thomas usually cost quite a bit less than those to the BVI. If you choose this route, remember that the last ferries to Tortola usually leave St. Thomas around 4:30 P.M.

By Sea

At least four ferry companies offer daily ferry service between Tortola and St. Thomas. Ferries run between Charlotte Amalie and Red Hook, St. Thomas, and Road Town and West End, Tortola. The trip from West End to Red Hook is about 30 minutes; from West End to Charlotte Amalie is about 45 minutes; and from Road Town to Charlotte Amalie is about an hour. Expect to pay about $45 round-trip, regardless of the route you choose. There is an additional $5 departure tax. If you are going to the St. Thomas airport, be sure to get a ferry that will take you all the way to Charlotte Amalie (you'll save on the taxi).

Up-to-date ferry schedules are printed in *The Welcome* (www.bviwelcome.com) and on its website. There is no need for advance ferry reservations, but it is always a good idea to confirm the schedule a day or so before your trip.

Ferry companies operating between the U.S. and British Virgin Islands are **Native Son** (284/494-4617, U.S. 340/774-8685, Charlotte Amalie and Red Hook to West End and Road Town); **Smith's Ferry Service** (also called Tortola Fast Ferry) (284/494-4495, U.S. 340/775-7292, Charlotte Amalie and Red Hook to West End and Road Town) and **Road Town Fast Ferry** (284/494-2323, U.S. 340/777-2800, Charlotte Amalie to Road Town).

From St. John, **Inter-Island Boat Services** (284/495-4166, Cruz Bay to West End) makes four daily trips.

If you eschew crowds, charter the **Virgin Islands Water Taxi** (Red Hook, St. Thomas, 340/775-6501, www.watertaxi-vi.com) for $200 from Red Hook to West End (five-person minimum).

GETTING AROUND

Tortola is a relatively small place—12 miles long and about three miles wide—but it is not necessarily easy to get around. There is no public transportation, the steep hills make walking and biking challenging for most of us, and taxis and rental cars are pricey.

If you expect to do a lot of exploring or to sample numerous restaurants, it is wise to rent a car. Taxi fares add up. Many visitors on a budget choose to rent a car for one or two days to explore the island and then stay put for the rest of their vacation.

In recent years, companies renting motor scooters have popped up. Scooters are generally cheaper than cars and can be a fun way to get around the island for a day. Clearly, they have their limits, however; if it rains you get wet, and they expose you to greater risk than a car.

Nearly any taxi will take you on a two-hour island tour ($50 for three people; $15 for each additional person), stopping at the best-known sights. But for that price, most people are better off renting a car and driving themselves.

Taxis

Taxis and the rates they charge are regulated by the government, but it is still a good idea to agree up front on a rate. Official taxis will have white license plates beginning with the letters TX. The fare for one to three people from the airport to Road Town is $18. From Road Town to Cane Garden Bay expect to pay about the same. The law requires taxis to wait for 10 minutes for you without charge.

Taxi stands are located at most heavily trafficked places. In Road Town, try the **Waterfront Taxi Stand** (284/494-6456) next to the Road Town ferry dock or the **Road Town Taxi Stand** (284/494-8755) on Wickham's Cay. The **Beef Island Taxi Association** (T. B. Lettsome International Airport, 284/495-1982) operates at the airport. The **West End Taxi Association** (284/495-4934) is located opposite the West End ferry dock. **Nanny Cay Taxi Stand** (284/494-0539) is next to Nanny Cay Hotel.

If you need an early morning taxi, call the night before. Choose the taxi association closest to you, and expect to pay extra if they come to pick you up.

Rental Cars

There are a plethora of car rental agencies on Tortola. Almost all of them rent two- and four-door SUVs, ranging from small Suzuki Sidekicks to large Mitsubishi Pajeros. Expect to pay about $50 per day for a rental that seats four people, and more for larger ones. It is usually worthwhile to compare prices, because there can be substantial variation among rental companies. You will have to pay $10 more for a temporary driver's license (obtainable at the rental agency) and can choose from a range of insurance packages.

U.S.-based rental chains including **Hertz** (West End and T. B. Lettsome Airport, 284/495-4405) and **Avis** (Road Town and West End, 284/494-3322) have offices here.

In Road Town, **Itgo Car Rental** (Mill Mall, 284/494-2639) has some of the cheapest rates on the island. Other reliable agencies include **Denzil Clyne Jeep and Car Rental** (West End, 284/495-4900), **Jerry's Car Rental** (West End, 284/495-4111), and **Del's Jeep and Car Rental** (Cane Garden Bay, 284/495-9356).

Scooters and Bicycles

For scooter rentals, try **Aaron Jeep, Car, and Scooter Rental** (Road Town, 284/494-8917, fax 284/494-8918). A two-person scooter will cost $42 per day.

A bike is not a practical means of transportation for most visitors. You must either be in excellent shape to climb the hills or need a simple way to get around within a contained community, like Cane Garden Bay or West End. If you do bike, try to avoid heavily trafficked roads, since many drivers are unaccustomed to sharing the road. Always wear a helmet and reflective clothing.

Bikes and related equipment can be rented from **Last Stop Sports** (Purcell, 284/494-1120, 8:30 A.M.–5 P.M. Mon.–Fri., 10 A.M.–4 P.M. Sat.) for $25–30 a day.

TORTOLA

VIRGIN GORDA

Virgin Gorda, or the Fat Virgin as Columbus saw it, is the third largest island in the British Virgins and the second most populated. Lying northeast of Tortola, Virgin Gorda is a study in contrasts. The southwestern peninsula is a flat, dry landscape colored by vivid bougainvillea and bright century plants. Some of the best beaches in the region are found here, plus the Baths National Park, where pools of turquoise water invite exploration.

The northern end of Virgin Gorda is mountainous and lush—the single paved road winds steeply through wild forest, along Gorda Peak National Park, and down to the villages of Gun Creek and North Sound, which cling to the hillside overlooking one of the best harbors in the Virgin Islands. Sir Francis Drake once used North Sound as a staging area for a 1595 attack on Puerto Rico, but today it is noted most as a magnet for sailing and water sports enthusiasts.

Just about 3,000 people call Virgin Gorda home, and they are a particularly welcoming bunch. At Spanish Town, the main settlement in the south, life revolves around the marina, where some of the most popular restaurants and shops are found. The side streets are lined with neat West Indian–style homes, many fronted by colorful gardens. Others are built imaginatively around the giant granite boulders of the area. Goats and sheep wander through the village, causing occasional traffic jams.

Often, visitors come to Virgin Gorda for the Baths—its genuinely remarkable world-famous beach—but stay for the special feeling of contentment they find here; people just seem happier on Virgin Gorda. Maybe it's the slow pace

HIGHLIGHTS

◖ Spanish Town: Neat and colorful, Spanish Town is one of the oldest settlements in the Virgin Islands. Share the road with goats and sheep (page 192).

◖ Coppermine National Park: A crumbling stone chimney breaks through the bright blue sky at Coppermine Point, a windswept headland. Watch the waves crash below and the birds fly overhead (page 193).

◖ The Baths: Huge granite boulders create an endless array of pools and grottos perfect for exploration at the British Virgin Islands' most famous sight (page 194).

◖ Spring Bay National Park: The "other" Baths, this beach maintains its serenity most days, making it a venue popular with locals and ideal for relaxation (page 196).

◖ The Dog Islands: Protected by the National Parks Trust, this cluster of islands near Virgin Gorda has pristine reefs for snorkeling (page 197).

◖ North Sound: Called by some a saltwater lake, this broad bay is protected from rough seas and ideal for sailing. Secluded beaches and friendly beach bars await exploration (page 197).

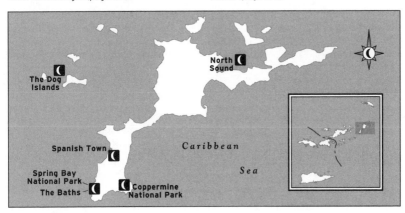

LOOK FOR ◖ TO FIND RECOMMENDED SIGHTS, ACTIVITIES, DINING, AND LODGING.

of life, the small-town feel, or the pride islanders have in their home. Whatever the secret, visitors will notice that it is nearly impossible to keep up a bad mood for very long on Virgin Gorda.

It is no surprise, then, that Virgin Gorda is home to some of the most exclusive resorts in the British Virgin Islands. Little Dix Bay, opened by Laurance Rockefeller in 1964, still wins awards for its five-star service and luxury, while the Bitter End at North Sound is an unrivaled choice for water sports lovers. There are a handful of more modest accommodations, but there are no campgrounds; by and large, Virgin

Gorda is not a destination for budget travelers. Neither is it a place for nightlife, shopping, or, to any great extent, exceptional dining. Instead, Virgin Gorda's main draw is its natural beauty, friendly people, and tranquility. In fact, there are few islands that so perfectly blend comfortable, high-quality accommodation with an unspoiled natural environment.

PLANNING YOUR TIME

Virgin Gorda is small enough (just 8.5 square miles) that it is pretty easy to see most of the sights in a day. Rent a car and combine a trip to

VIRGIN GORDA

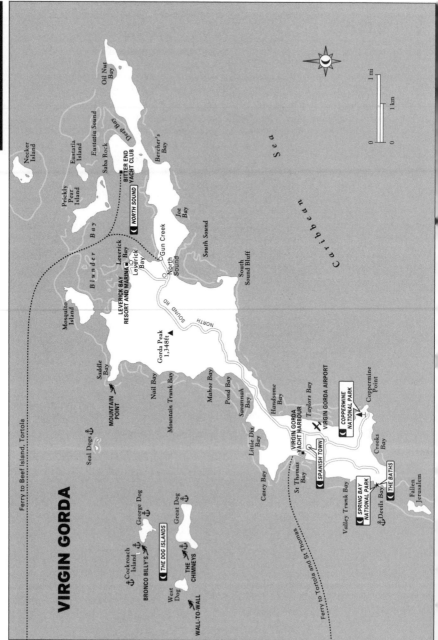

VIRGIN GORDA

Ferry to Beef Island, Tortola

Necker Island

Prickly Pear Island

Eustatia Island

Saba Rock

Oil Nut Bay

Deep Bay

Eustatia Sound

Blunder Bay

Mosquito Island

Leverick Bay

Leverick Bay

LEVERICK BAY RESORT AND MARINA

NORTH SOUND

BITTER END YACHT CLUB

Gun Creek

North Sound

Joe Bay

South Sound

Bercher's Bay

Caribbean Sea

Saddle Bay

MOUNTAIN POINT

Gorda Peak 1,348ft

NORTH SOUND RD

South Sound Bluff

Seal Dogs

Nail Bay

Mountain Trunk Bay

Mahoe Bay

Pond Bay

Savannah Bay

Handsome Bay

Coppermine Point

Cockroach Island

George Dog

BRONCO BILLY'S

THE DOG ISLANDS

Great Dog

Taylors Bay

VIRGIN GORDA AIRPORT

COPPERMINE NATIONAL PARK

Little Dix Bay

VIRGIN GORDA YACHT HARBOUR

SPANISH TOWN

St Thomas Bay

Crooks Bay

West Dog

WALL-TO-WALL

THE CHIMNEYS

Casey Bay

Valley Trunk Bay

SPRING BAY NATIONAL PARK

Devils Bay

THE BATHS

Fallen Jerusalem

Ferry to Tortola and St Thomas

1 mi

1 km

0   0

the **Baths** with one to windswept and remote **Coppermine Point National Park.** Admire the quaint village of **Spanish Town** before setting out to **Spring Bay,** one of the best beaches on the island. Two days will give you time to hike to the top of Gorda Peak or explore **North Sound** by dinghy or boat.

If your top priority is relaxation, then stay longer. Plan an afternoon at Savannah Bay or Valley Trunk Bay, little-visited beaches in the Valley. The **Dog Islands** are the perfect day-trip destination for divers and snorkelers.

Most accommodations on Virgin Gorda are in the Valley, the flat southern end of the island. Staying here is convenient: you are near restaurants, beaches, shops, gas stations and the main ferry dock. North Sound accommodations are more self-contained—many of them full-service resorts—where the focus is on privacy, exclusivity, and, to a large degree, water sports. While the trip between the Valley and North Sound is short—a mere five miles—the size of the mountain between creates a substantial barrier in both mind and fact.

Day trippers from St. Thomas, Tortola, or other islands will enjoy Virgin Gorda. Arrive by ferry and take a taxi to the Baths, or rent a car and explore on your own. Most days, the last ferry leaves Virgin Gorda at 3:30 P.M., but on Wednesdays and Saturdays from December to July you can catch the late-night ferry returning to Tortola at 6 P.M. or 10:30 P.M.

DRIVING TOUR

It is fun and easy to drive around Virgin Gorda, and the roads are generally quite good. This drive starts in the Valley, heads to North Sound, and ends at the Coppermine.

Begin at the ferry dock and follow Little Road out of town, past Handsome Bay and Savannah Bay. Pass the turnoff to Nail and Maho Bays, and head up and over the mountain. Be sure to engage a low gear, and watch out for other traffic that will no doubt blow right by you at speeds you cannot imagine. The BVI Tourist Board has built a couple of overlooks along the road, which make good stops. On clear days, you will be able to see Anegada.

After about four miles, you reach the colorful village of North Sound. Be sure to put the car in low gear for the steep descent through the village to Gun Creek, where you can catch a ferry to many different North Sound hotels and restaurants. There is a quiet bar overlooking the ferry that makes a good pit stop and a small market where you can pick up provisions for a picnic. The shade of the tamarind tree next door is a good place to eat it. Retrace your path back up the hill, taking a detour to Leverick Bay on the way, if you wish. Make your way back to the Valley, stopping at Little Dix Bay for a stroll through the gardens and meal at the restaurant, and follow Lee Road (the main drag) past the marina and heart of Spanish Town. Keep your eyes peeled for the Roman Catholic Church on the left after the marina. Climb its steep driveway to the parking lot, which has great views of the Valley.

Get back on Lee Road. At the roundabout, turn left and follow Tower Road past the grocery store, gas station, school, Spring Bay, and eventually to the Baths (watch the speed bumps). If the time is right, go for a swim or grab a bite to eat at Mad Dog Bar near the Baths parking lot.

Finish your drive with a detour to Coppermine National Park. To get there, backtrack past the schools, and look out on your right for Long Road, a long, straight, hot road. Follow it, then turn right again onto Coppermine Road, which dead-ends at the Coppermine. The Mine Shaft is a good choice for a pick-me-up along the way.

Sights

Virgin Gorda is a long, meandering island. The Valley, in the south, is flat and rectangular. Roads here are laid out roughly in a grid, but the absence of road signs makes it hard to find locations using a map. The best method is to spend a few minutes just driving around the Valley until you get your bearings, or ask for directions.

The rest of the island could not be easier to navigate. One road connects the Valley with North Sound and Leverick Bay. Once you overcome the initial shock of its steepness, it is easy to maneuver.

THE VALLEY

The Valley is the wide, flat southern end of Virgin Gorda, home to Spanish Town, four national parks, a world-class marina, and the giant boulders that define this island. Most travelers arrive on Virgin Gorda aboard one of the ferries that dock up to the St. Thomas Bay jetty, a short walk from the marina and town center.

◖ Spanish Town

Some say that Virgin Gorda's main settlement, Spanish Town, got its name from the Spaniards who settled there in the early 1500s. Others say that Spanish Town is a corruption of the early name, Penniston, which the settlement was known as.

In 1680, Spanish Town became the first seat of government in the British Virgin Islands. At the time, the town was a little more than an outpost—it became the capital only because the man nominated to be governor lived there. In 1717, the first census of the island found 317 whites living on Virgin Gorda and 303 blacks, more than were living on Tortola at the time. In 1742, the capital of the territory moved to Tortola, where it has remained since.

Today, Spanish Town is one of the most picturesque villages in the British Virgin Islands. Unrestrained by hills, it sprawls along a gentle slope, an attractive mix of homes, shops, churches, and schools. It is a nice place to walk as long as you avoid the brutal midday hours when the sun bores down from above. Islanders swear that the sun is hotter on Virgin Gorda, and they may be right.

A particularly nice walk follows Crabbe Hill Road along the "back" of the Valley, closest to the western shore. Just past the turnoff to the airport is the **Methodist Church,** one of the oldest churches in the British Virgin Islands. Some of the graves at the adjoining burial ground are marked with conch shells. Just past the Methodist Church is the local library and a little

---

VIRGIN GORDA'S COPPERMINE

Virgin Gorda's copper deposits have their roots in ancient geologic events. When Columbus sailed through in 1493, he is said to have grown excited by the sight of green streaks in the island's cliffs: they were telltale signs of the presence of copper.

Little is known of the early Spanish mines, built in the early to mid-1500s. It was not until 100 years later that another large-scale mining operation took place on Virgin Gorda. In 1840, the Virgin Islands Mining Company of Liverpool, England, opened the mines. They closed a mere two years later, however, due to bankruptcy. The mine reopened a few years later, this time with 40 Cornish miners working alongside the island's newly freed Africans. The mine was worked until 1867.

Geologists say that some 10,000 tons of ore were extracted from the mine. Today, Coppermine Point is deserted, except for occasional tourists who come to enjoy the remote, beautiful setting.

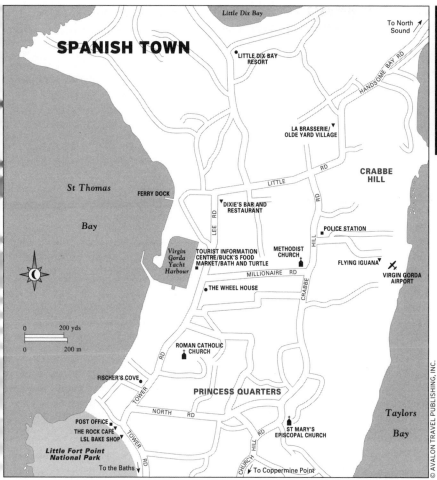

SPANISH TOWN

Little Dix Bay

To North
Sound

LITTLE DIX BAY
RESORT

HANDSOME BAY RD

LA BRASSERIE/
OLDE YARD VILLAGE

CRABBE
HILL

St Thomas

LITTLE   RD

Bay

FERRY DOCK

DIXIE'S BAR AND
RESTAURANT

LEE   RD

HILL   RD

POLICE STATION

*Virgin
Gorda
Yacht
Harbour*

TOURIST INFORMATION
CENTRE/BUCK'S FOOD
MARKET/BATH AND TURTLE

METHODIST
CHURCH

FLYING IGUANA

VIRGIN GORDA
AIRPORT

MILLIONAIRE   RD

THE WHEEL HOUSE

CRABBE

0   200 yds

0   200 m

ROMAN CATHOLIC
CHURCH

TOWER   RD

FISCHER'S COVE

PRINCESS QUARTERS

*Taylors
Bay*

NORTH   RD

POST OFFICE

THE ROCK CAFE
LSL BAKE SHOP

TOWER   RD

RD

CHURCH   HILL   RD

ST MARY'S
EPISCOPAL CHURCH

*Little Fort Point
National Park*

To the Baths

To Coppermine Point

© AVALON TRAVEL PUBLISHING, INC.

farther is the community clinic. **St. Mary's Episcopal Church** sits on the brow of the hill and is another of the very earliest buildings on Virgin Gorda. The school next door is of more modern construction.

Little Fort National Park

Tourism material misleads visitors into thinking they can visit Little Fort National Park, the location of a pre-Columbian Indian settlement and Spanish fortress. In truth, this 36-acre park, located behind the post office, is

inaccessible—there are no signs, trails, or easy access points. For the best views, sail by.

◖ Coppermine National Park

The newest national park in the British Virgin Islands, the Coppermine is a remote, windswept spot overlooking the rocky, rough north coast and the island's airport. Legend has it that Spanish settlers first mined silver here in the mid-1500s, and that Indians may well have built mines here even earlier than that. The ruins you see today date back to 1838, when Cornish miners established a copper mining operation here. It had a short, unprofitable life and closed four years later. The mines were reopened in 1859 and were worked until 1867. Some preliminary preservation work has taken place here to stabilize the ruins, but there is little in the way of facilities. A parking lot, sign, and unofficial trail are all you can expect. But it is a dramatic setting, and well worth the trip. If you're lucky, a plane will land at the airport while you are here, adding to the drama.

The Baths

Virgin Gorda's Baths are probably the most famous sight in the entire British Virgin Islands. Formed tens of millions of years ago when volcanic lava cooled into huge chunks of granite, the Baths are a landscape of clear, saltwater grottoes set on top of powder white beaches. There are endless pools for exploring and swimming.

War journalist Martha Gellhorn visited Virgin Gorda in 1942 as part of a Caribbean tour to assess World War II's impact on the region. The war, she observed, seemed too far away to be true

© SUSANNA HENIGHAN

the Baths

on Virgin Gorda. She spent an afternoon at the Baths and described it like this: "This cove was a place where nothing had changed since time began, a half circle of white sand, flanked by huge squarish smooth rocks, the rocks overlapping to form cool caves and the water turquoise blue above the furrows of the sandy bed."

You may recognize the Baths from the television commercials that have been shot here over the years. Offshore reefs, plus the intricate underwater boulders, make snorkeling fun, and you can take a 0.25-mile hike that clamors around, over, and under the boulders.

Before potable water made its way to Virgin Gorda in the 1960s and 1970s, the island's boulders played an important role in water collection. Pools of rainwater formed on top of many of the large rocks, which islanders used to water livestock, wash clothes, and for bathing. In places, the boulders also provided shelter from the wind, sun, and rain if you happened to need it.

The Baths are protected by the BVI National Parks Trust and are the most visited national park in the British Virgin Islands. After years of local debate, in 2004 the Trust began charging a small entrance fee at the main entrance to the Baths National Park (284/496-6314, 11 and up $3, under 11 free). Proceeds go to help maintain the Baths and other parks in the territory—a worthy cause. Some visitors have discovered that you can park at Spring Bay down the road and swim the Baths to avoid paying the fee, an unethical and shortsighted practice. If you come early in the morning (before 8 A.M.) or late in the evening (after 5 P.M.), you may well get in free anyway, because no one is there to collect the fee.

A 0.25-mile trail to the beach begins just beyond the entrance gate. The trail cuts through dry, scrubby forest, often navigating around and over large rocks. Watch your step. The trail ends at the Baths proper, a smallish beach fringed by coconut palms, sea grapes, and the setting of some of the most dramatic boulders. It is often a beehive of activity, especially if you visit when a large cruise ship has brought passengers from Tortola. There are usually a

WHERE DID THE BOULDERS COME FROM?

During the Tertiary Period of geologic history, about 70 million years ago, molten rock seeped through the floor of the young Caribbean Sea. The lava was hot – it reached temperatures as high as 2,000 degrees Celsius – and when it came into contact with the cool seawater, it solidified into granite.

As it cooled, the rock also shrank, causing cracks to form. Because of the characteristics of granite, it cracked at right angles, creating a series of rectangular rocks, stacked neatly on top of each other, like a block of cheese cut into cubes. Through faulting and uplifting over the next 60 million years, many of these granite cubes reached the earth's surface.

Over the last one million years, the boulders have been aged and weathered by the elements. The rhythm of waves, jolt of earthquakes, and flow of water have been written on the faces of the boulders. Time has also caused many of the right-angled boulders to transform into smooth-sided or spherical shapes.

© ROBERT S. BONI

Virgin Gorda's boulders have a long history.

few vendors set up in the shade, selling T-shirts and sarongs and offering to braid your hair. A small beach bar sells drinks and snacks. The National Parks Trust has built bathrooms, showers, and changing rooms at the beach (although sometimes there's no water—check first), and there is usually a warden around who can answer your questions.

Devil's Bay is another 0.25-mile hike from the Baths. Look just beyond the small NPT booth for the trail, which meanders around, over, and under boulders before turning you out at a large expanse of white sand. The hike around the rocks is challenging, and you will get wet. It takes about 20 minutes each way.

You can also hike directly from the parking lot to Devil's Bay, although the trailhead is difficult to find from the top (it is much easier to find from the beach). Ask at the National Parks Trust gazebo for directions. You can also swim from the Baths to Devil's Bay, snorkeling as you go.

The Baths are located on Virgin Gorda's exposed southern shore, and there is often a swell here. When the sea is rough, it can be dangerous (and unrewarding, since waves kick up a lot of sand and sediment) to snorkel. On days like this, stick to swimming, beaching, and hiking. If you're not sure, just ask one of the park wardens if the sea looks too rough to snorkel. Overestimating you ability, or underestimating the power of the sea, can be deadly.

◖ Spring Bay National Park

Spring Bay National Park, located about half a mile from the Baths, has the same captivating landscape and beautiful beach as the Baths, but often with far fewer people. This beach is especially popular with island residents who don't want to fight the crowds at the Baths or make the trek down to the beach. The boulders here are a little smaller and less concentrated than at the Baths, but they are still lots of fun to swim around and explore. There are picnic tables and trash cans here, but no bathroom facilities.

Look for signs to Spring Bay just before Guavaberry Spring Bay Apartments on the road to the Baths. Park in the lot, and follow the trail about 20 yards to the beach.

Look for the trail that departs from the right-hand (northern) end of Spring Bay to get to **Valley Trunk Bay,** an exquisite white sand beach bordered by private homes.

Fallen Jerusalem

Named for the image of a ruined city it evokes, this island lies between Round Rock and the southern tip of Virgin Gorda and looks like a tail extended off Virgin Gorda's Baths. The 30-acre island is a national park, and NPT moorings on the north side of the island enable visitors with private boats to explore it. On calm days, the snorkeling here is exceptional—imagine the beauty of the Baths without the crowds. You can also clamber endlessly around the rocky shore, imagining it is ruined streets and courtyards. Likely, the only other creatures you will see are the seabirds that nest here.

Fallen Jerusalem is a tiny island and national park off the southern tip of Virgin Gorda.

MID-ISLAND

At 1,370 feet, Gorda Peak is the highest point on Virgin Gorda and one of the highest in the Virgin Islands. More than 260 acres, including the peak and all land above the 1,000-foot contour, is national park. Much more remains unspoiled due to difficult topography. On the western shore, the green hillsides cascade down to a string of white sand beaches.

Gorda Peak National Park

Gorda Peak National Park, declared in 1974 after the land was donated by Laurance Rockefeller, is one of the best examples of dry forest remaining in the region. Although the park is relatively small, just 265 acres, the percentage of rare and endangered species is remarkably high. For example, keep a lookout for the billbush, a shrub you won't find elsewhere in the Virgin Islands. While it appears to have leaves, the stiff dark appendages are really modified stems. It puts out tiny scarlet flowers that smell, surprisingly, like boiling potatoes. Other rare species include the Christmas orchid, St. Thomas prickly ash, and the Virgin Gorda gecko, the smallest lizard in the world. Gorda Peak's richness led it to be chosen as a UK Darwin Initiative site for the preservation of biodiversity.

Two trails cut through the forest to a lookout tower near the peak. The main trail (the second you will encounter when driving from the Valley) provides the most direct route (about 0.75 mile) to the summit. There is a picnic table about halfway up.

The National Parks Trust publishes an informative brochure on Gorda Peak. Look for a copy at the BVI Tourist Board office at the marina.

Savannah Bay

Savannah Bay is a long stretch of powder white sand about a mile north of Spanish Town. The water here is shallow for quite a long way out and relatively protected, making it a good beach for children. There is shade beneath the sea grape trees and excellent snorkeling on the offshore reef.

◖ The Dog Islands

West Dog, Seal Dog, West Seal Dog, East Seal Dog, and Great Dog islands join with Cockroach Island to form the Dogs, the site of some of the best snorkeling and diving in the British Virgins. Totally undeveloped and uninhabited, the Dogs lie scattered between Virgin Gorda and Tortola. Their closeness to Virgin Gorda makes them a popular destination for dive operators. These islands are protected by the National Parks Trust, and visitors should use the NPT moorings provided.

◖ NORTH SOUND

North Sound is the general term used to describe all the land- and sea-based locations near Virgin Gorda's northern tip. North Sound proper is the protected, circular body of water formed by the narrow northernmost finger of Virgin Gorda, together with a smattering of small islands that protect it from ocean swells. It is almost always calm, and usually a beehive of marine activity.

The tiny, colorful village of North Sound overlooks this body of water. Homes here seem to cling to the hillside, and the rum shacks that look deserted during the day turn lively at night. On Sundays, church bells ring out over the valley. During the week, children walk to the Robinson O'Neal Memorial Primary School on the Leverick Bay Road. The North Sound post office is believed to be the world's smallest.

Even smaller, Gun Creek sits at sea level facing the ferry dock that links Virgin Gorda with the islands and bays that circle North Sound. Here you will find a small grocery, the North Sound clinic, and a few more bars.

With its manicured gardens, electric gates, and named estate houses, Leverick Bay stands in contrast to North Sound and Gun Creek.

There are no roads past Gun Creek, so you must explore North Sound by boat. Biras Creek, Bitter End, and several restaurants on other North Sound islands provide free ferry service for guests wanting to explore their properties (and eat or drink in their restaurants). You can also rent a small boat

COURTESY OF BRITISH VIRGIN ISLANDS TOURIST BOARD

boats in North Sound, Virgin Gorda

and putter around North Sound on your own. If you're an adventurous soul (and capable boater), you will have a great time roaming around the quiet bays, empty beaches, and beach bars of North Sound.

Mosquito Island

This 125-acre island sits off the northeastern coast of Virgin Gorda, forming part of the barrier that keeps the North Sound calm and protected. Mostly undeveloped, Mosquito has a small luxury resort, restaurant, hiking trails, and two great beaches. Nonguests are welcome if they have dinner reservations.

Prickly Pear Island

This 243-acre island located in the center of North Sound, Virgin Gorda, was declared a national park in 1988. Prickly pear cacti (thus the name) cover the hillsides that slope down to several pristine beaches. Four salt ponds provide habitat for migratory and resident birds, while red mangroves on the southern shore are home to fish, sea urchins, and other marine creatures. North Beach has especially good swimming and snorkeling. A hiking trail has been made connecting North Beach and the southern shore.

Saba Rock

Too small to really count as an island, Saba Rock is a fleck in the middle of North Sound and home to a popular restaurant, hotel, marina, and nautical museum. Visiting yachts get up to 250 gallons of water free. The **Saba Rock Nautical Museum and Gift Shop** showcases some of the wreck finds of underwater explorer Bert Kilbride.

Necker Island

It really does not get any more exclusive than Necker Island, the 74-acre private island owned by Sir Richard Branson of Virgin Atlantic and hot-air balloon fame. You and your friends can rent the island for between $20,000 and $42,000 per night. Not surprisingly, Necker Island does not welcome non-resort guests. If you do try to anchor your boat here and swim ashore to one of the beaches, you will certainly have a story to tell back home.

Entertainment, Events, and Shopping

NIGHTLIFE

Virgin Gorda nightlife is generally subdued, but there are still plenty of places to meet people and a few spots where you can shake a leg if you want to. Pick up a copy of the *The Limin' Times* for a complete rundown on nightlife and events.

The Valley

There is live music nightly at **The Rock Café** (Tower Rd., 284/495-5482), where you can always count on a lively crowd. The piano bar at dinner gives way to up-tempo calypso, reggae, and soca later in the night. **Fischer's Cove Hotel and Restaurant** (Lee Rd., 284/495-5252) and **The Bath and Turtle** (Yacht Harbour, 284/495-5239) have live music most weekends and are popular among visitors and locals. The dance floor at **Chez Bamboo** (Lee Rd., 284/495-5752) heats up on Friday nights with a jazz or blues band. **The Mine Shaft** (Coppermine Rd., 284/495-5260) has live music on Tuesday and Friday nights, plus proprietor Elton Sprauve throws a popular full moon party once a month.

North Sound

The **Bitter End Yacht Club** (284/494-2745) and **Leverick Bay Resort** (284/495-7421) have entertainment most evenings, of the resort variety. The bar at **Saba Rock** (284/495-7711) is often crowded with visiting yachters; there is sometimes live music or a DJ.

EVENTS

Virgin Gorda Easter Festival

Every spring, Virgin Gorda throws a swinging, high-spirited party. The Virgin Gorda Easter Festival includes nightly entertainment in the festival village, set up in the school yard. There are also beauty pageants, calypso competitions, a food fair, and jouvert, an early-morning street party with thumping bass lines and energetic dancing. It all climaxes with a parade through the streets of Spanish Town on the Monday following Easter. The BVI Tourist Board office at the Yacht Harbour (284/495-5181) can provide you with a schedule.

Virgin Gorda Music Festival

Musicians perform at the annual Virgin Gorda Music Festival on Thanksgiving weekend. Call the Virgin Gorda branch of the BVI Tourist Board (284/495-5181) to find out who's on tap to perform.

Whit Weekend Festival

Not to be left out, the tiny community of North Sound has its own festival over Whit Weekend. (Whit Monday, a public holiday, usually falls in May.) Traditional games, local food, music, and a whole lot of meeting and greeting are the main attractions. The festivities take place under a tent at the Robinson O'Neal Memorial School in North Sound.

Spanish Town Fisherman's Jamboree

Fischer's Cove Beach Hotel (284/495-5252) hosts a fishing tournament on Easter weekend, adding to the revelry of the annual Easter Festival. Anglers, including children, can compete for a wide range of prizes. The weigh-in always winds up as a rollicking party with music and plenty of fish tales.

SHOPPING

Virgin Gorda is not known for its shopping, and it won't ever be. Most islanders make the journey to St. Thomas regularly to stock their households. But visitors will find a handful of quaint shops with gifts and souvenirs.

The Valley

The yacht harbor is the shopping hub of the Valley. Shops here cater to visitors and residents; there are souvenir shops right next to food markets and the bank. **Dive BVI** has a good selection of snorkel and dive equipment, plus T-shirts and gifts with a nautical theme. Check out **Thee Artistic Gallery** for crafts and books and the **Virgin Gorda Craft Shop** for local crafts. There are also stores selling perfume, electronics, local music, and a wide range of souvenirs. There is also a clutch of gift shops at the top of the Baths.

North Sound

Bitter End Yacht Club has several shops. The Reeftique has clothing, books, and gifts, while the Trading Post has postcards, magazines, film, sunscreen, and the like.

On Saba Rock, **The Saba Rock Nautical Museum** is part museum, part gift shop. Here you can see artifacts collected by diving legend Bert Kilbride and buy wreck-inspired jewelry and gifts. At Leverick Bay, there is a **Pusser's Company Store.**

Sports and Recreation

The most fun can be had on Virgin Gorda when you get out and about in the natural environment.

Hiking

The trail at **Gorda Peak National Park** is uphill but not severe, and the view from the top is worth it. Take the second trailhead for the most direct route. Take the first for a longer walk. Whichever you choose, be sure to walk slowly and admire the tropical flora on your way.

There are also trails at Baths National Park, on Mosquito Island, and Prickly Pear Island.

SAILING

Day sail operators will take you out for a day of sailing and snorkeling around Virgin Gorda. **Double D Charters** (Yacht Harbour, 284/495-6150 or 284/499-2479, www.boatcharterbvi.com) offers day sails on its *Northern Sun* and *Free Spirit*.

If you would rather set your own course, **Euphoric Cruises** (Yacht Harbour, 284/495-5542 or 284/494-5511, www.boatsbvi.com) rents a range of powerboats.

In North Sound, **Leverick Bay Watersports** (Leverick Bay Resort, 284/495-7376, fax 284/495-7014, www.watersportsbvi.com) rents four-person dinghies, monohull sailboats, and two-person sea kayaks for between $50 and $80 per day. They also rent more upscale powerboats for between $200 and $350 per day.

If you're interested in learning to sail, or brushing up on your skills, **Nick Trotter Sailing School** (Bitter End Yacht Club, 284/494-2746, www.beyc.com) is the place to go. Instruction takes place using the Yacht Club's fine fleet, in North Sound's calm and protected waters.

Yachting Facilities

There are three major marinas on Virgin Gorda. **Virgin Gorda Yacht Harbour** (The Valley, 284/495-5500, www.vgmarina.biz) is a 111-slip, full-service marina and boatyard just south of St. Thomas Bay, the ferry terminal in the Valley. The draft here is 9.5 feet, but there are plans to dredge soon for greater access. Overnight rates vary, $1–1.95 per foot, per day, and go down if you stay for a week, a month, or longer. If you're in transit, you can dock here free for one hour and at $5–7.50 for each hour after that depending on size. There are moorings outside the marina; pay for them at the Yacht Harbour.

At North Sound, **Leverick Bay Resort** (284/495-7421, www.leverickbay.com, $1 per foot) has 25 slips with a controlling draft of 22 feet. Amenities include fuel, water, laundry, Internet access, a hotel, restaurant, and chandlery. Yachts can stop in here for a few minutes at no cost. Or try **Bitter End Yacht Club** (284/494-2745, www.beyc.com), which has 20 slips and a draft of 30 feet. Bitter End is a full-service marina, including a repair shop, with all the expected amenities except laundry service.

WATER SPORTS
Snorkeling

The favorite place to snorkel on Virgin Gorda is at the **Baths.** Within the pools, you can examine the underwater boulders. To see fish, swim beyond the boulders on the ocean side or head to **Devil's Bay** and snorkel around the rocky edge of the bay. You may also want to don a mask to explore the reefs around Savannah Bay and Pond Bay. You can snorkel at the Baths right off the beach.

Diving

Dive operators around Virgin Gorda often take divers to **Mountain Point** at the end of the island's westernmost tip, where overhangs and caves make for exciting diving. Conditions here can be rough in the winter. Another nice dive site is **The Invisibles,** named because it lies almost invisibly under the sea east of Necker Island, north of Virgin Gorda. A twin-rock pinnacle here attracts reef fish as well as the occasional pelagic species.

Dive operators and day sails from Virgin Gorda often take passengers to the Dogs. **The Chimneys,** at the western end of Great Dog, is a site popular with both divers and snorkelers, who can admire underwater archways and tunnels. Other popular sites are **Bronco Billy's,** reputedly named by Jacques Cousteau himself, between Cockroach Island and Seal Dog, and **Wall-to-Wall,** which is usually packed with schooling fish.

Another popular site for Virgin Gorda dive operators is the *Chikuzen,* a wreck lying northwest of the island. The *Chikuzen,* a 246-foot refrigeration ship, sank in 1981 and its carcass attracts pelagic fish species, eagle rays, sharks, and many more species.

There are dive shops in the Valley and North Sound. **Dive BVI Ltd.** (Yacht Harbour and Leverick Bay, 284/495-5513 or 800/848-7078, www.divebvi.com) has been around for more than 30 years and gets consistently high marks from customers. They rent diver propulsion vehicles (underwater scooters) to divers with proper certification.

Or try **Kilbride's Sunchaser Scuba** (Bitter End, 284/495-9638 or 800/932-4286, www.sunchaserscuba.com), named after Bert Kilbride, its founder and one of the BVI's first underwater explorers and discoverer of many wrecks.

Expect to pay about $90 for a two-tank dive.

Parasailing, Kiteboarding, and Kayaking

North Sound is the perfect place to try water sports of a more exotic variety. Parasailing is exhilarating and offers great views. **Leverick Bay Watersports** (Leverick Bay Resort, 284/495-7376, fax 284/495-7014, www.watersportsbvi.com) will get you flying for a 10-minute ride for $50.

Or try the newest water sport around, kiteboarding, at **Carib Kiteboarding** (Bitter End Resort, 284/495-7740, www.caribkiteboarding.com), where beginners can learn the sport or advanced kiteboarders can sharpen their skills and go on excursions. Lessons run about $300 for two hours.

If your blood runs cold at the thought of such excitement, stay in the slow lane. Kayaks are also available from Leverick Bay Watersports.

Fishing

It is a relatively short sail from Virgin Gorda to the deep-sea fishing grounds in the North Drop and the fly-fishing grounds around Anegada—shorter than from St. Thomas or Tortola. So if you've ever dreamed of catching a giant marlin or wahoo, here's your chance. *Big Ting* (Yacht Harbour, 284/443-2795) offers deep-sea fishing, fly-fishing, and shore fishing on a 45-foot Bertram. **Leverick Bay Charter Services** (284/495-7421) sets sail in 46-foot Custom Hatteras for deep-sea fishing trips. **Princess 1 Fishing Charters** (Yacht Habour, 284/495-7480) offers deep-sea fishing trips on 31-foot and 38-foot Bertrams and Bradleys.

Accommodations

Accommodations on Virgin Gorda range from modest apartment-style suites to all-inclusive luxury hotels. The total number of rooms is quite small, however, so book early, especially in high season.

VILLAS

There are dozens of luxury villas on Virgin Gorda, many of which provide privacy in extraordinary settings. There are villas near the Baths, the Coppermine, Mahoe Bay, Nail Bay, and Leverick Bay.

Villa rental agencies will help match you with a villa that fits your needs and budget and assist with trip planning if you like. Villas typically rent by the week, although shorter or longer stays can usually be arranged. Rates typically range $1,500–$5,000 per week.

Virgin Gorda Villa Rental (Leverick Bay, 284/495-7421, U.S. toll free 800/848-7081, Can. toll free 800/463-9396, fax 284/495-7367, www.virgingordabvi.com) manages 40 different villas at Leverick Bay and Mahoe Bay. **My Private Paradise** (284/495-9814, U.S. 202/554-8880, toll free 800/862-7863, fax 284/495-9814, U.S. fax 202/554-8887, www.myprivateparadise.com) manages more than 20 villas in the Valley, Leverick Bay, and Mahoe Bay. **Purple Pineapple Rental Management** (284/495-3100, fax 305/723-0855, www.purplepineapple.com) also rents villas on Virgin Gorda.

THE VALLEY
Under $125

The Wheel House (Lee Road, 284/495-5230, U.S. toll free 866/468-6284, fax 284/495-5262, $90 winter, $70 summer) is also called the Ocean View Hotel and has modest but comfortable rooms at the lowest rates on Virgin Gorda. Located in the heart of Spanish Town and set above a popular restaurant and bar, this is not a quiet retreat. But it does have comfortable beds and good a/c, and it's close to shopping, restaurants, and the marina.

You will receive a hearty welcome at the **Bayview Apartments** (Spanish Town, 284/495-5329, fax 284/495-5960, http:\bayviewbvi.com, $110 winter, $75 summer) a complex of three two-bedroom apartments set amid lush gardens in a residential section of Spanish Town. Rooms are furnished in rattan with tropical colors and have a full kitchen and balconies.

$125-175

Another option is centrally located **Fischer's Cove** (The Valley, 284/495-5252, fax 284/495-5820, www.fischerscove.com, $160–200), where you can choose between a private studio cottage or a more traditional hotel room. Cottages come with kitchenettes, ceiling fans, and a comfortable sitting room. Hotel rooms have balconies that face either the garden or the ocean. Some rooms are air-conditioned. The restaurant on-site is popular with locals and serves three meals a day.

$175-225

For accommodations near the Baths, your first and best choice is **C Guavaberry Spring Bay** (The Valley, 284/495-5227, fax 284/495-5283, www.guavaberryspringbay.com, $210 winter, $130 summer). Circular, with high ceilings and exposed beams, these guesthouses are comfortable, private, and within walking distance of the island's best beaches. There are both one- and two-bedroom units. Each comes with a full kitchen and an AM/FM radio. There is no cable TV, Internet, or air-conditioning; count on breezes and ceiling fans to do the cooling. There is a small commissary (but no restaurant) on the property, so you can even avoid a trip to the grocery store if you like. The best thing about Guavaberry Spring Bay is the charming setting—units are nestled between giant boulders, coconut palms, and brightly colored bougainvillea. Guests can walk down to Spring Bay right next door or take a slightly longer hike to the Baths.

$225-300

The newest rooms on Virgin Gorda are at **Olde Yard Village** (The Valley, 284/495-5544, U.S. toll free 800/653-9273, fax 284/495-5986, www.oldeyardvillage.com, $275–295 winter, $225–245 summer), a condominium development on the outskirts of Spanish Town built on the site of the Olde Yard Inn, a longtime favorite. The Village includes one-, two-, and three-bedroom condos, all of which come with a full kitchen, air-conditioning, telephone, cable TV, and modern, new decor and appliances. There is a pool and restaurant on the property, but no beach or beach view.

Over $300

Little Dix Bay Resort (Little Dix Bay, 284/ 495-5555, U.S. toll free 888/767-3966, fax 284/495-5661, www.littledixbay.com, $650– 1900 winter, $375–1000 summer) was the first resort in the British Virgin Islands and continues to set the standard for barefoot elegance in the region. Opened by Laurance Rockefeller in 1964, Little Dix offers comfortable accommodations in a spectacular setting. Rooms are tastefully decorated with exposed stone, wood finishes, and tile floors. Guests are treated to a free bottle of rum and mixers upon arrival, complimentary morning and afternoon coffee, and use of the resort's snorkel gear, sunfish boats, waterskiing equipment, fitness center, and tennis courts. Guests here can read brand new fiction and nonfiction works from the resort's library—some even before their worldwide release. The resort prides itself on top-notch service, and with a guest-to-staff ratio of 3-to-1, you can count on individualized attention. All in all, Little Dix epitomizes class.

The resort is set on one of Virgin Gorda's most lovely beaches. Nonguests may want to come just to stroll through the acclaimed gardens or eat in top-notch restaurants. For many years, Little Dix was the only show in town, so much so that it built the island's marina, airport, and even ran the only private school on the island for years. Today, Little Dix focuses only on the hotel. Recent years have seen the addition of a world-class spa, villas, brand-new rooms, and an oceanfront swimming pool.

MID-ISLAND

The hotels at mid-island are a real getaway. If you want to see the island or sample its restaurants and shopping, you will need a rental car.

$175-225

At the end of a bumpy dirt road, **Nail Bay Resort** (Nail Bay, 284/494-8000, U.S. toll free 800/871-3551, Canada toll free 800/487-1839, fax 284/495-5875, www.nailbay.com, $200–295 winter, $155–220 summer) combines luxury villas and apartment-style hotel accommodation. Rooms in the "village," or hotel, range from hotel-style studios to three-bedroom apartments. Nail Bay also has a number of large, luxury villas—ideal if you want a more private place to stay. Nail Bay has been involved in a drawn-out dispute with both the government and some of its private homeowners over whether or not it has met environmental protection standards laid out for the development. Up to now, the dispute has not impacted its day-to-day operations.

$225-300

Located along a quiet beach halfway between the Valley and North Sound, **Mango Bay Resort** (Mango Bay, 284/495-5672, fax 284/495-5674, www.mangobayresort.com, $245–435 winter, $170–315 summer) has nine beachfront villas with front doors just steps away from the ocean. Hillside villas provide impressive views of the shoreline below. Units come with air-conditioning, telephone, dial-up Internet, and daily maid service. All but the most modest rooms have a full kitchen, or you can choose to eat at the award-winning restaurant just down the beach.

NORTH SOUND
$125-175

Nestled amid an upscale community of snowbirds and vacationers on North Sound, **Leverick Bay Resort Hotel** (Leverick Bay, 284/495-7421, U.S. toll free 800/848-7081,

Canada toll free 800/463-9396, fax 284/495-7367, www.leverickbay.com, $149 winter, $119 summer) has 18 hillside rooms overlooking the resort marina. Rooms are fully equipped with a/c, cable TV, phones, coffeemakers, refrigerators, and two double beds. The resort has a restaurant, swimming pool, water sports center, spa, shops, and small grocery. The location is somewhat remote, though, so you will want to rent a dinghy to explore North Sound and a car to explore the island.

$175-225

Saba Rock is so small that there is little here except for **Saba Rock Resort** (North Sound, 284/495-7711, fax 284/495-7373, www.sabarock.com, $175–285 winter, $150–235 summer). Rooms, which range from small studios to suites, are equipped with a/c, satellite TV, coffeemakers, and small fridges. In addition, two villas ($400–550) have full kitchens.

Over $300

Elegance and seclusion are the primary attractions at **Biras Creek Resort** (North Sound, 284/494-3555, U.S. toll free 800/223-1108, U.K. toll free 800/894-057, fax 284/494-3557, U.S. fax 310/440-4220, www.biras.com, $840–910 winter, $615–685 summer) a small, all-inclusive resort on North Sound. Accommodations are in individual cottages, many of which face the beach. Cottages, set amid coconut palms and sea grape trees, come with a/c, outdoor showers, ceiling fans, telephones, CD players, refrigerators, tea- and coffeemakers, private verandas, and bikes to get around the sprawling resort grounds. Three meals a day, plus afternoon tea, at the resort's private dining room are included in the room price. Most meals are served in a stone house overlooking the bay, where there is also a lounge, snooker room, and DVD-equipped large-screen television. Bercher's Bay, the beach the resort faces, is a picturesque string of windswept white sand, best for beachcombing and walks. There

are miles of hiking trails on the property, and guests also have free use of the resort's dinghies to explore North Sound—a real plus.

The Bitter End Resort (North Sound, 284/494-2746, U.S. toll free 800/872-2392, fax 284/494-4756, www.beyc.com, $690–800 winter, $465–490 summer) is one of the Virgin Islands' most interesting and celebrated resorts. It is a land-based resort that delivers an ocean-centered vacation. Guests have access to the resort's extensive fleet of top-notch sailboats while at the same time staying in tasteful oceanfront accommodations. Villas have two twin beds or one king-size bed, ceiling fans, refrigerators, coffeemaker, and showers with sea views. The wraparound porches come with a double-size hammock. Suites come with a/c and TV (on request). Guests can also choose to stay onboard one of the resort's sailing yachts.

Bitter End is a sports lover's dream, with a wide array of water sports (most of them free for guests), hikes, fishing expeditions, and sailing classes. In addition, Bitter End hosts a wide variety of sailing, fishing, and water sports–themed weeks every year, including a women's sailing week, and the annual Pro Am Regatta, where guests get to sail with world famous skippers in a mini-regatta.

The rich and famous revitalize at **Necker Island** (284/494-2757, fax 284/494-4396, www.necker.com, $3,000 and up), Sir Richard Branson's private island. Up to 26 people can stay in swank Balinese-style cottages, but you have to rent the whole island for between $20,000 and $42,000 per night. Needless to say, guests are treated to gourmet dining, luxurious pampering, and can choose from a wide array of activities, from boat excursions to board games. Several times a year Necker Island invites not-quite-so-moneyed guests with "Celebration Weeks" and "Revitalization Weeks," where you can rent a room "house-party style." The rate for these events starts at $21,500 per week, per couple.

Food

Eating out on Virgin Gorda is expensive. In many cases, however, it is worth the expense. Casual spots specializing in West Indian food are the best place to meet and mingle with island residents.

THE VALLEY

For fun, unpretentious dining and excellent sunsets try ◖ **Mine Shaft Café and Pub** (Coppermine Road, 284/495-5260, 10 A.M.–10 P.M., $7–25). The diverse menu features ribs, roti, curry shrimp, jerk chicken, and steak, plus fresh fish and lobster. And don't miss the deadly Cave-In house drink. You can work off some of your meal on the mini-golf course.

The Flying Iguana (Airport Road, 284/495-5277, 7 A.M.–9 P.M., $7–35) is a friendly little café overlooking the Virgin Gorda airport. Chef Puck serves standard favorites from the grill, plus his "Duck by Puck," steak, rack of lamb, and fresh fish. For breakfast (7 A.M.–3 P.M.), choose from smoked salmon or lobster omelette, French toast Grand Marnier, or eggs Benedict.

People come all the way from Tortola to pick up their favorite bread, cake, or pastries from **LSL Bake Shop** (Tower Road, 284/495-5151, 7 A.M.–11 P.M. Mon.–Sat., 4–11 P.M. Sun., $8–30). In addition to baked goods, LSL serves breakfast, lunch, and dinner in its cozy, air-conditioned dining room. This is a popular place for lunch, when students from the nearby school and others stop in for the local lunch.

At **The Rock Café** (Valley, 284/495-5482, 4 P.M.–midnight, $15–37) you can enjoy Caribbean and international cuisine at tables set amid boulders or inside the air-conditioned dining room. This is a popular stop for happy hour, and there is live music at the piano bar nearly every night. House specialties include Sicilian-style swordfish and spaghetti with fresh Anegada lobster.

Spanish Town

Dixie's Bar and Restaurant, (Spanish Town, 284/495-5640, 7 A.M.–9 P.M. Mon.–Sat., $5–10) across from the ferry dock, is a popular breakfast and lunch diner, serving hearty West Indian and American-style food. It is also a great place to soak up local culture, especially in the morning when it seems that just about everybody in Virgin Gorda stops by for a cup of bush tea and something to eat. At lunch you can try local specials like stewed mutton and curried chicken, or play it safe with a sandwich or burger.

There is always a crowd at the **Bath and Turtle** (Virgin Gorda Yacht Harbour, 284/495-5239, 7:30 A.M.–10 P.M., $8–25), a patio pub surrounded by the shopping mall at the marina. The menu is diverse, with pizza, quesadillas, curried chicken, seafood, and pasta. The bar here is lively and friendly.

La Brasserie (Olde Yard Village, 284/495-6994, noon–3 P.M. and 5:30–8:30 P.M., $14–26) is a poolside restaurant serving Mediterranean-inspired meals. Entrees include salads, pastas, grilled sandwiches, pizza, and fresh lobster.

Fischer's Cove (Spanish Town, 284/495-5252, 7:30 A.M.–10 P.M., $6–36) serves three meals a day in its casual, beachfront dining room about five minutes from the marina in town. Try the chicken roti, lobster salad, or coconut-dipped shrimp.

◖ **Chez Bamboo** (The Valley, 284/495-5752, 3–10 P.M., $20–40) is a stylish New Orleans–style supper club on the east shore of Virgin Gorda. Try the conch gumbo, Nassau grouper *en papillote,* or strip steak with a creamy Worcestershire sauce. Desserts include delicacies like chocolate bourbon mint cake. There is often live jazz or blues on the veranda Friday nights. The food here is imaginative—some of the best on the island.

Little Dix Bay Resort has two main restaurants, **The Pavilion,** serving breakfast and lunch, and **The Sugar Mill,** serving intimate, upscale seaside dinners.

The Baths

There is something extra special about the piña coladas at **◖ Mad Dog's** (The Baths, 284/495-5830, 9 A.M.–7 P.M., $4–8), but don't try to find out the secret—they won't tell you. This inviting, open-air café serves sandwiches, burgers, and hot dogs all day, with lots of cold drinks. Beat the rush to get one of the comfortable loungers on the porch, and you won't know where the afternoon has gone.

The food plays second fiddle to the view at **Top of the Baths** (The Baths, 284/495-5497, 8 A.M.–10 P.M., $8–30) where the dining room overlooks spectacular boulders. The menu features pasta, salads, sandwiches, and fresh seafood. Diners can take advantage of the freshwater pool.

Markets

Buck's Food Market (Yacht Harbour, 284/495-5423) has canned and packaged food, and lots of frozen meat and vegetables. It is the main grocery store on the island. **The Wine Cellar** (Yacht Harbour, 284/495-5250) has wine, cheeses, baked goods, and gourmet items.

MID-ISLAND

Giorgio's Table (Mahoe Bay, 284/495-5684, noon–3 P.M. and 6:30–9:30 P.M., $28–37) is an island favorite for elegant Italian dining. Set on the waterfront at Mahoe Bay, Giorgio's serves homemade ravioli, lobster, pampas beef filet, and other specials. Reservations are required for dinner.

NORTH SOUND

Bitter End Yacht Club (North Sound, 284/494-2745, www.beyc.com, $40–50 dinner) has two restaurants: the **Clubhouse Grille,** which serves breakfast, lunch, and dinner daily and **The Pub** on the beach, with drink specials, burgers, pizza, and casual fare. Non-resort guests can catch the free Gun Creek ferry. Dinner reservations are requested.

◖ Fat Virgin's Cafe (Biras Creek, 284/495-7052, 10 A.M.–9 P.M., $8–20) on the dock at Biras Creek Resort serves casual but hearty fare for lunch and dinner. Ask about the soup of the day, or try the chicken roti, baby-back ribs, or flying fish sandwich.

Biras Creek welcomes nonguests with reservations to its prix fixe dinners at **The Castle** (284/494-3555, 7–10 P.M., $75), overlooking North Sound. Dinner here is a five-course affair with dress code. There are seatings at 7 and 7:30 P.M.

On Prickly Pear Island, the **Sand Box Bar** (284/495-9122, $15–30), serves lunch and dinner daily. The beach bar also has ice, showers, and overnight moorings for visiting yachters.

Markets

The biggest market in North Sound is **Buck's Food Market** (Gun Creek, 284/495-7368), located about 100 yards from the Gun Creek dock. Yachters can provision at the Bitter End Yacht Club's **Emporium. The Chef's Pantry** (Leverick Bay, 284/495-7154) has groceries, a deli, and bakery.

Practicalities

INFORMATION AND SERVICES

Tourist Offices

The **BVI Tourist Board** (284/495-5181, 8:30 A.M.–4:30 P.M.) operates a visitor information office at the Virgin Gorda Yacht Harbour. Friendly and knowledgeable staff here can give you maps, brochures, and advice about visiting Virgin Gorda.

Maps and Charts

The best map of Virgin Gorda is found in the pocket-sized, free, and widely available road map of the BVI. For a detailed topographical survey map, you will have to visit the Survey Department (Road Town, 284/494-3459, 8:30 A.M.–3 P.M. Mon.–Fri.) on Tortola.

Nautical charts, plus a lot of other marine equipment, can be purchased at the **Virgin Gorda Yacht Harbour Chandlery** (The Valley, 284/495-5628, www.vgmarina.biz). There is also a shipyard and repair service here.

Libraries and Media

The **Virgin Gorda Public Library** (Crabbe Hill Rd., 284/495-5516, 9 A.M.–5 P.M. Mon.–Fri., 9 A.M.–1 P.M. Sat.) has a small collection of books and magazines.

There are no Virgin Gorda newspapers; the national BVI papers are available at supermarkets around the island. Listen to Radio ZBVI (780 AM) at 7 A.M., noon, and 5:45 P.M. for local, regional, and international news. The free Tortola-based *Limin Times,* published on Thursdays, includes Virgin Gorda nightlife and upcoming events.

Emergencies

There is no hospital on Virgin Gorda. The **Iris O'Neal Clinic** (Crabbe Hill Rd., 284/495-5337) sees patients daily 8:30 A.M.–4:30 P.M. Nurses are available after hours: call 554. **Apex Medical Center** (Millionaire Rd., 284/495-6557) and **Medicure Ltd.** (Ocean View Hotel, 284/495-6833) are the island's two private medical clinics. Medicure also operates a pharmacy (284/495-5479, 9 A.M.–5 P.M. Mon.–Fri., 9 A.M.–1 P.M. Sat.).

Virgin Gorda's main police station is in the Valley (Crabbe Hill Rd., 284/495-2222), with an outpost in North Sound. In an emergency, dial 999 or 911. For maritime search and rescue, contact **Virgin Islands Search and Rescue** (284/494-4357, emergency 767).

Banks

The residents of Virgin Gorda said a big "hallelujah" in 2005 when a new bank opened a branch on the island, finally giving them a choice of banking institutions. Both **FirstBank** (Lee Rd., 284/495-6229) and **FirstCaribbean International Bank** (Virgin Gorda Yacht Harbour, 284/495-5217) have ATMs and can assist with banking transactions.

Post Offices and Communications

There are post offices in the Valley (Lee Rd., 284/495-5224) and North Sound (284/494-1898), where you can buy stamps and money orders and send mail all over the world. For courier services, try **Rush-It** (284/495-5821).

You can check your email at **Java Connection** (Leverick Bay, 284/495-7154) or **Trinity Financial Services** (Yacht Harbour, 284/495-5437) for $4 for 10 minutes. Trinity also has fax service.

Customs and Immigration

Immigration and customs officers meet all international flights and ferries arriving on Virgin Gorda. Tourists must have a return ticket and prearranged accommodations and can receive a tourist visa of up to 30 days in the first instance. If you need to apply for an extension, visit the **Immigration Department** (Millionaire Rd., 284/495-5621) in the government administration building. Customs officers can be reached at their headquarters at the ferry dock (284/495-5173).

Launderettes

Steven's Laundry and Cleaners (Virgin Gorda Yacht Harbour, 284/495-5525, 8 A.M.–noon, 4–8 P.M.) is the best choice for doing laundry in the Valley. You'll pay $3 for a wash.

GETTING THERE
By Air

Virgin Gorda's tiny airport (VIJ) is located along the eastern shore of the Valley, about a mile from the ferry dock. The dirt runway is wedged between two hills, so takeoffs and landings can be heart-stopping. Because of the conditions, flights can only arrive and depart in daylight. Nonetheless, flying is the most convenient way to arrive. You can avoid the hassle of arriving on Tortola and then arranging taxis and ferries to Virgin Gorda. You also get the pleasure of short lines and quick service at the small airport.

Air Sunshine (284/495-8900, U.S. toll free 800/327-8900, www.airsunshine.com) has four flights daily to Virgin Gorda. Expect to pay $125 one-way. **Seaborne Airlines** (340/773-6442, toll free 888/359-8687, www.seaborneairlines.com) has announced that it will offer seaplane flights from St. Thomas to North Sound in 2006.

By Sea

Ferries sail daily to Virgin Gorda from St. Thomas, Tortola, and Beef Island. Ferries from St. Thomas and Tortola arrive at the St. Thomas Bay jetty in Spanish Town. Those from Beef Island arrive at North Sound. You don't need advance reservations on most of the ferries (with the exception of the North Sound Express), but always call to confirm the schedule ahead of time. Fare is about $25 round-trip.

Between St. Thomas and Virgin Gorda: **Speedy's** (284/495-5240) has round-trip ferries from St. Thomas to Virgin Gorda on Tuesdays, Thursdays and Saturdays. Boats depart St. Thomas at 8:45 A.M. and 5 P.M. on Tuesdays and Thursdays and 3:30 P.M. on Saturdays.

From Tortola to Virgin Gorda: Two ferry companies run boats from the Road Town ferry dock to the Spanish Town ferry dock. Round-trip adult fare is $25; one-way fare is $15. Seniors and children 5–11 years pay $10 one-way and $15 round-trip.

Speedy's (284/495-5240, www.speedys-bvi.com) comfortable, air-conditioned catamaran departs Road Town Mon.–Sat. at 9 A.M., 10:30 A.M., noon, 1:30 P.M., and 4:30 P.M. There are additional trips on Saturday at 5 P.M.; on Monday and Friday at 6 P.M.; on Tuesday and Thursday at 10 A.M. and 2:45 P.M. and on Wednesday and Saturday (December through July) at 6:45 P.M. and 11 P.M. On Sundays and public holidays, Speedy's departs Road Town at 9 A.M., 1:30 P.M., and 5:15 P.M.

Smith's Ferry Service (284/495-4495, www.smithsferry.com) departs Road Town Mon.–Fri. at 7 A.M., 8:50 A.M., 12:30 P.M., and 3:15 P.M. On Saturday, Smith's departs Road Town at 7 A.M., 8:50 A.M., 12:30 P.M., and 4:15 P.M. On Sunday, Smith's departs Road Town at 8:50 A.M., 12:30 P.M., and 4:15 P.M.

From Beef Island to North Sound and the Valley: Reservations are required on the **North Sound Express** (284/495-2138), which runs a circular route between North Sound, Beef Island, and the Valley. Ferries leave the Trellis Bay, Beef Island, ferry terminal at 8:15 A.M., 11:15 A.M., 1:45 P.M., 4:15 P.M., 6 P.M., and 8 P.M. The ferry terminal is within walking distance (about .3 mile) of the Terrance B. Lettsome International Airport, but if you are carrying lots of luggage, opt for a taxi. (Better yet, get a taxi to deliver your luggage and walk off your airplane legs.)

GETTING AROUND
Taxis

Taxis are plentiful in the Valley, especially from the ferry dock to the Baths. Expect to pay $4 per person one-way from anywhere in the Valley to the Baths, Spring Bay, or Valley Trunk Bay ($3 if you ride in a taxi that has more than three passengers). If you tell your taxi driver what time you want to be picked up for the trip back to the ferry dock, he or she will come. Otherwise, just wait in the Baths parking lot, where it is usually easy to catch a ferry back to the dock. (Give yourself plenty of time if you are catching a ferry.)

Taxis elsewhere are slightly more complicated to arrange and significantly more expensive. You will pay $6 per person one-way from the Valley to Savannah Bay, Pond Bay, Mahoe Bay, and the Coppermine. It is a whopping $24 to get from the Valley to North Sound (taxis with four or more people on board should charge $6 per person one-way).

A 90-minute island tour including the Valley, the Coppermine, the Baths, Gorda Peak, and Leverick Bay costs $45 for between one and three people, and $15 per person for groups of four or more.

If you need a taxi pick-up, call **Mahogany Rentals and Taxi Service** (284/495-5469), **Gafford Potter Taxi Service** (284/495-5329), or the taxi stand at the Virgin Gorda Yacht Harbour (284/495-5252).

Car Rental

Getting a rental car gives you the freedom to explore Virgin Gorda at your own pace, although at a hefty price. The most bare-bones rentals here run more than $40 per day and quickly climb to over $80. You will need to buy a temporary BVI driver's license for $10 if you rent a car.

Speedy's (Crabbe Hill Rd., 284/495-5240) has a large fleet of Jeeps and sometimes offers special ferry and car rental packages. Other rental companies, all in the Valley, are **L&S Jeep Rental** (284/495-5297), **Mahogany Car Rentals** (284/495-5469), and **Island Style Jeep and Car Rental** (284/495-6300). Book early to avoid being stuck with the biggest and most expensive vehicles.

By Boat

If you want to explore North Sound, you have to do it in a boat. **Leverick Bay Watersports** (Leverick Bay Resort, 284/495-7376, fax 284/495-7014, www.watersportsbvi.com) rents four-person dinghies for $80 per day, monohull sailboats for $60 per day, and two-person sea kayaks for $50 per day. They also rent more upscale powerboats for between $200 and $350 per day.

JOST VAN DYKE

A short sail from Tortola and St. Thomas, Jost Van Dyke is a getaway among getaways. The five-square-mile island shares a common topography with the other Virgin Islands: rich green hillsides that cascade toward perfect white beaches. But Jost Van Dyke (YOST van dike) possesses a character of its own, thanks to the thousands of sailors who visit every year and the influence of one world-famous islander.

Named after an early Dutch settler (some say pirate), Jost Van Dyke was a sleepy island community well into the 1960s. Islanders fished, farmed, and traveled to nearby islands for work. But then, in 1968, a young Philiciano "Foxy" Callwood changed things when he started selling drinks and food from a beach shack at Great Harbour. It turned out that Foxy had a serious knack for hospitality. As

his reputation as an easygoing entertainer and gracious host grew, so did the number of sailors putting Jost Van Dyke in their sights.

Today, Foxy's is still the best-known thing on Jost Van Dyke but is by no means the only reason to come here. Watering holes in Great Harbour, Little Harbour, White Bay, and the East End cater to the yachting crowd. If you are happiest with a drink in your hand and the sand beneath your feet, you can't do much better than Jost Van Dyke.

If you have the will to wander away from the beach bar, you will find an idyllic island still content with the simple life. White Bay, on the south shore, is one of the best beaches in the whole Virgin archipelago. A network of unpaved roads through the island's hills can double as hiking trails and afford explorers

HIGHLIGHTS

[(Great Harbour: The most picturesque seaside village in the Virgin Islands, the "capital" of Jost Van Dyke consists of a sandy track along the waterfront and a few quiet side streets. Coconut palms, a majestic harbor, and a stately old church round out the appeal (page 213).

[(White Bay: One of the nicest beaches in the Virgin Islands, White Bay is divided in two by a rock promontory. The offshore reef is good for snorkeling; the sand is good for relaxing (page 215).

[(Bubbly Pool: Tucked away on the remote east end of Jost, this is a favorite of hikers and

explorers. A nice, private place for a dip, the pool fills with froth and bubbles when the surf is up (page 216).

[(Sandy Cay: A perfect desert island. Relax on the white sand beach, snorkel on the reef, or hike the loop trail and look for banana quits and boobies (page 216).

[(Beach Bars: No island has better beach bars than Jost Van Dyke. Foxy's is the most famous, thanks to master entertainer Foxy Callwood, but others, such as Soggy Dollar, Taboo, and Sidney's Peace and Love, are just as memorable and even more welcoming (page 217).

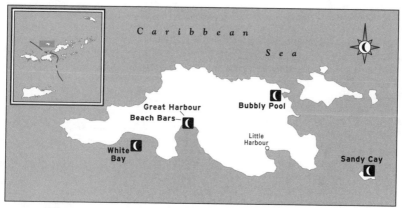

LOOK FOR [(TO FIND RECOMMENDED SIGHTS, ACTIVITIES, DINING, AND LODGING.

with unmatched views. Adventurers can hike to the mysterious Bubbly Pool and snorkel at Diamond Cay National Park. Jost is a great jumping-off point for exploring the out islands of Sandy Cay, Sandy Spit, and Little Jost Van Dyke, where visitors will find still emptier beaches and the remains of an 18th-century sugar plantation.

Most people get to Jost Van Dyke on charter yachts, which explains why there are still relatively few hotel rooms on the island. Still, you can find high-quality, low-fuss places to

stay on Jost, including an excellent beachfront campground. Daily ferry service makes Jost accessible to those without their own yachts.

PLANNING YOUR TIME

Jost is a quiet place—most visitors will be ready to move on after a few days. But if you want to get on the fast track to complete relaxation, by all means, plan a longer stay. Just don't forget to pack some books.

One of the most popular ways to explore Jost is pub-crawl style, starting out at either

JOST VAN DYKE

JOST VAN DYKE

On the Cay
Hollow Point

Long Point

Majohnny
Hill ▲

North
Side Bay
Point

North Side
Bay

C a r i b b e a n   S e a

Saddle
Bay
Point

Saddle
Bay

West End Point

Water Rock
Bay

▲West End Hill

PERFECT PINEAPPLE

SANDCASTLE/
SOGGY DOLLAR

WHITE BAY
CAMPGROUND/
IVAN'S STRESS
FREE BAR

🌙 GREAT HARBOUR

🌙 BEACH BARS   CLINIC   CHRISTINE'S
                              ▼BAKERY
                    RUDY'S ⚓ ⚓ ■   FOXY'S TAMA
                    CORSAIRS   BAR AND
                    ALI BABA'S   RESTAURANT
                    CUSTOMS AND   ● SEA CREST
                    IMMIGRATION   INN
          FERRY
          DOCK

🌙 WHITE BAY

Castle
Bay

Stoney
Bay

WHITE BAY
VILLAS

*Great
Harbour*
⚓

Dog
Hole

B
B
R

the East End or White Bay and sailing your way along the coast and into the numerous watering holes along the way. Jost Van Dyke has some of the best **beach bars** in the Virgin Islands, including the world-famous Foxy's Tamarind Bar in Great Harbour.

Day-trippers confined to land or those with less interest in beach bars should stroll through **Great Harbour,** the island's main settlement and home to what is probably the most picturesque Main Street in the Virgins—a sandy path fringed by coconut palms and the lapping sea. In Great Harbour you get a peek at island life: schoolchildren dressed in uniforms, small stores selling the basic necessities, and a stately old church.

Just over the hill from Great Harbour is the aptly named **White Bay,** a ribbon of white sand so beautiful it's almost unbelievable. You can

rent kayaks or other water sports toys to pass the time, but the most popular activity here is just lying back and enjoying the surroundings.

If you stay longer than a day, you will have time to make a day trip to **Sandy Cay,** where you can snorkel, hike the short loop trail, or relax on the beach. You could also visit the East End, where you can go to Diamond Cay National Park or hike to the **Bubbly Pool,** a secluded grotto that fills with bubbles when the surf is up.

Jost Van Dyke offers a good mix of nothing and something to do; you can spend a few days exploring on foot or by water, and spend some more relaxing on your boat or the beach. If you are staying a week or more, plan at least one day trip to Virgin Gorda or Tortola for a change of pace.

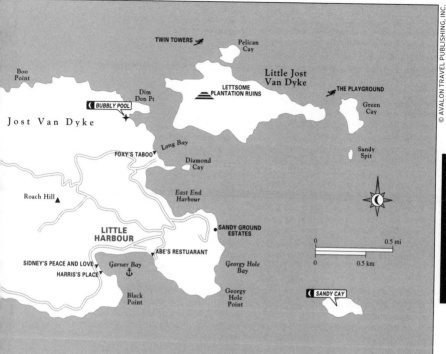

© AVALON TRAVEL PUBLISHING, INC.

JOST VAN DYKE

Sights

Jost Van Dyke is four miles long and three miles wide at its broadest point. Its ridge climbs to 1,054 feet at Majohnney Point and stretches from east to west like a meandering backbone. Development is limited to four bays along the southwestern coast of the island, although a few hilltop homes are now under construction.

A single road connects White Bay, Great Harbour, Little Harbour, and the East End; it takes about 15 minutes to drive the four miles from end to end. A new road has been cut along the ridge. It is unpaved and treacherous without four-wheel-drive.

Ferries arrive at Dog Hole, on the far western end of Great Harbour. It is easy to walk from the ferry to any place in Great Harbour, and

as long as you don't mind a bit of exercise, you can walk from there to White Bay as well.

SOUTH SHORE

Three bays along the southeastern shore of Jost Van Dyke constitute the extent of human settlement on the island.

(Great Harbour

Great Harbour looks like paradise: a fringe of white sand, coconut palms rising above the village, a beautiful old church, and unblemished green hillsides towering above it. Whether you arrive by ferry or private boat, your first real glimpse of Jost Van Dyke will probably be of Great Harbour. Get your camera ready.

Great Harbour's main street is a sandy path

ISLAND SLOOPS

Before the age of modern yachts, motorboats, and cruise ships, a different breed of watercraft plied the waters around the Virgin Islands. Small, wooden, and high-bowed, sloops were once the primary means of water transportation around the island. Known by the misnomer Tortola sloop, these vessels were built and used throughout the British Virgin Islands.

The sloops were built by Virgin Islanders, often using white cedar (*tabebuia heterophylla*), a tree native to the Virgin Islands. Shipwrights scoured the island for cedars that were the appropriate size and shape for their next project. White cedar eventually became the national tree of the British Virgin Islands.

There are no known plans or drawings for a Tortola sloop. Boatbuilders learned how to construct them from each other, and they kept their construction plan in their head. The construction process was carried out primarily using basic carpenter's tools such as a saw, hammer, chisel, and – most importantly – adze.

Island sloops are notable for their high bow and pronounced sheer, with a long overhang at both bow and stern. The mast is stepped on the keel and located one-third of the way between the bow and stern. The boom extends well beyond the transom and is usually the same length as the overall boat. Most Tortola sloops are less than 30 feet long.

As the islands' economy grew and diversified in the second half of the twentieth century, the art of boatbuilding faded from prominence in the community. For many years, the only active shipwrights were elderly men; the younger generation showed no interest in learning this art form.

But there is hope still for the island sloop. The Virgin Islands Studies Programme at the H. Lavity Stoutt Community College in Tortola has bought three Tortola sloops: *Moonbeam*, a 20-foot sloop built in the 1980s, *Youth Instructor*, a 25-foot boat built in 2000, and *Vigilant*, a 25-foot sloop built in the 1880s. Steps have also been taken to interview shipwrights and educate the community about its rich maritime heritage.

Meanwhile, the Jost Van Dyke Preservation Society finished a traditional island sloop in 2006 with the help of high school students, island residents, and some marine experts. Ask about the JVD 32 around Foxy's Tamarind Restaurant in Great Harbour.

There is a sculpture and display about the sloops at the **Marine Studies Center** (tel. 284/494-4994) at H. Lavity Stoutt Community College in Paraquita Bay on Tortola.

© SUSANNA HENIGHAN

an island sloop under sail

Great Harbour, Jost Van Dyke

that runs parallel to the beach. Fronting this are most of the town's restaurants and bars, as well as the Jost Van Dyke Methodist Church and the island's two-story Administration Building, where police, customs, immigration, and an island administrator have offices. Foxy's Tamarind Bar is located on the far eastern end of the harbor.

The heart of Great Harbour proper lies on the narrow side roads that veer off from the main street and on Back Street, which runs parallel to Main Street at the back of the village. This is where you will find the school, library, shops, laundry, gas station, and other evidence that people actually do live on Jost Van Dyke.

As would be expected, there is no large-scale shopping on Jost, but its small boutiques can be fun to explore. In Great Harbour, try Wendell's World (284/495-9969) for jewelry, crafts, and natural beauty products. Jost Van Dyke Watersports (284/495-0271, 8 A.M.–5 P.M.) stocks snorkeling and diving equipment, as well as a small selection of gifts and books. The Ice House (8 A.M.–6 P.M.) on Back Street sells handmade Christmas ornaments, used paperbacks, and locally made jams, jellies, and

salad dressings. The Foxhole (294/495-9258) at Foxy's Tamarind Bar and its sister shop at Foxy's Taboo at the East End sell T-shirts, gifts, and all sorts of Foxy-inspired items.

◖ White Bay

As you reach the top of the hill heading west out of Great Harbour, look down for the spectacular sight of White Bay before you, a ribbon of snow-colored sand and turquoise waters. White Bay is by far the nicest beach on Jost, and one of the best in the entire Virgin Islands. The sand is smooth and clean; it is fringed by low palms, sea grapes, and a few rustic buildings. The beach is cut in half by a small rock promontory. You can follow a path over the rocks or swim around them. An offshore reef rewards snorkelers.

The bay is popular among the yachting crowd despite the fact that there is no dock. Boats weigh anchor and passengers wade or swim ashore, hence the Soggy Dollar Bar at the beach's western end, named for the damp money fished from wet pockets and wallets.

The eastern end of White Bay is quiet; a small but excellent campground huddles among the sea grape trees here, and a few tasteful guest-houses look down from the hillside above. The western end is home to a half dozen beach bars and restaurants and a small hotel. The only real nod to commercialism here is at the far western tip of the beach, where on some days small cruise ships unload hundreds of passengers for a beach picnic. A sports center there rents kayaks, pedalboats, and other water toys and takes visitors on ATV tours of the island. The good news is that if this type of thing doesn't appeal to you, it's pretty easy to ignore.

Little Harbour

About 2.5 miles to the east of Great Habour is its smaller sister, Little Harbour. Small houses cling to the hillside here, overlooking the small bay and a narrow beach. A handful of shore-side restaurants, bars, and shops attract visiting yachts. The road dips down into Little Harbour, then steeply up and then down again toward the East End.

EAST END

A few years ago, the East End of Jost Van Dyke was largely unknown to visitors. There was no reason for most people to venture that way since only a few people lived there and there were no restaurants, hotels, or well-known attractions. But in 2003 Foxy Callwood opened Foxy's Taboo, built a dock, and began to draw visitors to one of the most beautiful parts of Jost Van Dyke.

The East End differs in character from other parts of Jost. The land around Taboo is flat and somewhat desolate; the flora includes cactus and other dry-weather plants. The small beach next to Taboo is rocky—not good for swimming—but the area is beautiful in an empty kind of way. The 1.25-acre **Diamond Cay National Park** juts out from the mainland just south of Taboo and is a nesting site for boobies and pelicans.

(Bubbly Pool

Ask at Foxy's Taboo for a map to the Bubbly Pool, or just head northward from the restaurant and look for the path—it's not hard to find. You will bypass the salt pond and climb over a low rise before descending into the cove where you will find the pool. The Bubbly Pool is most interesting when the northern swell is up—generally during the winter months. When the surf is up, waves pound into the boulders and break up into a fountain of fizz and bubbles. On a calm day, it is a nice, private place for a dip.

(Sandy Cay

Sandy Cay, a six-acre island less than a mile offshore Jost Van Dyke, is in many respects a perfect desert island. It has a sandy white beach, coconut palm trees, a nice offshore reef, and a wooded interior. Most visitors can pass a few hours here relaxing on the beach, swimming, or snorkeling. Others take the short (20-minute) hike that circles the interior salt pond and takes you past rocky cliffs favored by nesting seabirds. Conditions are also favorable for windsurfing and kiteboarding.

For many decades, Sandy Cay was owned by multimillionaire philanthropist Laurance Rockefeller. Just before his death in 2005, Rockefeller donated the island to the British Virgin Islands government on the condition that it become a national park. Rockefeller always believed in maintaining public access to the island, and the short trail that circles the island is well maintained. There are no moorings, however, and no trash cans, picnic tables, or bathrooms. Visiting sailboats should anchor off the sandy beach. The beach is susceptible to swells, especially in winter.

Sandy Spit

Add two shipwrecked souls to Sandy Spit and you have the desert island depicted in so many cartoons. It takes about five minutes to walk around the island, which consists of a beach and palm tree. This is a popular stop for charter boats, day sails, and day-trippers from Jost Van Dyke. You can also kayak here from the east end of Jost Van Dyke.

Little Jost Van Dyke

Little Jost Van Dyke lies so close to its namesake that you can wade there. Little Jost, a

the Bubbly Pool: one of Jost Van Dyke's best-kept secrets

155-acre (0.25-square-mile) island, is most famous as the birthplace of Dr. John Coakley Lettsome, the esteemed Quaker doctor and founder of the London Medical Society. Lettsome was born on Little Jost in 1744 while the islands were beginning their transition from cotton and indigo production to sugar. Lettsome was one of a pair of twin boys—reputedly the seventh pair delivered by his mother and the only to survive! Lettsome was schooled in England and returned to the Virgin Islands as a young doctor for six months in 1768, during which time he freed the family's slaves and quickly earned the princely sum of 2,000 pounds, which he used to further his education when he returned to England.

Dr. Lettsome never returned to his birthplace again, and the ruins of the Lettsome estate remain virtually untouched on Little Jost Van Dyke. They sit atop the low hill on the far western point of the island and are visible from Jost Van Dyke. Modern-day visitors can wander through what is left of the ruins or visit one of the secluded beaches along the northern shore.

You can wade across to Little Jost from Big Jost on your own (wear water shoes or booties) or go with a guide on a daylong snorkeling or kayaking trip. Charter yachts will also find quiet anchorages.

◖ BEACH BARS

No island in the Virgins has a better handle on the beach bar than Jost Van Dyke. Indeed, this island's beach bars may seem like the stuff of fantasy, but they are as real as can be. Sand between your toes, a cool ocean breeze, the low hum of calypso, deadly sweet concoctions, and an abundance of good cheer—that is the Jost Van Dyke beach bar.

It is never too early to go pub crawling, and if you arrive at a bar that seems closed, don't fret. Just help yourself. Many bars on Jost employ the honor bar system, and nothing embodies the generous spirit of the island better than this. (Don't forget to leave your payment on the way out.) Invariably, the afternoon hours, from 3 P.M. until sunset, are the best time to visit a beach bar. That is when you are sure to find a few new friends at the bar and some fitting calypso music in the background.

JOST VAN DYKE

JUST WHAT THE DOCTOR ORDERED

Exact recipes vary, but everyone agrees that rum, orange juice, pineapple juice, and cream of coconut are key ingredients in Jost Van Dyke's famous cocktail, the Painkiller. Here's one take on this popular drink, now served all over the Virgin Islands. If you prefer, you can serve this drink over ice cubes instead of blending it with crushed ice.

1 cup crushed ice
2 oz. dark rum
3 oz. pineapple juice
3 oz. orange juice
2 oz. cream of coconut (Coco Lopez)
Blend ingredients together. Garnish with a slice of orange and grating of fresh nutmeg.

You really must try a painkiller while you are on Jost. This concoction of rum, pineapple juice, coconut, and nutmeg is the quintessential island cocktail and goes perfectly with Jost Van Dyke's laid-back feel. For beer drinkers, the best news of the last few years is that Foxy has built a small microbrewery at his bar, so you can now get fresh, high-quality brews there. As far as I know, this is the only real microbrewery in the Virgin Islands.

Jost Pub Crawl

You will need a boat to embark on this entire pub crawl, and it should go without saying that your skipper needs to sip on virgin coladas to stay safe. A good starting point is **Foxy's Taboo,** the most straitlaced of the island's beach bars. Taboo is actually a bit removed from the beach; it is built on a wooden platform overlooking Diamond Cay and Little Jost Van Dyke.

Sail around to Little Harbour and stop at **Sidney's Peace and Love** (help yourself in the freezer if no one is around) and **Harris Place,** beach bars separated only by a narrow strip of sand—ideal for children. These places are generally quiet and uncrowded. Bring your own entertainment.

Great Harbour has the greatest number of beach bars, and you can explore them on foot. Sail into the harbour, pick up a mooring, and dinghy in to the shore. **Foxy's Tamarind Bar** on the eastern end of the harbor is the biggest and best-known of these. T-shirts left (or lost) by previous visitors adorn the walls, and you can study the business cards of attorneys, businesspeople, and other type-A personalities who succumbed to Foxy's painkiller and piña colada. There is live entertainment on weekends, and Foxy sings calypso most afternoons. When you're ready for a change of scenery, wander down the main drag at Great Harbour, and you will also find **Ali Baba's, Corsairs,** and **Rudy's.**

Save the best for last: Jost Van Dyke's quintessential beach bars are at White Bay. Start at **Ivan's Stress Free Bar,** next to the White Bay Campground. Mix your own cocktail at the honor bar, enjoy it out on the beach, and then head down to the **Soggy Dollar,** the supposed originator of the painkiller.

Entertainment and Recreation

ENTERTAINMENT

For all its quietude, Jost Van Dyke is not a dull place. Several bars and restaurants offer live entertainment regularly, and the whole island lights up a couple of times a year for festivals and parties. Foxy is the main entertainer at **Foxy's Tamarind Bar** in Great Harbour, probably the most popular nighttime establishment on the island. Live music can also be found on certain nights at **Rudy's** or **Corsairs.**

At White Bay, **Ivan's Stress Free Bar** has live entertainment on Thursdays, the same time as his weekly barbecue. The **Soggy Dollar Bar** has live music Sunday afternoons, and other bars in White Bay have entertainment occasionally.

Festivals and Concerts

Jost Van Dyke knows how to throw a party. From its earliest days as a tourist destination, Jost was famous for its special style of island revelry, thanks in large part to the influence of Foxy Callwood, proprietor of Foxy's Tamarind Bar in Great Harbour.

The biggest party of the year takes place on **New Year's Eve** (known locally as Old Year's Night). Hundreds of boats fill the anchorages around Jost and people throng to bars in all four bays. Foxy normally brings in some high-profile entertainers for the event. Over at White Bay, Ivan Chinnery hosts a low-key musical weekend at his campground.

What small-scale charm existed during the early years of Jost's New Year's celebration is long gone. In 1999 Foxy's made several high-profile lists of places to be ring in the year 2000. While the number of revelers has receded slightly since that millennial year, Jost is still jam-packed by a party-hearty crowd every New Year's. Special ferries run between Jost and St. Thomas, St. John, and Tortola for the big event.

The island's annual events also include **Foxy's Wooden Boat Regatta,** a celebration of classic wooden boats held Memorial Day Weekend. Recently, the regatta has also become a showplace for the traditional island sloops being preserved and maintained by H. Lavity Stoutt Community College on Tortola.

Foxy also throws a Music Fest every March, with headliners from throughout the Caribbean, and hosts smaller parties on Halloween, Christmas Eve, and Thanksgiving. Find out more at www.foxysbar.com.

And Jost holds its annual island festival, complete with a rag-tag parade, over Labor Day weekend. Don't expect much—but as with all things Jost, expect it to be a good time.

WATER SPORTS

With plenty of equipment available for rent, good guides for hire, and a number of excellent snorkel and dive sites, Jost Van Dyke is a great place for the water sports enthusiast. There is good snorkeling at White Bay, but the best reefs are found at Diamond Cay, and the out islands of Sandy Cay, Sandy Spit, and Little Jost Van Dyke. The best nearby dive sites are **the Playground,** between Green Cay and Little Jost, and **Twin Towers,** a challenging site north of Little Jost. **Watson's Rock, Tobago Canyons,** and **Mercurius Rock** are dive sites near Great Tobago, a small island bird sanctuary of the western tip of Jost. Exploring underwater can be as simple as donning a snorkel and going for a look around or as involved as spending a day diving unmarked dive sites with a guide.

The layout of Jost, and the number of nearby cays, makes the area ideal for kayaking. Armed with food, water, sunblock, and plenty of energy, visitors can craft their own expeditions. If you are going to paddle away from shore, be sure to equip your kayak with a flag or other marker to catch the eye of passing motorboats. A collision between a kayak and motorboat off Jost Van Dyke in 2002 killed an American tourist and demonstrated that accidents can, in fact, happen in paradise.

If high-powered water sports are more your cup of tea, you can rent water skis or jet boats, a souped-up personal watercraft, or even spend

White Bay is a favorite for day-trippers from St. Thomas.

hours bouncing on a huge trampoline over the water at White Bay.

You can rent a wide range of equipment or sign up for guided eco-tours at **Jost Van Dyke Watersports** (Great Harbour, 284/495-0271 or 284/496-7603, www.jvdwatersports.com). This outfit is the hands-down best water sports shop in the British Virgin Islands. It has developed a range of eco-tours that combine water sports, land exploration, and education; it will craft a special day trip to meet your needs if you like. Guides will take you off the beaten track (if such a thing exists on Jost!) and are excellent sources of information about the island. Eco-tours cost $40–70; a daylong kayak rental will run $20.

For divers, Jost Van Dyke Watersports boasts 30 unmarked dive sites around Jost Van Dyke and the Tobagos. They will take experienced divers on real blue-water expeditions. They also have some of the best prices around for sportfishing. Expect to pay about $100 for a two-tank dive and about $700 for a day of fishing.

BVI Sea and Land Adventures (284/499-2269 or 284/495-4966, U.S. 340/775-7292, fax 340/774-5532, www.bviadventure.com, 9 A.M.–5 P.M. daily), at the far western end of White Bay, rents a wide range of beach toys and water sports equipment, including kayaks, water skis, jet boats, and pedalboats. Rates range from $20 an hour for a kayak or $120 an hour for water skis or a jet boat. These folks also have a **trampoline** set up over the water; for $5 you can bounce all you want—a surprisingly fun activity, especially for a small group. Just don't forget your sunscreen.

ANCHORAGES

White Bay is a popular anchorage, although in winter the ground swells can make it uncomfortable for overnight stops. **Great Harbour** is a large, well-protected anchorage, although it can be difficult to get your anchor to hold. Dinghy ashore.

You can anchor on the western end of **Little Harbour** or pick up one of the moorings on the eastern end. On the East End, **Foxy's Taboo** (284/495-0218) has moorings and slips for boats wishing to visit the restaurant and bar.

LAND PURSUITS

There are no formal hiking trails or maps on Jost. Nonetheless, those who enjoy exploring on their own two feet will find plenty of ground to cover. The ridge road is a great place for walking, and once you climb the steep hills to get there it is not too demanding. You can reach the ridge by following the roads up from the western end of White Bay, the western end of Great Harbour (behind Rudy's), and the eastern end of Little Harbour. Jost Van Dyke Watersports can help you find goat trails and paths that cut through the wilderness and plans to offer hiking trails in the near future. Experienced backcountry hikers can delight themselves exploring the undeveloped west and northwest parts of Jost.

If you hike, do not underestimate the punishing sun, steep hills, the possibility that the weather could suddenly change, or the possibility that you could be walking much longer than you expect. The potential to get lost or hurt grows if you venture into the wilderness. Don't forget to bring plenty of water, sun protection, and food. Tell someone where you are going and when you expect to be back. Bring a means of communication with you if you can.

A new way of exploring was introduced to Jost Van Dyke in the early 2000s: all terrain vehicles. These open-air vehicles that resemble riding lawn mowers can now be seen climbing the steep ridge road and making their way through Great Harbour. BVI Land and Sea Adventures offers guided ATV tours for about $65 an hour.

Biking on Jost Van Dyke is not for the faint of heart. While the distances are short, the climbs can be brutal on the way up and terrifying on the way down. If you are sufficiently experienced, you can rent a bike from BVI Land and Sea Adventures at White Bay for about $25 a day.

Accommodations

The largest hotel on Jost Van Dyke has six rooms, and most accommodations are in individual villas. There is also an excellent campground and a few no-frills apartment-style rooms. Most visitors to the island sleep aboard sailboats. Land-based accommodation is found exclusively in Great Harbour or White Bay, although some villas are under construction along the ridge.

Under $125

At **[** **White Bay Campground** (White Bay, 284/495-9358) guests sleep steps away from the best beach on the island. The campground is well maintained and perfectly low-key. It offers a choice of of bare campsites (you bring the tent), large canvas tents (already equipped with beds and linens), and charming, simple wooden cabins (equipped with bed, linens, electricity, and a light). Expect to pay about $15 for a bare site, $35 for a tent, and $50 or more for a cabin.

Campground guests can use the community kitchen (simple but adequate for basic meal preparation) and a shared bathhouse. The campground kitchen, office, and honor bar are decorated with seashells, island fliers, and photos left by previous guests. The aptly named Stress Free Bar on the premises serves lunch most days.

Campers are vulnerable to the scourge of insects, but good strong insect repellent, mosquito coils, and vigilance in keeping your cabin door or tent flaps closed will prevent these pests from ruining your vacation. Keep in mind that dry weather and wind keep mosquitoes at bay. Sand flies, tiny gnat-like nuisances, come out around sunrise and sunset.

$125-175

The brightly painted **Sea Crest Inn** (Great Harbour, 284/495-9024, U.S. 340/776-4197, www.bviwelcome.com/seacrestinn, $130 winter, $90 summer) overlooks Great Harbour and is just steps away from most of its bars and restaurants. The concrete block structure houses a half dozen one-bedroom apartments, each equipped with a small balcony, kitchen, queen-size beds, air-conditioning, and cable TV.

Perfect Pineapple (White Bay, 284/495-9104, $130) has three rooms equipped with small kitchens and air-conditioning behind Gertrude's Beach Bar and Restaurant, a few yards from the beach. There are also a one-bedroom apartment ($200) and a two-bedroom house ($300) that come equipped with satellite TV and air-conditioning.

$225-300

The six-room **(€ Sandcastle** (White Bay, 284/495-9888, fax 284/495-9999, www.sandcastle-bvi.com, $225–275 winter, $140–200 summer) lies under the shade of coconut palms along beautiful White Bay. The hotel's four octagonal cottages are modest but comfortable, with king-size beds, outdoor showers, and a lounge area. The two newer concrete block apartments are air-conditioned. The hotel and its many return guests prize peace and quiet, so rooms don't come with television or phones.

Children under 10 are welcome only during a special "family week" in the summer.

It doesn't get much better than the **White Bay Villas and Seaside Cottages** (410/571-6692 or 800/788-8066, fax 410/571-6693, www.jostvandyke.com, $200–560 winter, $160–450 summer), a handful of one-, two-, and three-bedroom villas perched on the hillside overlooking White Bay. Besides the exquisite view, you get cooling breezes and access to amenities like cable TV, VCR, telephone, and a full kitchen. Knowledgeable on-site staff can help arrange activities and even provide childcare.

Seclusion and luxury are the name of the game at **Sandy Ground Estates** (East End, 284/494-3391, fax 284/495-9379, www.sandyground.com, $280 winter, $200 summer) on the east end of the island. The property consists of eight luxury one- and two-bedroom villas overlooking beautiful Sandy Ground beach. No beaches in the BVI are private, but this one may as well be because it is all but blocked from the sea by an extensive reef. The estate is difficult to access by road; if you're staying here it makes more sense to rent a dinghy than a car.

Food

Dining options on Jost Van Dyke have increased in recent years, and there is a fair amount of variety for such a small island. Most island eateries specialize in West Indian–style food, but you can find international favorites too. Prices are generally high; expect a modest dinner for two to cost at least $40. Lunch is a bit more affordable. If you are staying somewhere with a kitchen and plan to cook, it is wise to shop for most groceries on Tortola—selection is generally poor and prices high in the small shops on Jost.

Consider the opening and closing times given here as mere approximations, since many restaurants on Jost do not have set hours. As one White Bay restaurant proprietor said, "I have no doors, so I'm always open." But stroll

in at 10 P.M. and ask for a steak, and you may be disappointed. In fact, many restaurants, especially the smaller ones, ask for dinner reservations. Most restaurants that serve breakfast claim to be open by 8:30 A.M., but if you're on a tight schedule (or even if you're not) it is a good idea to call the night before and make sure someone will be there in the morning.

Great Harbour

The largest settlement on Jost Van Dyke also has the greatest number of places to eat and drink. A stroll down the sandy main street is all you need to introduce yourself to the choices.

At the eastern end of Great Harbour sits **Foxy's Tamarind Bar** (284/495-9258, 8:30 A.M.–late Mon.–Sat., 11:30 A.M.–late Sun., breakfast $8, lunch $12, dinner $15–25), Jost Van Dyke's first and foremost eatery and watering hole. The food here is secondary to the man himself, legendary Foxy Callwood. Callwood started out with a small shack on the beach, where he sold rum and soft drinks. Today, his Tamarind Bar is a sprawling complex that includes three bars, upstairs dining area, yard and stage, microbrewery, and gift shop. Foxy performs his signature mix of calypso and comedy every afternoon and early evening.

Foxy's is known for its weekend barbecue feast featuring chicken, ribs, and seafood. The lunchtime menu includes salads, pasta, rotis, and burgers; dinner is grilled fish, lobster, chicken, and steak. Dinner reservations are requested by 5 P.M.

☚ Rudy's (Great Harbour, 284/495-9282, 11 A.M.–9 P.M., $15–25) at the eastern end of Great Harbour is a family-run restaurant specializing in West Indian dishes, including grilled lobster, fish, and barbecued chicken. On special occasions, Rudy roasts a pig. The food here is simple, plentiful, and delicious. Most dinners cost around $20, but expect to pay $30 or more for lobster. On Thursdays Rudy puts on a lobster buffet.

Near the middle of Great Harbour's main street is **Corsairs** (Great Harbour, 284/495-9294, 7 A.M.–late, breakfast $8, lunch $7–15, dinner $14–25), where pirate kitsch meets an international menu. Corsairs were French privateers who terrorized Dutch and Spanish settlers in the earliest days of European settlement of the British Virgins. Today, the pirate theme is alive and well at Corsairs. The menu includes sandwiches and burgers as well as a wide selection of Mediterranean pasta and pizza.

For another take on West Indian fare, try **Ali Baba's** (284/495-9294, 8:30 A.M.–10 P.M., $12–25) just a few steps from the police, immigration, and customs station in Great Harbour. At Ali Baba's you won't find any explanation for its name, but you will find finger-licking West Indian conch, ribs, fish, lobster, and chicken. Breakfast is also served. Dinner reservations are requested by 6 P.M.

For a change of pace, **Christine's Bakery** (284/495-9281, 8 A.M.–5 P.M., $4–10) is a short walk down the side street next to the police station. This casual café serves omelettes, pancakes, and French toast for breakfast. It is also the place to come for fresh homemade bread, lunchtime sandwiches, and local food.

Wendell's World (284/495-9969, 8 A.M.–11 P.M., $6–12) sells fried chicken, burgers, and snacks near the center of Great Harbour.

White Bay

It is, indeed, hard to hold onto your worries at **Ivan's Stress-Free Bar** (White Bay, 284/495-9358, 11 A.M.–4 P.M. Fri.–Wed., 11 A.M.–late Thurs., $8–12) on the beach at White Bay. The bar is open all day—if no one is there to serve you, just serve yourself and leave the money. Lunch includes sandwiches and burgers, nearly all for under $10. Seating is under a huge tamarind tree in the yard, or on a beach chair in the sand. On Thursday nights, proprietor Ivan Chinnery goes all out with his popular barbecue buffet.

The number of eateries on the western end of White Bay has grown in recent years. But the most popular remains the **☚ Soggy Dollar Bar** (White Bay, 284/495-9888, 9 A.M.–3:15 P.M., $6–15), named after the damp bills handed over by sailors who wade ashore from visiting yachts. The Soggy Dollar claims to be the birthplace of the Painkiller, a delicious concoction of rum, pineapple juice, orange juice, and cream of coconut. If you want food to go with your rum, try cinnamon rum French toast at breakfast or the flying fish sandwich for lunch.

At night, the Soggy Dollar undergoes a Cinderella-type metamorphosis to become the **Sandcastle** (284/495-9888, $35), which serves a four-course gourmet meal by reservation only. Local chef Oliver Clifton gives guests a choice of meat, poultry, or seafood nightly, with soup, salad, and dessert. Reservations are required by 4 P.M.

Farther down the beach, **Gertrude's Beach Bar** (284/495-9104, 9 A.M.–late, $8–20) serves omelettes, eggs, and sandwiches for breakfast. Try garlic shrimp, chicken roti, ribs, or grilled mahimahi for lunch or dinner.

JOST VAN DYKE

Also on White Bay you will find **Jewel's Snack Shack** (284/495-9286, 11 A.M.–4 P.M., $4–8), which is exactly what it sounds like—a stand selling burgers, hot dogs, fries, and cold drinks. **One Love** (284/495-9829) sells cold beer and tropical drinks.

East End

Who can argue with a place called (**Sidney's Peace and Love?** Especially if it serves fresh lobster and lets you mix your own drinks. Sidney's (Little Harbour, 284/495-9271, 9 A.M.– late, dinner $15–40) lives up to its name with its friendly staff and low-key attitude. Lobster is the specialty here, but you can also get fresh steamed fish, conch, ribs, chicken, and more. Dinner reservations are requested by 5 P.M. and dinner is served around 7:30 P.M. Breakfast is bacon, eggs, and toast and runs about $6.

A few steps down the shore from Sidney's is **Harris' Place** (Little Harbour, 284/495-9302, 8:30 A.M.–late, $10–35), a waterfront restaurant serving three meals a day. Breakfast is available from 8:30 A.M.; ask ahead if you need it earlier. Lunch is served 11:30 A.M.–2:30 P.M. and features burgers, sandwiches,

and fresh seafood for $4–15. Dinner is fresh lobster, baked fish, barbecued chicken and ribs, and roast pork for $19–40. On Monday Harris' serves a special lobster buffet for $40, and on Thursday there is a seafood buffet for $27.

Across the bay from Sidney's and Harris' Place is **Abe's Restaurant** (284/495-9529, 11 A.M.–9 P.M., $8–40), where you can get lunch from 11:30 A.M. In addition to sandwiches and burgers, Abe serves fresh lobster, fish, and barbecued chicken. Dinner is served at 7 P.M.

(**Foxy's Taboo** (East End, 284/495-0218, 11 A.M.–11 P.M., $10–30) is a world away from other restaurants on Jost. Physically, it is set on the dramatic and remote East End of the island. Foodwise, Taboo offers much greater variety than other restaurants. Lunch includes fresh fish, pasta, homemade pizzas, and the best burgers on Jost Van Dyke. Dinner features gourmet seafood, steak, lamb, and chicken dishes for $18 and up. Taboo is a good base for exploring Diamond Cay, Little Jost Van Dyke, and the Bubbly Pool. Staff there can help point you in the right direction and may even furnish a map.

Practicalities

INFORMATION AND SERVICES

There is no official tourist information booth on Jost; check the covered bulletin board near the Administration Building for notices and announcements. Jost Van Dyke Watersports (Great Harbour, 284/495-0271, 8 A.M.–5 P.M. daily) runs an unofficial tourist information center out of its dive shop and is a good source of information about the island.

If Jost is your first stop in the British Virgins, be sure to check in with Customs and Immigration as soon as you arrive. Officers can be found in the two-story Administration Building in the center of Great Harbour (284/494-3450 or 284/495-9374). Police officers are stationed in the same

building (284/495-9345). If you have an emergency, dial 999.

The island's health clinic (Great Harbour 284/495-9239) is staffed by a live-in nurse. Mail service is provided by the District Officer, Carmen Blyden, whose office is located in the back of the Administration Building (Great Harbour, 284/495-3450, 8:30 A.M.–4:30 P.M. Mon.–Fri.).

The diminutive Jost Van Dyke Public Library is located in a building near the island school and is open 11 A.M.–5 P.M. Monday–Friday. You can buy used paperbacks at the **Ice House** (Back Street, 8 A.M.–6 P.M. daily), which also sells ice and water.

Jost has a number of small groceries selling canned foods, frozen meats, water, drinks, bread, and other staples. **Rudy's** (Great Harbour, 284/495-9024, 8 A.M.–8 P.M. daily) sells groceries behind the restaurant. **Nature's Basket** on the alley between Main Street and Back Street is open daily 8:30 A.M.–noon and 2–6 P.M.

Little Harbour has the **Little Harbour Marina** (284/495-9835, 8 A.M.–6 P.M. Sun.–Fri.), which sells water, ice, fuel, and other sundries. The marina also offers Internet access for $5 per half hour. Abe's (Little Harbour, 284/495-9329, 8:30 A.M.–8:30 P.M.) also runs a small grocery selling ice, water, and soft drinks.

There are no banks or ATMs on Jost, so plan ahead.

GETTING THERE AND AROUND

People who don't get to Jost on a private or charter yacht come by ferry. **New Horizon Ferry Service** (284/495-9278) makes the 25-minute trip between Tortola's West End and Jost five times a day. It leaves West End, Tortola, at 8 A.M., 10 A.M., 1 P.M., 4 P.M., and 6 P.M. Mon.–Fri., and 9 A.M., 10 A.M., 1 P.M., 4 P.M., and 6 P.M. on weekends. Round-trip fare is $20 per person. There is no need for advance reservations, but expect to pay with cash.

Jost's small size and limited road network make renting a car a luxury, not a necessity. If you are willing to do some walking, it is fairly easy to navigate White Bay and Great Harbour on foot—although you should be prepared for a tough climb in between them. Walking to Little Harbour on the East End is possible, but a much more serious undertaking.

If you opt for wheels, **Abe and Eunicy** (Little Harbour, 284/495-9329) will rent you a two-door or four-door Jeep for $50–80 a day.

Mountain bikes are available for $25 a day from **BVI Land and Sea Adventures** (284/499-2269 or 284/495-4966, U.S. 340/775-7292, fax 340/774-5532, www.bviadventure.com), although you should consider the challenging topography before opting to bike.

If you're handy on the water, consider renting a dinghy as a fun alternative to a car. You will enjoy the freedom of being able to scoot over to nearby Little Jost, Green Cay, and Sandy Cay, as well as being able to easily get to different bays on Jost itself. **Jost Van Dyke Watersports** rents inflatable dinghies, complete with fuel, safety equipment, and a briefing, for $60 a day. If you prefer a more demanding means of water transport, rent a kayak for $20 a day.

Taxis will happily run you between the various bays on Jost or take you on a sightseeing tour along the Ridge Road. Abe's Taxi (284/496-8429) and Jost Van Dyke Safari Service (284/495-9329) are good bets. Taxi rates are set by the government. Expect to pay $10 for a journey from Great Harbour to the Sandcastle and $12 from Great Harbour to Little Harbour. Per-person rates go down when you have more than three people. Ask upfront about rates to avoid any confusion.

JOST VAN DYKE

ANEGADA

Flat, empty, and so low-lying that early explorers feared it would slip beneath the sea, Anegada and its accompanying charms are singular among the Virgin Islands. Its attractions are simple: fresh seafood, solitude, and miles of empty, white beaches. Adventurers can complement the quiet times with expeditions through the island's wild interior, a land of epiphytes, wild orchids, and rare iguanas. Wherever you go, there is little chance of meeting a crowd. More likely, you won't see anyone at all.

Anegada lies 14 miles north of Virgin Gorda and is perched on the windward edge of a massive underwater plateau. The 15-square-mile island stands guard over the Anegada Passage, a 6,000-foot underwater chasm used as a thoroughfare by ocean liners and cargo ships. The nearby North Drop, where the sea depth plunges from 30 fathoms to more than 200, teems with large game fish. The island is buffered by the Horseshoe Reef, the third largest reef in the world, which extends south and east of the island like an underwater tail. The reef is as famous for the danger it poses to mariners as it is for its size and beauty.

Anegada peaks a mere 25 feet above sea level at its highest point. The west end of the island is dominated by salt ponds, wetlands home to rare and endangered wading birds, including flamingos. The eastern third of the island is a scraggly limestone wilderness, a surprising land of loblolly trees, cactus, epiphytes, wild orchids, and bright yellow century plants. The island is home to the Anegada rock iguana, an ancient-looking lizard that has been the focus of intense conservation efforts since 1997.

© SUSANNA HENIGHAN

HIGHLIGHTS

◖ **The North Coast:** Want a beach? You got it. Anegada's north coast is more than 10 continuous miles of powder white sand. Walk, beachcomb, kayak, swim, or sunbathe (page 231).

◖ **Western Salt Ponds:** Anegada's Western Salt Ponds are home to fish, wading birds, and a flock of wild flamingos. In 1999 they were declared a wetland of international importance (page 231).

◖ **Iguana Headstart Facility:** The critically endangered Anegada rock iguana – which looks like a remnant from the dinosaur age – is

the focus of intense conservation efforts and can be seen at a headstart facility in The Settlement. Lucky hikers can cross paths with the lizards while exploring the Anegada outback (page 233).

◖ **The Anegada Outback:** Wander along a goat path through a land of epiphytes, wild orchids, yellow century plants, flowering frangipani, limestone caves, and sweet birdsongs (page 233).

◖ **The Flats:** Silver and elusive, the bonefish that populate the flats are every fly fisher's dream. Try your hand at catching one (page 235).

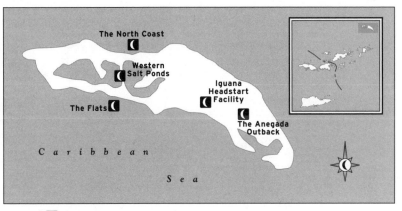

LOOK FOR ◖ TO FIND RECOMMENDED SIGHTS, ACTIVITIES, DINING, AND LODGING.

The island's only town, The Settlement, is a sparse collection of homes, shops, churches, and government buildings barely touched by the current of change that has swept through other Virgin Islands. Anegada's laid-back lifestyle is not an invention for tourists. It's the real thing.

Most visitors arrive by air, landing at the one-room Capt. Auguste George Airport at the center of the island. The flurry of activity generated by an arriving plane is probably the most you will see during your whole stay.

Boats can sail up to several docks along the island's southwestern shore, but only after navi-

gating a perilous course through reefs that have ensnared more than 300 ships since people started to keep track. While beautiful to look at, the beaches along the southern coast are not standouts for swimming and snorkeling. That honor belongs to the North Coast beaches: windswept, wild, and nearly always empty. No land stands between Anegada's North Coast and the other side of the Atlantic, and the waves that beat these beaches deposit an intriguing jumble of natural and man-made rubbish.

Anegada is spectacular, but it's not for everyone, least of all people who want to do

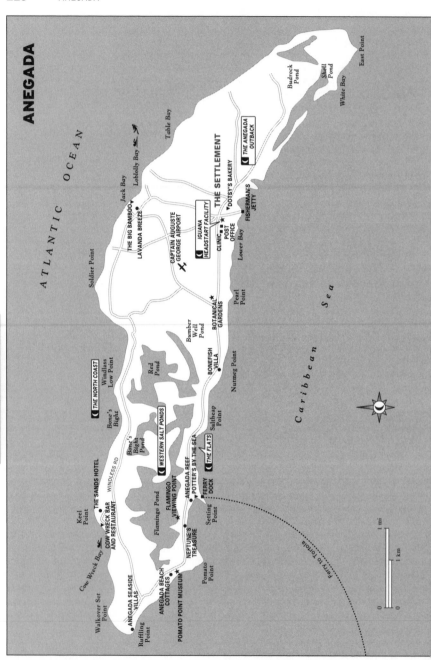

ANEGADA

ANEGADA

ATLANTIC OCEAN

East Point

Shell Pond

White Bay

Budrock Pond

Table Bay

Loblolly Bay

Jack Bay

THE SETTLEMENT

Dooty's Bakery

THE ANEGADA OUTBACK

FISHERMAN'S JETTY

Soldier Point

THE BIG BAMBOO

LAVANDA BREEZE

CAPTAIN AUGUSTE GEORGE AIRPORT

IGUANA HEADSTART FACILITY

CLINIC

POST OFFICE

Lower Bay

BOTANICAL GARDENS

Pearl Point

Bumber Well Pond

THE NORTH COAST

Windlass Low Point

Keel Point

THE SANDS HOTEL

COW WRECK BAR AND RESTAURANT

Cow Wreck Bay

Walkover Set Point

Ruffling Point

ANEGADA SEASIDE VILLAS

ANEGADA BEACH COTTAGES

POMATO POINT MUSEUM

NEPTUNE'S TREASURE

Pomato Point

Setting Point

FERRY DOCK

ANEGADA REEF

POTTER'S BY THE SEA

FLAMINGO VIEWING POINT

WESTERN SALT PONDS

Flamingo Pond

Bone's Bight Pond

WINDLESS RD

Bone's Bight

Red Pond

BONEFISH VILLA

Nutmeg Point

Saltheap Point

THE FLATS

Caribbean Sea

Ferry to Tortola

0   1 mi

0   1 km

something besides enjoy the beauty of their surroundings and the society of their companions. But for travelers wishing to truly get away, this is the place to come.

PLANNING YOUR TIME

For most people, Anegada's chief attraction is *not* planning their time. The established must-dos—seeing the rare **Anegada rock iguanas,** taking a stroll along the dramatic **North Coast,** and spotting flamingos at the **Western Salt Ponds**—can easily be accomplished in a day. In fact, Anegada is a popular and worthwhile day trip destination. Package day trips are available, but independent travelers can easily craft their own by flying to Anegada and renting a car or bicycle.

The closer you look at Anegada, the more there is to see and the more there is to do. While you can visit all of Anegada's principal sights and sample its atmosphere in a day, the beauty of the island comes into clearer focus the longer you stay. During an extended stay you will have time to try **fishing** on the Anegada flats or the North Drop, or kayak the beautiful southern shore. You could also hike in the **Anegada Outback** and spend a day birdwatching around the ponds. Visitors wanting to experience the Anegada wilderness, above or below water, should not expect any frills. Aside from a couple of people offering fishing trips, you will be on your own.

Overnight visitors to Anegada should assess just how much solitude they want. Solitude can be jarring. Some people stay for weeks and leave rejuvenated; others feel stir-crazy after just a few nights. Regardless of your disposition, it is wise to pack a good book (or two) and a deck of cards, since most hotels do not have television and there is next to no nightlife.

HISTORY

Pre-Columbians used Anegada as a supply station on their interisland voyages, drawing water from wells underneath the rock shelf and gathering fish and conch from the sea. Later on, pirates took shelter along Anegada's secluded shores and tempted passing ships onto its dangerous reefs. Bone's Bight on the island's North Coast was named after a pirate who favored this patch of the island.

Anegada's arid climate, poor soil, and relative isolation precluded the development of large-scale plantations that were widespread in the Virgin Islands during the 18th and 19th centuries. Instead, early settlers on Anegada quickly realized that the "wrecking industry" was the most lucrative the island offered. A Royal Geographic Society writer who visited Anegada in 1832 reported that the cry "vessel on the reef" was the only thing that roused the island's inhabitants. "Scarcely is the news announced than boats of every description, shallops and sailing vessels, are pushing off with all haste toward the scene of the action," he wrote. These settlers supplemented their wreck booty with small-scale farming of cotton, corn, ground provisions, and livestock.

Toward the end of the 19th century, the number of wrecks dwindled with the establishment of a lighthouse on nearby Sombrero Island and the identification of the dangerous current responsible for pushing so many ships onto Anegada's reef. Without the wrecks, Anegadians turned to farming and, increasingly, fishing to survive. With no refrigeration, the fishermen's catch was preserved using salt from the Western Salt Ponds. Islanders also gathered wood for charcoal production or collected the gummy sap of a native tree used in traditional boatbuilding. For many, however, the best way to survive these difficult years was to leave. Anegadians emigrated in large numbers to the U.S. Virgin Islands, the Dominican Republic, and the United States mainland seasonally or permanently. Those who remained continued to farm and fish, buoyed by regular remittances sent by family abroad.

All this changed in 1967, when a British businessman, Kenneth Bates, made a deal with the British administrator of the islands to lease, for 199 years, four-fifths of Anegada and build a hotel, marina, and accompanying infrastructure—all tax free. Anegadians were to be left on what some termed "a reserve" in the area around The Settlement.

EARLY VISITOR

In 1831, Robert Schomburgk, a member of the nascent Royal Geographical Society, was staying on St. Thomas when an American ship, the *Lewis*, was wrecked on the Anegada reef. Having heard that this was, by far, not the first ship to suffer such a fate, Schomburgk visited Anegada to make soundings of its passages and chart the reefs around it. Schomburgk wrote about this visit in the *Journal of the Royal Geographical Society* the next year, and his account remains one of the most keenly observed descriptions of the island.

Schomburgk found more than wrecks to report on when he visited the "strange spot" of Anegada. He found a gray siliceous substance covering the southern shore, in which he claimed which he claimed to find footprints of birds, animals, and Indians.

The southern part of the island was a mass of shelves, between which were large crevices and caves. The island's only trees grew out of these shelf holes, thriving in the rich, damp soil found within. Nearby, Schomburgk found a number of funnel-shaped shelf-hole wells, from which vast supplies of freshwater could be pulled. More remarkably, while camping near Cow Wreck Beach, Schomburgk was shown how to dig a hole into the sand to procure an abundant supply of freshwater.

Schomburgk was impressed by the relative health of Anegada; its people did not suffer from elephantitis and knew nothing of fish poisoning. Schomburgk theorized that the latter was due to the absence of poisonous manchineel trees on the island. The only real scourge Schomburgk noted were the mosquitoes, which swarmed day and night, sometimes in such force as to kill wild goats.

But Schomburgk's greatest observations were of the currents that swept around Anegada. In his studies, Schomburgk found evidence of a strong northwesterly current in the area, which he believed to be responsible for pushing many ships bound for other ports in the Caribbean onto Anegada's reefs. Schomburgk's findings were later confirmed, a discovery that led to a significantly fewer ships being lost on the Anegada reefs.

This sweetheart deal soon went sour. Islanders objected to the generosity of the giveaways and complained that the agreement had been negotiated without their input. At the same time, the government had given Bates a similarly generous offer to reclaim and develop land at Road Harbour on Tortola. The public protested this, too.

Bates was eventually run out of town, but not before the British government paid him off to the tune of $5.8 million. As a result of the failed Bates development, Anegadians continue to wrestle with a landownership quagmire and remain skeptical of any government proposal for their island.

Although flawed, the Bates episode left Anegada with some basic infrastructure it desperately needed: roads and an airstrip, for example. It also stoked desire among islanders for some kind of development that would bring them greater prosperity and demonstrated that Anegadians wanted to be the ones to lead it.

In 1977 Lowell Wheatley opened the island's first hotel, the Anegada Reef, which quickly became popular among sailors who delighted in Anegada's beaches, seafood, and end-of-the-earth atmosphere. Gradually more Anegadians opened guesthouses, hotels, and restaurants to cater to tourists who turned up on visiting sailboats or small planes. But despite the development, Anegada remains an island that keeps many secrets for her visitors.

Sights

Anegada's main road begins at the airport and circles around the Western Salt Ponds, following the south, west, and north shores of the island before heading back to the airport in the center of the island. The southern coast has the greatest concentration of restaurants and hostelries; the North Coast is empty but for a few beach bars and one hotel. The island's main town, The Settlement, is a few miles southeast of the airport. The roads on Anegada are almost universally bad, save the short paved stretch from The Settlement to Setting Point. The eastern third of the island is difficult to access by car; some narrow rough tracks are all there is.

In general, people on Anegada will be where they are supposed to when they are supposed to be there. Stores and restaurants will generally open on time and taxi drivers will be prompt. However, the smallness of the island necessitates some flexibility. If the owner of the restaurant has to travel to St. Thomas to shop, the restaurant may not open, and so on. So call ahead if you can, or ask around if something seems out of whack.

The North Coast

The North Coast is what most people come to Anegada for, and it does not disappoint. Stretching from Loblolly Bay at the east and winding all the way to West End Point, the North Coast is more than a dozen miles of unblemished, uncrowded, perfectly white beaches. The waves from the often-wild Atlantic Ocean crash onto the barrier reef several hundred yards offshore; smaller waves make their way onto the beach, depositing intriguing ocean riffraff. Beach quality varies along the shore depending on predominant currents and waves, but nowhere are the beaches rough or rocky.

A number of small roads branching off from the main loop road provide access to the Coast, but many people choose to base themselves at either **Cow Wreck Beach** or **Loblolly Bay,** home to two of the most popular restaurants and beach bars. Both have good snorkeling, but the reef is closer to shore and easier to access at Loblolly.

It is possible to walk the six miles from Cow Wreck to Loblolly, but be sure to prepare for the powerful sun and make plans for a pick-up. You can also kayak along the inside of the barrier reef; just remember that the current runs east to west. Beachcombing is another fun way to explore the Coast.

Western Salt Ponds

Anegada's Western Salt Ponds, declared a wetland of international importance under the Ramsar Convention in 1999, cover more than a third of the island. They are home to migrating sea- and shorebirds and are an important spawning area for a type of mullet fish. Before refrigeration, islanders used salt from the ponds to preserve meat and fish.

A path cuts through the dunes to the North Coast.

© SUSANNA HENIGHAN

ANEGADA

PINK FLAMINGOS

Flamingos are by far the most well-known birds to inhabit Anegada's Western Salt Ponds. Robert Schomburgk, writing in the *Journal of the Royal Geographical Society* in 1832, described the flocks of roseate flamingos that then lived in Anegada's salt ponds.

"It is a splendid sight to see several hundred drawn up in a regular form, resembling the figure of a cross, approaching from the west, flapping their mighty wings, and the sun reflecting his rays upon their rose-coloured breasts, the air resounding with their cry, which, consisting of several cadences, has been compared by the inhabitants to singing."

Flamingos were prized for their feathers and meat, however, and by the 1950s the elegant pink birds were all gone. So it was good news in the 1990s when the joint efforts of the BVI National Parks Trust, the Bermuda Aquarium and Natural History Museum, and several private individuals resulted in the reintroduction of flamingos to the island. The 20 birds were settled in the Western Salt Ponds, where, to the delight of conservationists, they have reproduced steadily and attracted several volunteers looking for a new place to live.

The best place to see the flamingos is from the end of the short access road opposite Neptune's Treasure along the southern coast. Look for a small Western Salt Ponds sign to be sure you're at the right place. Follow the one-lane road to the edge of the pond, and then look closely ahead of you: You will see the pink of the flamingos in the middle of the pond. Binoculars are the best way to watch the birds, and a telephoto lens will be required if you want pictures of them. Don't try to get close to the flamingos.

The ponds are a bird-watcher's paradise. The U.K.-based Darwin Initiative (www.seaturtle.org/mtrg) maintains a list of species present, and it is growing with every trip the Darwin scientists take to the island. A trained eye will spot ducks, plovers, sandpipers, herons (including Great Blue Herons), kingfishers, falcons (including peregrine falcons), and flamingos.

The ponds are surrounded by scrubby plants, including several species of mangrove and a number of succulents, including one that Anegadians typically added to salads for a sharp, briny flavor. You will need a guide to help you identify this plant; don't start nibbling on everything you see. Keep your eyes open for Anegada's endemic plant species: *acacia anegadensis* (poke-me-boy), *metastelma anegadensa* (wire wist), and *cordial rupicola* (black sage).

The Western Salt Ponds are a minimalist landscape: flat, mostly empty, with understated colors. Most tourists don't give them a second glance. But those who do are rewarded; they are uniquely beautiful and can be a nice place to walk if you grow weary of the beach—just keep track of your route so you don't get lost. A number of narrow roads feeding off the main road that circles the island provide easy access to the ponds. Keep in mind that the ponds expand and contract depending on the amount of rainfall, so be careful not to drive too close and get stuck in soft spots. Also be mindful that these lands are protected, and fishing, hunting, and otherwise extracting materials and animals from the ponds are illegal.

Pomato Point Museum

On the picturesque southwestern point of Anegada is the Pomato Point Restaurant, home of the Pomato Point Museum (Pomato Point, 284/495-9466, 8 A.M.–8 P.M. Mon.–Sat., free admission), where you can inspect a private collection of Anegada shipwreck paraphernalia. The collection features old coins, cannonballs, crockery, silverware, and other items salvaged from some of the hundreds of shipwrecks off the coast of Anegada. The museum is located in a small room off the dining area and is open whenever the restaurant is; it is open some Sundays.

The Settlement

The Settlement, Anegada's only village, is as low-key as the rest of the island. Located a few hundred yards from the southern shore and a short drive from the island's airport, The Settlement is where you can pick up basic supplies, see a nurse, mail a letter, and find most of the island's 150 residents.

The village sprawls along a couple of miles of road, with the newer concrete buildings—including a power plant—at the outskirts of town. Homes are simple and yards barren, aside from clotheslines, parked cars, and the occasional flowering plant. Many homes here have been in use for several generations and are excellent examples of traditional Virgin Islands architecture and building practice. The village center is a simple crossroads, identifiable by the general store and small grocery that sit there.

The Settlement is a pleasant place for a leisurely stroll or bike ride, especially if you want to take in something of the way of life of Anegada's residents. Like the rest of the island, there are no road signs here, so ask someone for directions if you are having trouble finding your way around.

At the end of the road heading south from the village center is the fisherman's jetty, a dilapidated public dock used by local fishermen and protected by mangroves. The piles of discarded conch shells have been placed here by several generations of fishermen. This is a good place to put in a kayak if you want to explore the southern shore.

The island's school, community center, and Methodist Church lie along the road heading north from the village center. The roadsides here are lined by low walls, many now crumbling. These walls were built by previous generations of Anegadians to protect their garden plots. As impossible as it may seem, Anegadians have long been farmers, growing guinea corn, cotton, ground provisions, and fruit.

A short distance west of the village center is the birthplace of Theodolph Faulkner, an Anegadian who was instrumental in leading a 1949 march in Road Town to demand greater self-government for the territory. A bust of Faulkner and a small plaque have been placed outside the old home.

Most cars just whiz by Anegada's unofficial **botanical gardens,** an oasis of color and greenery on the outskirts of The Settlement. The privately maintained gardens are located at the intersection of the road that follows the island's southern coast and the road that slants northward to the airport. There is no sign, and the white picket fence protecting the gardens from marauding livestock is often locked, but you can easily look over the fence to admire the tropical plants. Ask at Faulkner's Country Store if you want to know more about the gardens.

(Iguana Headstart Facility

A series of low cages adjacent to the government administration building are home to dozens of critically endangered Anegada rock iguanas. The BVI National Parks Trust operates the headstart facility, where hatchlings are housed until they grow large enough to survive on their own.

Iguanas do live in the wild, but they are difficult to find. The animals are shy, and they sense your presence long before you know they are there. If you do get near one, you will likely hear it scampering away through the bush before you can lay eyes on it. If you really want to glimpse an iguana—and they are worth seeing—visit the headstart facility.

The facility is open daily during daylight hours, just be sure to close the gate behind you when you leave. For information, contact the National Parks Trust headquarters (Road Town, 284/494-2069, fax 284/494-6383, www.bvinationalparkstrust.org) or ask around for Rondel Smith, the National Parks Trust warden on Anegada, who is a good source of information about the lizards.

(The Anegada Outback

The eastern end of the island, outside The Settlement, is a wild, unspoiled, and impenetrable land, called by some the Anegada Outback. Residents just call it the Bush. It is, at first glance, unwelcoming and harsh, but those who brave the thorns and sun of this landscape are richly rewarded by sights of unusual

ANEGADA'S IGUANA

Before the 1960s, iguanas outnumbered people on Anegada. The creatures, which look like leftovers from the dinosaur age, roamed the island's limestone wilderness nesting in the summer, while finding plants, fruit, and the occasional centipede for food.

The Anegada rock iguana, also called the stout iguana, grows up to six feet and can live up to 80 years. It is native to the entire Puerto Rican bank – the islands that stretch from Puerto Rico to St. Croix – but development has pushed the animals out of every island except Anegada, where for many years it was unbothered by hunting, human encroachment, or predators.

But following the failed Bates development in the late 1960s, the iguanas' luck ran out. The stone walls that once partitioned islanders' agricultural land were demolished, releasing livestock, including cows and goats, which promptly moved into large areas of the iguanas' habitat. Then the population of feral cats started to grow. Cats, it turned out, have quite a taste for iguana hatchlings. The combination of cat predation and competition for habitat from livestock caused the number of iguanas to plummet.

By the early 1980s, the situation was dire; estimates put the population at fewer than 300 animals. In response, an American scientist working with the local government began an effort to save the iguanas. In 1984 and 1986, Dr. James Lazell arranged for a total of eight Anegada iguanas to be relocated to Guana Island, which had been rid of all iguana predators. The lizards thrived; the original eight have begotten a population of more than 300. Animals from the Guana Island population have since been relocated to both Necker and Norman Islands.

Back on Anegada, islanders grew unhappy that the iguanas closely associated with their island were being removed to other places while nothing was being done to protect the diminishing population on Anegada. So, in 1997 the BVI National Parks Trust opened the iguana headstart facility with a half dozen young hatchlings collected from the wild. Six

years later, the first of the headstarted animals were reintroduced into the wild. Animals are now released annually.

The headstart facility is designed to prevent young iguanas from falling prey to cats, but it does not address the long-term challenges that face Anegada's iguanas. Scientists say their survival will depend on the establishment of a formal national park system on Anegada, as well as a program to eradicate feral cats. Island residents, while largely supportive of both plans, point out that land titles need to be given to residents before a national park is created. Many feel the iguanas removed in the 1980s were taken without permission and so are skeptical of an alternative plan to relocate some iguanas to uninhabited Fallen Jerusalem, where they would have a better chance of survival.

In the meantime, the Parks Trust continues to maintain the headstart facility while efforts are made to address the longstanding land conundrum that stands in the way of a permanent refuge for the iguanas.

an Anegada rock iguana in the wild

oliage, beautiful flowers, and a sense of silence
emarkable even for Anegada.

Flora includes wild orchids, delicate pink
lowers that poke up above the neighboring
ushes on a single thin stem. There are also
hickets of white frangipani, and huge cen-
ury plants that bloom bright yellow in the
ate spring and early summer. Anegada is home
o several species of plants that exist nowhere
lse in the world, including a prickly flowering
ush known to islanders as "poke-me-boy" and
small flowering vine once used to manufac-
ure fish traps. In many places, the plants grow
miraculously from gnarled limestone earth.

The only way to explore the Outback is on
oot. Only a few roads penetrate the wilderness, and they peter out after just a few hundred yards.

The North Drop

The North Drop is a deep ocean trench that
uns north of the Virgin Islands, reaching
depths of 200 fathoms and more in places.
Anegada is the closest of the Virgin Islands to
his famed sportfishing ground, where anglers
can do battle with blue marlin, wahoo, dorado,
una, and other prized fish.

The game fish are attracted by clouds
of baitfish—squids and flying fish among
them—that congregate to feed off the upwell-
ing currents that come out from the Drop.
Even those who do not troll the North Drop
themselves can enjoy its fruits; most island restaurants serve fresh tuna, swordfish, and others
plucked from the deep.

(The Flats

Anegada's other fishing ground is the flats, the
shallow expanse of sea along the southern coast
of the island, where fly fishers come to tackle
bonefish, one of the most elusive and challenging game fish around. Extending along
the southern shore from Setting Point eastward to the tip of the island, the flats are also
a good area for kayaking or puttering around
on a small boat. (Make sure it is small, though,
because the draft is quite shallow.)

To find the easiest place to explore the flats,
look for the small bridge along the southern
coastal road and an abandoned bar and restaurant called the Pink Flamingo. If you want
to fish, however, it is best to hire a guide who
can take you to the best and most reliable areas
for fishing.

ANEGADA

Sports and Recreation

WATER SPORTS
Fishing

Fly fishers in the know have for decades made
the long trip to Anegada to fish for the elusive,
slender bonefish that feed on its offshore flats.
Former president Jimmy Carter dedicated an
entire chapter in a memoir, *An Outdoor Journal,* to his experience fly-fishing on Anegada
and concluded that the tiny torpedoes are indeed one of the ultimate challenges of fly-fishing. Bonefish, or "gray ghosts," have strength
disproportionate to their small size and spook
easily; the smallest disturbance can cause a
whole school to beat a frenzied retreat. They
can be found on the flats from Setting Point
eastward to the end of the island, but if you re-

ally want to catch one, you should hire a guide
to show you the best places to fish and share
a few tips. Garfield Faulkner (284/495-9569)
and Clinton Vanterpool (284/495-8045) are
two experienced guides. Expect to pay about
$300 for a half-day trip and $475 for a whole
day. The Anegada Reef Hotel (Setting Point,
284/495-8002, fax 284/495-9362, www.ane-
gadareef.com) can also make arrangements for
a bonefishing trip.

Anegada is also a convenient jumping-off
point for sportfishers headed to the North
Drop, where they can troll for tuna, wahoo,
blue marlin, and other deep-sea game fish. **Just
A Little Bit II** (284/499-1938 or 284/495-
8047, U.S. 954/609-6138, fax 284/495-9461),

an Anegada-based boat, offers sportfishing and sightseeing trips. Many boats based on Tortola, Virgin Gorda, and St. Thomas fish these waters. The Anegada Reef can arrange North Drop fishing trips, too.

Kayaking

Kayaks are ideal crafts to explore Anegada's shoreline, as they coast over reefs that snare other kinds of boats. Kayak parallel to the shoreline inside the reef along the North Coast, or put in at the fisherman's dock south of The Settlement and paddle through the mangroves and flats along the southern shore to Setting Point.

Kayaks are available for rent from **The Purple Turtle** (Setting Point, 284/495-8062, 8:30 A.M.–6 P.M. daily) and **Cow Wreck Beach Bar and Restaurant** (284/495-8047, fax 284/495-9461) on the North Coast. Expect to pay between $40 and $50 to rent a two-person kayak for a full day and about $10 for an hour. Check at The Purple Turtle for suggested routes and helpful tips.

Snorkeling and Diving

With its expansive reefs and numerous shipwrecks, Anegada might at first blush seem to be a snorkeling and diving paradise. But it is not as simple as that. Most of the Horseshoe Reef lies just a few feet below the open ocean, exposed to powerful ocean swells that prevent delicate coral from growing—most of the reef here is stubby and compact. And since most of the 300-plus ships wrecked off Anegada were wooden, they rotted away on the ocean floor long ago. A no-anchor policy on the Horseshoe Reef also makes the logistics of snorkeling or diving here difficult, and dive operators have been asked not to take guests there.

But don't despair. There is excellent snorkeling at **Loblolly Bay** on the island's North Coast. Enter the water just west of the Big Bamboo restaurant and swim the short distance out to the reef, where you should look for a series of deep holes and caves that cut through the reef. You can dive here as well if you bring your own gear, but the area is pretty shallow and snorkeling is considered the best

way to view it. Watch out for the waves; if the swell is up snorkeling or diving here can be dangerous and unrewarding—the waves stir up sand that blocks visibility.

If you are determined to dive an Anegada shipwreck you will have to find a knowledgeable guide willing to take you out. No one advertises such outings so ask around at dive shops on Tortola and Virgin Gorda—you might get lucky. Two of the best wreck dives around Anegada are the *Parmatta* and *Rocus*, both of which lie several miles offshore on the southeastern tip of the Horseshoe Reef and are for experienced divers only.

SAILING

Visiting charter yachts will need special permission to sail to Anegada; the barrier reef is dangerous. If you have the experience to sail here yourself or have a skipper, then a trip here is well worth the time.

The **Anegada Reef Hotel** (Setting Point, 284/495-8002) has moorings for visiting yachts. Ashore you will find ice, a restaurant, and bar. **Potter's By the Sea** (Setting Point, 284/495-9182) also has moorings, ice, a restaurant, and a dinghy dock.

LAND PURSUITS
Bicycling

Being flat, Anegada presents easier terrain for bicycling than any of the other Virgin Islands. On the paved roads, biking is an easy way to get around and explore. You can also bike the miles of packed sand roads, a challenging but by no means impossible undertaking. Be sure to bring plenty of water and wear sun protection; there is not much shade out there. It takes about three hours to cycle the road that circles the Western Salt Ponds, more if you stop frequently to rest or investigate the narrow paths that crisscross the area.

You can rent bikes and motorized scooters from **T&A's Bike Rental,** located at the Cash and Carry (Setting Point, 284/495-9932, 9:15 A.M.–6 P.M. Mon.–Sat., 1–5 P.M. Sundays) for $15 a day or $10 a half day. A daylong scooter rental will cost you about $40.

Hiking

Hiking on Anegada is an adventure, not just an outing. There are no marked trails, no hiking guides, and no maps. But there are lots of opportunities for exploration along goat paths that crisscross the eastern wilderness, the Anegada Outback.

A good place to start hiking is at the end of the main road heading east through The Settlement. As you pass the outskirts of the village, the road will narrow until it is nothing more than a footpath. If you walk all the way to the eastern tip of the island you will find conch shell middins left by pre-Columbians centuries ago.

Take safety precautions if you decide to hike. Tell someone where you are going and when you expect to be back. Bring water and food and wear good shoes, long pants, and long sleeves to protect you from thorny plants and trees (of which there are a lot). Wear a hat and sunscreen. If you can, bring a cell phone or hand-held radio. Take a map and remain alert to where you are going so you won't get lost. Start early in the morning when it is cooler, and never hike at night when it is easy to get hurt or lost.

walking through the "Anegada Outback"

Accommodations

Under $125

Adventurers can camp at **Cardie's Camping** (Setting Point, 284/495-9625 or 284/499-9890), adjacent to Cardie's Shipwreck Restaurant and Bar. For $20 a night you will get a wooden platform and access to a bathroom, showers, and grill. Restaurants and a grocery store are within walking distance.

The North Coast **Sands Hotel** (Keel Point, 284/495-8065 or 284/495-8030, U.S. 340/777-3217, www.anegadasandshotel.com, $75 summer, $85 winter) is one of the best deals on Anegada. With its sweeping views of the North Coast and Western Salt Ponds, you may not even notice that it is not right on the beach. The two-story concrete hotel maintains a 100-yard path to nearby Keel Point Beach, where there is an umbrella for beachgoers.

Rooms are plain but comfortably equipped with air-conditioning, kitchenettes, balconies, and ceiling fans. It is one of the only places to stay on Anegada with cable TV.

Located on a shady corner of the island's south shore is the clean and cozy **❰ Neptune's Treasure Guesthouse** (Bender's Bay, P.O. Box 2711, Anegada, 284/495-9439, www.neptunestreasure.com, $90 summer, $110 winter). The nine-room guesthouse is owned by the friendly and welcoming Soares family, who also operate a long-line fishing business. The family's catch winds up at restaurants on Anegada, Virgin Gorda, and Tortola. The guesthouse has nice views looking south to Virgin Gorda and Tortola. Guests enjoy air-conditioning, in-room coffeemakers, and first dibs on the day's catch at the hotel restaurant.

ANEGADA

$125-175

For perfect sunset views, try the **Anegada Beach Cottages** (Pomato Point, 9052 New Classic Ct., Elk Grove, CA 95758, 284/495-9234, U.S. 916/683-3352, mckenzie@surfbvi.com, www.anegadabeachcottages.com, $125). The beach in front of the three cottages is long, hard-packed, and well protected, making it ideal for swimming and walking. Cottages come with ceiling fans, a full kitchen, and small porch, but no television or phone. The beach is a 50-foot walk away. One of the cottages can sleep up to four people for $175 per night. The cottages are a short walk from Pomato Point Restaurant.

(Bonefish Villa (Nutmeg Point, 284/495-8045, $135 summer, $160 winter) is a two-bedroom shoreside villa well equipped with air-conditioning, television, a phone, and full kitchen. It is located on the southern coast between Setting Point and The Settlement. Expect to pay $10 extra per night for more than two guests. The villa also rents through St. Thomas–based McLaughlin Anderson (340/776-0635 or 800/537-6246, fax 340/777-4737, www.mclaughlinanderson.com).

$175-225

(Anegada Seaside Villas (West End, P.O. Box 2710, Anegada, tel./fax 284/495-9466, www.anegadavillas.com, $170 summer, $200 winter) is a cluster of a dozen brightly painted one-bedroom concrete cottages located on the island's spectacular western tip. They are equipped with full kitchens, outdoor grills, stereos, and balconies, but no phone, TV, or air-conditioning. The beachfront location could not be more dramatic. The villas can sleep up to four people, but you will pay $25 per night for each extra guest.

$225-300

The Anegada Reef Hotel (Setting Point, 284/495-8002, fax 284/495-9362, www.anegadareef.com, $250 summer, $275 winter) is an island institution. Located at Setting Point and equipped with a large dock, the hotel and adjoining restaurant are well positioned to attract the yachting crowd. It is a gathering place for locals, too. Anegadian Lowell Wheatley and his wife, Sue, ran the property for nearly 30 years, until Lowell's death in 2003. His children now operate the establishment. The 20-room hotel is intentionally no-frills; if you want television and telephones, go elsewhere. The rooms are clean, neat, and comfortable, however. The room price includes all meals, but you will pay extra for lobster.

Over $300

If you want luxury and room to stretch out, choose **Lavenda Breeze** (Loblolly Bay, 284/495-8045, 845/255-1616, or 888/868-0199, www.lavendabreeze.com, $320 summer, $440 winter) a three-bedroom villa with a wraparound porch and views of beautiful Loblolly Bay. Amenities include satellite television, a full kitchen, VCR, DVD, washer, dryer, maid service, and more. If you would rather not cook, the house is a short walk from two restaurants.

Food

Eating out on Anegada means one thing: seafood. Fresh lobster, fish, and conch are the island's specialties, and restaurants serve little else. Consequently, they do them well. Most of the seafood is caught by local anglers and is a source of income for many island families. If you expect to tire of seafood (and its relatively high price tag) bring groceries and plan to do some cooking yourself. But you would be remiss not to enjoy at least one Anegada lobster.

Nearly all restaurants ask you to make dinner reservations by 4:30 P.M., either by phone, in person, or on VHF radio. Plan on paying $40 for a lobster dinner and $30 for fish or conch. Dinners include generous side dishes. For lunch, some restaurants serve sandwiches and burgers in addition to their regular seafood menu. Always call ahead or make a back-up plan because some restaurants close down unannounced when few tourists are around or the owners have something better to do.

The Settlement

Dotsy's Bakery (The Settlement, 284/495-9667, 9 A.M.–7 P.M. Mon.–Sat.) serves breakfast, lunch, and dinner in a small West Indian–style building in the heart of the island's only town. It is located near the end of the road heading south towards the fisherman's jetty. The menu includes West Indian specialties like conch, fish, and barbecued chicken for about $15, and burgers, sandwiches, and pizza for about $10. A standard breakfast will cost $5–10. This is also the place to buy fresh bread and local pastries.

South Shore

Located adjacent to the hotel by the same name, the seaside **Anegada Reef** (Setting Point, 284/495-8002, daily) serves breakfast 8:30–10 A.M., lunch 12:30–2 P.M., and dinner at 7:15 P.M. Like most Anegada restaurants, its dinner specialties are lobster and fish, but the menu also includes chicken, ribs, and other meats. Expect to pay $40 for a lobster dinner, $25 for chicken, and $17 for a vegetarian din-

ner. At lunch, the Reef serves sandwiches for about $8 and salads, including its signature lobster salad, for about $10. Early birds get a full English breakfast for about $9. If you are looking for company and a drink after dark, the Anegada Reef's bar is the place to go.

Colorful **(Potter's By the Sea** (Setting Point, 284/499-9637) is a cheerful beachfront restaurant with superb sunset views and a welcoming atmosphere. It opens daily for lunch 10 A.M.–2 P.M. and serves dinner at 7:30 P.M. Its sunset view makes it a great happy hour stop. Potter's serves island specialties including lobster and fish. Expect to pay $15–20 for most lunch entrées, and more for lobster. Dinners range $20–35.

Look for a cluster of coconut palm trees to find **(Neptune's Treasure** (Bender's Bay, 284/495-9439, daily), a family-run seafood restaurant on the southern coast. The Soares family catches its own seafood on one of its long-line fishing boats. You can dine outdoors on the deck or inside the screened dining room, a plus when mosquitoes are in attendance. The restaurant opens nightly for dinner with specialties of grilled lobster and fish. Lunch is served Monday–Friday. Breakfast is available daily 8:30–10 A.M.

At the western tip of Anegada's south shore is Pomato Point, home to the **Pomato Point Restaurant** (284/495-9439, 8 A.M.–9 P.M. daily) and the best blended drinks on the island. The breezy dining room is a short walk away from the beautiful and calm Pomato Point beach, perfect for swimming, walking, and sunbathing. Dinner and lunch specialties include lobster, fish, and conch. Expect to pay $20–30 for a very filling meal. Diners can examine the shipwreck artifacts at the Pomato Point Museum while they wait for their food or sip a cocktail.

North Coast

Ask most people, and they will tell you that the best food on Anegada is served at the **(Big**

Bamboo (Loblolly Bay, 284/495-2019, 10 A.M.–9 P.M. daily). To find it, follow the road that heads northeast out of The Settlement and pass turnoffs for Flash of Beauty and other Loblolly businesses. The road dead-ends at the Big Bamboo, located on the western end of the Bay. Open daily for lunch and dinner, the Big Bamboo specializes in pan-seared grouper, grilled lobster, and other seafood, but you can also order chicken. Lunch entrées range $15–30 and dinner ranges $25–35. Reservations are required for dinner. Meals come with potatoes, rice, and vegetables. The adjacent bar serves blended drinks and ice-cold beers. After you eat, relax in a hammock under the sea grape trees, lie in the sand under a beach umbrella, or go for a snorkel at Loblolly Bay.

You will feel like you have reached the end of the world when you get to the **Cow Wreck Bar and Restaurant** (Cow Wreck Beach, 284/495-8047, 11 A.M.–8 P.M. daily). Located at the end of a series of low sand dunes, this bar and restaurant squats on one of the most dramatic stretches of beach on Anegada. The area got its name when the *Rocus,* a ship carrying animal skeletons to a bonemeal factory in the United States, wrecked off Anegada in 1929 and the bones washed ashore here in great numbers. You can still see some of them scattered around the restaurant as part of its decor. Lunch here includes burgers, salads, fried chicken, and seafood. Expect to pay between $8 and $17. Dinner specialties are lobster, fish, and conch and cost between $20 and $40. Cow Wreck is known locally for its superb conch dishes. Dinner reservations are requested.

Practicalities

There are no luxury hotels on Anegada, nor ATMs, bookstores, or tourist information desks. Visiting here is an adventure; if you need something, bring it with you.

INFORMATION AND SERVICES

There is no tourist information center on Anegada; the best sources of information are the people you encounter. Your hotel proprietor, waiter, or taxi driver will be able to answer most of your questions. They may even provide the service you are looking for.

Good **maps** of Anegada are hard to find. The road maps provided by car rental agencies provide minimal information. If you expect to do a lot of exploring, obtain detailed survey maps and nautical charts on Tortola before you arrive.

For general government services, including **postal services,** visit the **District Office** (The Settlement, 284/494-8048, 8:30 A.M.–4:30 P.M. Mon.–Fri.).

The **Anegada Clinic** (The Settlement, 284/495-8049, 8:30 A.M.–4:30 P.M. Mon.–Fri.) is staffed by a nurse, but a doctor visits once a week.

The **Anegada Community Library** (The Settlement, 284/495-9464, 8:30 A.M.–4:30 P.M. Mon.–Thurs., 1–4:30 P.M. Fri., 8:30 A.M.–noon Sat.) keeps a tiny collection of books and magazines.

The **Anegada Police Station** (The Settlement, 284/495-8057) can be contacted 24 hours a day. For emergencies, dial 911 or 999. For emergencies at sea, contact Virgin Islands Search and Rescue by dialing 767 from any land line or cellular phone in the BVI.

There are no banks or ATMs on Anegada. Some businesses do not take credit cards, so plan ahead.

Communications on Anegada are still quite basic. After all, it wasn't long ago that most people communicated by radio only; in fact, calling a restaurant or business on Channel 16 is still a good way to get in touch with them. Most hotels do not provide phones for guests; you will have to ask to use a phone at the office or use the pay phone located at Setting Point near the Anegada Reef Hotel. The

home in The Settlement

Purple Turtle (Setting Point, 284/495-8062, fax 284/495-2231, 8:30 A.M.–6 P.M. daily) has internet, phone, and fax service. You can go online for 15 minutes for $5. Staff here can also help you plan outings and fishing trips or make dinner reservations.

Public notices and event announcements are posted on telephone poles around The Settlement and Setting Point, and at the airport. No one sells newspapers on Anegada; the best way to stay in touch with the outside world is to tune in on a radio. ZBVI, station 780 AM, airs news daily at 7 A.M., noon, and 5:45 P.M.

Supplies

Needless to say, Anegada is not a place for serious shopping. Getting what you need is the focus here.

Groceries and a hodgepodge of other sundries can be obtained at the **Faulkner's Country Store** (The Settlement, 7 A.M.–noon and 3–7 P.M. Mon.–Sat., 8 A.M.–noon Sun.) The newer **Cash and Carry** (Setting Point, 284/495-9932, 9:15 A.M.–6 P.M. Mon.–Sat., 1–5 P.M. Sun.), across the street from the Anegada Reef, sells

bulk groceries and some local produce. Most Fridays there is an outdoor barbecue.

For household goods, video rentals, and various hardware, try **Pal's General Store** (The Settlement, 284/495-9745, 8 A.M.–sunset Mon.–Sat.), a bright pink one-room shop across from Faulkner's Country Store in The Settlement.

The best recreational shopping is found at **The Purple Turtle** (Setting Point, 284/495-8062, 8:30 A.M.–6 P.M. daily), which is stocked with beachwear, gifts, children's books and toys, and even some gourmet food.

GETTING THERE AND AROUND

Anegada is a 10-minute flight from Tortola, and between 40 minutes and an hour by ferry, depending on sea conditions.

Several air carriers provide scheduled and charter flights to the island on small, three- to nine-seater aircraft. The views alone are worth the trip. **Clair Aero Services** (Beef Island, 284/495-2271) flies between Tortola and Anegada on Mondays, Wednesdays, Fridays, and

Sundays and will also pick up passengers from St. Thomas or Virgin Gorda if you book ahead. It accepts reservations by phone, and it is a good idea to make one. Round-trip fares are $60 per person from Tortola ($66 if you pay by credit card) and considerably more from the other islands. **Fly BVI** (Beef Island, 284/495-1747, www.fly-bvi.com) offers an Anegada day trip that runs $125 per person from Tortola and $175 per person from Virgin Gorda; it includes airfare, taxis on Anegada, and a lobster lunch.

If you would rather arrive by sea, **Smith's Ferry Service** (Road Town, Tortola, 284/494-4454) makes two round-trips to Anegada every Monday, Wednesday and Friday. The ferry departs Road Town at 7 A.M. and 3:30 P.M., and returns from Anegada at 8:30 A.M. and 5 P.M. Fare is $50 round-trip. Call ahead to confirm availability. A number of day-sail operators on Virgin Gorda and Tortola will make a day trip to Anegada if you reserve ahead.

Taxis will be there to meet you if you arrive with a scheduled flight or ferry on Anegada. If you are traveling with a charter, ask your charter company to arrange for a taxi or recommend one to you. **Tony's Taxi** (284/495-8037) is a good bet.

A rental car will give you the freedom to explore all corners of the island at your own pace. Expect to pay about $55 a day for a four-door Suzuki from **D.W. Jeep Rentals** (Nutmeg Point, 284/495-9688). The **Anegada Reef Hotel** (Setting Point, 284/495-8002) rents four-seater Jeeps for $65 as well as a safari bus for $75. For information about bike rentals, see *Sports and Recreation* in this chapter.

There are no road signs or street lights, so expect to get a little turned around—especially at night—even if you have a map. Driving hazards are few, but be aware of the livestock that roam the island, sometimes stopping to rest in the middle of the road.

BACKGROUND

The Land

The Virgin Islands are small tufts of green set in the Caribbean Sea, 1075 miles from Miami and 40 miles from Puerto Rico. Steep and forested islands, their hillsides tumble elegantly to the shoreline. The coast, lined by powder-white sand and fringed by protective coral reefs, is pleasantly scalloped. Some bays are especially wide, flat, and sheltered.

Geography

The Virgin Islands are at the northernmost tip of the Lesser Antilles, the string of islands that form an arc stretching from Puerto Rico in the north to Trinidad in the south.

The islands are at 18 25 north and 64 40 west, roughly the same latitude as Mumbai, Honolulu, and Mexico City. They lie at the confluence of the Atlantic Ocean and the Caribbean Sea. The Atlantic Ocean lies to the north and east of the islands, while the Caribbean is to the south and west.

The Virgin Islands comprise more than 90 individual islands, many of them nothing more than uninhabited rocks surrounded by sea. They have a combined coastline of 167 miles and a combined landmass of 193 square miles, about twice the size of the Vatican City.

With the exception of Anegada, which is

© SUSANNA HENIGHAN

BY THE NUMBERS

U.S. VIRGIN ISLANDS

Size: 144 square miles

Population: 108,700

Annual Overnight Tourists: 540,000

Annual Cruise Ship Tourists: 1.8 million

Life Expectancy: 78.9 years

GDP: $2.5 billion

Annual Budget: $560 million

St. Thomas
Size: 32 square miles
Population: 52,200

St. Croix
Size: 84 square miles
Population: 54,300

St. John
Size: 28 square miles
Population: 4,300

BRITISH VIRGIN ISLANDS

Size: 59 square miles

Population: 22,700

Annual Overnight Tourists: 291,231

Annual Cruise Ship Tourists: 300,415

Life Expectancy: 76.27 years

GDP: $2.5 billion

Annual Budget: $121 million

Tortola
Size: 21 square miles
Population: 18,200

Virgin Gorda
Size: 8 square miles
Population: 3,800

Jost Van Dyke
Size: 3 square miles
Population: 150

Anegada
Size: 15 square miles
Population: 150

a coral island, the Virgins are volcanic. They emerged from the Caribbean Sea some 65 million years ago as a result of alternating periods of undersea mountain-building, followed by periods of uplift and periods of explosive volcanism. The highest point in the islands is Sage Mountain (1,709 feet above sea level) on Tortola.

Up until the Pleistocene era, about 100,000 years ago, the British Virgin Islands, St. Thomas, and St. John, plus their related satellite cays were joined with Puerto Rico to form a single landmass. When the sea level rose, all but the uppermost mountains and highest valleys were submerged by water, and the islands we know today were formed.

St. Croix, divided from St. Thomas by a two-mile-deep trench, was always separate from the rest of the Virgin Islands, however. As a result, unique plant and animal species can be found there.

While the Virgin Islands form a single geographical unit, they are divided into two distinct territories with separate histories, economies, and administrations. The U.S. Virgin Islands, the more westward of the Virgins, comprise St. Thomas, St. Croix, and St. John. The British Virgin Islands comprise Tortola, Virgin Gorda, Jost Van Dyke, Anegada, and dozens of smaller islands and cays. The primary cities are Charlotte Amalie on St. Thomas, Christiansted on St. Croix, and Road Town on Tortola.

The boundary between the U.S. and British islands winds between St. John and Tortola and between Hans Lollick (U.S) and the Tobagos (U.K.). The territories are separated by as little as one mile of water in places.

Earthquakes

The Virgin Islands lie within an active earthquake zone registering some 900 measurable quakes each year. Most are minor—so weak you don't feel them—but occasionally there are more significant events, usually marked by a loud rumbling noise and shaking.

The possibility exists for the islands to experience a major earthquake. The most significant earthquake in modern history took place in 1867, causing tsunamis that inundated the cities of Charlotte Amalie, Frederiksted, Christiansted, and Road Town. Massive seagoing ships at anchor were deposited well inland.

The islands' seismicity comes from the fact that they lie just south of the boundary of the North American and Caribbean plates, where there is gradual subduction and displacement. The Puerto Rico Seismic Network at the University of Puerto Rico (http://red-sismica.uprm.edu/english) and the Seismic Research Unit at the University of the West Indies (www.uwiseismic.com) monitor the islands' seismic activity.

CLIMATE

The climate of the Virgin Islands is sub-tropical and humid, moderated by easterly trade winds. Seasonal changes in weather are subtle. The hottest month of the year is July, when high temperatures can reach 90 °F. During the coolest winter months, December and January, high temperatures reach the low 80s. Humidity generally ranges from 70 to 80 percent, peaking in July.

Historically, the Virgin Islands receive about 40 inches of rain per year. The wettest months are September, October, and November, when it seems to rain just about every day. January, February, and March are the driest months. Rain arrives quickly, falls heavily, and moves off just as suddenly as it came. If you visit during a rainy month, you will quickly realize that the best prescription against getting wet is to just seek shelter and wait out the rain.

The windiest months are December and January, when the so-called Christmas Winds pass through. These delightful air currents of 25–30 knots bring cool air from northern climes, making these months ideal for sailing and generally cooler. From November to June you can count on northeast winds of 15–20 knots consistently. In May, June, and July the summer doldrums hit and winds taper off; southeast winds of 10–15 knots are common. These are the worst months for sailing, and some of the

hottest. In September and October the weather tends to be unsettled.

Days are longer in the summer, with sunrise coming close to 5 A.M. and sunset around 7 P.M. At the peak of winter, sunrise is much closer to 6 A.M. and the sun sets at 6 P.M. Tides are minimal this close to the equator; with a range of about 12 inches, you probably won't even notice tidal fluctuations.

Hurricanes

The Atlantic Hurricane Season begins on June 1 and ends November 30, peaking in September. An old rhyme puts it fairly accurately: "June, too soon. July, stand by. August, it must. September, remember. October, all over."

The word hurricane comes from the Taino Indian word *Jurakan,* their god of malevolence and destruction. For these ancient seafarers, the destructive capacity of a hurricane was compounded by the fact that they arrived virtually unannounced.

In more modern times, the only warning one had of a storm was a sudden drop in barometric pressure just before the storm would strike. Older residents of Road Town, in the British Virgin Islands, can still remember the days when a government agent would monitor the barometer and ride through town on horseback warning people when the pressure took a sudden downward turn.

Today, the National Hurricane Center in Florida tracks and predicts hurricanes, and islanders have several days' notice before a storm strikes. Keeping an ear out for the tropical weather forecast is a daily feature of life in many households.

Evacuation is not generally practiced—except for tourists. Most people ride out the storm by boarding up windows and hunkering down with canned food, lots of extra water, flashlights, and battery-operated radios. Some homes also have standby generators. Builders use the latest hurricane-resistant building technology: impact glass for windows and hurricane clips for roofs, for example. Mariners moor their boats at established hurricane holes, coves where wind and wave action are

WEATHER

	January	February	March	April	May	June	July
Rainfall	1.86	1.53	1.58	2.68	3.36	2.42	2.45
High Temp	85.4	85.4	86	86	87.7	89.4	90.1
Low Temp	72.1	71.9	72.5	74	76	77.5	77.9

blocked. On top of that, local disaster management offices are well equipped and experienced in mitigation and response.

The Virgin Islands have experienced several devastating hurricanes. Storms in 1867, 1916, and 1924 wiped out whole towns. In 1989, Hurricane Hugo razed the Virgin Islands, St. Croix in particular. Hurricane Marilyn in 1995 dealt an especially devastating blow to St. Thomas. In 1999, Hurricane Lenny doused the entire region with heavy rains.

In addition to damage to buildings, roads, and boats, hurricanes can exact a cost to the natural environment. Waves from a hurricane can damage coral reefs, and the terrestrial destruction affects habitat for a number of creatures. Some species, including many predators, benefit from the disturbance of a hurricane, however.

Travelers who book trips to the Virgin Islands during hurricane season, and especially during the peak month of September, would be wise to also buy trip insurance in case your plans are disrupted by a storm.

CORAL REEFS

There are some 386 square miles of coral reef in the Virgin Islands, more than twice the total landmass of the territories. The Horseshoe Reef around Anegada, in the British Virgin Islands, is one of the largest barrier reefs in the world. Buck Island, near St. Croix, is surrounded by 31 square miles of barrier reef.

The most common type of reef in the Virgin Islands is the fringing reef, which runs parallel to the shore, providing protection for coastal areas. In other places, coral has begun to grow on underwater rocks and other hard surfaces.

Ecology

Home to some two million plant and animal species, coral reefs are the most biologically diverse ecosystem in the ocean and the second most diverse in the world—only the tropical rainforest supports more plant and animal species.

There are almost a thousand different coral species, each with its own growth and reproduction pattern. Each also has its own unique style: some resemble wrinkled brains and mushrooms, while others look like pillars, tabletops, moose antlers, wire strands, and cabbages.

Coral reefs provide a habitat for a wide range of sea creatures, including mollusks and urchins. Sea fans, anemones, and sponges fasten onto the coral. Small creatures find nourishment and protections amid the coral, and in turn attract large sea species like sea turtles, rays, and sharks.

The building block of the coral reef is the coral polyp, a tiny, soft creature that attaches itself to hard surfaces in shallow sea areas. Polyps can range from the size of a pinhead to that of a football. The polyps have slit-like "mouths" at the top surrounded by tentacles, which they use to sting and trap food—mainly plankton. Cells on the bottom of the polyps produce calcium carbonate, which builds islands and reefs. When a polyp dies, it hardens into "rock," creating the reefs that we know.

August	September	October	November	December	Annual
3.37	5.29	5.35	5.7	2.95	38.54
90.5	89.9	89.2	87.4	85	87.8
77.8	77.3	76.4	75	73.1	75.1

Coral reefs grow slowly. While some reefs can grow as much as two feet per year, most grow only a few inches. The coral reefs that exist in the Virgin Islands have been growing for millions of years.

Small algae called *zooxanthellae* live symbiotically within coral polyps. The algae get shelter and food from the polyp, while the polyp gets food from the algae via photosynthesis. Photosynthesis requires sunlight, so coral reefs can only grow where the ocean is shallow and clear. Coral also requires ocean currents, which bring it plankton, the tiny organisms that sustain it, and warm ocean temperatures—between 75 and 85 degrees.

The polyps and algae are a food source for other sea creatures, and the reef's caves and crevices are ideal locations for breeding and protection from large predators. More than one-quarter of all marinelife is found in coral reefs.

Life on the Reef

Coral reefs are cities under the sea. Even when the surface of the sea is glassy and there is not a sound except the wind, the underwater reef is teeming with life. It is a joy to float above and observe.

There are two main types of coral: hard coral and soft coral. Hard coral, the bricks and mortar of the coral reef, takes on a fantastic array of shapes and colors. **Elkhorn coral** looks like clusters of antlers reaching out sideways toward the surface of the ocean. **Brain coral** are spheres imprinted with a pattern that makes them look remarkably like brains. **Pillar coral** grow like candelabras reaching to the sea surface, and **staghorn coral** look like great colonies of orange starfish. Pay particular attention to **fire coral,** yellow stony coral that looks something like giant lichen. A brush against one of these can leave you with painful cuts.

Like hard coral, soft coral is made up of colonies of coral polyps. But unlike hard coral, soft coral have skeletons consisting of needles encased in softer, more flexible material. **Sea fans** are a common kind of soft coral. Others resemble whips and plumes.

A host of other sea creatures live among the coral. **Sea anemones** are soft, translucent tentacled creatures often seen anchored in cracks between the reef. The sharp, black barbs of **sea urchins** can easily be seen poking out from under and between rocks. There are many types of **sea sponges,** soft, multicelled animals that act as filters for the ocean. Crustaceans including **lobsters** and **crabs** are also found on the reef, often beneath a dark ledge. It takes a practiced eye to find these reclusive animals.

Fish, of course, are the star of the show on the coral reef. They dart around, nibbling, weaving in and out of the current, showing colors ranging from deep purple to bright yellow and every hue in between. One of the most common reef fish is the **parrot fish,** which come in colors ranging from red to rainbow to black. Look closely and you will see its distinctive fused teeth, which it uses to scrape chunks of coral into its mouth. Using a mill at the back

SNORKEL TIPS

A troublesome snorkel mask can make snorkeling frustrating and dangerous. When masks are not worn properly, water seeps in around the edges, ruining visibility and stinging eyes. These tips will help you snorkel with confidence:

1. Test your mask to see if it fits properly. Do this by placing it on your face without the band and taking a deep breath in. If the mask fits properly, it will stay on your face. If your mask does not stay put, try another size or check for things that could be breaking the seal: beards or moustaches, hair, eyeglasses, or sunscreen.

2. Fogging is also a problem. You can prevent fogging by rubbing the inside of your mask with spit or a dish-soap wash. Commercial defogging solutions are also available.

3. Make sure that your mask strap is not too tight, and that it is positioned just below the widest part of your head. Your mask should be secure, but comfortable.

4. Fins help in snorkeling because they reduce the amount of energy you have to use to get around. Your kick should be smooth. Be careful not to accidentally kick or brush up against coral.

5. If you tend to get chilled easily, it is a good idea to wear a wetsuit or surf shirt.

6. A floatation belt or jacket helps snorkelers who do not naturally float or who want extra security.

7. Underwater visibility is best on sunny days, when the sea is calm.

© SUSANNA HENIGHAN

Starfish are one of thousands of creatures that live in waters around the Virgin Islands.

© SUSANNA HENIGHAN

sand dollars

of its throat, parrot fish grind the coral into a powder, which is excreted as sand.

The yellowtail **damselfish** begins life a vivid shade of dark blue with bright blue spots before turning to a nondescript brown as an adult. Look for the feelers on the lower lip of the **goatfish.** One of the most common types of reef fish is the **wrasse,** a small fish often with bright stripes of color near its head. **Triggerfish,** one of many types of fish that can change colors based on its surroundings, are distinguished by their tails, which extend to two long points.

Some fish have very distinctive shapes. **Trunkfish** are easy to spot because of their triangular build. Long and thin, the **trumpetfish** eats by sucking unsuspecting fish into its vacuum-like mouth. You will often encounter them standing on their head to mimic some part of the underwater landscape. Colorful **angelfish** are flat and can grow to be the size of a dinner plate. They swim elegantly around the reef and will surely catch your eye. **Butterfly fish** resemble angelfish but are distinguishable by a large black dot near their tails, meant to confuse predators.

Look out for **squids,** easily recognized by their large, white eyes that look almost human. Most reef squid are small—about a foot long—and can be seen swimming around just like a fish. **Octopus,** on the other hand, often hides.

One of the greatest joys of snorkeling on the reef is seeing a school of fish. Near shore, you may find yourself engulfed in a mass of tiny fry. Pop your head above water and you will no doubt see pelicans diving for dinner. On the reef, schooling species include goatfish, grunts (named for a noise they make), and spadefish. You may also encounter schools of jacks and silversides.

You will also see larger sea creatures on the coral reef, attracted by the presence of so much potential food. **Hawksbill turtles,** one of the three kinds of sea turtle in the Virgin Islands, look for food and shelter around the reef. **Green turtles** prefer sea grass beds, and **leatherbacks** are most often seen in the open ocean.

FLORA

From gardens to wild forests, the Virgin Islands are host to a rich diversity of plantlife, many of it remarkable for its adaptation to the dry, inhospitable climate of the islands.

At the Seaside

The tree most associated with the beach is the **coconut,** a member of the palm family. Coconut trees are hearty and useful. Their fronds, or leaves, can be used to make thatch roofs and mats. The coconut seed, when green, contains coconut milk, a sweet and somewhat viscous drink. When dried, the nut contains coconut meat, which can be used in cooking, baking, or even industry. Coconut trunks can be used for lumber, and the oil is used in cooking and beauty preparations.

Surprisingly, coconuts are not native to the Caribbean. They originated in the western Pacific and eastern Indian Ocean and were brought to the region by early Portuguese voyagers. Coconut trees are adaptable and can withstand significant periods of drought.

Another common seaside plant is the **sea grape,** or *coccoloba uvifera,* a member of the buckwheat family. These adaptable trees grow along both protected and windswept shores. Many bathers find shade and shelter tucked beneath sea grape branches at the beach. The sea grape has round leaves, reaching up to about six inches wide. They produce strings of edible grapelike fruits in cluster, turning from green to purple in fall. The fruits have large pits, and range from sour to sweet. They are quite tasty.

Don't try to eat the fruit of the **manchineel,** or *hippomane mancinella,* tree, a tree so toxic that its sap can take the paint off a car. The fruit of these trees can kill, and even brushing against one can lead to uncomfortable rashes. Manchineels have shiny, dark, elliptical leaves that droop on long, yellowish stalks. Look closely at the junction of the leaf and leaf stalk and you will see a tiny raised dot about the size of a pinhead. Manchineels are the only beach trees with this feature.

Manchineels produce shiny, green fruits that look like apples. Don't eat them! Also avoid touching the leaves, scratching yourself on the bark, or using the wood for a fire. It is even a bad idea to take shelter under a manchineel during rain, since the rainwater can wash tiny bits of the sap onto your skin.

Around the House

Virgin Islanders love to plant colorful gardens around their homes. With the palette of colors and plant types available to these tropical gardeners, it is easy to see why.

One of the favorite decorative trees is the **flamboyant,** or flame tree, which produces a bright red crown of blossoms every June. When it is not in bloom, the flamboyant's wide canopy makes it a great shade tree. Another favorite for color is the **bougainvillea,** a hearty bush that can grow to great heights if allowed. Bougainvillea comes in a dazzling array of colors including red, pink, orange, and white. The "blooms" are actually modified leaves, called bracts, which they produce to attract pollinators to their small, white flowers.

Hibiscus are also bound to catch your eye. These bushes produce brightly colored flowers that can grow as large as seven inches across. Practiced gardeners compete annually at flower shows for the best hibiscus bloom. Locals also use the petals to make a sweet, red drink aptly called "hibiscus."

Often used as a natural fence, **oleander** is a plant worth identifying, if only because of its capacity to poison. Oleander puts out five-petaled blossoms of pink, purple, and white. Do not ingest any part of the plant—it is deadly.

One of the most beautiful decorative shrubs in the islands is the **poinsettia.** Once you see one of these growing over your head with dense red bracts brilliant in the sun, you will never think the same about the pitiful potted ones you see every Christmas. **Yellow allamanda** is another favorite among Caribbean gardeners, for its bright yellow flowers and neat, shiny leaves.

In the Forest

Wet tropical forests can be found at Sage Mountain on Tortola and in Caldonia, the hilly, damp

Sea grapes are a tasty seaside snack in the late summer and early fall.

forest on St. Croix's northwestern tip. Plant species here thrive in low light and moisture. Instead of building defenses against grazing cattle and drought, plants here have developed bitter-tasting and toxic leaves to defend against insects that thrive in the damp forest.

Bromeliads are members of the epiphyte family that nest among the branches of larger trees, gathering nutrients from the air and storing rainwater in its leaves. Bromeliads look like the leafy top of a pineapple; some produce beautiful flowers.

One especially beautiful forest plant is the **tree fern,** or *cyathea arborea.* A straight, single stem rises leafless, topped off by delicate fern leaves. These trees look like normal ferns at first; they reach their full diameter on the ground before starting to grow upward.

Dry tropical forests are common; in fact, most of the wooded areas you see around you would fall into this category. In these ecosystems, trees and plants are adapted for long periods of drought.

One of the telltale signs that you are in a dry forest is the presence of the **turpentine tree,** or

bursera simaruba. This beautiful tree has dozens of familiar nicknames: gumbo limbo, West Indian birch, gommier, and tourist tree are a few. It is easily identified by its peeling, red bark and its graceful limbs.

There is an abundance of cactus types in the Virgin Islands. **Turk's cap cactus** are almost perfectly round balls that sit right on the ground, with a reddish "cap" atop. The fuchsia fruits are edible, and a particular favorite of birds. These cactus are said to tilt toward the equator, which earned them the nickname compass plant.

Prickly pear cactus are characterized by flattened oval pads that pile on top of and around one another to form a single plant. The deep, dark red fruits are edible, but be sure to peel them first to get rid of the prickles.

Some of the largest and most majestic trees you will see in the Virgin Islands are **Kapok** trees, also called **silk cotton trees** *(ceiba pentranda).* These trees can grow to magnificent heights—up to 75 feet—with trunks as wide as a car. Kapok trees produce large pods full of short, lustrous fibers. This fiber has been used to stuff pillows, lifejackets, and furniture.

One of the most beautiful tropical flowering trees is the **frangipani,** often seen in gardens as well as in the wild. At first glance you may wonder if the tree is even alive—there are very few leaves. Look again, though, and you will see the lovely white flowers and long, dimpled leaves. In the spring, at the beginning of the dry season, colorful frangipani caterpillars come to munch on the leaves.

Other important features of the dry forest are the **aloe** and **century plants.** Aloe grows wild throughout the dry forest and is a useful plant, since the gooey substance that oozes out when you crack a leaf can be useful in treating burns and cuts. Century plants are the flowering stalk of the agave, which bloom in the spring. Look out over the landscape of the dry forest at that time, and you will delight in counting the number of bright yellow chimneys you see. In recent years, a blight brought by imported century plants affected century plants on Tortola, St. Thomas, and other islands.

On the Farm

Fruit trees are hardly limited to the farm; many households plant them around the house for their obvious utilitarian purpose. **Sugarcane** makes a good natural fence, since it grows tall and straight. A member of the grass family, sugarcane takes about a year to mature. Most gardens around the Virgin Islands have a small patch, not for sugar production, but for chewing and eating on its own. Another fixture in many backyard gardens are **banana** and **plantain** "trees". These fast-growing plants are distinguishable by their long, slatted leaves. After the plant has produced, it is cut down, and a new one will sprout in its place. The whole process takes about nine months.

There are an abundance of magnificent fruit trees in the Virgin Islands. **Avocado pear** trees are handsome, especially when they droop with the weight of ripe avocados every summer. These tropical avocados are large and bright green but just as tasty as the small, black fruits familiar in the supermarkets of North America. Another fruit tree sure to catch your eye is the **breadfruit,** which grows to towering heights and has large, lobed, handsome leaves. The fruit grows to be as large as a basketball and ripens during the summer. It is basically tasteless but can be seasoned and roasted, boiled, or fried. The fruit is not highly prized, however, and often goes uneaten.

Other common fruit trees are the guava, mango, and papaya. **Guava** trees are bushy and produce small, lemon-sized fruits used to make guava candy and preserves. The **mango** is probably the most popular tropical fruit; its sweet, juicy flesh is the perfect finish to any meal. The trees themselves are handsome, with long, droopy leaves that produce dense shade. Few household yards are without a mango tree of their own. **Papayas,** the other favorite tropical fruit, ripen just below the leaves on the fast-growing papaya tree. Pick these out by their tall, slender stalk and round, intricately lobed leaves.

FAUNA
Mammals

The only indigenous mammal in the Virgin Islands is the bat. All others were introduced by people who migrated through and eventually settled in the islands. Amerindians introduced dogs, pigs, guinea pigs, and agoutis (although the latter two have not survived in the wild). European settlers introduced a wide range of domesticated animals, including goats, sheep, and horses.

Europeans are also responsible for two of the islands' worst pests, the rat, which arrived as a stowaway on ships, and the mongoose, introduced to kill rats that had taken up residence in sugarcane fields. The mongoose was a disappointment to rat control; it was active during the day while rats slept and could not climb trees in pursuit of the more agile rodents. Instead mongooses fed on lizards, birds, turtle eggs, and chickens. They have been responsible for wiping out whole species of lizards on some islands. Today, mongooses remain a problem for conservationists and farmers.

Birds

Birds are some of the most delightful animals of the Virgin Islands, and birders will be rewarded by colors, acrobatics, and songs of the island birds.

Near the sea, there is usually no better show than the one put on by **pelicans,** who glide (look: no wing flapping) far above the ocean surface only to crash down with incredible force, gathering tiny fish and other sea creatures in its pouch. Pelicans have special air chambers on their chest and special film over their eyes to cushion the sea landing.

One of the most easily identifiable shore birds is the **magnificent frigate bird,** sometimes called a man-o-war. This long-winged, black bird with a forked tail and bent wings looks like a leftover from the dinosaur era. Male frigate birds have a strip of bright red skin on their throat, which they blow up like a balloon to attract females during mating season. Frigate birds catch fish at the surface of the sea, but their biggest food source is in the air; they chase other seabirds fiercely until they drop their catch. Then the frigate bird glides down to catch it.

Look out as well for **brown boobies, laughing gulls, royal terns,** and **tropic birds.** Boobies, now endangered, got their name from the Spanish word "bobo," meaning dunce. They are large and excellent divers. Caribbean gulls are smaller than the seagulls many are used to; listen to their song—"ha, ha, ha, ha." Tropic birds are elegant and beautiful. Look for the long streamers that extend from their tails.

Inland, birds are smaller and much more difficult to watch. Flower gardens tend to attract **doctor birds** and **green-throated caribs.** One of the favorite birds of the islands is the **bananaquit,** a ubiquitous and cheerful creatures you will see in flower gardens and the forest. They have a wheezy, squeaky call and build untidy nests of grass and leaves. They often have bright yellow bellies, set off by black round the head.

Many open-air restaurants suffer an abundance of **Carib gackles,** medium-sized birds that make sport of eating crumbs, leftovers, and even whole meals from diners' plates. There are two kinds of dove on the islands: **common ground dove** and **Zenaida dove,** also called turtle dove.

The Charlotte Amalie High School chose the **chickenhawk** as its football mascot in the late 1990s when football made its debut in the U.S. Virgin Islands. These common hawks can be seen soaring high above farms, fields, and woodland. They keep an eye out for favorite food sources: snakes, lizards, frogs, and rats.

Another bird that is easy to see is the **cattle egret,** a long-legged, white heron that follows cattle, sometimes on their backs. These birds are natives of Africa and were first reported in the Caribbean in 1933.

Reptiles and Amphibians

Many travelers are taken aback by the pulsing, almost deafening, song of the bo-peeps, or **coquis** at night. The call of these small frogs is often at first mistaken for the sound of crickets or cicadas. In the rainforest, they sing all day; in drier habitats, they sing only at night. Listen closely, and you will hear that they are saying their name: "ko-kee, ko-kee."

Less melodious is the song of the **giant toad,** brown, blotchy creatures that can grow as large as a softball. They hide out during the day, but often sing the praises of the rain at night.

One of the most delightful animals in the Virgin Islands is the lizard. Newcomers never fail to delight in their omnipresence, agile movement, and—in some cases—impressive shows. The most common kind of lizard is the **ground lizard,** a small, brown lizard that munches on insects. **Tree lizards** change colors to suit their surroundings, and males have rounded sacs under their throats. When they want to be threatening, the males will inflate their pouch and do "push-ups" in place. The third common type of lizard is the **house gecko,** or wood slave. These helpful creatures are used to people and are often found inside. House geckos have Velcro-like feet that allow them to climb on just about any surface. They feed on insects (great for killing mosquitoes that make it inside) and are active at night.

Crabs

It is easier to see the zigzagging tracks of the **ghost crab** than to spot the animal itself, which can scurry sideways so quickly it seems to disappear. Ghost crabs live on the beach, burrowing into the sand for protection and safety. Farther inland, it is the **land crab,** or white crab, that dominates. These large, whitish crabs have one claw larger than the other, and are sometimes eaten. Another very common crab is the **hermit crab.** Although associated with the sea, these crabs are found miles away from the shore, and high up on mountainsides. Many take up residence in the West Indian top snail shells. When hermit crabs outgrow their shell, they have to find a new one. Hermit crabs will eat about anything, including rat poison, carrion, and feces. Their flesh is a traditional fish bait.

ENVIRONMENTAL ISSUES
Coral Reefs

Coral reefs around the world are dying, and those in the Virgin Islands are no exception. The impact of coral disease, pollution, and careless humans take a high toll on these delicate ecosystems. Scientists don't know exactly how much of the reefs around the Virgin Islands have been lost, but they know that some have. Old-timers, and even not-so-old-timers, say that reefs are smaller and less healthy and support fewer types of fish than they once did. You have to go far from shore to see a truly unspoiled, undisturbed reef.

There are several causes for this decline. Discharge of raw sewage into the sea causes algae growth, which smothers the coral reef. Other types of marine pollution, such as oil spills or industrial wastewater discharge (such as at the rum factory on St. Croix) have a more direct, deadly impact on reefs. White band disease affected elkhorn coral in 1976, 1989, and again between 1997 and 2001. More recently, sea fans have been affected by fungal growth believed to be linked to Sahara dust.

Pollution, disease, and environmental stress are killing coral all around the Virgin Islands.

One of the most serious threats to coral reefs is sedimentation, caused when dirt and dust is eroded into the sea and settles on the reef, smothering and killing the coral. The greatest source of erosion is coastal development, although on steep islands like Tortola, St. Thomas, and St. John, hillside development can be just as damaging. Another cause of coral decline is careless boaters, who drop anchor or, even worse, drag an anchor, over coral reef. Snorkelers and divers can also hurt the reef when they touch it. Be aware of your fins when you snorkel or dive, and don't accidentally brush them against the reef.

Some steps have been taken to address these threats, although more needs to be done if the islands are going to avoid even more destruction of their greatest resource. In the U.S. Virgin Islands, fairly stringent local and federal environmental regulations are applied to control pollution and check coastal development. However, there continue to be problems with marine pollution and development that occurs despite loud and reasoned environmental-based argu-

Mangroves are a critical part of the island ecosystem, but many acres of mangroves have been destroyed for coastal development throughout the Virgin Islands.

ment. In both territories, moorings have been placed in some popular anchorages to prevent anchor damage. Little can be done about coral disease, except to provide support and training to the scientists who are studying it.

Other problems still exist, as well. The British Virgin Islands still don't have a public sewage treatment system, and raw sewage is pumped directly into the ocean. Likewise, in the sailing capital of the world, there is no rule requiring holding tanks, so yachts are free to discharge sewage directly into the sea. In the U.S. Virgin Islands, persistent problems with its aging sewage system cause similar problems. In both territories, no one seems able, or willing, to put a check on coastal or hillside development.

Fishing

Virgin Islanders have fished for centuries to feed their families and bring in income. Many fishermen use seine or gill nets to capture schooling mackerel, yellowtail snapper, and jacks. Others use fish traps, locally known as fish pots. These traps are made of wire

mesh built on a wooden or metal rectangular frame. Depending on local conditions, they are set singly or strung together. Some fishermen use buoys to identify where they left their pot—others rely on memory or GPS coordinates. Fish caught in these traps are sometimes called pot-fish. You will also see children and adults standing near the water's edge with a line—they are hoping to bring home supper.

Used in moderation by fishermen who appreciate the need for balance in nature, none of these fishing methods is necessarily destructive. But there is increasing evidence that the Virgin Islands fishery is declining. A 1991 study on the fishery in the U.S. Virgin Islands found that the average size of many popular species, including parrot fish, grunt, and triggerfish, is declining while large grouper, the single most important commercial species, is all but gone. Another study of the fishery around St. Croix conducted from 1997 to 2001 showed a 10 percent decrease in the average fish weight over the period and a 40 percent decline in the number of fish per fish-pot

CLOSED SEASONS

British Virgin Islands

Conch	June 1–Sept. 30
Whelk	June 1–Sept. 30
Lobster	March 1–June 30
Margate	Jan. 1–March 31
Nassau Grouper	March 1–May 31
Red Hind	Jan. 1–March 31
Turtle	April 1–Nov. 30

U.S. Virgin Islands

Conch	July 1–Sept. 30
Whelk	April 1–Sept. 30
Jewfish (Goliath Grouper)	no harvest
Nassau Grouper	no harvest*
Turtle	no harvest

*in federal waters

haul. There is no data on the British Virgin Islands fishery, although anecdotal evidence suggests that fish numbers and sizes are decreasing there as well.

The fishery is declining due to several factors, but it boils down to this: too many fish are being taken from the sea. Conservationists say that fish pots are one source of the problem because if they are lost—if they come loose from the rope or the fisherman can't find them—then they become floating death traps. Fish swim in but can't swim out. The fish that enter the trap eventually die, attracting more fish. Others say that more and more fishermen are not following traditional fishing rules: they take fish that are too small or while they are spawning. Scarcity of fish has also pushed some fishermen to use scuba gear and fish guns—a practice that also upsets the balance between man and nature.

Quite a bit is being done about the loss of fish stock, but its success depends on better enforcement and on viewing fishermen as partners, not adversaries. Both the U.S. and British Virgin Islands have closed seasons for many of the most popular, and most vulnerable, species of fish, as well as other creatures like lobster and conch. There are also size limits. Both territories also have no-take areas. In the U.S. Virgin Islands there has been a push for fishermen to use biodegradable fish pots, which break down if they are lost in the ocean.

Consumers should not be afraid to buy fish due to overfishing concerns. Instead, familiarize yourself with closed season rules. If someone tries to sell or serve you something that should be off-limits, it has either been frozen or caught illegally. Ask.

Garbage Disposal

Garbage disposal is a major logistical challenge for islands where land is at a premium and shipping is expensive. Neither the U.S. nor the British Virgin Islands have mastered the challenge—at least not yet.

There is virtually no recycling in either territory, apparently because the cost of shipping recyclables off-island cannot be recouped through recycling revenue. An on-again, off-again can recycling program on St. Thomas is a private initiative, as is a battery recycling program in the British Virgin Islands.

Instead of recycling, the U.S. Virgin Islands have landfills on St. Thomas, St. Croix, and St. John. These are poorly managed and cannot handle the growing amount of waste being produced. Landfill fires—sparked by spontaneous combustion from the heat generated by the garbage—pose health and environmental risks. On St. Croix, smoke from the landfill fire impedes operation of the neighboring international airport.

In the British Virgin Islands, authorities burn trash on the smaller islands of Jost Van Dyke, Anegada, and Virgin Gorda. The incinerator on Tortola is terribly swamped with more garbage than it can handle, and huge piles of garbage are building up outside the incinerator. These too have caught fire. There are plans for a new, larger incinerator to come on stream in 2006, however.

Reduction of waste has posed challenging for both territories, since so many goods arrive on container ships, wrapped in cardboard or plastic, on wooden pallets. Packaging is a big part of life. Sadly, there has been little to no political leadership on this issue, which could probably be solved, or at least addressed in a more successful way, with a little imagination and cross-border cooperation.

Freshwater

You will notice discreet signs in many bathrooms and kitchens asking you to preserve water. Water is a precious resource on these islands with no lakes or rivers and few springs. Most homes, and a good many businesses, have cisterns—large concrete storage tanks—below their floor slab, where rainwater collected on the roof is stored. In times of rain, cisterns can sometimes overflow. In times of drought, every last drop is rationed. Cistern water is generally used for showers, washing, cleaning and flushing. It should be boiled for drinking or cooking.

The other main source of freshwater is seawater desalination plants, which use reverse osmosis technology to make freshwater out of saltwater. In the British Virgin Islands, most of the public water supply comes from a series of desalination plants around the territory. Desalinated water is safe to drink and does not taste salty.

Despite the existence of technology to make freshwater from the ocean, water is still considered a precious resource, if for no other reason than if your cistern should run dry, it is expensive to buy. Guests should do their part to conserve water.

Sewage

It is a little bit too tempting to dump one's raw sewage straight into the ocean. After all, it is free and easy to do so, and the ocean is so big, what does it matter, right? When the Virgin Islands were more sparsely populated than they are today, when millions of people did not visit them annually, and when the islands were not already under environmental stress, that view may have been correct. But today, dumping raw sewage into the ocean is an environmental problem, causing beach closures and impacting the health of coral reefs and other underwater habitats.

The U.S. Virgin Islands' wastewater treatment system is old and overwhelmed. There are frequent malfunctions that cause wastewater to flow, untreated, into the ocean. In the British Virgin Islands, there is no wastewater treatment system at all, except in the community of Cane Garden Bay. Sewage from Road Town is collected and pumped untreated into the sea. In other areas, residents rely on septic tanks.

History

The Virgin Islands have been defined by their history. The islands possess a rich legacy of pre-Columbian settlement, and the physical, cultural, and economic footprint of the plantation era—its contradictions, cruelties, and extravagance—remains. In more modern times, waves of immigrants have enriched the island's culture, and economic and natural challenges have defined the Virgin Islander's resilient character.

EARLY PEOPLES

Four waves of pre-Columbian people settled in the Virgin Islands: the Ciboney, Igneri, Taino, and Kalinago peoples. Each group arrived in the Virgin Islands from South America, and each brought new advances in crop cultivation, social structure, and tools.

Ciboney

The first humans are thought to have been present in the Virgin Islands as early as 2,200 B.C. These earliest islanders, called Ciboney by the Spanish and Ortoiroid by today's archaeologists, were fisher-foragers who did not make pottery or cultivate plants. They lived nomadically and used crude stone tools to prepare food. Shellfish was probably an important part of their diet.

The Ciboney lived in crude shelters, fashioned out of palm fronds and other material at hand. Social organization was primitive; families who lived and traveled together constituted a single band, without organized leadership. Archaeological evidence of these Stone Age people has been discovered at Krum Bay, St. Thomas, and Brewer's Bay, Tortola.

Igneri

The next wave of Indians were the Igneri, or Saladoid, people, who migrated from South America around 400 B.C. and lived undisturbed in the Virgin Islands for almost 1,000 years. They cultivated crops including yucca and cassava. In addition to fish, the flesh of the *agouti,* a ratlike animal they raised, was their primary source of protein.

The Igneri knew how to make pottery and produced thin griddles on which they cooked cassava. They lived in communal round houses.

Taino

Much more is known about the third and most sophisticated group of Pre-Columbians to live in the Virgin Islands. These people, defined by a different style of pottery and more advanced cultivation and social systems, have become known as Taino (the Arawaks of popular legend). Tainos lived throughout the Virgin Islands; archaeologists have found evidence of Taino settlement at some 32 sites on Tortola alone. The Salt River Bay area of St. Croix is widely believed to be an important Taino settlement and has been studied extensively. Digs at Cinnamon Bay, St. John, and Hull Bay, St. Thomas, have unearthed evidence of Taino settlements at those locations.

Tainos traveled between islands in large canoes. Their *caciques* (chiefs) arbitrated disputes, oversaw cultivation and hunting, and made decisions about the future of the village. Cacique was a hereditary position.

Ornamentation was important to the Tainos for it was linked to their religious beliefs. In their worship they used zemis, idols made of wood, stone, bone, shell, and clay, through which they worshiped the gods and sought to exert control over them. The Taino goddess of wind and water, Juraken, is the namesake of today's hurricanes. Some zemis were believed to influence the weather, crops, hunting, wealth, and childbirth. Religious leaders called *behiques* communicated with the gods and healed the sick and injured.

Taino villages were typically a ring of circular huts. The cacique lived in large rectangular houses with his wives; commoners lived in round thatch-roof huts with dirt floors and one door. They slept in hammocks.

FEMALE CARIB.

a female Carib (Kalinago) Indian, as depicted in a 19th-century leaflet

Tainos enjoyed parties. They created castanets out of little plates of stone and used them to make music. Both men and women played a ball game using a rubber ball. Evidence of ball courts has been found at Belmont, Tortola, and Salt River Bay, St. Croix.

Kalinago

The final wave of pre-Columbian peoples arrived in the Virgin Islands shortly before Christopher Columbus' "discovery" of the islands. The Kalinago (popularly known as Caribs) were a martial society, which had made its way northward from South America, con-

quering the more peaceful Tainos along the way. Defeated Taino males were killed or taken as slaves, while Taino women were absorbed into the Kalinago society.

It was a Kalinago village that Columbus and his men set upon on November 1493 when they sailed into Salt River Bay, St. Croix, but archeologists do not know whether the Kalinago had reached St. Thomas, St. John, or the other islands at that time. No evidence has been unearthed that they had, and since Columbus and his fleet did not stop at any of the other Virgin Islands, no documentary evidence exists either.

The myth that the Kalinago were cannibals has never been substantiated, and, if they did eat human flesh, it is almost certain they did so for ceremonial purposes only. More likely, the myth came from the Kalinago's fierce nature and the fact that their way of honoring the dead was to hang their bones in pots from the rafters of their homes—a practice misinterpreted by the Spanish who came into contact with them. The Spanish, who originated the myth of the cannibalistic Carib, benefited from its spread because it justified their ruthless extermination of the islands' Indian populations.

Like the Taino, Kalinago marriages were polygamous, although not every man could afford to have more than one wife. For Tainos, it was the caciques who were most likely to have multiple wives; for the Kalinago it was the warriors. Believing that it made them more beautiful, the Kalinago flattened the front and back of their children's heads.

The Kalinago's social organization was looser than that of the Taino; Kalinago culture emphasized physical prowess and individualism. While settlements had a leader, his authority was limited. War-chiefs were chosen from among villagers based on their skill in battle. Kalinago lived separated by gender; the men lived together in large building called a carbet, while the women lived in smaller houses. Tobacco was the standard of exchange.

Kalinago military dominance was due to the culture's focus on training and their development of more deadly weapons than the

Taino. Young Kalinago men were trained as children to be warriors, and the values of courage and endurance were highly valued. The bow and arrow was the most common Kalinago weapon; poison from deadly plants was used on the tip of the arrow to increase the chance of death. The Kalinago depended on the element of surprise in achieving military victories.

Demise

Within 100 years of Spanish arrival in the Caribbean, there were no more Indians living in the Virgin Islands. Some were captured as slaves to work in Spanish gold mines, and others fled southward to islands farther away from the Spanish strongholds of Puerto Rico and Hispaniola. The Caribbean island of Dominica still has a "Carib" community—descendants of these Indians.

Other Indians stayed put and fought their new Spanish neighbors. St. Croix's Caribs, as the Spanish called them, violently opposed Spanish settlement of the region; the new Spanish settlement on Puerto Rico was the target of numerous Indian raids and attacks between 1510 and 1530. On one raid, the Indians killed the newly appointed governor of the colony. In response to the Indians' aggression, the Spanish crown formally gave its settlers in the region license to hunt and kill Indians in 1512, a move that marked the beginning of the end for the remaining Virgin Islands Indians. Although the Indians continued to raid and attack Puerto Rico between 1520 and 1530, they were ultimately no match for the Spanish. By 1590, and probably well before that on most of the islands, Indians had disappeared from the Virgin Islands.

Today, there are no native Indians in the Virgin Islands. Only a few of their words—such as hurricane, hammock, and barbecue—remain.

EXPLORATION

Christopher Columbus (or Cristóbal Colón, as the Spanish knew him) sailed through the Virgin Islands in November 1493 during his second voyage to the New World. The Admiral's first voyage in 1492 had taken him

CHRISTOPHER COLUMBUS
1492 - 1992

COURTESY OF LIBRARY OF CONGRESS

to the Bahamas, Cuba, and Hispaniola. On Christmas Eve, 1492, his flagship, the Santa Maria, grounded on a reef and sank off Hispaniola. Columbus and his men salvaged what they could from the ship to build a settlement for the 40 men he would have to leave behind at what he called La Navidad.

The aim of Columbus' second voyage was settlement. Seventeen ships and more than 1,000 men departed the Canary Islands on October 13, 1493. The fleet made good time across the Atlantic and spotted the island of Dominica on November 3, 1493. They sailed northward along the northern Leeward Islands until November 13, when they reached a large, fertile, and well-populated island that Columbus decided to name Sancta Cruz (The Holy Cross).

Columbus sent some of his men ashore at Salt River Bay for freshwater and, some reports claim, to capture Indians who could tell him where he was. When the advance party was returning to the fleet, it encountered an Indian canoe, in which there were four Carib men, two Carib women, and two Taino slaves. A fight between the two parties ensued; Columus' men overturned the canoe while the Caribs peppered the Europeans with poison arrows. Columbus' party was impressed by the Indians' prowess as warriors. Columbus' son, Don Fernando, wrote later about one Carib who kept shooting after the canoe was upset as if he had been on dry land."

Columbus named the area in front of Salt River Bay Cape of Arrows after the skirmish. In the end, one member of Columbus' party died, and one Carib was killed. The rest of the Indian party was taken as prisoners and eventually transported to Spain. It was, no doubt, a terrible fate for these captured Indians. A glimpse of their treatment is given by Columbus crewmember Michele de Cuneo, who recorded matter-of-factly the details of his sexual assault on "a very beautiful Carib woman whom the Lord Admiral gave to me."

After the skirmish at St. Croix, Columbus divided his fleet; the small caravels, including the one in which he rode, sailed northward through what is now Drake's Channel. As he sailed, Columbus was impressed by the number of small islands before him and named them as Virgines after the then-popular myth of St. Ursula and her 11,000 virgin martyrs killed by the Huns. St. Ursula remains on the official seal of the British Virgin Islands. The second half of Columbus' fleet remained south and sailed straight for the eastern end of Puerto Rico, where the two parties met up and continued on their way to Hispaniola.

Although Columbus did not stop to explore these islands, he did name many of them. During the passage he named Virgin Gorda (Fat Virgin) and gave Tortola the name Santa Ana, which did not stick.

Other early explorers passed through the islands but did not settle. Ponce de Leon led voyages in the area in the early 16th century; Sir Sebastian Cabot and Sir Thomas Pert passed through in 1517 after exploring Brazilian waters. Sir John Hawkins sailed through in 1563 with his first cargo of African slaves for Hispaniola. On a third voyage, Hawkins sailed with young Francis Drake. Later, after being knighted, Drake returned to the Virgin Islands in 1585, where he mustered his fleet in North Sound, Virgin Gorda, that same year for a disastrous attack on the Spanish settlement on Puerto Rico. The main passage through the island group now bears Drake's name. Eleven years later, the Earl of Cumberland used the same North Sound as a staging area for a more successful attack on Puerto Rico.

Piracy

The stories of pirates in the Virgin Islands are long on legend and short on fact, but that has not stopped many of these tales from remaining popular today. St. Thomas' Bluebeard and Blackbeard's Castles really have nothing to do with piracy—they were fortifications built to protect Charlotte Amalie harbor from enemy attack. History knows nothing about a pirate "Bluebeard." Blackbeard is the pirate Edward Teach, who plundered Caribbean trading ships from 1716 to 1718. Whether he had any special affiliation with St. Thomas is unknown, but he did travel through the Virgin Islands.

The true history of piracy in the Virgin Islands is relatively short. From 1680 to 1684, under the leadership of brothers Adolph and Nicolaj Esmit, St. Thomas developed a reputation for tolerating and even indulging piracy. In 1683, Adolph Esmit was accused of offering safe harbor to *La Trompeuse,* a pirate ship captained by Jean Hamlin. The British ship *HMS Francis,* captained by Charles Carlile and sent to hunt the pirate ship, sailed into St. Thomas harbor and found *La Trompeuse* alongside five other known pirate vessels. While Carlile made plans to burn the pirate ship, Esmit sheltered the pirates, including Hamlin himself, who reportedly found accommodation at Fort Christian, the official residence. Esmit flouted English threats by not only refusing to hand Hamlin over to them, but also by selling him a new ship.

The Esmits lost power in 1684, and later governors of St. Thomas were not so tolerant of the illegal trade. In 1698, pirate Bartholomew Sharp was imprisoned for life and his property confiscated; a year later St. Thomas governor

TREASURE ISLAND

The inspiration for *Treasure Island* came to Robert Louis Stevenson while he was on a wet Scottish holiday with his father and stepson. Encountering an old, handpainted map of an imaginary island, Stevenson made notes about his new idea. "It was to be a story for boys; no need of psychology or fine writing; and I had a boy at hand to be a touchstone," he wrote. The story's most famous character, Long John Silver, was modeled after his friend and collaborator W. E. Henley.

Stevenson's story was first published in 17 weekly installments under the title *The Sea-Cook* in *Young Folks* magazine. He wrote using the pseudonym "Captain George North" and was paid £30.

Two years later Stevenson revised the periodical text and created *Treasure Island*, published in 1883 by Cassell and Company in London. It sold briskly and has become a classic. The original map that served as its inspiration was lost, and Stevenson considered the replacement, included in some early editions, to be a poor copy. Today, the legend lives on that the island setting of *Treasure Island* is the British Virgin Islands' Norman Island.

COURTESY OF LIBRARY OF CONGRESS

Robert Louis Stevenson wrote *Treasure Island* based on a map of a fictional West Indian island.

Johan Lorentz forbade Captain Kidd from entering St. Thomas harbor.

Tales of piracy abound in the British Virgin Islands, too, fueled by the legend of treasure found on Norman Island.

COLONIZATION

Early European settlements in the islands were tenuous. The Virgin Islands, like the rest of the Caribbean, was the stage for European battles for supremacy. Alliances and enemies changed quickly; depending on your perspective, marauding ships were either pirate or patriot. Disease, war, and economic uncertainty made life difficult and unpredictable.

From 1493 until the late 1500s, settlements in the Virgin Islands were actively discouraged by the Spanish, who had established a colony on nearby Puerto Rico. Some historians say

that the Spanish established a small mining outpost on Virgin Gorda in the first half of the 16th century, further discouraging other European powers.

By the beginning of the 17th century Spanish supremacy was fading, and other European powers grew intent on settling the islands. There is evidence of Dutch and English settlements on St. Croix as early as 1625. In the British Virgin Islands, there are records of English settlement in 1640 and 1646, and a French settlement in 1648. Early settlers were a hardy bunch, drawn by the lure of adventure, possibility of profits, and, in some cases, desperation.

British Virgin Islands

The earliest European settlement on Tortola dates back to 1649, when Dutch settlers arrived on Tortola. They lived in relative peace ntil war broke out between the Dutch and the English in 1665. During that war the English attacked Tortola, destroyed the Dutch settlements, and took 67 African slaves they found here. This is the first record of the presence of African slaves in the British Virgin Islands.

The Dutch returned after the 1665 attack and three years later a report describes the population of Tortola as "80 Irish, English and Welsh under the Dutch." The English and Dutch did not remain at peace, however, and during another war in 1672 the Dutch settlement was again attacked by the English. This time, the Dutch surrendered before a drop of blood could be shed. The islands became British, and they remain so today.

The future remained uncertain for settlers of the British Virgin Islands even after the Dutch surrender in 1672. During peace negotiations after the war between England and the Netherlands, it was agreed that the Virgin Islands would eventually be handed back over to the Dutch. This never happened, but the uncertainty over the islands' future discouraged large-scale settlement and investment. The islands became home to people who could not get land on other, more prosperous, islands.

U.S. Virgin Islands

Meanwhile, the Danes grew interested in establishing a Caribbean colony. St. Thomas, still unsettled and possessing a good natural harbor, caught their eye.

St. Croix's early years were a time of shifting alliances and uncertainty. Although Columbus claimed St. Croix for the Spanish when he sailed by in 1493, the Spaniards made no attempt to colonize the island, probably because of the continued presence of hostile Indians there. Early European settlers on St. Croix were English, French, and Dutch adventurers who established fragile settlements amid the threat of attack. By 1650, the French had the upper hand in these disputes. They developed a small-scale plantation colony, where they produced indigo, cotton, and sugar.

The Danes' first attempt at colonizing St. Thomas came in 1665, under the leadership of Captain Erik Nielson Smith. Settlers of a number of different nationalities were recruited and began to establish trading facilities and clear the land for plantations. The colony weathered attacks from English privateers, sickness, and even a hurricane before it was abandoned 19 months later.

The Danes' second attempt at colonization took place in 1672, when the *Faero* set sail for the West Indies with 190 people on board. The Danes had recruited a diverse bunch of settlers for St. Thomas. The 128 Danish West India Company employees were indentured servants, contracted to work for the Company for between three and five years. The remaining 62 people were recruited from prisons and poorhouses in Denmark.

When the *Faero* arrived on St. Thomas in May 1672, their numbers had declined to just 104—seven had escaped and 77 died. During the first seven months of the colony's life, another 75 people died, leaving a bare 29 people in the nascent colony. Dutch, German, English, French, Norwegian, Swedish, Scottish, Irish, Flemish, and Jewish settlers arrived and grew the colony. By 1680 there were 156 whites and 175 slaves on the island.

An eight-year tax holiday announced in 1688 drew even more settlers, including French Huguenots and many more Dutch. By 1715 the island's population had increased to 547 whites and more than 3,000 slaves. St. Thomas' plantation economy grew in tandem with its population. In 1688 there were 90 surveyed plantations on the island; by 1720 there were 164. Cultivation on the island peaked in 1725, with 177 plantations.

Meanwhile, the French abandoned St. Croix in 1696 in favor of Haiti, and the island was virtually unoccupied until 1733, when it was sold to the Danes. It was the first time title to a West Indian island had been exchanged by means other than warfare. Denmark sent its first shipment of materials and men to St. Croix in August 1734, under the command of Frederik Moth, who had been named governor of the island. About 150 British people, who were living on the island with about 450 slaves, were allowed to stay if they pledged allegiance to the king of Denmark. The island was promptly surveyed and subdivided into 400 estates, which were sold to aspiring planters from Europe and the surrounding Caribbean colonies. The opportunity attracted Danes, Scots, English, Dutch, Irish, and Sephardic Jews.

St. John was the last of the Virgin Islands to be substantially settled by Europeans. Danish attempts to settle the island in 1675 and again in 1684 failed, in part because of disturbances by the English, who had claimed nearby Tortola in 1672, and in part because the Danes were focused on establishing their colony on St. Thomas. By the early 1700s, St. Thomas was thriving and its harbor was one of the busiest in the Caribbean. Agriculture had taken a backseat to commerce, and planters were looking for an island that could serve as the plantation headquarters of the colony. St. John fit the bill.

In 1718, the Danish West India Company sent 20 planters, five soldiers and 16 slaves to St. John to begin dividing, settling, and cultivating the island. To lure settlers, the Danes offered a seven-year tax hiatus and welcomed all nationalities. The deal attracted a number of established St. Thomas planters, who remained on St. Thomas but hired overseers to manage their St. John plantations. The opportunity also drew a number of poor settlers who started by cultivating cotton, indigo, and tobacco in the hopes of raising the capital required to set up a sugar plantation.

PLANTATION ERA

Political stability and the availability of capital led to growth of the Virgin Islands' plantation economy. On the flat, fertile plane of St. Croix, plantations were set neatly next to each other, windmills dotting the landscape. On the other, more hilly islands, slaves cleared whole hillsides of native forest and terraced the slopes for the cultivation of sugar. The plantation era was one of contradictions and great cruelty. For planters, it was often a gamble; fortunes were won and lost in a single growing season. For the enslaved Africans who produced the wealth, it was brutal and dehumanizing.

Slaves were transported to the Virgin Islands on overcrowded slave ships. Many did not survive this horrific "Middle Passage."

Africans who survived the devastating Middle Passage from Africa's west coast were auctioned in markets at Charlotte Amalie, Christiansted, and Road Town and worked, some to death, on the plantations. Those who survived performed the grueling work of clearing land and planting and harvesting sugarcane.

Danish West Indies

By the end of the 18th century, St. Croix was second only to Jamaica in sugar production per acre. In 1800, the island had the fourth largest sugar product in the Caribbean. The colony's success meant planters and their families could afford to lead lives of great opulence. Many of the island's elaborate estate houses date back to the period from 1760 to 1820, the heyday of the plantation period.

On St. John, the plantation era began with Danish settlement. The 1733 slave rebellion caused some planters to pull out of the island but others remained. Many St. John plantations were owned by absentee planters.

While St. Croix and St. John grew in importance as sugar islands, St. Thomas turned its focus away from agriculture and toward trade. Delegations from the colony to Denmark in the early 18th century led to easing of trade restrictions, which allowed ships of all nations to trade in St. Thomas on payment of fixed import and export duties. Over the coming decades, trade restrictions were further eased, until St. Thomas became a free port in 1764. Denmark's declared neutrality allowed St. Thomas to flourish even in times of war.

British Virgin Islands

The British islands got off to a slow start with the plantation industry. Uncertainty about the islands' ownership and future discouraged investment, so while the Danish West Indies were being cultivated with sugar (which required major capital investment), plantations on the British islands continued to produce cotton, indigo, ginger, and coffee—all of which required little investment but yielded much more modest profits.

The plantation era began in earnest in the British Virgin Islands in 1747 when an Englishman named James Purcell was appointed Lt. Governor of the territory. Purcell lobbied for local government and traveled to Liverpool, England, to seek financing for Tortola's planters. Purcell's efforts bore fruit. Financing was provided, and plantations all around the island turned to sugar cultivation.

It is during this time that whole hillsides of native timber were cut down to make space for sugar fields and many of the fortifications now in ruin around the island were built. James Purcell died in 1759 and was succeeded by his brother, John Purcell, who continued to govern over peace and prosperity. In 1774, the same year that sugar production reached its peak on Tortola, representative government was established for the first time—another sign of the colony's growing importance.

SLAVERY

Prosperity for planters meant something entirely different for the Africans brought to the islands to provide the labor that fueled the plantation economy. During the most prosperous years of plantation life here, slave ships sailed to St. Thomas, St. Croix, and Tortola with cargo directly from Africa. Newly arrived Africans were given one week of "seasoning" to recuperate from the horrific Middle Passage from Africa before being put to work; mortality rates among newly arrived slaves were as high as 30 percent.

Slave Life

Most slaves lived in mud and thatch huts on their plantations, except for the slave driver, or Bomba, who often lived in a wooden house. Field slaves worked from sunup to sundown, with longer hours during the arduous sugar harvest period. Slaves were often given small patches of land on which they were expected to produce food for themselves and their families, which was augmented by meager provisions from their owner. Each slave was supposed to receive one new piece of clothing each year but on some occasions got none.

Slaves in the British Virgin Islands were subject to unfettered brutality, in part because of a Slave Code now noted as one of the most repressive in the entire Caribbean region. One report from Tortola tells of a planter stabbing a slave through the heart because he did not like the meal she prepared. In another case, slaves who executed a rebellion on Josiah's Bay Plantation in 1790 were tortured for days and then put to death in a public execution. In the Danish islands, authorities responded to the 1733 St. John rebellion by instituting repressive rules against slave gatherings.

The miracle of slavery is that the slaves not only survived but developed a rich culture and strong character despite oppression and brutality. Most plantations allowed slaves one and a half days off each week. On Saturday afternoons they were expected to cultivate their own crops, on which they depended for food, and on Sundays they rested.

Many slaves found ways to earn money, some developing skills that allowed them to buy their freedom and the freedom of their

QUELBE MUSIC

The traditional music form of the Virgin Islands is quelbe music, also called scratch or fungi. A quelbe band consists of a banjo, conga drum, squash, and a triangle. Other instruments sometimes include guitar, bass, saxophone, or flute. Quelbe musicians use objects close at hand to construct their instruments, although today some have adopted more modern instruments. The banjo was often made out of an old sardine can. The squash was a dried local gourd, serrated and then scratched with a comb or wire-pronged stick. The baseline was usually provided by someone blowing into the discarded tailpipe from a car.

Quelbe music developed on sugar plantations, where slaves used materials at hand to provide a rhythm and melody to which they could tell stories, share jokes, and spread gossip. The music was influenced by African rhythms and the sound of Danish and British military bands. After slavery ended, quelbe music grew in popularity as the restrictions of slavery ended and the music form could spread freely. Many older Virgin Islanders have sweet memories of nights spent dancing to the sound of their village quelbe band.

Quelbe music still tells stories and jokes, often with a risqué undertone. Quelbe is especially popular at Christmastime, giving a new and refreshing take on Christmas music. Traditionally, quelbe bands would go serenading in the wee hours of Christmas morning, wishing their neighbors a merry Christmas.

Today, quelbe music is being preserved by a handful of bands. In the British Virgin Islands, the Lashing Dogs and Loverboys perform fungi music (as it is called there) at bars and festivals. In the U.S. Virgin Islands, Jamesie and the Allstars, Stanley the Ten Sleepless Nights, Bully and the Kafooners, and Blinky and the Roadmasters carry on the tradition. Jamesie Brewster, the leader of Jamesie and the Allstars, is the subject of a forthcoming documentary. You can hear a snippet of his music at www.jamesieproject.com.

The traditional accompaniment to quelbe music is the quadrille, a kind of square dancing introduced to the Virgin Islands from the French Caribbean and influenced by English and Irish planters. Quadrille or not, it is impossible to stand still listening to quelbe music. St. Croix culture bearer and writer Richard Schrader wrote in his book *Maufe, Quelbe and t'ing* that when Jamesie Brewster performs, "trees shake their branches and grass bends down low." That just about sums it up.

---

families. A market was held on Sunday mornings in Charlotte Amalie, Christiansted, Frederiksted, Road Town, and other villages, where slaves would bring produce and other goods to sell. Slaves also depended on their religious beliefs. Before missionaries began Christianizing slaves in the late 1700s, many slaves practiced the religions of Africa, labeled obeah today. These religions involved belief in various gods, and also knowledge of bush medicine and other healing methods. Recognizing the threat of the slaves' religious gatherings and beliefs, authorities passed laws making obeah illegal. It remains illegal in the British Virgin Islands today.

EMANCIPATION

By the turn of the 19th century, doubts were increasing about slavery. Abolitionists in the United States and Europe were gaining strength, and social changes were bringing about a greater awareness of human rights and freedoms. The Haitian revolution of 1804 had forced the issue of slavery and freedom to the forefront. Between 1834 and 1886, slavery would be abolished in the Caribbean.

The end of slavery did not automatically address the social and economic oppression experienced by Africans in the islands, but it was the first in a long series of steps toward equality and empowerment, a process that continues today.

British Virgin Islands

As the plantation industry in the British Virgin Islands grew, doubts were developing in England over slavery. Abolitionists fought for decades against the slave trade and slavery itself, eventually prevailing in 1807 when Parliament ended the transatlantic slave trade. The Act meant no more Africans could be brought to the New World as slaves but did not necessarily improve the lives of slaves already in the region. Nor did it end the slave trade within the Caribbean and many slaves from small, declining territories like the British Virgin Islands were sent to colonies still experiencing growth.

In 1811, the trial and hanging of Tortola planter Arthur Hodge for the murder of his slave, Prosper, further fueled concern over the treatment of slaves in the British West Indian colonies. The case received attention in England and throughout the West Indies, and testimony about Hodge's brutal treatment of Prosper and other slaves further turned public opinion against slavery.

Also, the slaves themselves were changing. Methodist missionaries arrived on the island in 1789 and were the first Christians to minister directly to the slaves. The Methodists soon had a following of more than 2,000 slaves and in 1823 the Methodist church opened the first Sunday school on the island, a small but important step toward education.

In 1790 and 1821, slaves at Josiah's Bay rioted in response to rumors, first the rumor that their owner was withholding freedom from them and second that their owner was going to ship them to Trinidad. While both riots were ultimately put down, they frightened planters.

Economic forces also caused planters to lose interest in their plantations. Sugar prices fell during the first half of the 19th century, after the discovery of a way to extract sugar from the sugar beet, which could grow in Europe. At the same time, the cost of maintaining slaves was higher since they could no longer be worked to death and then replaced. Finally, a major hurricane hit the islands on September 22, 1819, destroying 100 of the 104 plantations in cultivation. Many planters decided not to rebuild after the storm.

These factors and others led to end of slavery in the British West Indian colonies, including the British Virgin Islands, on August 1, 1832. Historians disagree on how the Proclamation was communicated in the British Virgin Islands. Some say it was read aloud at the Sunday Morning Well in Road Town, where a plaque now hangs. Others say it was more likely announced in churches around the Territory.

Today, Tortola celebrates its annual Emancipation Festival on the first Monday in August in commemoration of the slaves' first days of freedom.

Danish West Indies

Slavery persisted in the Danish colonies for 16 years longer than in the British islands. After the British ended slavery in 1832, Denmark knew it had to plan for emancipation in its colonies. In 1840, the Danish king proposed a scheme where slaves would be given an extra day off per week, during which they could work for their owner for wages and eventually buy their freedom. While some planters agreed to giving slaves an additional free day, few agreed to pay them, and the proposal was not accepted.

In 1847 another proposal was made, this one accepted by both Danish officials and planters. Under the plan all babies born to slaves would be free from that date on, but adult slaves would have to wait 12 years before freedom would be granted. While the Danes had consulted extensively with planters on the plan, no one had thought it necessary to consider the opinion of the slaves themselves, a decision that proved to be shortsighted. On July 3, 1848, thousands of slaves on St. Croix rose up, led by a young slave named Buddhoe, to demand their freedom. The disturbance moved through the countryside to Fort Frederik, where the slaves lay down their single demand: freedom. A deadline of noon came and went with no sign of freedom or the governor, Peter von Scholten, who had the authority to grant it. In response, the slaves wrested the hated "justice post," where many slaves had been beaten and killed, from its position near the fort and threw it in the water. Buddhoe uttered an ultimatum: "Freedom by four o'clock or we burn the town."

Von Scholten arrived in Frederiksted before 4 P.M. and went into the fort, where he consulted with planters and officials. Von Scholten, faced with a crowd of some 8,000 slaves, rejected their counsel, instead uttering the words that soon became famous: "From this day forward, all unfree in the Danish West Indies shall be free."

AFTER EMANCIPATION

The end of slavery marked the beginning of a long economic decline in the Virgin Islands. The Danes and British did very little to support the newly freed slaves, and many of the planters pulled out. Left virtually alone, the former slaves turned to subsistence farming, fishing, and small-scale trade to survive. St. Croix was the only island that maintained a sugar industry significantly beyond the end of slavery; its last sugar mill closed in the 1960s.

British Virgin Islands

In the British colonies, slavery was followed by a period of apprenticeship, a stepping stone between slavery and freedom. Under apprenticeship former slaves were no longer subject to the brutality they knew under slavery and were free to move about the island as they wished. But they were required to remain on the plantations where they once were slaves, where they worked for a small salary.

Apprenticeship ended around 1840, and by then the sugar industry was close to its death. In 1839, five years after the end of slavery, Tortola produced 423 hogshead of sugar. In 1852, it produced just one. During this time, most English planters left.

The freed slaves became yeoman farmers, merchants, and seamen. Farmers kept cattle, raised fruits and vegetables, fished, and cleared timber to make charcoal, most of which was sold to St. Thomas. In fact, aside from small scale production for local use and the brief burst of rum production during American Prohibition, the islands said goodbye to sugar for good.

What few whites remained on the island fled after riots broke out in 1853. Angered over the government's decision to double the cattle tax

overnight, islanders gathered in Road Town to protest the tax and demand the release of two men arrested because of their refusal to pay it. Eventually, the rioters broke into the prison where the men were being held, took the firearms, and spent two days burning and destroying Road Town and what plantations remained throughout the island. Only one Road Town building survived the fire and is still known as the "fireproof building."

The second half of the 19th century was quiet in the British Virgin Islands. Some islanders persevered by hard work, while some migrated to the United States and other places that promised more opportunity. The British government neglected the islands. The only schools were operated by the Methodist and Anglican churches, and health care was primitive. The Legislative Assembly, still a white only establishment, disbanded in 1902 and responsibility for the islands fell to a British governor stationed in Antigua, where it remained for 50 years.

Danish West Indies

While emancipation was achieved in 1848 black laborers in the Danish West Indies were still forced to work under slave-like conditions. Immediately after slavery was abolished the Danish administration enacted rules designed to prevent newly freed slaves from leaving their plantations. Rules required laborers to enter into one-year contracts with their employer at terms set out by law: a five-day work week, and wages of 5, 10, or 15 cents a day depending on whether the slave was skilled or unskilled. Laborers were told they could apply to change employers only once a year. In addition, passport requirements were designed to limit the number of people who could leave the islands all together.

Rules or no, many blacks did not remain on the plantations. On St. John, where the sugar industry collapsed almost immediately after the end of slavery, the population of the island fell from 2,228 to 994 between 1850 and 1880. Those people who remained turned to subsistence farming, fishing, and trade to survive.

On St. Croix, while many former slaves were restricted from leaving the island, they did leave the plantations to live in town, where they sought employment as servants, port hands, or artisans. To fill a shortfall of agricultural labor, St. Croix was opened to immigrants from the nearby British islands, Barbados, and St. Eustatius.

Fireburn

Discontent with working conditions and restrictions on free movement came to a head on St. Croix in October 1878, when a riot broke out in Frederiksted, fueled by rumors that the Danes had stopped issuing passports and that police had killed a laborer. A crowd in Frederiksted stormed the fort but was unable to scale the internal gate. They turned instead on the town and nearby plantations, setting fire to town houses, businesses, great houses, sugar mills, and crops. Crowds of laborers roamed the island for days, armed with sticks and fire. Leaders included three Crucian women, Mary Thomas ("Queen Mary"), Rebecca Frederik, and Axelline Saloman.

It took the Danes two weeks to put down the "Fireburn," as the riots have come to be known. In the final analysis, nearly 900 acres of agricultural land were destroyed, 60 laborers were killed, and three soldiers perished. More than 400 laborers were arrested; 75 of these were sentenced to jail. Mary, Rebecca and Axelline, the "Queens of the Fireburn," were sent to Denmark to serve their sentences. They returned to St. Croix and worked as street vendors until their deaths.

The Merchant Island

St. Thomas did not fare much better than its sister islands. Cholera outbreaks there in 1853 and 1866 killed an estimated 3,200 people. A devastating hurricane in 1867, followed by an earthquake and tidal wave in the same year, destroyed the island's reputation as a safe harbor.

The beginning of the steam age and advances in communications contributed to the island's decline. St. Thomas harbor was too small for the large steam ships of the late 19th century, and the advent of telegraphic connections allowed merchants to acquire market information without making the journey in person. The number of steamships calling on St. Thomas peaked in 1880 and declined ever since.

Meanwhile, the island saw an influx of people. Former slaves left plantations on St. Croix and St. John in high numbers, many of them heading to Charlotte Amalie, where they sought work on the docks and in subsidiary trade businesses.

THE 20TH CENTURY

A few attempts were made in the early 20th century to diversify and strengthen the economies of the then-Danish West Indies and the British Virgin Islands. On St. Thomas, the National Bank of the Danish West Indies was established in 1904 after the St. Thomas Bank ceased operations in 1898. A new shipping authority was created in 1904 to encourage trade. In 1912, the Danish West Indian Company was founded, and in 1915 its headquarters were moved to St. Thomas. (Its offspring, the West India Company, is still the largest cruise ship agent on the island.)

On St. Croix, plantations turned to other crops, such as citrus, coconuts, and tomatoes. Cattle also began to be an important part of the island economy. On St. John, the Danish Plantation Company opened experimental bay rum factories in 1903 in hopes of providing some economic stimulus for the island. Bay rum proved to be a successful export, and several former sugar factories were converted to bay rum plants. One of the largest was at Cinnamon Bay.

On the British islands, authorities established an agriculture station in 1902, which was supposed to introduce new crops and agricultural skills to the islanders.

World War I and the Transfer

Despite feeble attempts to the contrary, the Danish West Indies' economy worsened due to the outbreak of World War I. Shipping ground to a near halt, and living conditions were poor. In

Peasant houses in Lavelle, St. Croix, in 1941. The United States neglected the islands' social and economic needs for many years after their acquisition in 1917.

1916, inspired by a successful strike by sugarcane workers on St. Croix, St. Thomas coal-carriers struck. Led by George A. Moorhead, the strike was successful and led to a doubling of the wage, from $.01 to $.02 per basket.

While St. Thomas and the other Danish West Indies were an increasing financial liability for Denmark, the United States saw them as islands of potentially strategic importance. The U.S. needed to protect approaches to the Panama Canal and also wanted to prevent the islands from winding up in the hands of a foreign nation hostile to America. U.S. interest in the islands also coincided with a growing imperialist attitude in the country.

The sale was negotiated between 1915 and 1916, and the official transfer took place on March 31, 1917, still observed as Transfer Day in the territory. The U.S. paid $25 million for the three islands.

From 1917 until 1931, the islands were administered by the U.S. Navy, and little emphasis was placed on developing democratic institutions or meaningful economic growth. How-

ever, some accomplishments were made. Naval officials reorganized hospitals, vaccination programs were put in place, and a sanitary code passed. Concrete water catchments were built on St. Thomas following a 1924 drought, and schools were built and opened.

On St. Croix, thousands of Puerto Ricans were encouraged to migrate to the island to provide agricultural labor. New Deal–era homesteading programs provided some economic opportunity for Crucians and served to subdivide several of the largest plantations. The 1934 program saw the subdivision of about 5,000 acres at estates Whim, LaGrande Princess, Northside, and Bethleham. Under the scheme, settlers could buy six acres of land for about $18 a year, paid over 20 years.

Economic Growth

World War II was a minor economic boom for the islands. Construction of military installations on St. Thomas drew more laborers away from the farm, and when the building boom was over they did not go back. In 1952, the U.S. Virgin

THIRD TIME'S THE CHARM

While the United States did not acquire the islands of St. Thomas, St. John, and St. Croix until 1917, America's interest in the islands dated back more than 50 years earlier.

At a dinner party in Washington, D.C., in January 1865, U.S. Secretary of State William Seward approached the Danish minister in Washington, Waldenmar Raasloff, with a proposal to buy the islands. But discussion on the proposal was delayed by a number of circumstances.

In January 1866, Seward visited the islands and was impressed, but he did nothing for more than a year. Negotiations finally began in May 1867, and an agreement was made in October of that year. The treaty provided for U.S. acquisition of St. Thomas and St. John for $7.5 million, with the understanding that inhabitants of the island would first be allowed to voice their support or opposition through a plebiscite. Following that, ratification would be needed by the Danish Rigsdag and the U.S. Senate.

The vote was carried out on January 9 and 10, 1868. A total of 1,244 people voted in favor of the sale; 22 against. Islanders were hopeful that affiliation with the United States would lead to more economic opportunities.

But the 1867 treaty languished in the U.S. Senate. Post-Civil War America was not interested in expansion overseas, and many believed that Seward, unpopular over his purchase of Alaska, had overstepped his authority in negotiating the treaty, despite the fact that Presidents Lincoln and Johnson had approved of the purchase. The devastating hurricanes and earthquake of 1867 did not help matters.

One observer put it this way: "Immediately everyone began to make fun of the treaty, as one for the annexation of hurricanes and earthquakes, and the subject was fairly laughed out of court."

The parties tried again in 1900, and another treaty was negotiated in 1902. This time, the treaty was drafted in Washington and was placed first before the U.S. Senate. The sum agreed was $5 million for all three islands: St. Croix, St. Thomas, and St. John. No vote was required in the islands, where many residents were still smarting over the U.S.'s rejection of the previous sale.

This time, however, it was the Danes who stood in the way of the sale's completion. The upper house of the Danish parliament found itself in a 32-32 tie on the treaty, and so it was vetoed.

Negotiations began again in 1915, between Dr. Maurice Egan, the U.S. minister to Copenhagen, and the Danish foreign minister. This time, talks went smoothly. The United States public was behind the sale, and Danish interest in the islands was waning. In January 1916, the parties agreed to a sale price of $25 million. The treaty was approved by the U.S. Senate on September 7, 1916. In Denmark, the matter went to a national referendum before being approved by both houses of the Legislature.

In the Virgin Islands, public opinion was in favor of the sale. Formal transfer ceremonies were held on St. Thomas and St. Croix on March 31, 1917. The Danish Dannebrog was taken down, and the U.S. Stars and Stripes was raised.

Islands Tourist Development Board was formed, and travelers began to discover St. Thomas.

While St. Thomas and St. John were focusing solely on tourism, St. Croix was opening its doors to industry. Tax incentives approved in the 1960s encouraged the development of the island's industrial economy. In 1966 Hess Oil and Harvey Alumina established industrial centers on the island. Some of the early hotels—Carambola and the Buccaneer—date from this period too.

One of the early visitors to the islands was Laurance Rockefeller, the grandson of John D. Rockefeller. Rockefeller visited the islands during the early 1950s on a Caribbean cruise and immediately saw their potential, as national parks and tourist destinations. He and his agents quickly began negotiating with landowners to buy up large tracts of St. John.

Rockefeller spent an estimated $2 million to buy more than 5,000 acres of land on St. John, which was handed over to the government when the Virgin Islands National Park was declared at a ceremony on December 1, 1956. The same day, Rockefeller reopened Caneel Bay Plantation, a luxury resort completely surrounded by park land. St. John's nature-based tourism industry was born.

The Cuban Revolution in 1959 proved to be the launch pad for the Virgin Islands' tourism industry: there was a seven-fold increase in the number of tourists between 1959 and 1969.

Having made his mark on the U.S. Virgin Islands, Rockefeller moved on to the British islands, where he bought large tracts of land on Tortola and Virgin Gorda to become national parks, and he developed Little Dix Bay Hotel on Virgin Gorda, which opened its doors in 1964.

Modern Challenges

Hurricanes Hugo in 1989 and Marilyn in 1995 dealt a terrible blow to the islands—St. Croix and St. Thomas in particular—razing whole homes and destroying hundreds of hotel rooms.

Hugo killed three people and left an estimated one-third of St. Croix's residents homeless. The island's hillsides were totally denuded, and damage to buildings was widespread. Even today, island residents who lived through that storm speak of two segments of their lives: before Hugo and after Hugo.

Marilyn struck the Virgin Islands on September 15–16, 1995, and St. Thomas bore the worst of the storm. There was an estimated $2.1 billion in direct damage, eight people died, and 21,000 homes were damaged or destroyed. The Charlotte Amalie waterfront was dotted with boats that had been carried ashore by the storm surge, including a U.S. Coast Guard cutter.

Despite the terrible damage, many island residents say that media coverage of both hurricanes, which focused on isolated incidents of looting and overstated the destruction, was responsible for compounding the islands' post-hurricane woes.

The U.S. Virgin Islands are in a state of perpetual fiscal crisis. In 2004, the islands received $800 million in federal grants and direct funding; residents received a further $228 million in personal federal benefits. Despite this, the poverty rate remains high—almost 50 percent on St. Croix, and about 30 percent territory-wide—and the quality of public services is low. St. John is the exception—its economy is growing quickly and, many say, recklessly—fueled by investment from U.S. mainlanders seeking an upscale island retreat. Native St. Johnians are being squeezed out of the picture.

The U.S. Virgin Islands government continues to pin its hopes on the cruise ship industry: an expanded cruise dock and new shopping mall at Crown Bay opened in early 2006. It is designed for the largest class of cruise ship. Waterfront development near the Anne Abramson Pier in Frederiksted, St. Croix, is designed to lure cruise ships back to that island after they pulled out in 2002. It is yet to be seen whether this will happen.

Modern BVI

The British Virgin Islands have enjoyed a much greater degree of stability and prosperity during the last 40 years than the U.S. Virgin Islands. Following the establishment of Little Dix Hotel in 1964, the islands' tourism industry grew, fueled by a large and successful charter yacht fleet. Meanwhile, the territory adopted the International Business Companies Act in the early 1980s, marking the beginning of a flourishing offshore finance sector. In addition to IBCs (shell companies), the BVI now specializes in reinsurance, mutual fund administration, insolvency, and trusts. Many of the BVI's clients are located in Hong Kong, China, and Singapore.

Despite its economic gains, the BVI has social problems it needs to face. Crime has become a problem, and while the islands remain far safer than many destinations in the world, islanders are eagerly looking for ways to stem the growing tide of petty crimes, armed robberies, and murders. The influx of immigrants who come to work in the tourism and financial services sector is also causing tension; many native British Virgin Islanders feel that they are losing their unique culture and heritage, while locals are not benefiting enough from the economic growth.

Government and Economy

U.S. VIRGIN ISLANDS

The U.S. Virgin Islands are an unincorporated territory of the United States, subject to U.S. laws. Virgin Islanders are U.S. citizens and the U.S. president is the head of state, although Virgin Islanders do not vote in presidential elections.

Since 1970, the governor of the U.S. Virgin Islands has been chosen by popular election. Before that, the governor was appointed by the U.S. president. As the head of the executive branch, the governor chooses commissioners to oversee departments, proposes the territory's annual budget, and signs (or vetoes) legislation. The governor is assisted by a lieutenant governor, elected as part of a gubernatorial ticket, like the U.S. president and vice president.

Charles W. Turnbull, a Democrat and former history professor, concludes his second four-year term as governor in November 2006 and won't be eligible to seek another term in office.

The 15-member unicameral legislature is elected every two years. The Senate passes laws and can petition the U.S. Congress to make changes to the Organic Act, the territory's constitution. Seven of the 15 senators are elected from the St. Croix district and seven are elected from the St. Thomas-St. John district. The final member is chosen at large but must be a resident of St. John.

Virgin Islanders also choose a nonvoting delegate to the House of Representatives who can take part in debates and serve on committees but does not have a vote on the floor. Donna Christian-Christenson's term expires in 2006, but she may run again.

Elections

Elections for governor are held every four years; elections for Senate and delegate to Congress every two. The vast majority of Virgin Islanders align themselves with the Democratic Party, so much so that political parties are largely irrelevant in local elections. Personality and political alliances are much more important; party affiliation is easily shrugged off when found inconvenient.

Election season is marked by spirited debates, lots of political banners and signs, and a seemingly endless sequence of open-air political rallies.

Judicial and Penal Systems

There are both local and federal courts in the U.S. Virgin Islands. Territorial court judges are appointed for 10-year terms by the governor and hear civil and criminal cases based on local laws. U.S. District Courts in St. Thomas and St. Croix are part of the Third U.S. Circuit, the same as Pennsylvania, New Jersey, and Delaware. The Third Circuit Court of Appeals is the territory's appeals court; cases from the Virgin Islands can be appealed all the way to the U.S. Supreme Court.

The Virgin Islands have a higher crime rate than many U.S. cities of similar population. In 2005, there were more than 40 homicides, many of which are linked to drugs and gangs. Violence does not often affect tourists, although visitors should avoid urban areas at night and use common sense in other situations. From 1990 until 2005 there were six tourist homicides in the U.S. Virgin Islands.

The U.S. Virgin Islands have one of the world's top 10 inmate-to-population ratios: 490 per 100,000 people, according to recent figures. These inmates are housed at prisons on St. Thomas and St. Croix.

Economy

The U.S. Virgin Islands' economy is highly dependent on tourism—80 percent of the $2.5 billion GDP comes from that industry. Some two million people visit the U.S. Virgin Islands every year, most of them aboard cruise ships. There are small agriculture, manufacturing, and industrial sectors, too. St. Croix is home to one of the world's largest oil refineries.

Despite the large number of visitors, the

The BVI Financial Services Commission regulates its booming financial services industry.

U.S. Virgin Islands economy is struggling. The government is bloated and inefficient, providing poor services at high prices. Slumps in tourism following Hurricane Hugo in 1989, Hurricane Marilyn in 1995, and the terrorist attacks of 2001 have hampered economic growth. In 2004, many of the public high schools lost accreditation, a development symbolic of the problems with the education system.

Some 29 percent of households in the Virgin Islands have incomes below the federal poverty line, and more than 40 percent of children grow up in poverty. The median income in 1999 was $24,704, 41 percent lower than the national median income in the same period. Unemployment is near 10 percent. Nearly half of all households are headed by a single mother.

There is considerable variation among the three islands, with St. Croix having the greatest extent of poverty and St. John the least. For example, where nearly 50 percent of children on St. Croix are living in households below the poverty line, only 22 percent of children on St. John fall into the same category. Unemployment also varies by island: While unemployment in 2005 was at 6.5 percent in the St. Thomas-St. John district, it was two whole percentage points higher on St. Croix.

BRITISH VIRGIN ISLANDS

The British Virgin Islands are an overseas territory of the United Kingdom, one of five remaining U.K. colonies in the West Indies. Power is shared between a locally elected government and the British governor, who is appointed by the Queen. The local government is responsible for most areas of administration, including finance. The British governor administers the courts, the police, and the public service and is responsible for external affairs. In 2005 the local government petitioned the U.K. for changes to its constitution that would transfer more authority to the local government and strip away some of the governor's powers.

Since 1978, the territory has paid for itself. British aid is minimal and is used for areas of special interest to the British government. In the early 1990s the U.K. government paid for a new prison; in 2001 it contributed to the building of a new residence for the governor. Smaller

...ms of money from the U.K. go to support environmental and good-government projects.

The BVI has a ministerial government, modeled after the Westminster system. Ministers, who are the chief policymakers in the government, are chosen from among members of the majority in legislative council. Together, the ministers form the executive council, which meets weekly to make policy decisions. The chief minister, together with the governor, guides executive council and leads the government.

The public service is nonpartisan. Ministers are supported by permanent secretaries and other officials who do not change when a new party comes to power. They are obligated to serve the government of the day, whether they voted for it or not.

Laws are proposed and passed in the 13-member legislative council. Council meetings, which take place about every six weeks, are broadcast live on television and radio and can be interesting to listen to. Debate is decorous, but in between the references to "honorable members" you will pick up some very carefully worded barbs. Most meetings include question-and-answer segment not unlike the British question time aired on C-SPAN.

Both the court system and government of the British Virgin Islands is well respected in the region and the wider world. A corruption scandal involving the territory's financial secretary in 2002 was dealt with swiftly: the offender was put in prison and lost his job. It was the first case of its kind in the BVI, and no others have followed.

While the BVI government is not especially modern, and while it sometimes reacts very slowly, it is generally effective, transparent, and accountable.

Elections

Elections must be held at least every four years, or sooner if the ruling party requests, or if the ruling party, or coalition, seems to have lost its ability to control the government.

The last elections were held in 2003, when the National Democratic Party won eight seats, unseating the longstanding Virgin Islands Party and former chief minister, Ralph T. O'Neal. Led by Chief Minister Orlando Smith, the NDP promised more transparency, better accountability, and more focus on social, environmental, and health issues. In 2005, following the death of one of its members, the NDP won a by-election, a victory that seems to indicate the public is generally pleased with the direction the new government is taking. The next elections will be held sometime in 2007.

There are about 10,000 registered voters in the BVI—about half of the population. Immigrants who have settled in the territory must obtain citizenship—called belonger status—before they can register to vote.

Judicial and Penal Systems

The BVI is part of the Eastern Caribbean Supreme Court, which administers courts in eight different eastern Caribbean jurisdictions. Judges and magistrates are rotated among the jurisdictions. Rarely will a judge or magistrate from the Virgin Islands preside over court there. The law is based on English common-law, and courtroom practices follow those used in England. Appeals are heard by the three-judge Eastern Caribbean Court of Appeals. The final court of appeal is the privy council in the United Kingdom.

Lawyers and judges wear black robes with high white collars in court, but no wigs. In magistrate's court, the attire is business suits.

Prisoners serve their sentences in a hilltop prison on the remote northeastern corner of Tortola. Due to overcrowding, minimum security female prisoners are now housed in the old prison on Main Street in Road Town. There is no death penalty in the British Virgin Islands; the penalty for murder is life in prison without parole. No one really remembers when the last person was executed here, but that did not stop a loud public outcry in 1999 when the U.K. required all its territories to remove capital punishment from the law books.

Economy

The British Virgin Islands has a complex and in many ways contradictory economy. On one hand it is one of the most prosperous territories in the Caribbean, fueled by high-end tourism and financial services. In 2004, the BVI's gross domestic product was $2.5 billion, or $38,500 per capita.

There is virtually no unemployment; in fact, the territory's economy is so hot that the BVI must import more than half of its workforce. Despite this prosperity, some people in the BVI are poor. The minimum wage is a staggeringly low $4 per hour, and the cost of living is among the highest in the Caribbean. A 2002 study found that almost 25 percent of people in the BVI live below the poverty line. Many of the poorest workers are employed in the construction and tourism industries.

On the other end of the economic spectrum is financial services, the other pillar of the BVI economy. More than 400,000 international business companies are on the BVI's offshore registry, attracted by low incorporation fees, no taxes, and the BVI's political and economic stability. Since 1990, the territory has sought to diversify its offshore sector, with the addition of legislation for mutual fund administration, captive insurance, and special trusts. Financial services account for more than half of the government's annual revenues.

So far, the BVI has escaped inclusion on so-called offshore blacklists. Neither has it ever been named in any high-profile money laundering case. Thousands of European and American professionals work in the BVI's financial service industry, and the government has pledged to do more to open up opportunities for British Virgin Islanders in the industry.

The People

The Virgin Islands are diverse—residents hail from nearly every Caribbean island, plus Asia, Africa, Europe, and North America. Although both Virgin Island territories have administrative links with western countries—the United Kingdom and the United States—these islands and their people are distinctly Caribbean.

Three-quarters of the people in the U.S. Virgin Islands and some 83 percent in the British islands are black, descended from African slaves brought to Caribbean islands during the plantation era. In both territories there are Indian, Middle Eastern, and white minorities.

Both territories are made up of highly mobile people. In the U.S. Virgin Islands, some one-third of the population is foreign born, with most of the foreign immigrants coming from other Caribbean islands. The British Virgin Islands is highly dependent on immigrant labor in both its tourism and financial service fields—the latest figures suggest that more than 60 percent of the labor force in the BVI is foreign.

The presence of such a large number of immigrants has led to some degree of xenophobia in both the British and U.S. Virgin Islands, although it is stronger in the BVI. There are distinct "rungs" of the local society, beginning at the bottom with newly arrived immigrants and ending at the top with prominent local families whose ancestry is traceable in the Virgin Islands all the way to emancipation. Virgin Islanders are astute catalogers of people: they know, seemingly by instinct, who is "from here," who is "born here," who is "come here," and who is just passing through. Don't think for a moment that you can just blend in.

Virgin Islanders in both territories have strong ties with the United States, due largely to widespread outward migration that took place during the first 75 years of the 20th century. Many Virgin Islanders still travel to the United States to attend college—some do not return home. When you talk to a Virgin Islander, do not be surprised to learn that they are far more familiar with your country than you are with theirs. Although British Virgin Islanders are U.K. citizens, with the right to live and work in the U.K. and entire European Union, the destination of choice for British

Virgin Islanders seeking opportunity abroad remains the United States.

CULTURE
Daily Life

The tropical climate makes early morning a good time to get things done, and many households are up before sunrise. Many women rise early to prepare breakfast and lunch for their families. By 8 A.M. the sun is on full bore, and there is a general bustle toward school and work. Traditionally, children and working men and women returned home for lunch, and some still do. Increasingly, however, lunch is eaten out. For those unrestrained by rigid work or school commitments, midday makes the perfect time for a nap.

After-work time is golden. Between four and six, the heat of the day begins to subside, and the pressures of the day are past. This is the time when men stop "under the tree" to catch up with friends, or when neighbors linger to talk over the fence. School children, no longer concerned with keeping their uniforms clean, run ragged through the yard.

Darkness signifies the time to come home and settle in for the night. Virgin Islanders' belief in jumbies, evil spirits of the night, may have subsided in recent generations, but it has not gone completely. Evenings not spent at home may be spent playing sports or attending church group meetings or social events.

Saturdays are the traditional day for cleaning, cooking, washing, shopping, and general chores around the house. Most households try to get these things done in time for the Sunday Sabbath, when they go to church and spend the afternoon at home. Many families adhere to the tradition of Sunday dinner at home. Sunday afternoon is also the traditional time for family outings to the beach, playground, or ice cream shop.

Men and Women

On one hand, women in the Virgin Islands are ahead of their sisters in more "developed" countries. Because racist laws limited the rights of black men and women for centuries, women were never banned from voting, owning property, or obtaining an education because of their sex. During slavery, black women were expected to carry the same load as a man, and they did. After the end of slavery, women continued to work—and not just around the house. Women were farmers, laborers, fishers, and more.

When secondary education was introduced, girls were just as likely to go to school as boys. As a result, the first generation of educated local leaders included both men and women. Today, women are legislators, ministers, commissioners, judges, teachers, principals, and religious leaders. Although women have been elected to both territories' legislatures, a woman has not yet achieved the highest elected offices of governor or chief minister.

In recent years, women and girls have outachieved boys in secondary and tertiary education in the Virgin Islands, leading to concern that the education system unfairly favors girls. Indeed, boys are much more likely to drop out of school, fail, or be unemployed than girls. These trends have led some—men and women—to believe that women have actually gained the "upper hand" in Virgin Island society.

Despite the trappings of gender equality that abound in the public sphere, women still face inequality, particularly in their private lives. In the home, men and women often follow traditional male-female roles. Indeed, most men and women would probably agree that the man is the head of the household. Men have not embraced the notion of shared housework or, to a large extent, co-parenting. Neither have some men adopted the concept of monogamy.

Many couples live together and have children but do not marry. Having children out of wedlock is widespread and widely accepted (statistics from the British Virgin Islands show that 60 percent of births occur out of wedlock). Though an American term, the "baby mother" has existed for decades in the Virgin Islands. Now she has a name.

Infidelity on the part of men is widely accepted and practiced in the Virgin Islands. Married men have "inside children," born to their wife, and "outside children," born to their girlfriends. The language is telling: Women have children "for" a man rather than "with" him. Having many children with many women does not seem to hurt a man's reputation. In fact, all signs seem to indicate that the opposite is true. High-ranking government officials and popular politicians have well-known "outside children." Wives do not usually pursue divorce as a result of their husbands' infidelity. Being married brings a perceived elevation in status for a woman that many are reluctant to lose.

Inequality between men and women is about more than heartache or jealousy, however. Campaigns against domestic violence are only starting to gain traction in the islands—women who choose to leave abusive relationships still face an uphill battle for acceptance and support. The spread of HIV also makes marital infidelity a serious health issue for many women, for whom it is difficult to insist on condom use by their husbands.

Children

Virgin Islanders like and welcome children. Very few households do not know the presence of at least one child, grandchild, niece, or nephew. Traditionally children were raised by the whole community—neighbors freely disciplined other people's children, and any child knew they could get food, shelter, or help from any adult if they needed it. There is still a good deal of communal childrearing, although in many cases the community circle has shrunk to one's immediate and extended family and friends. "The family circle" is a phrase in common parlance.

Corporal punishment at home is common, although it is practiced in moderation and probably much less than it once was. Often the threat of the belt is enough to get a misbehaving child to do as they are told. In Virgin Islands culture, children are supposed to obey their parents at all times. Asking questions, talking back, or sharing their own opinion is considered undesirable, cheeky behavior. Children who are coaxed into conversations about their experiences, thoughts, and feelings are being spoiled.

Virgin Islanders are particularly aware of their children's behavior in public or with company and cannot understand why American and European parents are so unconcerned about their own rambunctious little ones.

Perceptions of Time

Island time is well known and well appreciated in the Virgin Islands. Very few things here start on time. Meetings start anywhere from 10 to 30 minutes late. Many offices and shops open later than their posted hours. Nighttime concerts or pageants are notorious, sometimes starting hours late.

If someone says they are coming "now" that means they are coming soon. If someone says they are coming "soon," look for them in a few minutes or hours. If someone says, "I'm coming to you," it means hold on, and I will take care of you in a few minutes. Impatience is an undesirable trait associated with Americans and Europeans.

Service in restaurants and shops runs on island time too. Unless you want to be perpetually annoyed during your vacation, just go with the flow. Maybe you will even start to appreciate the fact that just as no one else hurries, neither should you. Even if you can't adopt the island time mentality, don't try to fight it. Getting frustrated or angry does absolutely no good. If you are really in a hurry, simply inform the waitstaff right away and they will surely do what they can to speed things up.

There are some exceptions to the island time rule. If you get arrested and have to come to court, get there on time. Ferries and airplanes run generally on time. There are also individuals who are perpetually on time. If you have made arrangements with someone, try to find out if they are an on-time person or an island-time person.

Clothing

Virgin Islanders put considerable stock in their appearance. It is disrespectful, not to mention embarrassing, to show up in professional or religious environments without proper attire r without being properly groomed. Virgin Islanders wear their clothes well pressed and their shoes well shined.

Office attire tends to be conservative; the general trend toward casual office wear has not been accepted here. Church clothing is even more formal; many men wear suits and women don colorful and elaborate hats, with matching dresses and shoes. Casual functions, such as afternoon picnics and outdoor concerts, call for casual clothing: blue jeans and T-shirts, for example. Whenever you leave the house, however, you should look neat and clean. Many Virgin Islanders reserve shorts for the beach or sports field.

Few things offend a Virgin Islander more than seeing someone who is dressed inappropriately. They will let a slightly wrinkled shirt or scuffed shoes slide (but don't think they don't notice), but instances of gross fashion miscalculation are not forgiven easily. Bathing suits are not acceptable attire for town, for example. Shorts and a T-shirt are not appropriate for church.

Religion

Virgin Islanders are highly religious and churchgoing. Christian churches of nearly every persuasion exist in the Virgin Islands, although the Methodist, Moravian, Catholic, and Anglican have been here for the longest period of time. Statistics from the British Virgin Islands demonstrate this: of 20,000 churchgoers, 97 percent are Christian. Of those, 37 percent are Methodist, 19 percent are Anglican, and 12 percent are Catholic.

There is no attempt at separating church and state in the British Virgin Islands. Prayers open Legislative Council meetings; school days begin with prayer; and references to God are common in political discourse.

In the U.S. Virgin Islands, which are governed by U.S. laws including the separation of church and state doctrine, religion plays a less obvious but no less influential role in daily life.

There are small groups of non-Christians in both territories. Arab immigrants from Palestine and Syria form an Islamic society, while Indian immigrants from Guyana and Trinidad practice Hinduism. There are also some Rastafarians. These groups do not suffer outright religious discrimination, although they are rendered nearly invisible by the sheer size and influence of the Christian community.

Food

The food of the islands is influenced by the diverse cultures that have settled there, as well as the meats, fruits, and vegetables that are widely available. Traditional Virgin Islands dishes include **grilled or fried fish.** Grilled fish is often cooked with onions, peppers, and other seasonings wrapped in aluminum foil over a grill. Fried fish is traditionally cooked in hot fat over a charcoal fire. Often, you are served a whole fish (including the head). **Fungi,** a side dish made from cornmeal and not unlike polenta, is the traditional accompaniment to fish. More common side dishes today include potato salad, coleslaw, corn, and peas and rice.

Saltfish is another island favorite. Made from salt cod, saltfish is a pungent hash of flaked fish seasoned with onions and peppers. It is often served for breakfast, or cooked inside patties or **pâtés**—fried, meat-stuffed bread eaten for breakfast. **Whelk** and **conch** are two more popular seafoods. Whelk are generally smaller and more tender, and their flesh is darker than conch, which is white. Both shellfish are tenderized by pounding or pressure-cooking until they are soft. Conch in butter sauce is probably its most popular presentation; conch soup, made with dumplings and vegetables, is also popular.

Virgin Islanders also like to eat meat. Goat meat, called mutton, is the most commonly served red meat. **Stewed mutton** is flavorful and tender. **Goat water** is filling goat soup, often served late at night. **Oxtail,** which tastes like beef stew, is another popular red meat. **Souse** is made of pig's head and tail. Pork, served roasted and stewed, is also popular. Chicken is very popular and is consumed in many forms, including stewed,

Conch is a favorite shellfish, often served in butter sauce.

barbecued, and curried. **Chicken palau** is chicken cooked with seasonings and rice.

Vegetables and fruits are an important part of the Virgin Islands diet, but only as side dishes. Vegetarianism is not widespread, except among the Rastafarian minority. Local fruits are used to make drinks, including **guavaberry liqueur,** a sweet Christmas drink; **sorrel; soursop,** made using milk; **hibiscus,** made from the petals of hibiscus flowers; and **maubi,** made from the bark of a local tree. In addition, fruit punch made from guava, mango, passion fruit, pineapple, orange, and other fruits is popular.

Bananas and plantains are used a lot in cooking. **Green bananas** can be steamed and served as a starchy side dish. **Plantains** are fried or boiled and served with fish and other dishes. White **sweet potatoes,** often served boiled and sliced, are sweet like yams but much more starchy. **Pumpkin** is used to make delicious pumpkin soup, pumpkin rice, pumpkin bread, and pumpkin fritters. Another traditional soup is **kallaloo,** made from greens.

The most common grain is probably rice, and it is often cooked with pigeon peas, beans,

or seasonings. In the British Virgin Islands **peas and rice** are often cooked with a little bit of sugar. *Johnnycakes* are discs of fried hot bread, served alongside fish or chicken or just eaten as a snack. *Coconut bread* is a round, flat, mildly sweet loaf. **Fritters** of all kinds are popular, including pumpkin fritters, conch fritters, and banana fritters.

With the influx of travelers, gourmet cooks and immigrants, the cuisine of the Virgin Islands has changed. Besides the American influence of fast food and convenience food, island eating has been influenced by the Caribbean people who have migrated to the Virgin Islands. **Curries** and **rotis,** curried food wrapped in a chickpea and flour tortilla, have been imported from the southern Caribbean island of Trinidad. **Jerk-seasoned chicken and pork** is a Jamaican standard. Fried **flying fish** is from Barbados. Many traditional Puerto Rican recipes are highly seasoned; pork is a favorite of the Spanish tradition.

In addition, talented cooks have taken the traditional seasonings, flavors, and cooking methods of the Virgin Islands and created so

FISH, VIRGIN ISLANDS STYLE

Fish is an important part of the Virgin Islands diet. Here are two popular ways to prepare fish in the islands:

Creole Fish

4 lbs. fish (whole, steak, or fillet)

1/2 cup tomatoes, chopped

1/2 cup green pepper, chopped

1/3 cup lemon juice

1 Tablespoon oil

2 teaspoons salt

1 teaspoon minced onion

1 teaspoon fresh thyme

dash of pepper

pepper sauce (to taste)

Clean fish and preheat oven to 500 degrees. Place fish in a single layer in a baking dish. Stir together remaining ingredients and spoon over fish. Bake for 5-8 minutes, or until fish is tender and flakes easily with a fork. (Serves 10)

Steamed fish

1 whole fish, or fillet

salt and pepper (or native seasoning)

1/2 small onion, sliced

2 Tablespoons red pepper, diced

2 Tablespoons green pepper, diced

1 clove garlic, minced

minced hot pepper to taste

1 sprig fresh thyme

2 Tablespoons butter, cut into small pieces

Preheat oven to 450 degrees, or prepare a hot charcoal grill. Clean and season fish with salt and pepper, or native seasoning. Prepare other ingredients and set aside. Cut a piece of aluminum foil about four times the size of the fish.

Place half of butter pieces in the center of the foil. Place half of vegetables and seasonings on top of butter, and then put fish on top of this. Cover fish with rest of butter pieces and vegetables. Tightly close foil. Place on baking sheet in hot oven and bake until soft, 15-20 minutes, depending on thickness of fish. Can also be cooked over grill, turning halfway through.

Carefully remove fish from foil (the hot steam can burn you) and serve with seasoned rice, plantains, and sweet potatoes.

---

phisticated dishes in many of the best island restaurants. While they may not be traditional, these dishes are by all means Caribbean.

It is easy to find restaurants that serve traditional island food, but most do not cater to tourists. Nevertheless, they will be delighted to see visitors who are interested in tasting local foods.

Language

English is the predominant language of the islands, but some islanders speak Spanish. The Virgin Islands English dialect is at first very difficult for many visitors to understand, particularly when it is being spoken between Virgin Islanders. Listen carefully, though, and you will find yourself picking up more and more words. Many Virgin Islanders, especially those whose work brings them into contact with visitors, will slow down for your benefit.

Listen as well for dialects of other Caribbean islands. Each island has its own dialect, and once your ear becomes accustomed, you will be able to pick up the difference between, for example, a Jamaica and a Barbados dialect.

One of the most beautiful things about the language of the Virgin Islands is the colorful metaphors and sayings. Virgin Islanders are skilled at metaphor and suggestion. They are excellent orators and storytellers.

WORDS OF WISDOM

Virgin Islanders use proverbs to communicate subtle and straightforward advice. Here's a sample of some common proverbs:

God Almighty never shut he eye. (God is always watching.)

When rat see cat he never laugh. (Don't take those who can cause you injury lightly.)

Every fool got he own sense. (To each his own.)

Empty bag can't stand up. (A weak or virtueless person is but an empty sack.)

If wind don't blow, you won't see the fowl's bottom. (An ill wind can do good.)

Time longer than twine. (Time will tell.)

Bush have ears; long grass carry news. (Gossip and scandal spread in mysterious ways.)

If you play with a dog, he'll lick your mouth. (Familiarity breeds contempt.)

Trial make mention. (Merit comes to he who overcomes adversity.)

Sleep steal me. (I overslept.)

ESSENTIALS

Getting There and Around

GETTING THERE

Although they are surrounded by sea, most travelers will get to the Virgin Islands by air. With the exception of cruise ships and a twice-monthly passenger ferry from Puerto Rico, no passenger ships sail regularly to the islands. Mariners with their own yachts, plus time and sailing experience, can include the Virgin Islands on a tour of the Caribbean.

From North America

Major American airlines provide nonstop service to St. Thomas in the U.S. Virgin Islands, although the nonstop service tapers off some during the summer months. **American Airlines** (284/495-2559, U.S. toll free 800/474-4884), **Delta Airlines** (U.S. toll free 800/221-1212), **U.S. Airways** (U.S. toll free 800/622-1015), **United Airlines** (U.S. toll free 800/864-8331), and **Continental Airlines** (787/793-7373) have nonstop service from New York, Newark, Baltimore, Atlanta, and Miami and other hubs.

If your final destination is St. Croix or Tortola, you can fly to St. Thomas, and then transfer to another plane or a ferry to your final destination. Or route your trip through San Juan and transfer to a short connecting flight

© SUSANNA HENIGHAN

to your final destination. In many cases, the final leg from San Juan to your destination is offered through a code-share agreement with a regional airline: U.S. Airways has teamed up with **Caribbean Sun** (284/495-1711, U.S. toll free 866/864-6267, Caribbean toll free 800/744-7827, www.flycaribbeanstar.com); Continental is partnered with **Cape Air** (U.S. toll free 800/352-0714, www.flycapeair.com); and American Airlines works with **American Eagle** (www.aa.com).

In recent years, the so-called low-cost airlines have started to make headway into the Caribbean flying market, San Juan to be specific. **Jetblue** (800/538-2583, www.jetblue.com) has daily direct service from Dulles in Washington, D.C., and JFK in New York to San Juan. **ATA** (800/435-9282, www.ata.com) has flights from San Juan to hubs in Orlando and Chicago Midway. **Spirit Airlines** (800/772-7117) flies daily from Fort Lauderdale and Orlando to San Juan, with connections possible to many other American cities. Finally, **Independence Air** (800/359-3594, www.flyi.com) has flights from San Juan to Dulles in Washington, D.C.

Airfares vary considerably by season; average round-trip fares from major American cities to St. Thomas, St. Croix, or Tortola (Beef Island) range from $300 to $800. A fare below $400 round-trip is a good deal. The best way to find cheap fares is to start at the online search engines like www.cheaptickets.com and www.orbitz.com. Check the low-fare carriers too. Fare sales are common during the summer and shoulder season (March–October). Expect to pay premium fares to travel around Christmas or New Year's.

From Europe

British Airways (U.K. 0870/850-9850, www.ba.com) and **Virgin Atlantic** (U.K. 0870/380-2007, Caribbean toll free 800/744-7477, www.virgin-atlantic.com) fly from the U.K. to Caribbean hubs. British Airways flies daily from London-Gatwick to Barbados and five days a week from Gatwick to Antigua. Virgin Atlantic flies daily from London-Heathrow to Barbados and three days a week from Heathrow to Antigua.

From the Caribbean

It is very easy to get from San Juan to the Virgin Islands. **Caribbean Sun** (284/495-1711, U.S. toll free 866/864-6267, Caribbean toll free 800/744-7827, www.flycaribbeanstar.com); Cape Air (U.S. toll free 800/352-0714, www.flycapeair.com), **American Eagle** (www.aa.com), and **Air Sunshine** (284/495-8900, www.airsunshine.com) fly between San Juan and St. Thomas, St. Croix, and Tortola.

LIAT (888/844-5428, www.liatairline.com) and **Caribbean Sun** (800/744-7827, www.flysca.com) fly from Caribbean hubs in Antigua and Barbados, plus other islands, to the Virgin Islands.

By Ferry

The only ferry to the Virgin Islands departs from Fajardo, Puerto Rico, once a week. **Transportation Services of St. John** (340/776-6282, $60 one-way, $100 round-trip) runs the ferry, which departs Fajardo on Sundays at 1 P.M. It leaves St. John on Fridays at 7 A.M. and St. Thomas on Fridays at 7:30 A.M. Advance reservations are required.

Cruises

St. Thomas is one of the most popular cruise ship ports of call in the world. Nearly every cruise that passes through the eastern Caribbean stops at Charlotte Amalie. Major cruise lines also call on Road Town, Tortola, but with considerably less frequency. The mega-ships of **Carnival Cruise Lines, Celebrity Cruise Lines, Holland America Cruise Line,** and **Costa Cruise Lines** are among the most frequent visitors.

Several smaller ships also call in the Virgin Islands. **Arabella** (800/395-1343, www.cruisearabella.com) cruises around St. Thomas, St. John, and the British Virgin Islands every winter with no more than 42 people. The **American Canadian Caribbean Line** (www.acci-smallships.com) has no more than 100 passengers on its *Grande Caribe,* which cruises the Eastern Caribbean, including the Virgin Islands, in the winter. You could also check out **Seabourn Cruise Line** (800/929-9391, www.seabourn.com), noted for luxury, and **Star Clippers** (305/442-0550, www.starclippers.com), which offers a "Treasure Islands" cruise that visits many of the Virgin Islands.

GETTING AROUND
By Air
Flying is a fun, fast, but expensive way to get around the Virgin Islands. There are airports on St. Thomas, St. Croix, Tortola (Beef Island), and Anegada. In addition, seaplanes fly between San Juan, St. Thomas, St. Croix, and Virgin Gorda, and helicopters can fly to many more of the islands, including the private island retreats.

In addition to being fast and efficient, flying around the islands is beautiful. Any of the charter airlines in the islands will agree to take you up for a sightseeing flight.

Charter airline companies include **Fly BVI** (284/495-1747); **Island Helicopters** (284/499-2663); **Caribbean Wings** (284/495-6000); **Air Culebra** (284/496-8962 or 787/268-6951); and **Island Birds** (284/495-2002).

By Boat
Boats are the most popular and most natural way to get around the Virgin Islands. Visitors can build their whole vacation around a boat by chartering a sailboat. Land-based visitors can take day sails to out islands, rent a powerboat for the day, or catch an interisland ferry or water taxi to reach their destination.

By Taxi
Taxis are widely available on all the islands and can be a good way to get around if you are nervous about driving on the left or if you don't want to move around too much. Taxis tend to be expensive, however, and if you want to do a lot of exploring on land you would be better off renting a car and driving yourself.

Rental Cars and Motorcycles
Rental cars are available on all the islands. Unfortunately, if you want to island hop, you will

Sailing charter boats is one of the best ways to experience the Virgin Islands.

SETTING SAIL

Sailing is one of the most popular activities in the Virgin Islands, and a charter yacht vacation is one of the best ways to experience the Virgin Islands. Trade winds, mild weather, and generally calm conditions make the Virgin Islands favorable for sailing. Sailing is also the best and most natural way to visit many of the smaller "out islands" that so perfectly embody the spirit of the Virgin Islands.

The British Virgin Islands is the epicenter of the charter yacht industry – some two-thirds of overnight visitors to the BVI come to stay aboard sailboats. Tortola is the home base of the greatest number of charter yacht companies. There are also a handful of charter companies on St. Thomas, but most St. Thomas charterers head to St. John and the British Virgin Islands anyway.

Types of Charter Vacations

There are three basic types of charter yacht vacation: a sailing school experience, crewed charter, or bareboat charter.

Sailing school experiences combine a charter vacation with sailing instruction – you can choose your desired intensity of instruction.

Crewed charters are like villas on the ocean: they come with a full crew, usually a captain, cook, and mate, who take care of all the work. Your only responsibility is to relax and say what you want to do for the day, although if that even seems too much, the crew can plan a pleasant itinerary for you. While you can book crewed charters directly, the traditional method of booking has always been through a broker, who maintains contact with all the crewed charter boats in the Virgin Islands and can match you with a boat that fits your budget and your interests.

Bareboat charters are probably the most popular kind of charter vacation in the Virgin Islands. Bareboating simply means chartering without a crew, although you can hire a skipper if you want to simplify your vacation or don't meet the requirements to skipper your own boat. Charter companies require a sailing résumé on which you detail and demonstrate any courses or sailing experience you have. You will

also need to demonstrate your skills after you arrive. Don't try to oversell your skills – feeling underprepared will ruin your vacation. In some cases, a charter company will require you to hire a skipper for the first day or so to bring you up to a level they are comfortable with.

Bareboat charters come fully equipped to sail, and most charter companies offer an array of provisioning choices, ranging from a full provisioning service (they shop for you according to a list you provide) to none at all (you do your own shopping). You can also choose boats that come equipped with water sports toys (kayaks, snorkels, floaties, etc.).

When to Charter

There are significant seasonal considerations when planning a sailing vacation. The best and most consistent time for sailing in the Virgin Islands is winter (November–April), when winds average 15 to 20 knots from the northeast. The Christmas Winds of December and January are the best of the year.

In spring and summer the winds slack off to 10-18 knots, although this can still be a nice time to sail. It is best to avoid chartering August–October, when the weather tends to be unsettled and the chances of a hurricane are greatest.

Costs

The cost of a bareboat charter is comparable to the cost of renting a villa or a moderately high-priced resort. A crewed charter is equivalent to a luxury resort.

The high season cost of a 35-foot two-person bareboat averages about $3,000 per week, although you can pay $2,000-$3,500 depending on the age of the boat and add-ons. A 40-foot catamaran that sleeps four will cost about $5,000 per week. In summer, the rates go down 20–40 percent.

Additional costs to consider include provisioning, whether you pay for the company to do it or do it yourself, insurance, and the cost of hiring a skipper ($125 and up a day) and cook ($125 and up per day) if you choose.

Crewed yachts are more expensive, but you don't have to worry about add-ons – food, crew, and service are included. Expect a two-person crewed charter to cost about $5,000 for a week; a four- or six-person charter will cost between $8,000 and $12,000.

Booking a Charter

If a charter yacht vacation sounds good to you, contact any of the charter companies listed below. For information on crewed charters, the best sources of information are the **Charter Yacht Society of the BVI** (tel./fax 284/494-6017, www.bvicrewedyachts.com), which keeps a listing of all active crewed yachts, prices, and contact information. For the U.S. Virgin Islands, contact the **Virgin Islands Charterboat League** (340/774-39440). You can also contact a charter yacht broker. Reputable brokers include: **Swift Yacht Charters** (508/647-1554, fax 508/647-1556, www.swiftyachts.com) and **Ed Hamilton and Co.** (207/882-7855, U.S. toll free 800/621-7855, fax 207/882-7851, www.ed-hamilton.com).

Charter Companies

Tortola is home to the greatest number of charter boat companies. St. Thomas also has a few. In choosing between the two bases, consider the tradeoffs: St. Thomas is generally easier and quicker to get to, and groceries and other supplies are marginally cheaper. However, you have to sail for several hours and clear BVI Customs and Immigration before you reach the most popular cruising ground. Meanwhile, flying to Tortola may require an extra leg, and provisions are generally more expensive. However, when you set out on day one, you are nearby the best cruising attractions.

BVI Charter Companies

The largest charter yacht company on Tortola is **The Moorings** (Wickham's Cay II, 284/494-2331, U.S. 727/535-1446, U.S. toll free 888/952-8420, www.moorings.com). Its fleet features 32- to 52-foot monohulls and catamarans with between two and five cabins. Yachts in its exclusive line are less than two years old; the club line features older boats.

Sunsail (Hodge's Creek Marina, East End,

284/495-4740, fax 284/495-1767, U.S. toll free 888/350-3568, www.sunsail.com) is the second biggest fish in the BVI charter yacht market.

Smaller charter companies include **BVI Yacht Charters** (Inner Harbour Marina, Road Town, 284/494-4289, fax 284/494-6552, U.S. toll free 888/615-4006, www.caribbeancruisingvacations.com); **Conch Charters** (Fort Burt Marina, Road Town, 284/494-4868, fax. 284/494-5793, U.S. toll free 800/521-1989, www.conchcharters.com); **Voyage Charters** (Soper's Hole Marina, 284/494-0740, fax 284/494-0741, www.voyagecharters.com); and **Tortola Marine Management** (Road Reef, 284/494-2751 or 800/633-0155,. www.sailtmm.com).

Some of the lowest rates are found at **North South Yacht Vacations** (Nanny Cay Marina, 284/494-0096, U.S. 905/822-9146, U.S. toll free 800/387-4964, fax 284/494-7543, www.nsyv.com), which offers monohulls, catamarans and power yachts.

Several companies specialize in catamarans only. These include owner-operated **Barecat** (Soper's Hole Marina, tel./fax 284/495-1979, U.S. toll free 800/296-5287, www.barecat.com) and **The Catamaran Company** (Nanny Cay Marina, 284/494-6661, www.catamarans.com).

All the companies listed above offer bareboat or crewed charters. Most will also arrange for a sailing instructor, skipper, cook, and provisioning service.

USVI Charter Companies

CYOA Yacht Charters (Frenchtown Marina, 340/777-9690, U.S. toll free 800/944-2962) has a fleet of monohull, catamaran, and power yachts.

Locally owned and operated, **Island Yachts** (Red Hook, 340/775-6666, U.S. toll free 800/524-2019) gets high marks for its personalized service.

Other charter companies are **Regency Yacht Charters** (Estate Nazareth, 340/776-5950, U.S. toll free 800/524-7676), a worldwide charter yacht company, and **VIP Power and Sail Yacht Charters** (Compass Point Marina, 340/774-9224, U.S. toll free 866/847-9224).

have to deal with different car rental agencies (and often pay a different rental price) on each island. For the greatest comfort, rent a four-wheel-drive vehicle, which is handy for negotiating hills and unpaved mountain roads, especially on St. John, Tortola, and Virgin Gorda.

For the best rates, and to be sure that you'll have a car at all, reserve your rental car early, especially on small islands like Anegada, Jost Van Dyke, and Virgin Gorda, which have a relatively small rental fleet. Well-known U.S. car rental companies including Avis and Hertz have shops throughout the U.S. and British Virgin Islands. Budget and Thrifty have shops in the U.S. Virgin Islands.

Hitchhiking

Many residents catch rides in the Virgin Islands, but few tourists do. Hitchhiking is safer, and more widespread, in the British islands. It is not safe on St. Thomas or St. Croix.

Hitchhikers do not stick their thumbs out in the Virgin Islands. Instead, they simply stand on the side of the road and wait. Sometimes, they raise their arm out in front of them to show that they are looking for a ride.

Visas and Officialdom

U.S. VIRGIN ISLANDS
Visas

Travelers who do not qualify for visa-free entry to the United States will need a non-immigrant visa to visit the United States. Check with the nearest U.S. embassy to find out if you need a visa to travel to the U.S., or check the U.S. State Department website at travel.gov. Travelers from most European countries, Canada, and Australia do not need a nonimmigrant visa.

Taxes

There is no sales tax in the U.S. Virgin Islands, but hotels and guesthouses levy an 8 percent hotel tax on rooms. There is also a $2.50 per day charge on car rentals.

Residents of the islands fill out a federal tax return but pay the bill to the local tax bureau, which uses the income to finance local government.

Customs

The U.S. Customs and Border Protection Agency considers the U.S. Virgin Islands outside the customs territory of the United States mainland. This means that you will have to clear customs before you board your aircraft in St. Thomas or St. Croix, and that you will probably have to go through customs again when you arrive at your next stop in the U.S., whether it's Puerto Rico or the mainland. Fill your customs declaration form in completely and accurately, and you should have no trouble.

U.S. residents, including children, can bring back up to $1,200 in goods duty-free from the U.S. Virgin Islands. Additionally, $1,000 in goods can be imported at a flat rate of 5 percent, and you can mail an unlimited number of gifts up to $100 in value, excluding perfume, liquor, and tobacco products. U.S. residents over 21 can bring five bottles of liquor home, or six if one is locally produced in the Virgin Islands.

If you arrive via private boat from an international destination (including the British Virgin Islands), you must proceed directly to a port of entry to clear U.S. Customs and Border Protection. Ports of entry are at Charlotte Amalie, St. Thomas; Gallow Bay, St. Croix; and Cruz Bay, St. John. Hours are 8 A.M.–noon and 1 P.M.–4:30 P.M. daily. Telephone 340/774-6755 for more information. If you arrive after hours, raise your quarantine flag, stay aboard, and report to Customs as soon as it opens the next day.

Permits and Licenses

There are no work permit requirements in the U.S. Virgin Islands. As long as you are legal to live and work in the United States, you can do so in the U.S. Virgin Islands.

No cruising permit is required for boats in the Virgin Islands for less than six months. If you plan to stay longer, you will need to register your boat with the Department of Planning and Natural Resources (340/774-3320).

Bribes

Don't embarrass yourself by trying to bribe officials in the U.S. Virgin Islands. It is insulting to the officers, and you may well find yourself in serious trouble for doing it.

BRITISH VIRGIN ISLANDS

All visitors except Americans and Canadians must have a passport to enter the BVI. U.S. and Canadian citizens can enter using a birth certificate and government-issued ID. However, beginning on January 1, 2007, all travelers, including U.S. citizens, need a passport to re-enter the United States from the Caribbean. This means that American visitors to the British Virgin Islands are not required to have a passport to get in, but they need one to get back home. Canadians who have to go through the United States to get home also need a passport.

Visas

Visitors are allowed to stay in the BVI for up to one month in the first instance. Further tourist visas must be applied for once you are here. All visitors should have a return ticket home and prearranged accommodations.

Nationals of 91 different countries including China, Cuba, Guyana, Haiti, Russia, and Suriname need to apply for a visa at the local British Embassy before traveling to the territory. Americans, Canadians, Mexicans, and Western Europeans do not need a visa. Call the BVI Passport Office (284/468-3701 ext. 3038) for complete visa information.

Work Permits

All non-belongers must have a work permit to work in the BVI. British citizens are not exempt from this requirement. Work permits must be applied for by your employer while you are outside of the territory. In other words, it is not okay to come to the BVI, look for work, and apply for a work permit while you are supposedly on vacation. If you make the mistake of telling the immigration officer that you are looking for a job, you might very well be on the next plane home.

If you are interested in working in the BVI, find a job first. Vacancies are listed in the local papers. Once you are hired, you and your employer will have to navigate the formidable maze of labor and immigration officials in order to get a work permit and entry permit. Work permits are issued for one-year periods and must be renewed. While you are on a work permit, you cannot work for anyone else.

Taxes

There is no income tax in the BVI, although a payroll tax functions much like a flat income tax would. Employees' annual salaries over $7,500 are taxed at 8 percent. At the same time, employers pay 2–6 percent of their total payroll in taxes, depending on the size of the business.

There is no sales tax, but the government charges a 7 percent hotel tax, which is added to hotel bills, often along with a service charge. Most hotels do not include the tax in their published rates. There is also a departure tax of $5 by sea, $20 by air, and $7 for cruise ship passengers.

Customs

Customs duties are one of the reasons why goods and services are so expensive in the BVI. Duties range from zero to 20 percent, depending on the good and the purpose for which it is being imported. Most goods are charged a 10 percent customs duty. Everything coming into the country is subject to customs duty, including mail-order items and gifts. Residents returning to the BVI after more than 72 hours away are allowed the paltry sum of $50 duty-free. A retailer bringing items in for resale will pay the same customs duty as people bringing the same item in for themselves.

RASTAS WELCOME

From 1980 until 2003, Rastafarians and hippies were banned from entering the British Virgin Islands. The Legislative Council approved the ban in 1980 on the urging of Ralph T. O'Neal, then the minister in charge of immigration, in response to the growing popularity of Rastafarianism in the region and reports that Rastas and hippies had taken to living on beaches on Tortola and stealing fruit.

The immigration ordinance required that the "persons commonly known as Rastas and persons commonly known as hippies" be denied entry unless they had previous written permission from the minister for immigration.

The Rasta Law, as it became known, was roundly criticized by many within the community and outside of it. The territory was embarrassed when the late poet Audrey Lorde and a traveling companion of actor Morgan Freeman were turned away because of the law. Many African-Americans argued that it was racist, and human rights organizations criticized it as discriminatory. Immigration officers with no real guidance on how to enforce the law often simply saw it as a ban on people with dreadlocks.

Under growing public pressure, Ralph T. O'Neal, now chief minister, in 1999 commissioned a public opinion survey on the law. The results were not released until 2003, when the opposition National Democratic Party was elected. The survey found most islanders opposed the law.

Soon after the election, the new chief minister, Dr. Orlando Smith, announced that the Rasta Law had been rescinded.

There has been no massive influx of Rastafarians into the BVI since the ban was lifted, but British Virgin Islanders are pleased to have wiped this discriminatory stain from their territory's image.

Permits and Licenses

Charter boats pay a special charter boat permit fee to the Customs Department. The fee is $4 per person per day for boats based outside of the BVI and $2 per person per day for BVI-based boats December 1–April 30. The rate for BVI-based boats goes down to $0.75 per person per day during the summer.

You must obtain a fishing license before you can fish in the BVI. Fishing licenses are obtained from the Ministry of Natural Resources and Labour (284/468-3701 ext. 2147). Many crewed charter boats, plus all fishing charters, have the necessary license already. If you want to fish, your best bet is to sign up with one of these operators or take part in a fishing tournament.

Bribes

Offering a bribe is a highly disrespectful move that will backfire on you. Police, customs, and immigration officers do not accept bribes and will not welcome your suggestion that they do.

Tips for Travelers

CONDUCT

Yes, you are in the islands, but you should still follow basic common sense and etiquette.

Etiquette

Good manners are an essential feature of daily interactions in the Virgin Islands. The only way to begin a conversation with anyone is to first wish them a "good morning," "good afternoon," or "good night." Indeed, these should be the first words out of your mouth when you enter a room with others already inside, or walk up to a group of people. Of course, if the roles are reversed the only correct way to reply to someone else's "good morning" is to echo their words. Only then can you begin to talk of something else.

In some situations, it is also good manners to ask how the person is, or offer an observation about the weather before delving directly to the business at hand. This may not be appreciated by the immigration officer who has a whole line of people to deal with, but in slightly less congested situations, it is the right thing to do.

Very mannerly people will look you in the eye when they meet you on the street and wish you a good day, regardless of whether they know you or not. This is a delightful practice, and if you do it you will soon be overflowing with love for yourself, the people you meet, and the day ahead.

Probing questions are considered rude. You may very well wonder where your hostess lives, whether she went to school, if she has any children, or whether she is married, but for heaven's sake, don't ask her. Virgin Islanders cherish their privacy and resent your intrusion into things that do not concern you. If you really cannot bear not to know, then learn the very Virgin Islandish art of careful observation and listening.

Styles of Communication

Virgin Islanders like to joke with each other and have developed very thick skins for this very

purpose. Friends who meet each other on the street will immediately start giving each other a hard time about whatever comes to mind. If a barb is thrown your way, you are expected to respond in such a careful way as to throw an equally stinging barb back to the other person. This kind of exchange has nothing to do with embarrassing or insulting your friends, but is merely the way in which people interact. Even business conversations usually begin with a few moments of lightheartedness.

Body Language

Acknowledge people when you come into contact with them, either with a handshake, nod, or eye contact. A smile is appreciated, but don't take it too far. Virgin Islanders appreciate sincere friendliness, not fakeness. Stand at least a few feet away from the person you are speaking to.

Terms of Address

In keeping with the generally conservative and mannerly culture of the Virgin Islands, courtesy titles are used frequently and extensively. Until you are told otherwise, it is best to call people Mr. or Mrs. so-and-so. Police, immigration, and customs officials are often Officer so-and-so. Lawyers are Attorney so-and-so, and the list goes on.

On the opposite end of the spectrum from courtesy titles, nicknames are commonly used and generally lots of fun. Some people are better known by their nickname than their given name. The sports field, the ocean, and the playground are places especially conducive to nicknames, although those that are particularly evocative seem to find a foothold in every setting.

Table Manners

Virgin Islanders are not hung up on table manners. You would no doubt feel awkward slurping your food at a fine dining restaurant, but that has more to do with the restaurant itself than the country in which it is set.

While Virgin Islanders do not employ strictures about knives, forks, and elbows on the table, they do like to be left alone while they are eating. If you happen upon someone enjoying their lunch, don't interrupt them and don't expect them to stop eating to attend to you.

Drugs

Both the U.S. and British Virgin Islands have stiff drug laws. Marijuana, cocaine, and other drugs are illegal here. The islands are also a major drug transshipment point—for your own safety and health, don't get mixed up with drugs while you are in the islands.

OPPORTUNITIES FOR EMPLOYMENT
U.S. Virgin Islands

The tourism industry generates opportunities for employment in the U.S. Virgin Islands. Foodservice, retail sales, hotel management, and the marine industry are the areas where you will find the greatest number of jobs available. Salaries are not always generous, particularly in the service industry, and the cost of living in the islands can be quite high.

British Virgin Islands

In addition to tourism, job opportunities exist in the financial services industry. Accountants, lawyers, and those with special knowledge of offshore finance will find it quite easy to land a job in the islands. In tourism, opportunities exist particularly in the marine fields: sailors, diving professionals, and those with experience servicing boats are in demand.

Remember that you will have to apply for and receive a work permit (via your employer) before you can start work in the BVI. The application must take place while you are off-island. Work permits are issued only when the employer can demonstrate that there are no belongers qualified or interested in the job.

OPPORTUNITIES FOR STUDY
U.S. Virgin Islands

The University of the Virgin Islands (www .uvi.edu) is a four-year, accredited university with campuses on St. Thomas and St. Croix. Founded in 1963 as the College of the Virgin Islands, UVI offers both bachelor's and master's degree opportunities.

British Virgin Islands

H. Lavity Stoutt Community College (www .hlscc.edu.vg) is a two-year college founded in 1990. In addition to earning associate's degrees, HLSCC students can earn bachelor's degrees in certain fields through partnerships between HLSCC and other four-year institutions, including UVI. The New England Culinary Institute (www.necibvi.com) has a satellite school attached to HLSCC, and students enroll in a two-year course leading to an associate's degree in the culinary arts.

The University of the West Indies also has a satellite school on Tortola.

SPECIAL GROUPS
Women

Women are sometimes the target of harassment in the Virgin Islands, and women traveling alone should always be aware of their surroundings. Don't walk alone at night in town, and certainly don't try to catch a ride alone at any time. Catcalls, often in the form of a hiss, are common. The best way of handling them is to simple ignore the offender and walk on. Engaging him in a conversation, or even showing your displeasure, will probably just make the situation worse. If you feel threatened, walk quickly to a well-lit or busy area.

Women dining or drinking alone are a prime target for harassment. Bring a book and develop a very cold demeanor if you really want to be left alone. Likewise, a woman alone on the dance floor is a magnet for men. Often, it seems like it does not matter how many times you tell a man you do not want to dance with him. This can easily spoil a night of dancing. Some men consider all female visitors to be in the market for a steamy West Indian vacation romance. If you're not, don't let anyone think you are.

Gay and Lesbian

Homosexuality is not widely accepted in the Virin Islands, and many islanders are extremely homophobic. But where gay Virgin Islanders face an uphill battle for acceptance, gay and lesbian travelers are tolerated. For the warmest welcome and greatest freedom, gay and lesbian travelers should first consider St. Croix, which has several openly gay-friendly hotels and nightspots.

Virgin Islanders everywhere will turn a blind eye to your sexuality as long as you let them, so it is best to avoid open demonstrations of affection and obvious indications of your sexuality. Don't ask, don't tell is the unspoken and unwritten social contract for gays and lesbians in the islands.

In the British Virgin Islands, attitudes towards homosexuality were aired openly in 1999, when the British government mandated the removal of anti-sodomy laws from the books. Despite the fact that the law had never been used in a prosecution, public outcry was loud, vociferous, and, in some quarters, hateful. The outcry passed, the law was changed, and thousands of gay folks have visited in peace since.

Travelers with Disabilities

The U.S. Virgin Islands, which are governed by the Americans with Disabilities Act, are much better equipped for disabled travelers than the British Virgin Islands. Even so, getting around the islands will not be easy for those with physical disabilities. Many shops, restaurants, and hotels are not designed for wheelchairs, and even those hotels that claim to be accessible may not meet your needs. Always call the hotel directly and explain your exact needs before booking a room. Once you arrive on-island, do not be shy to speak up about whatever you need; hotel, restaurant, and shop staff members are normally very accommodating and will help to overcome whatever accessibility challenges exist.

The Cyril E. King Airport on St. Thomas uses a lift to transport wheelchairs from the plane to the tarmac. Accessible and affordable transportation is available through **Dial-A-Ride** (340/776-1277, fax 340/777-5383), but call at least a week ahead to arrange for an airport pick-up (don't expect taxis to accommodate a wheelchair).

St. John's **Estate Concordia** (www.maho .com) has pioneered accessible design through a partnership with the Rhode Island School of Design, which designed four accessible units at this eco-camp. Estate Concordia owner Stanley Selengut and the design experts are now working with the local government to improve accessibility around the island.

A good option for disabled travelers is a cruise. A 2005 Supreme Court ruling requires all cruise lines that operate in the United States, including those that are registered in other jurisdictions, to adhere to the Americans with Disabilities Act. Some cruise lines were already catering to disabled passengers; **Princess Cruises** (800/ PRINCESS, www.princess.com) and **Royal Caribbean Cruise Line** (U.S. toll free 866/562-7625, www.royalcaribbean.com) have received good marks from disabled travelers.

You can reach the TTY/TDD call relay operator in the U.S. Virgin Islands by dialing 800/440-8477. Gimp on the Go has a detailed review of St. John on the website (www.gimponthego.com) and www.allabilities.com includes links to other disabled travel resources. **Connie George Travel Agency** (Glenolden, Penn., 610/532-0998, U.S. toll free 800/532-0998, www.cgta.com) specializes in planning trips in the islands for disabled visitors.

Seniors

Seniors can and do travel to the Virgin Islands in great numbers. Don't expect senior discounts, however. **Elderhostel** (toll free 877/426-8056, www.elderhostel.org) organizes one or two trips per year in both the British and U.S. Virgin Islands, often focusing on historic preservation. The **American Association of Retired Persons** (www.aarp.org) publishes destination-specific travel advice for destinations around the world, including the Virgin Islands.

Children

The Virgin Islands provide a whole range of appealing activities for children: swimming, snorkeling, hiking, and water sports are especially suitable. However, a few hotels, especially in the British Virgin Islands, don't allow children under a certain age, so be sure to check first.

For parents who want a little time out from the kids, many larger hotels offer childcare service (be sure to check it out first before leaving your child there). In the British Virgin Islands, contact Tropical Nannies (284/495-6493, www.tropicalnannies.com).

Pets

Unless you are moving to the Virgin Islands, leave your pets at home. You will have to overcome serious administrative hurdles to bring your animal to the British Virgin Islands, and it is not much easier to get a pet into the U.S. Virgin Islands. It will not be easy to find a hotel that will let Fido stay with you.

Health and Safety

The most common health problem experienced by travelers to the Virgin Islands is sunburn. Nevertheless, the possibility exists for more serious problems, especially if you take risks swimming, diving, boating, driving, or with sexual behavior. Health care in the islands is generally good, although specialist services are limited, and ambulance service may be very slow, especially in remote or outer islands.

The U.S. Centers for Disease Control (877/FYI-TRIP, www.cdc.gov) maintains up-to-date health information for travel destinations around the world, including the Virgin Islands. This is a good resource for travelers.

Before traveling make sure you are up to date on all routine immunizations, including hepatitis A and B, tetanus, diphtheria, and measles. There is no risk of malaria or yellow fever in the Virgin Islands.

Dengue

While mosquitoes in the Virgin Islands do not spread malaria or yellow fever, there have been cases of dengue and dengue hemorrhagic fever. Dengue is a virus characterized by fever, headaches, and joint and muscle pain, sometimes accompanied by nausea, vomiting, and rash. Symptoms usually appear 4–7 days after the person is bitten by a dengue-carrying mosquito. There is no cure or vaccine for dengue. Treatment is available for the symptoms. In rare cases, dengue can be fatal, especially in cases of small children or older adults.

The only way to avoid dengue is to avoid mosquito bites. Use a mosquito repellent containing DEET, and stay within screened-in or air-conditioned rooms. Avoid being outside during the early morning and late afternoon hours favored by mosquitoes.

The Sun

Take precautions against the powerful tropical sun. Apply sunscreen 15–20 minutes before you go out, and reapply regularly. Wear hats and long-sleeved loose clothing to protect your skin. Avoid direct sunlight from 10 A.M. to 2 P.M.

Be especially careful when you are swimming or sailing, since the coolness of the water and breeze may make you forget how strong the sun is. Wear a T-shirt when snorkeling for long periods to protect your back, and be sure to apply sunscreen to the back of your legs.

The Ocean

Do not overestimate your swimming, snorkeling, diving, or sailing abilities. The ocean can be powerful, unpredictable, and deadly. Pay attention to weather forecasts. Yes, you are on vacation, but terrible things can still happen.

Swimming-related deaths occur annually in the Virgin Islands, usually when someone overestimates their ability or underestimates the physical challenge involved. If you have had heart trouble or are at risk for a heart attack, be especially careful. The only beaches with lifeguards are Magen's Bay on St. Thomas and Trunk Bay on St. John. All the rest are swim at your own risk.

If you are susceptible to motion sickness and plan to sail or ride in a boat, bring Seaands, the wristbands that help prevent motion sickness. Ginger is also a proven remedy. You could also pack over-the-counter motion sickness medicine like Dramamine.

Sharks live in Virgin Islands waters, but they mostly stay in deep waters well offshore. It is unlikely you will encounter a shark at all. You will, however, see barracudas if you snorkel. Barracudas tend to stay still in the water; do not bother them and they will not bother you. Moray eels live inside dark caves and crevices—don't reach into one of these unless you have checked it out with your light first. Learn to recognize sea urchins—their long, black spines are a giveaway. Step on one and you will be in a lot of pain.

Tropical Fish Poisoning

One of the most mysterious and worst tropical maladies is fish poisoning, a severe illness caused when you eat a fish containing ciguatera toxins. Symptoms of fish poisoning are severe nausea, diarrhea, vomiting, and weakness. In addition, there are neurological symptoms such as tingling feet and hands, itchiness, and the sensation of hot things feeling cold and cold things feeling hot. Muscle weakness and pain in the bones and joints are also symptoms.

Depending on the severity of the case, symptoms can range from mild to completely debilitating. If you experience any of the symptoms, think of whether you have eaten fish in the last 24 hours. In many cases, hospitalization is required to prevent dehydration.

Unless you swear off tropical fish all together, there is no sure way to avoid fish poisoning. There is no reliable way to tell if a fish will poison; the best thing is to avoid species that have been known to poison, including barracuda, grouper, snapper, jacks, and parrot fish.

Beach Pollution

Pollution caused by the discharge of untreated sewage from ageing sewerage systems on St. Thomas and St. Croix cause beach closures on those islands from time to time. The U.S. Virgin Islands Department of Planning and Natural Resources is responsible for testing the water quality of beaches, and alerting the public if pollution reached dangerous levels. Beach closures are announced in the local newspapers, and you will be alerted by notices posted around the beach. You can also contact DPNR at 340/773-1082 on St. Croix or 340/774-3320 on St. Thomas. Results of the weekly water quality testing are also posted on the DPNR website, www.dpnr.gov.vi.

In the British Virgin Islands, the authorities are not as fastidious about testing water quality, so use common sense. Popular anchorages, such as Road Harbour, Cane Garden Bay, and Trellis Bay, are probably are not the cleanest places to swim. Also, untreated sewage from the Road Town area is discharged into the sea at Slaney, west of Road Town. A sign at that location warns against swimming or fishing in that area.

Bothersome Insects and Animals

Mosquitoes tend to come out at dusk and dawn. They are worst in urban and suburban areas where trash, flowerpots, cisterns, and other containers serve as breeding grounds. They are also common around ponds. Mosquitoes are worst in the rainy season and are easily tempered by breeze.

Bring insect repellent, especially if you will be camping or staying in rustic accommodations. Always keep screen doors closed. Mosquito coils, which are burned like incense, work well, but the fumes bother some people. The most common brand is Baygon; these are widely available in stores around the islands.

Another pesky bug is the biting midge, known locally as the sandfly. These annoying bugs live in sand and come out during dusk and dawn. They resemble a gnat and deliver uncomfortable bites. Bug repellent works against them. Be careful not to track too much sand into your room, villa, or boat, or sandflies will follow.

There are no dangerous wild animals or snakes in the Virgin Islands. Many islands have large populations of feral cats and dogs, which can be problematic. Dog packs are known to attack livestock, especially at night. In the British Virgin Islands, look out for goats, cows, and chickens while driving.

Prescriptions

There are good, well-stocked pharmacies in St. Thomas, St. Croix, and in Road Town, Tortola, but to avoid hassle, bring any prescription medicine you need (in its original container) with you to the islands. It is also a good idea to bring the prescriptions themselves in case you need a refill.

Birth Control

Condoms are available at drug stores and grocery stores around the islands, and birth control prescriptions can be filled at pharmacies. The brands that you are used to may not be available in the British Virgin Islands, however.

Abortion is illegal in the British Virgin Islands but legal in the U.S. Virgin Islands.

Sexually Transmitted Diseases

The Caribbean has the second highest prevalence rate for HIV-AIDS in the world, behind sub-Saharan Africa. The countries of Haiti, Trinidad and Tobago, and the Bahamas have been worst affected; they have infection rates of 3 percent.

The Virgin Islands have relatively low rates of infection, although AIDS advocates say that much more needs to be done to arrest the spread of the disease. According to the latest figures, 1 in 300 people in the U.S. Virgin Islands is infected; in the BVI the rate is 1 per 500.

Unsafe sex is dangerous in any country, including the Virgin Islands. If you plan to have promiscuous sex (or even if you don't) pack condoms and use them.

Information and Services

MONEY

Both the U.S. and British Virgin Islands use United States currency. Travelers from Europe, Canada, and other parts of the world can exchange money at banks throughout the islands. Banking hours are generally 9 A.M.–2 P.M., although some banks have longer hours. There are no independent money changers.

Hotels, car rental agencies, charter boat companies, retail shops, and large restaurants almost always accept credit cards and travelers checks. In fact, many hotels and car rental companies will require a credit card. Some smaller establishments do not accept these forms of payment, however, and others require a minimum purchase amount to process a credit card payment. Always ask first.

Tipping

Tipping follows the same general pattern as in the United States: tip between 10 and 20 percent for restaurant service and a few dollars for someone who helps you with your bags. Taxi drivers can be tipped if you are especially impressed with their service, but a tip is not required.

Many hotels tack a 10 percent "service charge" on their bills. Many restaurants follow suit, tacking a 10 or even 20 percent service charge onto bills. Be sure to look closely at your restaurant bill before adding an additional tip.

MAPS AND TOURIST INFORMATION

Free, pocket-sized road maps are widely available throughout the Virgin Islands. These are handy and reliable and will meet the needs of most travelers. Maps are also printed in the free tourist-oriented magazines that are widely available.

Specialized hiking maps of St. John are available from the National Park Service headquarters in Cruz Bay. The NPS shops in Cruz Bay and Christiansted, St. Croix, have the best selection of maps in the islands.

If you want a good, detailed map of the entire Virgin Islands, you should buy it before you come. Map publishers Berndtson and International Travel Maps have high-quality maps available from major online map stores and booksellers, including Barnes and Noble and Amazon. You can also find them at www.vitrader.com. The National Geographic Society has an excellent map of the Virgin Islands National Park on St. John.

Detailed government survey maps of the British Virgin Islands are on sale at the Survey Department (284/494-3459). This office also sells what it calls a "tourist map" for $12, which is a detailed large format, foldout map of the BVI.

Nautical Charts

It is best to obtain nautical charts before you arrive in the Virgin Islands. This will allow you to plan your cruise ahead of time and avoid the frustration of looking for charts in the islands, where availability is often limited. While most charter companies provide a chart with the boat, you may find it is not as detailed as you want.

Chart series published by Caribbean Yacht Charts, Imray, the U.S. National Ocean Service (NOAA), the U.S. National Imagery and Mapping Agency, and British Admiralty are all fine for navigating in the Virgin Islands. The NOAA, Caribbean Yachting Charts, and Imray products are probably the easiest to find. A good source for nautical charts is www.nauticalcharts.com. The National Oceanic and Atmospheric Agency (www.nauticalcharts.noaa.gov) lists official NOAA chart retailers throughout the United States.

The U.S. National Ocean Service chart no. 25640 is the only chart that encompasses the entire U.S. and British Virgin Islands. Other charts, however, show greater detail. Single charts range $20–30; a complete, detailed set of charts for the Virgin Islands can cost several hundred dollars.

Electronic charts are the latest thing in sailing, but they can be very hard to obtain in the islands. Electronic charts produced by C-Map, Navionics, Garmin, and BSB/NOAA are good for cruising the Virgin Islands.

Tourist Offices and Libraries

You will find tourist offices and information desks in Road Town, Tortola; Spanish Town, Virgin Gorda; and Christiansted, St. Croix. The National Park Service office on St. John doubles as an information desk. On St. Thomas, the Department of Tourism's visitors bureau has spotty hours and is a poor source of information.

There are public libraries on St. Thomas, St. John, St. Croix, Tortola, Virgin Gorda, Anegada, and Jost Van Dyke. The larger libraries have Internet access.

Both the U.S. and British Virgin Islands have tourist offices in the mainland United States and Europe, plus useful websites.

The **British Virgin Islands Tourist Board** (www.bvitourism.com) has offices in Road Town, Tortola (284/494-3134); San Juan, Puerto Rico (787/999-6655); New York (212/696-0400, U.S. toll free 800/835-8530); Atlanta (770/874-5951); Los Angeles (213/736-8931); London (44/207-355-9585); Milano, Italy (39/02-667-14374); and Düsseldorf, Germany (49/2104-286671).

The **U.S. Virgin Islands Department of Tourism** (www.usvitourism.vi) has offices in St. Thomas (340/774-8784); St. Croix (340/773-0495); St. John (340/776-6450); New York (800/372-8784); Chicago (312/670-8784); Miami (305/442-7200); Los Angeles (213/739-0138); Atlanta (404/688-0906); Washington, D.C. (202/624-3590); London (44/208-994-0978); Milano, Italy (39/02-3310-5841).

FILM AND PHOTOGRAPHY

Film Processing

You can get your film developed in the Virgin Islands, although processing is generally expensive and may not be as high-quality as your photo shop back home. The best photo shop in the Virgin Islands is **St. Thomas' Blazing Photos** (340/776-5547), which has locations in Havensight Mall and Red Hook Plaza. You will also find film-processing shops in Road Town, Tortola; Cruz Bay, St. John; and Sunny Isle Mall, St. Croix. Most shops have embraced the digital revolution and provide printing services for digital cameras too.

Photo Tips

The Virgin Islands' endless summer is a photographer's best friend and worst enemy. The sunshine and blue sky make it nearly impossible to take ugly photos. For the best shots of the crystal blue water, choose an absolutely sunny day and seek out the highest elevation you can find.

While a sunny day almost guarantees good scenery photos, it makes photographing people difficult. If it is very bright, you may need to use a flash to fill in the shadows of a person's face. Remember the old rule to always put the camera's back to the sun, but watch out as well for squinty eyes.

It is well worth picking up a cheap, disposable underwater camera to bring with you. You can also buy them at shops throughout the islands, and just about every dive shop stocks them. Don't bother taking underwater shots on a cloudy day; you really need sunlight to boost the colors. Also try to avoid windy or rough days, when waves have churned up clouds of sediment. The built-in flash on many of the point-and-shoot disposable cameras is quite weak; don't try to take photos of things more than six feet away if you're depending on the flash.

The disposable waterproof cameras are handy even if you're not planning on underwater photography. Seawater and sun can damage your camera; if you anticipate lots of beach, boat, or surf photography, protect your camera by leaving it at home. If you insist on taking a regular camera to the beach or on a boat, pack it in a plastic bag. Better yet, use a "dry bag." Remember that even a mild saltwater spray can damage your camera.

Photo Etiquette

In the Virgin Islands, it is rude to take photographs of strangers without their permission. On some islands, St. Thomas in particular, there are a few outgoing entrepreneurs who make a living by posing in colorful Caribbean garb astride a donkey. If you want something a little more authentic than that, you will have to do some legwork of your own.

The only exception to this is at local fairs or cultural events, where it is okay to photograph performers or participants. If you can, however, it is still a good idea to ask first.

COMMUNICATIONS AND MEDIA
Postal Services

Postal service in both the U.S. and British Virgin Islands is reliable. The U.S. Virgin Islands are served by the U.S. Postal Service, and the same products and services available in the mainland are available at post offices in the islands, including overnight, registered, and priority mail. Zips codes for the U.S. Virgin Islands are 00801-00809. There is one post office on St. John, five on St. Thomas, and six on St. Croix. Postal rates are the same as in the mainland United States.

While not as sophisticated as the mail service in the U.S. Virgin Islands, the BVI Post Office is just as reliable. You can mail letters and packages, buy stamps, and purchase money orders. There is no overnight, insured, return receipt, or priority mail service, however.

It costs 50 cents to mail a letter from the BVI to the United States, Canada, and Europe, and 35 cents to mail a postcard. It takes 7–10 days (and sometimes longer) for a letter mailed in the BVI to reach the United States or Canada. Many a traveler has had the experience of already being home when their postcards start to turn up in friends' mailboxes.

In the British Virgin Islands, an alternative to using the local postal service is to send mail through one of the mailbox service companies. These businesses rent post office boxes to residents who want to be able to receive mail at a U.S. address. They also take your letters and packages and mail them at U.S. Virgin Islands post offices. While expensive, this can be the best way to send mail if you are in a hurry or need the added security of insurance or a return receipt.

Try Inland Messenger Service (Lower Main Street, 284/494-6440) or Khoy's Mailing Service (R. G. Hodge Plaza, 284/494-4539), both in Road Town. International couriers FedEx, DHL, and UPS also have offices in both territories.

Neither the U.S. or British Virgin Islands have a system of postal addresses. With the exception of downtown Christiansted in St. Croix, all customers use post office boxes to receive their mail. This is one reason why giving directions is so challenging in both territories.

Another strange fact is that because of the routing systems used by both the U.S. and British Virgin Islands postal authorities, mail between the two territories does not travel especially quickly.

Shipping Packages

In both territories, the most affordable way to ship a package back home is through the post office. This method is also quite reliable. In the U.S. Virgin Islands, you can bring your package to any post office. Rates depend on the destination but can be as low as $6 for a five-pound package to the United States, and $17 for air parcel post to the United Kingdom.

In the British Virgin Islands, bring your package to the parcel post desk at the Road Town Post Office, where you will have to fill out a U.S. Customs declaration form. It costs $14 to mail a five-pound package to the U.S. and $17 to mail it to the United Kingdom.

Telephone and Fax Services

Placing calls to and from the U.S. Virgin Islands is easy and relatively affordable. As part of the U.S., the territory is usually not considered an international call, although you should check your long-distance plan before making any calls. The area code is 340, and calls can be made on pay phones, using calling cards, or on cellular phones. Major U.S. cellular phone companies provide service in the U.S. Virgin Islands. Cingular and Sprint have the best service. Check your wireless plan for information on roaming charges.

In the BVI, Cable and Wireless West Indies has had an exclusive license (in other words, monopoly) for the provision of telephone, fax, and Internet services. CCT Boatphone has an exclusive license for cellular phone services. This is a bad thing for consumers and visitors; the calling rates here are among the highest in the world.

Plans to introduce competition to the telecommunications market in 2006 and 2007 should mean lower prices and better service.

But that is yet to be seen. For now, if you care the least bit about your spending, do not make the mistake of picking up the phone in your hotel room, charging a call on your credit card, or using the roaming feature of your cell phone until you check first to find out exactly how much that call will cost you. It is not uncommon for unsuspecting visitors to talk for anywhere from $1 to $4 a minute.

If you need to make an overseas call, one of the best ways of doing so is to purchase a Cable and Wireless calling card, which can be used at pay phones. You gain the advantage of setting an automatic budget for your call, although you suffer the indignity of making your call from a public pay phone, which can leave a lot to be desired. You can also dial 1-800-CALL-USA (800/225-5872).

If you're looking for cheaper alternatives, consider these: use a U.S. or international calling card with an 800 number. You will still pay a hefty per-minute charge for the "toll free" call ($0.25 on weekends and $0.45 during weekdays), but the overall cost of the call is much cheaper than it would normally be.

You can also try your U.S. or international cell phone. Many people are able to pick up signals from cell phone towers on St. John along the Sir Francis Drake Highway heading west on Tortola, from the area of the West End Ferry Dock, and even from parts of Virgin Gorda.

Internet telephone companies like Skype work in the BVI, but you will need an Internet connection first. As of now, no one is giving those away free.

Internet Access

Internet service is generally reliable in the U.S. Virgin Islands, and you can find Internet cafés in towns and near marinas. Rates are a little higher than in the mainland U.S.

Internet rates are quite a bit higher in the BVI, where Cable & Wireless West Indies is the monopoly provider. Dial-up rates are $13 and up, while ADSL Internet access costs upward of $100 per month, although a modified slower ADSL is available for as little as $50 a month. Internet service is moderately reliable.

The demand among travelers for Internet access has spawned a few cybercafés around the islands. Most charge around $5 for 15 minutes online.

Wireless Internet is not shared freely in the BVI. There are wi-fi hotspots maintained by BVI Marine WiFi (www.bvimarinewifi.com) at 10 popular anchorages, but you have to register, pay, and receive a password in order to log on. Rates are $19 per day or $99 per week.

Two-Way Radio

Radio is the best and most reliable way for mariners to communicate. All boats should be equipped with a VHF radio, and boat captains should make sure that not only they, but all members of the party, know how to use it. Channel 16 is used for standby and for emergency calls. Virgin Islands Radio, which can facilitate ship-to-shore calls, monitors channels 24, 85, and 87. Register and pay ahead of time with Virgin Islands Radio, and you will be able to make and receive local and international phone calls with their assistance. Channels 3, 4, and 6 are used for weather updates.

Be sure to review proper radio use before casting off. For example, channel 16 should only be used to establish contact with another party and not for conversations. In the case of a real emergency, use channel 16 and call, "Mayday, mayday, mayday," state the name of the vessel, and then "over" until someone responds. It is important to remain calm and speak clearly so you can be understood.

Local Newspapers and Magazines

The *Virgin Islands Daily News* is the best and most reliable newspaper in the Virgin Islands. It covers happenings in the U.S. Virgin Islands in great detail and often includes stories about the British Virgin Islands as well. It covers regional and international news and includes comics, TV listings, crosswords, weather, and more. The *Daily News* is published every day except Sunday and costs 75 cents (85 cents in the BVI).

The *St. Croix Avis* is a daily focusing on St. Croix news, widely available on that island. *Flair Magazine,* published on St. Thomas, includes profiles of Virgin Islanders and examines topical issues.

St. Thomas-St. John This Week and *St. Croix This Week* are monthly (yes, there's a contradiction there) magazines geared at tourists. Both contain calendars of events, useful phone numbers, and lots of advertising.

The British Virgin Islands are served by two different national weekly newspapers and one national twice-weekly. The *BVI Beacon,* published on Thursdays, is the best. Others are the *BVI StandPoint,* which comes out on Tuesdays and Fridays, and the *Island Sun,* published on Fridays. For entertainment news, pick up the Friday edition of the *StandPoint* or look out for the free entertainment guide the *Limin' Times,* a small glossy publication.

The *BVI Welcome* is a bimonthly glossy magazine for tourists with thoughtful articles, lots of useful information, and advertising. It is widely available at hotels, restaurants and other tourist-oriented places.

Local Radio and Television

There is an abundance of local radio stations in the Virgin Islands. Listening to local radio is a great way to soak up the local culture, pick up on Caribbean music, and find out where the big party is on the weekend.

Some good bets on the radio dial are: **Mongoose 104**(104.9 FM; oldies and classics); **Isle 95** (95.1 FM; reggae and urban); **Magic 97** (970 AM; news, talk, and Caribbean music); **WRRA** (1290 AM; blues, jazz, Calypso); **ZVCR** (106.9 FM; Caribbean); **ZBVI** (780 AM; news, Caribbean, oldies); **KISS 101.3** (urban); **105 JAMZ** (Caribbean, reggae); and **WVGN** (107.3 FM; NPR news). Not all radio stations can be picked up on every island.

WEIGHTS AND MEASURES

Despite being British, the British Virgin Islands use imperial measures: miles, feet, and pounds are the common parlance. Speed limits are posted in miles, gas is sold by the gallon, and groceries weighed in pounds and ounces. The same is true for the U.S. Virgin Islands.

Electricity is 110 volts, 60 cycles, the same as

in the United States. No transformers or plug adapters are required. Both the U.S. and British Virgin Islands experience occasional power outages, but many hotels and guesthouses have backup generators so you may not notice.

Time Zones

The Virgin Islands are on Atlantic Standard time, one hour earlier than Eastern Standard Time and four hours later than Greenwich Mean Time. There is no daylight saving time.

RESOURCES

Suggested Reading

HISTORY

Anderson, John L. *The Night of the Silent Drums.* Rome: Mapes Monde, 1992. John Anderson conducted exhaustive research into the 1733 slave rebellion on St. John and brought what he learned to life in this story, told through the eyes of a Danish plantation doctor who was sympathetic with the Africans' cause. Although fictional, the book is widely regarded as factual and accurate in its depiction of the events of 1733. The story was first published by Charles Scribner and Sons in 1975; the 1992 edition is beautifully illustrated with rare West Indian hand drawings and prints.

Andrew, John. *The Hanging of Arthur Hodge.* Xlibris, 2000. This self-published thesis is a comprehensive account of the 1811 trial of Tortola planter Arthur Hodge, who was hanged for the murder of one of his slaves. The event was an anti-slavery milestone in the Caribbean, and Andrew's telling is both informative and entertaining.

Armstrong, Douglas. *Creole Transformation from Slavery to Freedom: Historical Archeology of the East End Community, St. John, Virgin Islands.* Gainsville, Florida: University of Florida, 2003. This academic work looks closely at the social transformation that took place at the end of slavery in the Caribbean, through a close examination of the St. John East End community, which gained freedom 40 years before the 1848 emancipation in the Danish West Indies.

Bastian, Jeanette Allis. *Owning Memory: How a Caribbean Community Lost its Archives and Found its History.* Westport, Connecticut Greenwood Publishing Group, 2003. A former librarian and archivist in the U.S. Virgin Islands, Jeanette Bastian writes how the community was forced to develop its own history because the historical record was stored in Copenhagen and Washington, D.C., the seats of the two colonial powers.

Chernow, Ron. *Alexander Hamilton.* New York Penguin Press, 2004. The newest biography of St. Croix's most famous native son.

Cohen, Judah. *Through the Sands of Time: A history of the Jewish community of St. Thomas U.S. Virgin Islands.* Waltham, Massachusetts Brandeis University Press, 2004. This hefty work records the long and colorful history of St. Thomas' Jewish community, from its early roots in the 17th century to today.

Dookhan, Isaac. *A History of the Virgin Islands of the United States.* Jamaica: Canoe Press, 1994. First published in 1974, this was one of the first comprehensive histories of the U.S. Virgin Islands and remains a good introduction to the history of the islands. Dookhan, a Guyanese scholar also wrote a history of the British Virgin Islands, but it is out of print and extremely difficult to find.

Gill, Patricia. *Buddhoe.* 1976. This self-published work is a fictional account of the

1848 slave uprising on St. Croix and its charismatic leader.

Lewisohn, Florence. *St. Croix Under Seven Flags.* Hollywood, Florida: The Dukane Press, 1970. Well written and engaging, this hefty history of St. Croix is one of the best-told stories of the island ever written. Although it is dated in some respects, students of history will still appreciate Lewisohn's research and the numerous illustrations.

Low, Ruth Hull and Rafael Valls. *St. John Backtime: Eyewitness Accounts from 1718 to 1956.* St. John: Eden Hill Press, 1985. This attractive, slim volume contains excerpts of first-hand accounts of St. John, from the earliest days of Danish settlement to the 1950s. While some were authored by native St. Johnians, most provide an outsider's view of the island. It is also nicely illustrated.

O'Neal, Eugenia. *From the Field to the Legislature: A history of women in the Virgin Islands.* Westport, Connecticut: Greenwood Publishing Group, 2001. The former head of the local government's women's affairs desk wrote the first history of the women of the Virgin Islands in 2001. This academic work provides a valuable and rare picture of women's role in Virgin Islands society and history.

CHRONICLES

Benjamin, Guy H. *Me and My Beloved Virgin.* New York: Benjamin's Publishing Co., 1981. St. Johnian Guy Benjamin tells of growing up in Coral Bay, St. John, in the early part of the 20th century.

Melchior Sr., Ariel. *Thoughts Along the Way: Virgin Islands Reflections.* St. Thomas: Ariel Melchior Inc., 1981. One of the founders of the *Virgin Islands Daily News,* Ariel Melchior has compiled some of the best editorials from that newspaper, from its founding in the 1930s until the 1970s. The result is a fascinating picture of the U.S. Virgin Islands' struggle for self-government and a greater sense of identity.

Seaman, George. *Ay-Ay: an Island Almanac.* London: Macmillan Publishers, 1989. A St. Croix native, George Seaman grew up to be one of the island's greatest fans. In this memoir he shares his delight in the annual rhythm of seasons, animals, weather, and human events. Woven in are descriptions of the Crucian lifestyle, history, and a boyhood on a quiet Caribbean island.

Svalesen, Leif, Selena A. Winsnes (translator) and Pat Shaw (translator.) *The Slave Ship Fredensborg.* Indiana University Press, 2000. Underwater archeologist Leif Svalesen recounts the journey of the slave ship *Fredensborg,* which sank off the coast of Norway in 1768 on its way back from the Danish West Indies. The wreck was discovered in 1974, and Svalesen uses artifacts from the wreck, including the captain's log, to tell the detailed story of its journey. The book forms the basis of an exhibit at the Fort Frederik Museum in Frederiksted, St. Croix.

FLORA AND FAUNA

Barlow, Virginia. *The Nature of the Islands.* Dunedin, Florida: Chris Doyle Publishing, 1993. Exhaustively researched, beautifully written, and charmingly illustrated, this is the best and most accessible guide to the nature of the islands. This book is well-organized, and makes it easy to learn more about the plants, trees, and animals around the islands.

Lazell, James. *Island: Fact and Theory in Nature.* Berkeley: University of California Press, 2005. Scientist James "Skip" Lazell has lived on and studied Guana Island for decades, and this work examines the remarkable diversity of life that exists on this tiny British Virgin Island. His analysis raises questions about prevailing scientific wisdom, and evolves into an argument about the critical importance of biodiversity for life on earth.

Nellis, David W. *Puerto Rico and Virgin Islands Wildlife Viewing Guide.* Helena, Montana: Falcon Publishing, 1999. This guide includes descriptions and information about the major natural attractions in the Virgin Islands and

Puerto Rico, as well as full-color photos of common birds, lizards, and other animals.

Raffaele, Herbert A., Cindy J. House, and John Wiessinger. *Guide to the Birds of Puerto Rico and the Virgin Islands.* Princeton, New Jersey: Princeton University Press, 1989. This is the definitive and best guide to the birds of the Virgin Islands, with detailed descriptions of 284 species, 273 of which are illustrated. In addition, there are practical tips for birders visiting the area.

Stokes, F. Joseph. *Handguide to the Coral Reef Fishes of the Caribbean.* New York: Lippencott and Cromwell, 1980. This illustrated guide includes descriptions of hundreds of reef fish, plus tips on how to identify mystery fish.

Thomas, Toni. *Traditional Medicinal Plants of St. Croix, St. Thomas, and St. John.* St. Thomas: University of the Virgin Islands, 1997. This informative field guide contains detailed information about traditional uses of hundreds of plants, including appropriate warnings. Its information is applicable to the British Virgin Islands, too.

FOOD AND DRINK

Clarke, Clarice C., ed. *Native Recipes.* St. Thomas: University of the Virgin Islands Co-operative Extension Service, 1998. Produced by the University of the Virgin Islands, this is a good resource for traditional Virgin Islands cooking and recipes, including dishes that are hard to find in other Caribbean cookbooks. There is also nutritional analysis of recipes.

Morgan, Jinx and Jefferson. *The Sugar Mill Caribbean Cookbook.* Boston: The Harvard Common Press, 1996. Owners of the Sugar Mill Hotel and Restaurant on Tortola's north shore, Jinx and Jefferson Morgan offer an engaging Caribbean-inspired cookbook designed for cooks in North America and Europe, where Caribbean ingredients may be hard to find. Many of the recipes take an authentic Caribbean dish and add an elegant twist—often with superb results.

GUIDES

Lensfesty, Thomas Jr. and Thomas Lensfesty. *The Sailor's Illustrated Dictionary.* New York: Lyon's Press, 2004. A reference book like no other. Entries include types of knots, clouds, equipment and much more.

Gaffin, Pam. *St. John: Feet, Fins, and Four-Wheel Drive.* St. John: American Paradise Publishing, 2003. St. John resident Pan Gaffin provides practical and insightful advice about visiting St. John. The book outlines dozens of different driving tours, hikes, and "scrambles" on St. John.

Scott, Nancy and Simon. *The Cruising Guide to the Virgin Islands, 12th edition.* Dunedin, Florida: Cruising Guide Publications, 2005. Veteran Virgin Islands sailors Nancy and Simon Scott publish the definitive guide for cruisers. A sturdy cover and spiral binding make it as practical as it is useful. It is up-dated annually.

THE REGION

Columbus, Christopher and J.M. Cohen (editor). *The Four Voyages.* New York: Penguin Group, 1992. A new edition of Christopher Columbus' own account of his "discovery" of the Caribbean, including passages describing his encounter with Kalinago Indians on St. Croix in 1493.

Ferguson, James. *The Story of the Caribbean People.* Kingston, Jamaica: Ian Randle Publishers, 1999. This textbook is a useful resource on Caribbean history, from pre-Columbians to the modern issues of drug trafficking, money laundering, and tourism. While the Virgin Islands play only a minor role in Ferguson's telling, his history provides valuable context for students of the islands.

Kincaid, Jamaica. *A Small Place.* New York, Farrar, Straus and Giroux, 1988. The best portrait of the peculiar history and culture of a small Caribbean island ever written. Although based on Kincaid's native Antigua, *A Small Place* paints a true picture of the entire region. Students of the region turn to this thin tome time and time again.

Las Casas, Bartolome de. *A Short Account of the Destruction of the Indies*. New York: Penguin Group, 1992. The 1542 account of Spanish settlement of Puerto Rico and Hispaniola by a Spanish priest was an urgent indictment of the treatment of the Igneri and Kalinago Indians that were found in the region. The description is still as powerful and troubling today as it was then.

BEACH READS

Brandt, Kathy. *Dark Water Dive*. New York: Penguin Group, 2004. An underwater murder mystery set in the British Virgin Islands. Homicide detective Hannah Sampson explores the (fictional) underbelly of paradise.

O'Neal, Eugenia. *Just An Affair*. Columbus, MO: Genesis Press, 2003. A classic romance set in the British Virgin Islands. Charter boat captain Caryl Walker falls for a smooth-talking music CEO but loses her memory before she can tell her former lover to take a hike.

Wouk, Herman. *Don't Stop the Carnival*. Boston: Little, Brown and Co, 1965. The Caribbean classic, it is the story an optimistic hotel manager who sets up shop on what is widely believed to be Water Island near St. Thomas in the 1960s. Nothing goes as planned, but there is plenty of laughter and entertainment.

PHOTOGRAPHY

Handler, Mauricio. *British Virgin Islands: A photographic portrait*. Newton, Massachusetts: Twin Light Publisher, 2001. Veteran Virgin Islands photographer Mauricio Handler captures the natural beauty of the British Virgin Islands in this high-gloss coffee table hardback, widely available at bookstores around the islands.

Simonson, Steve and Peter Mullenburg. *The U.S. Virgin Islands*. Newton, Massachusetts: Twin Lights Publisher, 2003. Transports you right back to the beautiful islands with color photographs of St. Thomas, St. Croix, and St. John.

LITERATURE

Penn-Moll, Verna. *Johnny-Cake Country*. Colchester, Essex: Mount Sage Press, 1990. In this slim fictional account of life in the BVI, the former chief librarian of the BVI describes the contradictions and choices intrinsic in "development."

Vanterpool, Hugo F. *Dusk to Dawn: Hugo F. Vanterpool*. Kingston, Jamaica: Kingston Publishers Ltd., 1995. Adults and teens will enjoy this story of young Allan Todman.

White, Robb. *Two on the Isle: A memory of Marina Cay*. New York: W.W. Norton & Co., 1985. This book was originally published in the 1960s as *Our Virgin Island*. In it Robb White remembers three years spent living on Marina Cay in the British Virgin Islands in the late 1930s. The story was later turned into a movie starring Sidney Poitier and John Cassavetes, shot in the islands.

Internet Resources

TRAVEL INFORMATION

V.I. Now
www.vinow.com

This up-to-date website is designed to help travelers to the U.S. Virgin Islands plan their trip. There are restaurant, beach, and hotel reviews, calendars of upcoming events, a message board, ferry and cruise ship schedules, and a marketplace where you can buy books, maps, and V.I. souvenirs. Although advertising-driven, the content here is reliable and substantial.

U.S. Virgin Islands Department of Tourism
www.usvitourism.vi

The official Tourism Department website for the U.S. Virgin Islands. You can download marriage applications, hotel rate sheets, and press releases.

British Virgin Islands Tourist Board
www.bvitourism.com

The official Tourist Board website for the British Virgin Islands is well organized and frequently updated.

BVI Online
www.b-v-i.com

This travel site has lots of photos and insider information on visiting the British Virgin Islands.

BVI Welcome
www.bviwelcome.com

An online edition of the glossy visitor magazine, BVI Welcome has feature articles on the BVI and a searchable index of hotels, restaurants, businesses, and services. You can also access the online edition of the weekly *Limin Times* with information on the local bandstand, upcoming events, and parties.

NEWS

Virgin Islands Daily News
www.virginislandsdailynews.com

The website for the leading newspaper in the Virgin Islands, there is a searchable index of recent articles, tourist information, government guides, and a dining guide.

BVI Beacon
www.bvibeacon.com

The leading newspaper in the British Virgin Islands publishes synopses of the major stories of the week.

ZBVI Radio
www.zbviradio.com

The website of the oldest radio station in the British Virgin Islands. You can listen live through online streaming.

St. Thomas/St. Croix Source
http://sts.onepaper.com

An online rival of the Virgin Islands Daily News, the St. Thomas and St. Croix Source posts news daily, as well as a local calendar and dining guide.

SAILING

U.S. Office of Coast Survey
www.nauticalcharts.noaa.gov

The National Oceanic and Atmospheric Agency is the official publisher of nautical charts in the United States, including charts covering the U.S. and British Virgin Islands. Their website has information about the most recent chart updates, the location of chart agents all over the U.S., and provides instructions on how to order charts directly from the government. You can also download electronic nautical charts for free.

Caribbean Weather
www.weathercarib.com

This site maintains up-to-the-minute weather information for the Virgin Islands and the entire Eastern Caribbean, including official National Weather Service forecasts, tropical storm bulletins, and radar images. Ideal for mariners.

TELEPHONE DIRECTORIES

British Virgin Islands Yellow Pages
www.britishvirginislandsyp.com

A fully searchable online edition of the official phone book of the British Virgin Islands, including white pages, blue pages, and yellow pages.

U.S. Virgin Islands Phone Book
www.viphonebook.com

The fully searchable online edition of the most widely used phone book in the U.S. Virgin Islands.

HISTORY

Danish Archives
www.virgin-islands-history.dk

An English-language website maintained by the Danish Archives, this site contains information about the history of the Danish West Indies, plus access to many of the archives related to their history.

Index

A

abolitionists: 266-268
accommodations: *see specific place*; villa rentals
Adams Music Research Institute: 38-39
Agriculture Fair: 89-90
AIDS: *see* HIV-AIDS
air travel: general discussion 283-284, 285; Anegada 241-242; St. Croix 100-101; St. Thomas 59; Tortola 185; Virgin Gorda 208
Alice in Wonderland: 161
all-terrain vehicles (ATVs): 221
aloe: 252
Alton Augustus Adams Music Research Institute: 38-39
amphibians: 253-254
anchorages: 49, 86-87, 125, 168-169, 220
Anegada: general discussion 16, 226-227, 229; accommodations 237-238; food/restaurants 239-240; historical background 229-230; maps 228; planning tips 229; recreational activities 235-237; sightseeing tips 20, 23, 25, 27, 231-235; tourist information and services 240-241; transportation services 241-242
Anegada Outback: 27, 227, 233, 235
Anegada rock iguanas: 16, 233, 234
Angelfish Reef: 157
animals: 252-254, 295; *see also* fish/fishing
Annaberg School Ruins: 113, 115
Annaberg Sugar Mill Ruins: 20, 23, 115
Annaly Bay: 79
Apothecary Museum: 70
Apple Bay: 155, 182
archaeological sites: 77, 112, 123; *see also* petroglyphs
art galleries: 46, 91, 121, 165-166
arts community: 43-44
Art Thursday: 91
astronomical observatories: 82
August Festival: 164
avocado pear trees: 252

B

banana trees: 252
banks: 58, 99, 133, 184, 207
barracudas: 295
basket-making: 20, 115
The Baths: general discussion 15, 194-196; food/restaurants 206; recreational activities 201; sightseeing tips 20, 21, 23, 189

bats: 252
The Battery: 108
beach bars: 16, 211, 217-218
Beauregard Bay Beach: 83
Beef Island: 23, 24, 25, 150-151, 181
Bellamy Cay: 152
Belmont Estate: 171
biking: Anegada 236; Jost Van Dyke 221, 225; St. Croix 88; St. John 126; Tortola 171-172, 187
birds/birding: general discussion 253; Anegada 231-232; Buck Island National Monument 75; St. John 20, 112-113, 122
birth control: 296
Blackbeard's Castle: 36-37, 39
boating: 134, 167-168, 209, 285
body language: 291
Bolongo Bay: 44
Bomba's Full Moon Party: 163-164
bonefish: 16, 27, 235
bookstores: 184
botanical gardens: 26, 36, 80, 137, 145-146, 233
bougainvillea: 250
boulders of Virgin Gorda: 195
breadfruit trees: 252
Brewer's Bay Beach: 41
Brewer's Bay (Tortola): 148
bribes: 289, 290
Britannia House: 39
British Virgin Islands: colonization 262-263; government and economy 274-276; 19th century events 268; plantation era 265, 267; statistical information 244; 20th century

BEACHES

Anegada: 231
beach bars: 16, 211, 217-218
environmental issues: 295
itinerary tips: 23-24
Jost Van Dyke: 16
nude beaches: 26, 42
St. Croix: 75, 78-79, 81, 83
St. John: 15, 109, 111-113, 117-118
St. Thomas: 40-42, 44
Tortola: 148, 151-152, 155
Virgin Gorda: 15, 194-196
Water Island: 40

events 272; visitor guidelines 289-290
bromeliads: 251
Bronco Billy's: 201
Brown Bay: 124
Bubbly Pool: 16, 24, 211, 216
Buccaneer Beach: 83
Buck Island National Monument: 14, 19, 25, 62, 75-76
Buddhoe: 74, 267
bus service: 59, 101, 135
BVI Music Fest: 164
BVI Spring Regatta: 169

C

cacti: 80, 198, 251
Caldonia Rainforest: 26, 80
calling cards: 299
Callwood Rum Distillery: 22, 147-148
Camille Pissarro Gallery: 38
camping/campgrounds: 128-129
Cane Bay: 78
Cane Bay Wall: 84
Caneel Bay: 109
Cane Garden Bay: general discussion 15; accommodations 174-175; entertainment and nightlife 161; food/restaurants 180-181; recreational activities 20; shopping 165; sightseeing tips 22, 23, 147-148
Cane Garden Bay Beach: 148
cannibalism: 259
Cappoon's Bay: 155
Caribbean Community Theatre: 91
Caribbean Museum Center for the Arts: 75
Caribs: see Kalinago culture
Carrot Bay: 22, 154, 182
car travel: see rental cars; scenic drives
Carvel Rock: 160
casinos: 89
The Caves: 20, 24, 157
cell phones: 299
cemeteries: 146
Centre for Applied Marine Studies: 150
century plants: 16, 252
Charlotte Amalie: general discussion 14, 30, 32-33, 35; accommodations 51-52; food/restaurants 54-56; maps 34; shopping 40, 46; sightseeing tips 19, 23, 35-41
charters: general discussion 286-287; permits 290; St. Croix 86; St. Thomas 48; Tortola 166-167; Virgin Gorda 200, 201
Chenay Bay: 83
childrearing: 278

children, traveling with: 31, 293-294
The Chimneys: 201
Chocolate Hole: 124
Christian's Fort: 108
Christiansted: general discussion 14; accommodations 92-93; entertainment and nightlife 89; food/restaurants 96-97; maps 66-67; shopping 91-92; sightseeing tips 65-72
Christiansted National Historic Site: 19, 22, 62, 67-68, 70
Ciboney culture: 258
cinemas: 45
Cinnamon Bay: 20, 21, 23, 112
Cinnamon Bay Beach: 112
Cinnamon Bay Ruins: 112
Cinnamon Bay Self-Guided Loop Trail: 122
Cinnamon Bay Trail: 122
Cistern Point: 160
climate: 245-247
closed seasons (fishing): 256
clothing tips: 18, 278-279
Cocoloba: 125
coconut trees: 250
Coki Point: 24
Coki Point Beach: 44
Columbus, Christopher: 77, 142, 260-261
communication styles: 291
Cooper Island: 20, 24, 160-161
Coppermine National Park: 189, 193-194
Coppermine Point: 20
copper mines: 192
coquis: 253
Coral Bay: general discussion 115-117; entertainment and nightlife 119-120; food/restaurants 131-132; recreational activities 20, 25, 26; shopping 120-121; sightseeing tips 104
coral reefs: general discussion 246-247, 249; Anegada 236; environmental issues 254-255; St. Croix 75-76, 78; St. John 124, 125; Tortola 157, 161
Coral World Marine Park and Undersea Observatory: 21, 30, 43
courtesy titles: 291
Cow Wreck Beach: 20, 231
Crab Races: 90
crabs: 90, 254
Cramer's Park: 19, 83
credit cards: 296
crime: 273
cruise ships: 31, 59, 101, 272, 284-285
Cruzan Rum Distillery: 80-81
Cruz Bay: general discussion 15; entertainment and nightlife 119; food/restaurants 129-131;

recreational activities 21; shopping 120; sightseeing tips 106-109
culture: 277-281
currency: 296
Customs House (1841): 70
customs regulations: general discussion 288, 289; Jost Van Dyke 224; St. Croix 100; St. Thomas 58; Tortola 185; Virgin Gorda 207
cybercafés: 58

D

daily life: 277
Danish West India and Guinea Company Warehouse: 70
Danish West Indies: 263-265, 267-269
Davis Bay: 78
day sailing: 167
Dead Chest: 158
dengue fever: 294
Denis Bay: 111
desalination plants: 257
Devil's Bay: 195, 201
Diamond Cay National Park: 216
disabled travelers: 293
Diverse Virgin program: 85
dive sites: see scuba diving
Dog Islands: 26-27, 189, 197, 201
dolphin swimming experience: 170
Drake's Seat: 41
driving tours: 63-65, 106, 140-141, 191
drugs: 292
Druif Bay: 40
Drunk Bay: 20
dugout canoes: 167
The Dungeon: 154-155
duty-free shopping: 14, 288

E

Eagle Shoal: 125-126
earthquakes: 244-245
East End (Jost Van Dyke): 216-217, 224
East End (St. Thomas): 42-44, 53, 57
East End (Tortola): 148-152, 161, 166, 175-176, 181-182
economy: 269-272, 273-276
ecosystems: 246-247
ecotours: 48, 78, 79, 88
education: 292
8 Tuff Miles: 120
Elaine Ione Sprauve Museum and Library: 23, 108-109

elections: 273, 275
electricity: 300-301
Emancipation Day: 90
emancipation efforts: 266-269
Emancipation Gardens: 36
emergency services: 58, 99, 133, 184, 207, 240
Emmaus Moravian Church (1782): 116-117
employment opportunities: 292; see also work permits
Enid M. Baa Public Library (1818): 37, 57
entertainment and nightlife: see specific place
environmental issues: 254-257, 295
Estate Little Princess: 77
Estate Mount Washington: 80
etiquette: 291, 298
European exploration and colonization: 77, 260-264
executions: 144, 145

F

Fahie Hill Mural: 20, 22, 137, 146
Fallen Jerusalem: 25, 196
fauna: 247, 252-254, 295
fax services: 185, 299
ferry service: general discussion 284; Anegada 242; Jost Van Dyke 225; St. Croix 101; St. John 134; Tortola 158, 185-186; Virgin Gorda 208
film processing: 133, 297
financial services industry: 272, 276
Fireburn: 269
fire departments: see emergency services
The Fireproof Building: 145
fish/fishing: general discussion 247, 249; Anegada 16, 235-236; charters 48, 86, 201; environmental issues 255-256; fly-fishing 235; licenses 290; poisoning symptoms 295; sportfishing 16, 48, 86, 235-236; St. Croix 75, 78, 86; St. Thomas 48; Virgin Gorda 201
fish, Virgin Islands style: 281
flamboyant (flame tree): 250
flamingos: 232
The Flats: 227, 235
flora: 16, 232, 235, 250-252; see also botanical gardens
fly-fishing: 235
food/restaurants: 279-281; see also specific place
forests: 250-252
Fort Berg: 117
Fort Christian Museum: 21, 36, 37
Fort Christiansvearn: 22, 67-68
Fort Frederik Museum: 19, 22, 62, 64, 73-75
Fort Recovery: 155

FESTIVALS AND EVENTS

Agriculture Fair: 63, 89-90
Bomba's Full Moon Party: 163-164
Crab Races: 90
Crucian Christmas Festival: 63, 72
8 Tuff Miles: 120
Emancipation Day: 72-73, 90
Emancipation Festival: 267
Half Ironman: 63, 90
Jump-Ups: 89
Love City Triathlon: 120
Mango Melee: 63, 90
New Year's Eve bash: 16, 219
Rolex Regatta: 45
Spanish Town Fisherman's Jamboree: 199
St. John Blues Festival: 120
St. John Carnival: 120
St. Thomas Carnival: 30, 44-45
Taste of St. Croix: 90
Trellis Bay Full Moon Party: 23, 137, 163
Virgin Gorda Easter Festival: 199
Virgin Gorda Music Festival: 199
Whit Weekend Festival: 199

Francis Bay Beach: 112
Francis Bay Pond: 20, 25, 113
Francis Bay Trail: 122
frangipani: 16, 235, 252
Franklin A. Powell, Sr., Park: 107
Frederik Lutheran Church (1793): 36
Frederiksted: general discussion 14; accommodations 93-94; entertainment and nightlife 89; festivals and events 72-73; food/restaurants 97-98; maps 73; recreational activities 87; shopping 92; sightseeing tips 72-75
French Heritage Museum: 39
Frenchman's Cay: 154
Frenchtown: 19, 30, 39, 45, 55
Friedensthal Moravian Church (1850s): 71
Friends of the Virgin Islands National Park: 121
Full Moon Party: 23, 137, 163-164
fungi: see quelbe music

G

gambling: 89
game fish: see fish/fishing; sportfishing

garbage disposal: 256-257
gardens: see botanical gardens
gay and lesbian travelers: 292-293
gender issues: 277-278
geography: 243-244
geologic history: 195, 245
Gibney's Beach: 109
Ginger Island: 161
Ginger Steps: 161
Gli-Gli: 167
golf courses: 49-50, 87, 172
Gorda Peak National Park: 15, 197, 200
Gottlieb, Moses: 74
government: 273-276
Government House (St. Croix): 70
Government House (St. Thomas): 36
Grand Hotel (1840): 36
Grass Cay: 125
Great Harbour: general discussion 16, 213, 215, 220; food/restaurants 222-223; sightseeing tips 20, 211
Great Lameshur Bay: 124
Great Tobago Island: 27
Guana Island: 152
guava trees: 252
gyms: 126

H

Haagensen House (1827): 39
Hamilton, Alexander: 69
Hansen Bay: 117
Hans Lollik: 42
harassment: 292
Hassel Island: 40
Haulover Bay: 117
Havensight: 40, 46, 55-56
Hawksnest Bay: 109-110
Hawksnest Beach: 23, 109
health care: 294-296
helicopter service: 285
Heritage Trail: 22, 64
hibiscus: 250
historical background: 229-230, 258-272
historic churches: St. Croix 68, 71, 75; St. John 116-117; St. Thomas 36, 37; Tortola 144-145, 148, 150, 155; Virgin Gorda 192-193
historic homes: 37, 39
hitchhiking: 288
HIV-AIDS: 296
Hodge, Arthur: 144, 145
Holy Cross Catholic Church (1755): 71
Holy Trinity Lutheran Church (1792): 75

HIKING TRAILS

Anegada: 27, 237
Buck Island National Monument: 14, 76
Francis Bay: 25
Jost Van Dyke: 221
Reef Bay: 20, 21, 26, 118-119, 122-123
Salt River Bay: 78
St. Croix: 22, 82-83, 87-88
St. John: 15, 20, 104, 109, 112-113, 121-123
St. Thomas: 50
Tortola: 26, 147, 157, 171
Virgin Gorda: 15, 194-198, 200

homosexuality: 292-293
Honeymoon Beach (St. John): 109
Honeymoon Beach (St. Thomas): 40, 41
horseback riding: 88, 171
horse racing tracks: 50
hospitals: see emergency services
Hotel 1829 (1831): 37, 39
HOVENSA oil refinery: 83
Hull Bay: 42
humidity: 245
Hurricane Hole: 40
hurricanes: 17, 245-246, 272

I

Igneri culture: 77, 258
Iguana Headstart Facility: 20, 27, 227, 233
iguanas: 16, 233, 234
immigrants: 276, 290
immigration services: 58, 100, 185, 207, 224
immunizations: 294
The Indians: 157
indigenous people: 77, 229-230, 258-260
insects: 295
International Rolex Regatta: 45
Internet resources: 306-307
Internet services: 58, 100, 133, 185, 207, 299-300
The Invisibles: 201
Island Center: 91
island sloops: 214
island time: 278
itineraries: beaches 23-24; best of the Virgin Islands 19-20; family vacation 21; historical and cultural exploration 22-23; sailing

adventure 24-25; wildlife and wilderness exploration 26-27

JK

Jack and Isaac Bay Preserve: 20, 26, 62, 82-83
jazz concerts: 91
jewelry: 46, 91, 120, 165-166
jobs: see employment opportunities
Johnny Horn Trail: 122
Joseph Reynold O'Neal Botanical Gardens: 26, 137, 145-146
Josiah's Bay: 152
Jost Van Dyke: general discussion 16, 210-211; accommodations 221-222; East End 216-217, 224; entertainment and nightlife 219; festivals and events 16, 219; food/restaurants 222-224; maps 212-213; planning tips 211-212; sightseeing tips 20, 24, 213-218; South Shore 213-216; tourist information and services 224-225; transportation services 225; see also Great Harbour
judicial and penal systems: 273, 275
Jumbie Beach: 111, 124
Jump-Ups: 89
Kalinago culture: 77, 259-260
Kapok trees: 251-252
kayaking: Anegada 27, 235, 236; Jost Van Dyke 219; St. Croix 78, 83, 86; St. John 125; St. Thomas 42, 48; Tortola 151, 170; Virgin Gorda 201
Kelly's Cove: 157
kiteboarding: 15, 201

L

Lambert Beach: 151
Lameshur Bay: 26, 118, 124
language: 281-282, 291
launderettes: 59, 100, 133, 185, 208
Lavalette House (1831): 37
Lawaetz Family Museum: 19, 22, 79
LEAP (Life Environmental Arts Project): 80
Legislative Council Chambers: 145
Leinster Bay Trail: 122
libraries: general discussion 297; Anegada 240; Jost Van Dyke 224; St. Croix 99; St. John 133; St. Thomas 37, 57; Tortola 184; Virgin Gorda 207
licenses: see permits
Lind Bay Trail: 109
Lindbergh Bay: 41
Lind Point Trail: 121-122

Little Apple Bay: 15, 23
Little Elizabeth Beach: 152
Little Fort National Park: 193
Little Hans Lollik: 42
Little Harbour: 216, 220
Little Hawksnest Beach: 109
Little Jost Van Dyke: 16, 24, 216-217
Little Lameshur Bay: 124
Little Magen's Bay: 42
Little Maho Bay: 112
live music: 91, 120, 164, 199
lizards: 15, 253
Loblolly Bay: 20, 25, 27, 231, 236
lobsters: 16
Long Bay (Beef Island): 24, 151
Long Bay (Tortola): 23, 155
Lord God of Sabaoth Lutheran Church (1740): 71
Love City Triathlon: 120

M

magazines: 300
Magen's Bay: 19, 24, 30, 41-42
Magen's Bay Trail: 50
Maho Bay: 112, 124
mail services: 298-299
Main Street (Road Town): 142-145, 165, 178
mammals: 252
Manchineel Bay: 24
manchineel tree: 250
Mango Melee: 90
mango trees: 252
mangrove sites: 124, 150
Mangrove Wetland Preservation Project: 150
manners and conduct: 291-292
Maple Leaf: 125
maps: Anegada 228; Buck Island National
    Monument 76; Charlotte Amalie 34; Christiansted 66-67; Cruz Bay 107; Frederiksted
    73; Jost Van Dyke 212-213; Road Town
    162-163; Salt River Bay 77; Sir Francis Drake
    Channel 156-157; Spanish Town 193; St. Croix
    64-65; St. John 105; St. Thomas 32-33; Tortola 138-139, 149, 153; Virgin Gorda 190
map sources: general discussion 296-297;
    Anegada 240; nautical charts 132, 184, 207,
    297; St. Croix 99; St. John 132; St. Thomas
    57; Tortola 183-184; Virgin Gorda 207
Marina Cay: 152
marinas: 49, 86, 168, 200, 225
marine railway: 40
Marine Studies Center: 214
markets: Anegada 241; Jost Van Dyke 224-225;
    St. Croix 71; St. John 131, 132; St. Thomas 56;
    Tortola 180-181, 183; Virgin Gorda 206
Market Square (St. Croix): 70-71
Market Square (St. Thomas): 37
Markhoe Point: 160
marriage traditions: 116
media services: 57-58, 99, 133, 184, 300, 306
medical centers: see emergency services
Mercurius Rock: 219
Methodist Church (Virgin Gorda): 192
Mingo Cay: 125
miniature golf: 126
missionaries: 267
money: 296
mongoose: 252
Moray eels: 295
Morningstar Beach: 41
mosquitoes: 294, 295
Mosquito Island: 198
motion sickness: 294-295
motorcycles: see rental cars
Mountain Point: 201
Mountaintop: 41
Mount Healthy National Park: 20, 146-147
movies: 45
murals: St. Thomas: 37, 44; Tortola: 20, 22,
    137, 146

N

Nanny Cay: 154
nautical charts: 132, 184, 207, 297
Necker Island: 198
newspapers: general discussion 300; Internet
    resources 306; St. Croix 99; St. John 133; St.
    Thomas 57-58; Tortola 184; Virgin Gorda 207
New Year's Eve bash: 16, 219
19th century history: 266-269
99 Steps: 36
Norman Island: 20, 24, 156-157
North Coast: 20, 23, 25, 27, 227, 231
North Drop: 16, 235
North Shore Shell Museum: 22, 155
North Sound: general discussion 15; accommo-
    dations 203-204; entertainment and night-
    life 199; food/restaurants 206; shopping
    200; sightseeing tips 25, 189, 197-198
Nottingham Estate: 150

O

obeah: 266
ocean safety: 294-295

octopus: 249
oil refineries: 83
Old Administration Building: 143
Old Customs House: 144
Old Government House Museum: 23, 142
Old Prison: 144-145
oleander: 250
O'Neal Botanical Gardens: 137
Oppenheimer Beach: 109
orchids: 16, 80, 235
overlooks: 41

P

Painkiller: 218
papaya trees: 252
Paradise Point Tramway: 40
Paraquita Bay Agricultural Station: 150
parasailing: 201
passports: 17-18, 289
Peace Hill: 110-111
performing arts: 91, 164
permits: 288-289, 290
Peter Island: 157-158
petroglyphs: St. Croix 77; St. John 20, 21, 26,
    104, 119, 123; see also archaeological sites
pets, traveling with: 294
pharmacies: 133, 296
photography: 133, 297-298
piracy: 261-262
Pissarro, Camille: 38
planning tips: general discussion 17-18; Ane-
    gada 229; Jost Van Dyke 211-212; St. Croix
    63; St. John 104, 106; St. Thomas 30-31; Tor-
    tola 137, 140-141; Virgin Gorda 189, 191
plantain trees: 252
plantation era: 264-265
Planter's Burial Ground: 146
plants: 16, 232, 235, 250-252; see also botani-
    cal gardens
the Playground: 219
poinsettia: 250
Point Udall: 19, 82
poisonous fish: 295
poisonous plants: 250
police: see emergency services
politics: 273, 274-275
pollution: see environmental issues
Pomato Point Museum: 232
population: 276-281
postal services: general discussion 298-299;
    Anegada 240; St. Croix 99-100; St. John
    133; St. Thomas 58; Tortola 184-185; Virgin
    Gorda 207

prescriptions: 296
Prickly Pear Island: 25, 198
Princess Bay: 124
Protestant Cay: 71-72
proverbs: 282
pub crawls: 218; see also beach bars

QR

quadrille: 266
Quakers: 151
quelbe music: 163, 266
radio stations: 184, 300
railways: 40
Rainbow Beach: 75
rainfall: 245, 246-247
Ram's Head Trail: 20, 104, 122
Rastafarians: 290
rats: 252
reading suggestions: 302-305
recreational activities: see specific activity;
    specific place; water sports
recycling efforts: 256
Red Hook: 43, 46, 57
Reef Bay Trail: 20, 21, 26, 118-119, 122-123
Reichhold Center for the Arts: 45
religion: 279
rental cars: general discussion 285, 288; Ane-
    gada 242; St. Croix 101-102; St. John 135; St.
    Thomas 60; Tortola 186-187; Virgin Gorda
    209
reptiles: 253-254
resources: 302-307
restaurants: see specific place
Ridge Road: 22, 146-147, 180
Road Town: accommodations 173-174; enter-
    tainment and nightlife 161; food/restaurants
    178-180; maps 162-163; sightseeing tips 23,
    141-146
Road Town Methodist Church: 144
Rockefeller, Laurance: 216, 271-272
rock iguanas: 16, 233, 234
Rogues Bay: 148
rum distilleries: 22, 80-81, 147-148

S

Saba Rock: 198
Saba Rock Nautical Museum and Gift Shop: 198
safety tips: 60, 124, 292, 294-296
Sage Mountain National Park: 20, 26, 137, 147,
    171
Salt Island: 23, 24, 137, 158-160
Salt Pond Bay: 20, 117-118, 124

SAILING

general discussion: 285
anchorages: 49, 86-87, 125, 168-169, 220
Anegada: 236
boat rentals: 167-168, 209
charters: 166-167, 200, 286-287
day sailing: 167
Internet resources: 306-307
itinerary tips: 24-25
marinas: 49, 86, 168, 200, 225
nautical charts: 132, 184, 207, 297
regattas: 169, 219
schools: 168, 200
St. Croix: 86-87
St. John: 125
St. Thomas: 48-49
Tortola: 15, 166-169
Virgin Gorda: 200
yacht clubs: 49, 87, 169, 200

Salt River Bay: 77-78
Salt River Canyon: 78, 84
sandflies: 295
Sandy Cay: 16, 24, 211, 216
Sandy Ledge: 157
Sandy Point Wildlife Refuge: 26, 81
Sandy Spit: 216
Sapphire Bay: 44
Savan: 35
Savannah Bay: 197
Scale House (1856): 70
scenic drives: 22, 63-65, 106, 140-141, 191
scenic overlooks: 41
Schomburgk, Robert: 230, 232
scooter rentals: 187
scratch: see quelbe music
scuba diving: Anegada 236; Jost Van Dyke 219; St. Croix 26, 78, 84-85; St. John 125-126; St. Thomas 47-48; Tortola 15, 24, 160-161, 169-170; Virgin Gorda 197, 201; wreck dives 47-48, 125, 160, 201, 236; see also Wreck of the RMS Rhone
Sea Cow's Bay: 152
sea grapes: 250
sea grass beds: 124
sea life: 246-247, 249
seasons: 17, 245
sea urchins: 295
Secret Harbour: 44

seniors: 293
The Settlement: 20, 27, 233, 239
Seven Arches Museum: 38
sewage disposal: 255, 257, 295
Seward, William: 271
sexually transmitted diseases (STDs): 296
sharks: 295
shipwrecks: Anegada 229, 230, 232, 236; St. John 125; St. Thomas 47-48; Tortola 160; Virgin Gorda 201; see also Wreck of the RMS Rhone
shopping: Charlotte Amalie 40, 46; St. Croix 91-92; St. John 120-121; St. Thomas 14, 41; Tortola 165-166; Virgin Gorda 20, 199-200
Shoys Beach: 83
sightseeing tips: Anegada 231-235; Charlotte Amalie 35-41; Jost Van Dyke 213-218; St. Croix 65, 67-83; St. John 106-119; St. Thomas 32-44; Tortola 141-161; Virgin Gorda 192-198
Sir Francis Drake Channel: 155-161, 177-178, 183
Sir Olva Georges Plaza: 142-143
Slave Rebellion of 1733: 110-111, 265
slavery: 73-74, 110-111, 264-268
sloops: 214
Smith Bay: 57
Smuggler's Cove: 24, 154, 155
snorkeling: general discussion 248; Anegada 20, 25, 27, 231, 236; Buck Island National Monument 75-76; equipment 124; Jost Van Dyke 219; Norman Island 24; safety tips 124; St. Croix 14, 19, 83, 85-86; St. John 20, 26, 109, 111-113, 118, 123-124; St. Thomas 24, 47; Tortola 148, 157, 160-161, 169; Virgin Gorda 20, 196, 197, 201
snuba: 43
Solomon Beach: 109
Soper's Hole: 154, 182-183
Spanish Town: 20, 189, 192-193, 205
Spanish Town Fisherman's Jamboree: 199
spectator sports: 50, 172
sportfishing: 16, 48, 86, 235-236
Sprat Beach (St. Croix): 75
Sprat Beach (St. Thomas): 40
Sprat Hall: 22, 80
Sprauve Museum and Library: 23, 108-109
Spring Bay National Park: 23, 189, 196
Spyglass Hill: 24
Spyglass Wall: 157
squids: 249
staircases: 36-37
statistical information: 244
St. Croix: general discussion 14, 61-63; accommodations 92-96; East Island 81-83, 95-96,

98-99; entertainment and nightlife 89; festivals and events 63, 89-90; food/restaurants 96-99; maps 64-65; North Shore 76-79, 94, 98; planning tips 63; recreational activities 84-88; shopping 91-92; sightseeing tips 19, 26, 65, 67-83; tourist information and services 99-100; transportation services 100-102; West Island 79-81, 94-95, 98; *see also* Buck Island National Monument; Christiansted; Frederiksted

St. Croix Archaeology Museum: 70
St. Croix Environmental Association (SEA): 84
St. Croix Half Ironman: 90
St. Croix Landmarks Society Museum Store: 92
St. Croix LEAP: 80
Steeple Building: 22, 68, 70
Stevenson, Robert Louis: 156, 262
St. George's Anglican Church: 144
St. George Village Botanical Garden: 80
St. John: general discussion 14-15, 103; accommodations 126-129; entertainment and nightlife 119-120; festivals and events 120; food/restaurants 129-132; maps 105; North Shore 109-115, 121, 131; planning tips 104, 106; recreational activities 121-126; shopping 120-121; sightseeing tips 20, 23, 106-119; South Shore 117-119; tourist information and services 132-133; transportation services 134-135; *see also* Coral Bay; Cruz Bay
St. John Blues Festival: 120
St. John Carnival: 120
St. John's Anglican Church: 71
St. Mary's Episcopal Church: 193
St. Patrick's Roman Catholic Church (1848): 75
St. Paul's Anglican Church: 75
St. Peter and St. Paul Roman Catholic Church: 37
St. Peter Greathouse and Gardens: 41
St. Philips Anglican Church: 148, 150
street vendors: 179-180
St. Thomas: general discussion 14, 29-30; accommodations 51-53; East End 42-44, 53, 57; entertainment and nightlife 44-45; festivals and events 30, 44-45; food/restaurants 54-57; maps 32-33; Northside 41-42; planning tips 30-31; recreational activities 47-50; sightseeing tips 21, 32-44; tourist information and services 57-59; transportation services 59-60; *see also* Charlotte Amalie
St. Thomas Carnival: 30, 44-45
St. Thomas Reformed Church (1844): 37
St. Thomas Synagogue (1833): 37
study opportunities: 292
Sugar Bay: 44

sugarcane: 252
sugar mills: 20, 23, 80, 115, 118
sugar plantations: 114
sunburn: 18, 124, 294
Sunday Market Square (St. Croix): 71
Sunday Morning Well: 145
Sunset Jazz: 91
surfing: 15, 42, 152, 155, 170
swimming safety: 294-295

T
table manners: 291-292
Taino culture: 77, 119, 258-259
Tamarind Beach: 83
Taste of St. Croix: 90
taxes: 288, 289
taxis: general discussion 285; Anegada 242; Jost Van Dyke 225; St. Croix 101; St. John 134; St. Thomas 59-60; Tortola 186; Virgin Gorda 208-209
telephone services: 299, 307
television: 99, 300
temperatures: 245, 246-247
tennis courts: 50, 87, 126, 171
Thornton Estate Ruins: 154
Thornton, William: 154
Tillet Gardens: 43-44
time perceptions: 278
time zones: 301
tipping: 296
Tobago Canyons: 219
Tortola: general discussion 15, 136-137; accommodations 173-178; East End 148-152, 161, 166, 175-176, 181-182; entertainment and nightlife 161; festivals and events 23, 137, 163-164; food/restaurants 178-183; maps 138-139, 149, 153; planning tips 137, 140-141; recreational activities 166-172; Ridge Road 22, 146-147, 180; shopping 165-166; sightseeing tips 20, 22-23, 24, 26, 141-161; Sir Francis Drake Channel 155-161, 177-178, 183; tourist information and services 183-185; transportation services 185-187; West Island 152-155, 161, 166, 176-177, 182-183; *see also* Cane Garden Bay; Road Town
Tortola sloops: 214
tourism industry: 271-272, 273, 276, 292
tourist information: general discussion 297; Anegada 240-241; Internet resources 306; Jost Van Dyke 224-225; St. Croix 99; St. John 132; St. Thomas 57; Tortola 183; Virgin Gorda 207
tours: Charlotte Amalie 36-37, 39; ecotours

48, 78, 79, 88; walking tours 36-37; *see also* driving tours
Tower Fort: 155
trade winds: 245
traditional foods: 279-281
trampolines: 220
tramways: 40
transportation services: general discussion 283-288; Anegada 241-242; Jost Van Dyke 225; St. Croix 100-102; St. John 134-135; St. Thomas 59-60; Tortola 185-187; Virgin Gorda 208-209
travelers checks: 296
travel tips: 291-294
Treasure Island (Stevenson): 156, 262
tree ferns: 251
trees: 80, 250-252
Trellis Bay Full Moon Party: 23, 137, 163
tropical fish: 247, 249, 295
tropical forests: 250-252
Trunk Bay (St. John): 20, 21, 23, 104, 111-112
Trunk Bay (Tortola): 148
Trunk Bay Underwater Trail: 124
Trygborg: 36-37, 39
Turner Hole: 83
turpentine tree: 251
turtle dove myth: 142
Turtle Point Trail: 122
turtles: 26, 81, 249
20th century history: 269-272
Twin Towers: 219
two-way radio service: 300

UV

United States purchase of islands: 270, 271
U.S. Virgin Islands: colonization 263-264; government and economy 273-274; statistical information 244; visitor guidelines 288-289
Valley Trunk Bay: 196
vegetation: 16, 232, 235, 250-252; *see also* botanical gardens
Vertigo: 78
Very Long Baseline Array Telescope: 82
Vessup Bay Beach: 44
V.I. Legislature Building (1874): 36
Villa Notman (1860): 39
villa rentals: 51, 92, 126, 173, 202
Virgin Gorda: general discussion 15, 188-189; accommodations 202-204; entertainment and nightlife 199; festivals and events 199; food/restaurants 205-206; maps 190; Mid-Island 197, 203, 206; planning tips 189,

191; recreational activities 200-201; shopping 199-200; sightseeing tips 20, 23, 25, 192-198; tourist information and services 207-208; transportation services 208-209; The Valley 192-196, 199-200, 202-203, 205-206; *see also* North Sound
Virgin Gorda Easter Festival: 199
Virgin Gorda Music Festival: 199
Virgin Islands Folk Museum: 143-144
Virgin Islands National Park: 14, 108
visas: 288, 289

WXYZ

walking tours: 36-37
The Wall: 26, 62, 78, 84
Wall-to-Wall: 201
Water Island: 39-40
Waterlemon Cay: 20, 26, 104, 113, 124
water resources: 257
water sports: Anegada 235-236; Buck Island National Monument 76; equipment 171; Jost Van Dyke 219-220, 225; lessons 171; St. Croix 84-87; St. John 123-126; St. Thomas 47-49; Tortola 151-152, 166-171; Virgin Gorda 200-201
Watson's Rock: 219
weather: 17, 245-247
websites: 306-307
weights and measures: 300-301
West End: 20, 152-155, 161, 166, 176-177, 182-183
Western Salt Ponds: 20, 227, 231-232
Whim Plantation Museum: 19, 22, 62, 64, 79
White Bay: general discussion 16, 215-216, 220; food/restaurants 223-224; sightseeing tips 20, 24, 211
Whit Weekend Festival: 199
wildlife: 247, 252-254, 295
William Thornton Estate Ruins: 154
windmills: 146-147
winds: 245
windsurfing: 15, 42, 170
Witch's Hat: 125
women travelers: 60, 292
work permits: 288-289
World War I: 269-270
Wreck of the RMS *Rhone*: 15, 23, 24, 137, 159, 160
yachting: *see* charters; sailing
Yawzi Point Trail: 122
yellow allamanda: 250
Zion Hill Methodist Church: 155
zip codes: 298
zooxanthellae: 247

Acknowledgments

This book is the product of the six years I have spent living and working in the Virgin Islands. I owe its existence to the residents of these islands who welcomed me into their community and shared their way of life and their exceptionally beautiful home with a stranger. It also would not have happened without the support of those people who believed in me and encouraged me to pursue it. I would like to thank my family and friends in the Virgin Islands and Tennessee, especially my parents, Lucy and Rich Henighan, and my grandmother, Louise Barker, for your love and encouragement.

A number of people extended a warm welcome to me while I was traveling around the islands. On St. Croix, I would like to thank Connie Woveris of Villa Greenleaf; Bruce and Mathilde Wilson of Mount Victory Camp; Elsie Galloway of Hotel Caravelle; Lisa Blau and Divi Carina Bay; Mile Mark Watersports; and Joyce M. Hurd at Sprat Hall Plantation. Mary Boehm of Club Comanche Hotel, thank you especially for your last-minute hospitality. Jane Watkins of Watkins PR provided invaluable advice about visiting St. Croix. Bob and Leslie Richenbach provided insight on their adopted home.

On St. John, I would like to thank Melody Smith and Maho Bay Camps for your welcome, and Park Ranger Don Near for your insight. On St. Thomas, thanks to Wendy Snodgrass and Bellavista for your expert advice and hospitality and to Allegra Kean of Coral World.

I received assistance from Suzanne Duffy and Katie Rogers at M Booth and Associates and from Jamie Foley of the Zimmerman Agency. I would also like to thank the staff of the Caribbean Studies Unit of the Road Town Public Library in the British Virgin Islands for your patience and assistance.

Thank you to the editors and other staff at Avalon Publishing Group for your professionalism, patience, and good advice. Rebecca Browning, Kari Gim, Kevin McLain, Kat Smith, Stefano Boni, and Sabrina Young provided assistance through every step of the process. Special thanks to my editor, Cinnamon Hearst, for making this a better book.

Finally, I would not have been able to write this book without the love and support of my husband and my guide, Amarro Potter. This book is dedicated to him.

www.moon.com

For helpful advice on planning a trip, visit www.moon.com for the **TRAVEL PLANNER** and get access to useful travel strategies and valuable information about great places to visit. When you travel with Moon, expect an experience that is uncommon and truly unique.

MAP SYMBOLS

▤	Expressway	◖	Highlight	✗	Airfield	⚓	Beach
	Primary Road	○	City/Town	✈	Airport	🦈	Dive Site
	Secondary Road	◉	State Capital	▲	Mountain	⚓	Anchorage
▪▪▪▪	Unpaved Road	◉	National Capital	✚	Unique Natural Feature	🅿	Parking Area
▬▬▬	Trail	★	Point of Interest			🏛	Church
▪▪▪▪	Ferry	•	Accommodation	🌿	Waterfall	⛽	Gas Station
⊢⊢⊢	Railroad	▾	Restaurant/Bar	▲	Park	▨	Mangrove
▦	Pedestrian Walkway	▪	Other Location	⊓	Trailhead	▨	Reef
▥▥	Stairs	⋀	Campground	⌁	Golf Course	▤	Swamp

CONVERSION TABLES

°C = (°F - 32) / 1.8
°F = (°C x 1.8) + 32
1 inch = 2.54 centimeters (cm)
1 foot = 0.304 meters (m)
1 yard = 0.914 meters
1 mile = 1.6093 kilometers (km)
1 km = 0.6214 miles
1 fathom = 1.8288 m
1 chain = 20.1168 m
1 furlong = 201.168 m
1 acre = 0.4047 hectares
1 sq km = 100 hectares
1 sq mile = 2.59 square km
1 ounce = 28.35 grams
1 pound = 0.4536 kilograms
1 short ton = 0.90718 metric ton
1 short ton = 2,000 pounds
1 long ton = 1.016 metric tons
1 long ton = 2,240 pounds
1 metric ton = 1,000 kilograms
1 quart = 0.94635 liters
1 US gallon = 3.7854 liters
1 Imperial gallon = 4.5459 liters
1 nautical mile = 1.852 km

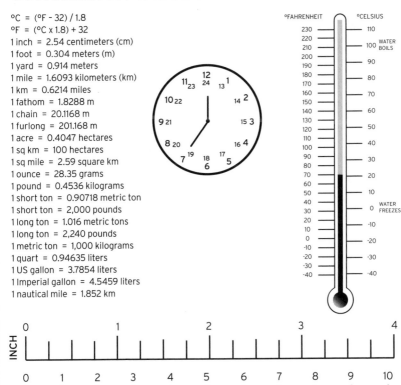

MOON VIRGIN ISLANDS

AVALON
publishing group incorporated

Avalon Travel Publishing
An Imprint of
Avalon Publishing Group, Inc.

1400 65th Street, Suite 250
Emeryville, CA 94608, USA
www.moon.com

Editor: Cinnamon Hearst
Series Manager: Kathryn Ettinger
Acquisitions Manager: Rebecca K. Browning
Copy Editor: Valerie Sellers Blanton
Graphics Coordinator: Stefano Boni
Production Coordinators: Amber Pirker, Jacob
  Goolkasian, Domini Dragoone
Cover & Interior Designer: Gerilyn Attebery
Map Editor: Kat Smith
Cartographer: Suzanne Service
Cartography Manager: Mike Morgenfeld
Indexer: Judy Hunt

ISBN-10: 1-56691-572-4
ISBN-13: 978-1-56691-572-4
ISSN: 1092-3357

Printing History
1st Edition – 1997
3rd Edition – September 2006
5 4 3 2 1

Text © 2006 by Susanna Henighan

Maps © 2006 by Avalon Travel Publishing, Inc.
All rights reserved.

Some photos and illustrations are used by permission and are the property of the original copyright owners.

Front cover photo: © Steve Simonsen
Title page photo: Courtesy of U.S. Virgin Islands
  Department of Tourism

Printed in the United States by Worzalla.

KEEPING CURRENT

If you have a favorite gem you'd like to see included in the next edition, or see anything that needs updating, clarification, or correction, please drop us a line. Send your comments via email to feedback@moon.com, or use the address above.